Greenwood's Library Year Book. 1897: A Record Of General Library Progress And Work

Thomas Greenwood

MR. J. PASSMORE EDWARDS.   From photo by F. Argall, Truro.

GREENWOOD'S

LIBRARY YEAR BOOK

1897

A Record of General Library Progress and Work

EDITED BY

THOMAS GREENWOOD

AUTHOR OF "PUBLIC LIBRARIES," "MUSEUMS AND ART GALLERIES,"
"SUNDAY SCHOOL LIBRARIES," ETC.

LONDON
CASSELL & CO., LIMITED
LA BELLE SAUVAGE, LUDGATE HILL, E.C.
1897

PREFACE.

In 1886, when the first edition of *Public Libraries* was published, the number of adoptions of the Public Libraries Acts then stood at 133. At the present time the number has reached over 330 adoptions of the Acts. The most sanguine friends of the movement . hardly dared hope for such a satisfactory rate of progress. This has been accomplished without, so far as I am aware, any person being paid a single shilling for his advocacy of these Institutions. It is the pardonable pride of many friends of Public Libraries that the movement rests absolutely upon voluntary labour. It is not unfair to place this fact side by side with the cost of administration of some of the organisations with which the Public Library movement now and again comes into collision.

A few years ago the goal of our efforts was placed at 400 adoptions of the Acts, when in 1900 the Jubilee of the Ewart Act will be celebrated. Present indications seem to encourage the hope that the number may be nearer 500 than the smaller total named.

All classes are clearly alive to the need of an ever-widening measure of national education. What is required is not a cramping and withering sectarianism, but a scheme the trend of which shall be in the direction of national large-heartedness, and the good educational equipment of our people for the inevitable struggle with the leading nations of the world.

The one great hope in this Public Library movement is that Public Libraries must ultimately form an integral part of our system of education, which shall embrace elementary,

b

secondary, and advanced. That Public Libraries are fully and comprehensively qualifying for this position, I am more than ever convinced.

To my large circle of correspondents in every part of the country, and leading foreign countries, who keep me so well advised of the progress made, I tender my heartiest thanks. I am obliged to many librarians who give me so much encouragement. To my colleague, Mr. James D. Brown, librarian, Clerkenwell Public Library, who has aided in the work of preparing this Year Book, I am gratefully indebted.

To my friend, Dr. Eduard Reyer of Vienna, I desire to express my thanks for having translated and incorporated in his *Handbuch des Volksbildungswesens* a good portion of the last edition of *Public Libraries*. Dr. Reyer's work in Austria and Germany is telling with considerable effect.

A survey of the whole question, as it presents itself in the various countries, shows that these Institutions are fulfilling, as they have never done before, a real place in the life of the people.

CONTENTS.

CONTENTS

LIST OF ILLUSTRATIONS.

x . LIST OF ILLUSTRATIONS.

GREENWOOD'S LIBRARY YEAR BOOK

1897

ABERDEEN UNIVERSITY PRESS.

GREENWOOD'S LIBRARY YEAR BOOK.

INTRODUCTION.

IT has been felt for many years among all classes of Library workers, that an annual publication devoted to general Library interests and collecting information regarding progress and work, would be useful and acceptable. Many persons have also deplored the lack of a book giving recent information concerning the Public Library movement, as, owing to its progressive nature, no work on the subject can keep abreast with it unless issued at frequent intervals. I have, therefore, tried to meet these needs by publishing this Year Book, in a form and at a price to insure its ready circulation. The information it contains is the latest available, and neither pains nor expense have been spared in the effort to secure up-to-date particulars. It is hoped, as the work progresses and its features become matured and better known, it may be established as a standard book of reference. The responses to the various circulars sent out were not so numerous as expected, and in some respects the work suffers somewhat from this indifference or neglect, but in future issues I trust this will be repaired. Meanwhile, I offer my cordial thanks to those who took the trouble to answer my questions. I have enlisted the services of some of the best-known experts in different departments of Library work and feel sure their efforts will prove useful to new librarians and suggestive to old ones. In this year's issue the more progressive features of recent accomplishment in Library work are dwelt upon, and in future issues further attention will be given to such advances in development, while not forgetting the claims of older and longer-established administrative methods.

By way of formal introduction, I propose to make some remarks on the whole question of municipal Libraries, dividing them, in imitation of the preacher, into three convenient heads, which may be specified as (1) What has been done; (2) What is being done; and (3) What remains to be done.

I. WHAT HAS BEEN DONE.

In the forty-six years which have passed since the Public Library Law was first promulgated in 1850, through the efforts

of William Ewart and his friends, great advances have been
made in the establishment of Libraries and improvement of
the methods employed in their administration. The early years
of the movement were marked by extreme caution in using the
powers provided by Parliament, while the efforts made by anti-
educationists and municipal niggards of all kinds, assisted
greatly in retarding its growth. Again, five years were
practically lost, owing to the inadequate provisions of the Act
of 1850. It gave no power to buy books, and limited the rate to
½d. in the pound of rateable value, so that it is not to be won-
dered at, if between 1850 and 1855 little progress was made. The
much greater latitude allowed by the Act of 1855 acted as a
stimulus to Communities, and gradually, but with increasing
strength, the movement forged ahead, gaining power with every
advance in educational law, till after 1870 it assumed the
appearance of a steady flowing stream, and so has continued.
The number of Libraries existing which have been established
under the various Public Libraries Acts is now 330, of which
265 are in England, 32 in Scotland, 17 in Ireland and 16 in
Wales. In the provision of Libraries the various divisions of
the United Kingdom show results as follows :—

Wales has one municipal Library for every 94,937 of its population.
England   ,,   ,,   ,,   ,,   103,708   ,,   ,,
Scotland   ,,   ,,   ,,   ,,   125,812   ,,   ,,
Ireland   ,,   ,,   ,,   ,,   276,764   ,,   ,,

Thus Wales is easily first, while Ireland drags woefully in the
rear. For the whole of the United Kingdom there is one
Library for every 116,000 inhabitants. This result has been
attained in the face of some of the most bitter and determined
opposition ever offered to any popular movement for the good
of the people. In reading what has been written against
Libraries, one would really believe that they were established
to destroy every impulse for good existing in the mind and
soul of man ; that they were communistic institutions of the
most violent sort; and that they destroyed every particle of
decency and self-respect in the composition of good citizens.
Well, most of this has been outlived, or, it may almost be said,
has been written in vain, for is it not the fact that every
large municipality in the country, save one (of which more
anon), and many of the smaller ones, have adopted these Acts
and now possess thriving and splendid Libraries ? It may well
be asked what semblance of truth or good sense these strong
statements possess, when we turn to the action taken in the
matter by such a hard-headed and thrifty county as Lancashire.
This is one of the most purely industrial areas in the world, it
is famous for its study of all economic and social questions, it
is the headquarters of the co-operative movement, and its
inhabitants have always been distinguished by a keen knowledge and appreciation of what is good for themselves.

If, then, the Public Library movement is wrong, and has an evil influence, how is it that Lancashire has been so blind and deluded, notwithstanding the traditional shrewdness of its inhabitants, as to allow thirty-two of its largest cities and towns to put such pernicious things as Public Libraries into active operation? Why is it that more than two-thirds of the people of Lancashire have declared in favour of Public Libraries, and cities and towns like Liverpool, Manchester, Preston, Oldham, Bolton, Blackburn, Salford, Rochdale, Warrington, Wigan, St. Helen's, Barrow-in-Furness, etc., rival each other in the value and extent of their Public Libraries? The same may be asked as regards Staffordshire, Cheshire, Yorkshire, London, Kent and Middlesex, which are distinguished by the activity which they have shown in the establishment of Libraries. The mere fact that every considerable town of any importance in England has adopted the Libraries Acts, should be enough to convince every one that such institutions have taken a strong hold on the affections of the people. That they are used far beyond the most sanguine hopes of their early promoters, for every kind of practical and recreative purpose, is undoubtedly the case. It has been claimed that the Libraries of the United States attain a higher level of work and organisation, but my own opinion, derived from personal observation, is quite the opposite. That the Public Libraries of the United States are better equipped all round as regards buildings, funds and apparatus, may be readily admitted, but that they are more used or stand higher in public estimation may be at once flatly denied. There is positively no comparison between the amount and variety of work accomplished in the Libraries of the two countries. In the United States the average Library income, as a rule, is double, and in many cases more than double, that available for British Libraries, and practically all of this is devoted to the work of the lending and reference departments. There are no newsrooms, no lectures, no museums, no art galleries, no classes, nor any of the other features which are to be found in most British Libraries as adjuncts to the Library work proper. Consequently where one finds a British Library spending perhaps £2000 per annum in serving books, newspapers, lectures, etc., to a population which uses these features perhaps 1,000,000 times in one year, the average American Library will spend perhaps £5000 in issuing 300,000 volumes for home and Library reading and providing magazine rooms to be visited 100,000 times in one year. Then again, outside of Massachusetts, there is no very general diffusion of municipal Libraries, and I doubt if in the whole of the United States there are any little rural, rate-supported Libraries, like those at Middle Claydon in Bucks, or Tarves in Aberdeenshire, doing good and great work on $50 to $150 per annum. In this opinion I am strongly upheld by both English and Continental librarians who have had opportunities of comparing the Library work of both countries. In one direction do the American Libraries excel those of the United Kingdom. That is in general organisation. The schemes of classification used, the high-class apparatus, and the better and more scientific administration of the details of management, are all points on which they leave the average British Library far behind. There are Libraries in Britain which are far advanced in every department, and yield in no respect to the best of their American rivals, but the fatal lack of funds wherewith to experiment or change, is an almost insurmountable bar to progress in a majority of the Libraries in the United Kingdom. It may be claimed, further, that on the Continent there is nothing in the way of Public Libraries which can be named in the same breath with the free and democratic institutions of Britain. The communal Libraries of France and Belgium, and the municipal Libraries of Germany, are so infested with bureaucratic restrictions and formalities, as to be practically caviare to the multitude. The municipal Libraries of Paris and Berlin, though doing good work, are very mediocre concerns compared to the fine and well-equipped parochial Libraries of London, and so it may be said generally of all the Continental Libraries under State or municipal control. They are managed as trusteeships, very strictly tied up, and so do not touch, in any general measure, the life and needs of the people.

II. What Is Being Done.

Without traversing the whole ground covered by the active operations of the modern Public Library, it is impossible in brief limits to give an idea of the varied and interesting work accomplished. There are several points, however, to which attention may be directed, and to the more important of these I will confine myself. With the advance of time and more liberal opinions, features of a novel and useful kind are constantly being added to the work of Libraries. With most of these I have sympathy and can heartily wish them additional extension and success, but I must confess the imitation Russian method of blacking-out betting news from newspapers is one which seems to me quite out of place in a rate-supported municipal Library. The action of Aston Manor, Middlesbrough and other towns in pursuing this course was not dictated, as some have supposed, by any high feeling of moral obligation towards the citizens at large, but was undertaken solely and confessedly with an object of discipline directed towards the preservation of good order. The argument used was to the effect that if any persons, but particularly persons interested in horse-racing, crowded round newspaper stands they constituted themselves a nuisance to all the other readers and therefore should be suppressed. It does not appear that the originators of the ink-roller plan of maintaining order ever thought of suppressing obstructers of the kind mentioned by a vigorous enforcement of their rules. They hit upon the less valiant expedient of defacing the newspapers which formed the attraction, and so saved the librarian and the local police a little trouble at the expense of much dignity. I am not going to argue the question of the immorality or otherwise of betting news, because it does not enter into the matter under discussion. It seems to me a very serious thing if Library Committees employ such a policy as defacing any printed matter considered good enough for display in a reading-room for the mere purpose of preserving order. It constitutes a violent assault upon literature and the newspaper press to deface any portion of a public paper because its attractions lead to crowding or disorder. There are other very plain remedies for such a condition of things, and it seems a very weak-kneed procedure to obliterate news of interest to many for the sake of quelling the delinquencies of a few. The ordinary rules of a Library against noise and talking are quite enough, when properly administered, to prevent any disorder. The action of Aston Manor succeeded only in bringing discredit upon all the Public Libraries in the country, without greatly abating the nuisance it was instituted to check. It is pleasing to record, however, that the lead of Aston was not taken by more than a few towns, and more pleasing to notice that Aston has now provisionally abandoned the practice. Perhaps a new caretaker has been installed, or the librarian has recently braced up his nerves to the task of reducing a few hobble-de-hoys to order! This blacking-out is practically the only innovation to which strong exception can be taken among the work being done in Public Libraries. Extension of liberty among the users of Public Libraries was one of those changes of policy which was certain to come sooner or later. That it has been inaugurated with success, and in London of all places, is one of those surprises which derive their chief pleasure from their unexpectedness. Librarians, both in England and America, have for years been flirting with what is called variously "free access" or "open access," but none of them ever dreamt of organising it as a system of lending for Public Libraries till in 1894 the Library authorities of Clerkenwell, acting under the advice of their librarian, Mr. J. D. Brown, established it without flourish or ceremony. This form of open access is radically different from the kind which is almost universal in proprietary, college and other Libraries, inasmuch as the whole method has been constructed on scientific lines designed to meet the peculiar difficulties and conditions of the case. Nothing of the sort had ever been tried before, and naturally it cost the older librarians a severe effort to swallow their traditional and *ex-officio* distrust of the public. But the outcry which was raised did not come from librarians of standing at all, but almost solely from an indi-

vidual who had pecuniary interests in a Library indicator
designed to facilitate the issue of books in a manner not too
irksome to the librarian. The efforts of this interested individual served to keep matters lively for about twelve months,
and as they were directed mostly to arousing the fears of timid
and lazy librarians he succeeded in giving certain newspapers
and their readers the impression that a revolution was going
on which, if successful, would ruin Public Libraries and lodge
most of the readers in jail! All that is, however, practically
ancient history, but is none the worse of mention, as future
inquirers may wish to learn the inner history of an agitation
fomented to serve pecuniary ends and scare the public from
obtaining fuller enjoyment of their own Libraries. I have no
sympathy whatever with the view that Public Library administration has reached the summit of perfection, especially as it
affects the convenience of the people, and I therefore hail with
pleasure the movement now in progress to free Libraries from
the dominion of red tape and mechanical obstructions between
readers and their books. I hold that neither Library Committees nor librarians have any legal or moral right to prevent
the public from handling, examining and choosing books in
the manner best suited to its convenience and needs. It is
little short of impertinence to condemn readers to spend hours
consulting bad catalogues at home and numerical indicators
at the Library in search of books which may or may not be
available, while denying them the advantages of examination
before registration, and giving no alternative selection in the
event of every hypothecated book being out. Librarians and
Committee-men never feel the wearisome inconvenience of
having to struggle in a crowd of other readers looking for small
numbers on a huge frame, consequently they are very apt to
imagine that no delays are experienced by borrowers charged
with the tiresome task of ascertaining what books on their
lists are in. Again, the ordinary catalogue-entry is no guide
to the character of a book, nor are indicator numbers, so that
a reader may, after infinite labour, withdraw a dozen books
and find none of them suitable for his purpose. There can be
no doubt that much of the ill-natured criticism to which Public
Libraries are subjected arises from this niggardly and suspicious
method of dealing with the people. I am in constant receipt
of newspapers from all over the country containing letters from
Public Library borrowers protesting against alleged defects in
administration, and most of these complaints have particular
reference to the difficulty of getting suitable books promptly,
because of indicators and such like mechanical obstructions.
It is devoutly to be hoped that borrowers will agitate till they
get rights similar to those which have been granted with
perfect safety and real economy at the Libraries mentioned in
another part of this Year Book as having successfully inaugurated the open access system. The scruples of prejudiced

librarians and timid Committees will soon be overcome if the public shows that it means to have its rights. What is working successfully and well in various parts of the country will work equally well on similar lines everywhere else, and no consideration of a selfish nature should be permitted to postpone a reform which is undoubtedly the most valuable and important ever introduced into Public Library administration. I am firmly of opinion that open access, both to Lending and Reference Libraries, is the policy of the future, and that within a very few years a great extension of the system will be witnessed. My observations of Library work all over Britain, America, Canada, South Africa and throughout Europe have long since convinced me that the utmost freedom must be ultimately given to the public in well-classified and arranged Libraries if they are to be used to the fullest advantage, and that a complete revision of policy must sooner or later be attempted. The Clerkenwell system seems the best for open Lending Libraries in the present stage of their development, and no Library Authority should adopt any other plan till it has well considered and examined the various open Libraries and formed an opinion as to how they meet public requirements as compared with Libraries conducted on old-fashioned restricted lines.

The articles on "Fiction" and "Sunday Opening" treat at some length of the leading aspects of both questions. The former is a matter, it seems to me, which concerns the public alone. If ratepayers and their families prefer to read novels rather than sermons and works on political economy, I, for one, cannot blame them. As they pay the piper they have every right to call the tune, in spite of the Chadbands and Pecksniffs of everyday life. The appreciation of imaginative literature on the part of the general public has much to recommend it, being but another proof that the English-speaking nations are not losing that love for pure literature which is a heritage from bardic times. I rejoice that so many copies of the works of Scott, Dickens, Kingsley, George Eliot, Meredith and Thackeray, not to speak of Shakespeare, Burns and Tennyson, are being continually worn out in the public service. There would be much greater reason to deplore decadence in public taste if such authors were neglected in favour of proselytising theology, restless and ever-changing science, or undermining political dogmas. The arguments against Public Libraries have been reduced to the fiction bogey, with occasional incursions towards the rate bogey and perhaps a glance at the pet objection of the Liberty and Property Defence League, that Public Libraries are the resorts of ragged scoundrels endowed with more fleas than money. I should have thought this last was a bid for conventional freedom which might fitly be recognised as coming within the scope of the League, and so call for its powerful protection ! The liberty of the individual to carry fleas apparently is not entitled to such defence. It is a great pity the liberties of the reading public cannot be protected from the aspersions of a clique of narrow-minded faddists who are apparently bent on imprisoning the public mind in the interests of the moneyed classes. As the fiction question is one which solely concerns the public, so is the Sunday opening question one almost entirely for the consideration and decision of communities. There is so much local sentiment bound up in the question that in its present state no general policy can be formulated or recommended. It must be remembered that what holds good in London is not appreciated in Cumberland, Wales or Scotland, so that local option should, in my opinion, remain the determining factor till the change of opinion now ripening has time to make itself felt. No doubt the action of the State Authorities in opening the institutions under their care will have an educational effect and point out the right way. On reviewing the present position of the Public Libraries of the country there is much reason for congratulating ourselves on their activity, and the great volume of useful work which they collectively get through every year. When it is considered that they are the means of circulating between 30,000,000 and 40,000,000 volumes per annum in every class of literature, and that only books of a wholesome character and high literary standard are comprised in this vast issue, it will be recognised that the value and influence of the work makes powerfully towards the cultivation of the higher faculties of the human mind. It is also a chief means of carrying on the educational system which has its origin in the board school and its culmination in the university. But the issue of books is only one department of the work carried on by the Public Libraries. The great reading-rooms, with their hundreds of newspapers, magazines, scientific, literary, technical and trade journals; their maps bearing on current political and scientific affairs; their directories, annuals, dictionaries and guides of various kinds, are nothing short of public bureaux of information on every topic of current interest. It is more than likely that in these very rooms, which some editors seem to imagine are consecrated to loafers with their attendant fleas and disease germs, newspapers hostile to the Public Library movement have their largest circle of readers. Does the editor of the *Figaro*, for example, ever think of this when he makes his onslaughts against Public Libraries? Or, what is more to the point, has he, or any other member of the journalistic fraternity, ever witnessed the sights and deficiencies so often commented upon? Busy editors are too prone to pass *ex cathedra* judgments on matters which cannot possibly come under their own notice, and I would like those gentlemen to rely a little more upon personal observation and less upon club-room *obiter dicta* when summing up the demerits of institutions about which they can only know very little. The other sides of Library work which are now flourishing and developing more and more every year consist of courses of lectures on literary and scientific topics; museum and art-gallery work; assistance in the work of university extension; educational work in connection with board schools and technical institutions; and generally of work connected with after-school education. But enough has been said as to the present position of Library work.

III. What Remains to be Done.

The leading want in connection with the Public Library movement is its extension to rural districts in some effective form. The conclusions of every expert who has examined the question are all against the parish as a unit for administration, while means are so meagre and conditions so hopelessly antagonistic. The same shortcomings and needs which led to parochial unions for poor law purposes must ultimately conspire to make the county the only workable area; but whether it is, for Library purposes, administered by the County Council or a special Educational or Library Board, remains to be determined. Educational experts are greatly at variance as to the advantages of central *versus* local control in matters of education, and there is a similar want of unanimity as regards Libraries. If ever the educational machinery of the country is consolidated, the Libraries will, as a matter of course, take their place as an important part of the system. Meanwhile, the villages and parishes are suffering from want of Libraries to bring sweetness and light into the dull monotony of rural life. Nothing can be done while it is left for each little Parish Council to raise its £5 or £20 for Library purposes, because the hopelessness of taking action on such means immediately presents itself whenever the question comes up for consideration. I am personally in favour of giving the County Councils power to adopt the Public Libraries Acts, just as if they were Urban Sanitary Authorities, leaving them to experiment with the various plans which have been suggested for establishing district reading-rooms and travelling Libraries on various scales of magnitude. The travelling Library system has undoubtedly possibilities connected with it not possessed by any other plan yet proposed, and the various schemes of Messrs. Ogle, Brown and Credland, elsewhere alluded to, are all worthy of serious attention. They each possess features of value, and only actual trial could demonstrate which was best.

Another urgent need arises in connection with the provision of Public Libraries for the smaller towns which have not yet adopted the Acts, though other places have shown the way. A fillip is required, and it seems to me that nothing could be more appropriate than the establishment of Libraries in these towns to commemorate the long and glorious reign of Queen

Victoria. The Library and Educational Laws were all sanctioned by her Majesty, and in a very few years the jubilee of the first Library Act will be at hand. What could be more useful, more appropriate and more patriotic, therefore, than to signalise the prosperous reign of the Queen by a splendid series of Public Libraries wherever they are required? There is scarcely a county in England which does not contain towns able to establish and support Public Libraries, just as easily and in the same manner as other places of similar size and importance. I give this rough list in the hope that it may prove an incentive to action :—

ENGLAND: Towns which might Adopt the Acts.

BEDFORDSHIRE : Biggleswade, Dunstable, Leighton Buzzard.

BERKSHIRE : Abingdon, Maidenhead, Newbury, Wallingford, Windsor.

BUCKINGHAM : Aylesbury, Buckingham, Marlow, Wycombe.

CAMBRIDGE : Ely, March, Newmarket, Wisbech.

CHESHIRE : Bollington, Congleton, Crewe, Sandbach.

CUMBERLAND : Cockermouth, Keswick, Longtown, Wigton.

DERBYSHIRE : Alfreton, Belper, Ilkestone, Matlock.

DEVON : Barnstaple, Crediton, Dartmouth, Dawlish, Exmouth, Honiton, Ilfracombe, Newton Abbot, Paignton, Tavistock, Teignmouth, Tiverton, Torquay.

DORSET : Blandford, Bridport, Dorchester, Shaftesbury, Sherborne, Weymouth, Wimborne.

DURHAM : Barnard Castle, Birtley, Bishop Auckland, Blaydon, Durham, Jarrow, Seaham.

ESSEX : Chelmsford, Dagenham, Harwich, Maldon, Romford, Saffron Walden, Southend.

GLOUCESTER : Cirencester, Stroud, Tewkesbury.

HAMPSHIRE : Alton, Basingstoke, Christchurch, Cowes, Newport, Ringwood, Romsey, Ryde, Sandown, Ventnor.

HEREFORD : Ledbury, Ross.

HERTFORD : Barnet, Berkhampstead, Bishop's Stortford, Hatfield, Hemel Hempstead, Hitchin, Rickmansworth, Tring.

HUNTINGDONSHIRE : Huntingdon.

KENT : Ashford, Broadstairs, Chatham, Dartford, Deal, Dover, Herne Bay, Margate, Sheerness.

LANCASHIRE : Accrington, Bacup, Burnley, Bury, Chorley, Prescot, Ulverston.

LEICESTER : Ashby-de-la-Zouch, Melton Mowbray.

LINCOLN : Boston, Gainsborough, Grantham, Grimsby, Louth, Spalding, Stamford.

LONDON : Bethnal Green, City, Deptford, Greenwich, Hackney, Islington, Lee, Limehouse, Marylebone, Paddington, Plumstead, St. Clement Danes, St. James' (Westminster), St. Olave, St. Pancras, Soho.

MIDDLESEX : Acton, Harrow, Hendon, Hornsey, Staines.

MONMOUTH : Abergavenny, Blaenavon, Monmouth, Tredegar.

NORFOLK : Cromer, Diss, King's Lynn, North Waltham, Thetford, Wymondham.

NORTHAMPTON : Daventry, Higham Ferrers, Rushden, Wellingborough.

NORTHUMBERLAND: Alnwick, Benton, Berwick-on-Tweed, Bedlington, Hexham, Morpeth.
NOTTINGHAM: Beeston, Radford, Retford.
OXFORD: Banbury, Chipping Norton, Henley, Woodstock.
RUTLAND: Oakham.
SHROPSHIRE: Bishop's Castle, Bridgnorth, Ludlow, Wellington, Wenlock.
SOMERSET: Bath, Crewkerne, Frome, Wells, Wellington, Yeovil.
SUFFOLK: Beccles, Stowmarket, Sudbury, Woodbridge.
SURREY: Banstead, Epsom, Godalming, Guildford, Redhill, Reigate.
SUSSEX: Arundel, Bexhill, Bognor, Chichester, Hastings, Horsham, Lewes, Littlehampton, Newhaven.
WARWICKSHIRE: Nuneaton, Stratford-on-Avon.
WESTMORELAND: Ambleside, Appleby.
WILTSHIRE: Calne, Chippenham, Devizes, Malmesbury, Marlborough, Swindon, Trowbridge, Wilton.
WORCESTER: Bewdley, Bromsgrove, Droitwich, Evesham, Malvern, Redditch, Stourbridge.
YORKSHIRE: Batley, Beverley, Birstall, Bridlington, Goole, Huddersfield, Knaresborough, Malton, Northallerton, Pontefract, Richmond, Ripon, Saddleworth, Scarborough, Selby, Wakefield, Whitby.

A very large number of District Council areas are not included in the above list.

Ireland stands in similar case, as likewise do Wales and Scotland. I therefore supply lists of towns in these countries which could also establish and support Public Libraries.

IRELAND: TOWNS WHICH MIGHT ADOPT THE ACTS.

Londonderry, Galway, Lisburn, Kilkenny, Wexford, Ballymena, Carrickfergus, Armagh, Portadown, Tipperary.

WALES: TOWNS WHICH MIGHT ADOPT THE ACTS.

Ystradyfodwg, Merthyr, Aberdare, Pembroke, Cardigan. Carmarthen, Ruabon, Llanelly, Aberayron, Brecon, Pwllheli, Conway, Llandudno, Bethesda, Denbigh, Aberavon, Llandaff, Llangollen, Flint, Mold, Neath, Dolgelly, Tenby, Haverfordwest.

SCOTLAND: TOWNS WHICH MIGHT ADOPT THE ACTS.

Glasgow, Leith, Greenock, Govan, Coatbridge, Hamilton, Motherwell, Dumfries, Stirling, Wishaw, Port Glasgow, Montrose, Rutherglen, Pollokshaws, Kirkintilloch, Clydebank, Johnstone, Irvine, Rothesay, Broughty Ferry, Barrhead, Musselburgh, Helensburgh, Larkhall, Cambuslang, Banff, Dalkeith, Fraserburgh, St. Andrews, Alexandria.

The case of Scotland is peculiar, in that it furnishes the only instance of a very large and important city which has no municipal rate-supported Libraries. Glasgow, which is the second largest city in the empire, and first in most affairs of

municipal enterprise, has failed so miserably in this matter of
Libraries, that a little inquiry may not come amiss at this
juncture.   The citizens of Glasgow seem for years past to have
become blinded to all save purely material affairs.   Their
worship of the bawbee has become chronic, and led by a Council
composed of hard-headed, and it must be assumed, close-fisted
business men, they have devoted attention only to the things
that *pey*, namely, tramways, sewage disposal, model lodging
houses, etc.   They have not established a single educational
institution of any sort for years; everything of that nature
belongs to the past.   To the Bailie Nicol Jarvies of long ago,
with their respect for learning, rather than to the vulgar and
blatant Bailies of recent times, belong all the existing
educational institutions which the city possesses.   The
University; the Stirling, Baillie and Mitchell Libraries,
Anderson's College, the Athenæum, in short, every educational institution of any importance owes its origin to the
labours of past worthies who could collect wealth without
worshipping it.   The opposition to the establishment of Public
Libraries in the Council has come from men who, comparatively speaking, and in their own picturesque vernacular,
scarcely know a "B fra' a bull's fit!"   One gentleman in
particular has by persistent bawling of such phrases as
"more rates" and "inopportune," positively frightened the
more intelligent members of the Council out of the free
exercise of their own judgment.   His chief aider and
abettor used to be a certain Bailie, whose vulgar performances on the magisterial bench filled every one with
amazement and disgust mingled with wonder that judicial
functions of any kind should be entrusted to such an
ignorant vulgarian.   The amusing familiarity with which
he was addressed by all and sundry as "Oor Jeems" and
"Jeems," shows the wonderful depths to which a City Council
can sink in the selection of its magistrates.   It is obvious that
a Council which was capable of appointing to office a man
of this intellectual calibre, could have but little sympathy
with any educational movement. So has Glasgow suffered on its
intellectual side, by remaining too long in the hands of a group
of mere materialists, headed by men of meagre education.
Tannahill sang of one Rab Roryson who owned a famous bonnet,
but was careful to explain, " 'Twas no for itsel', 'twas the head
that was in it".   In these later times the bailie bodies of Glasgow are wholly engrossed with the outsides of things and seem
more intent on furnishing hats than brains for the ratepayers.
Nor is there wanting a more sordid side to the picture. Though
one of the richest and most flourishing cities in the world,
possessing Library endowments amounting to at least £100,000,
and with three of the finest reference Libraries in the country,
Glasgow seems to be gasping for some Carnegie to come along
and bribe it into doing its duty.   It is to be hoped that before

long Glasgow will turn attention to the educational needs of the people, both as regards literary and technical subjects. At present the only culture which is flourishing seems to be that of money. Perhaps one day, if repentance does not come soon, Glasgow may awake to find that "siller" is not everything. The only places in England which can in any way be compared with Glasgow are Huddersfield, Ystradyfodwg and Burnley. But none of these is an ancient cathedral city, with a university of great importance and a population bordering on a million souls.

In some quarters it seems to be taken for granted that the Public Library service of the country has reached a point beyond which it cannot improve. Such, however, is not the opinion of those who look closely into the inner workings of the system. In some instances Library Committees and librarians have utterly failed to grasp the full significance of providing literature for the people in such a way as to meet even ordinary requirements. Then, again, partly owing to limited funds, librarians have been appointed who have no qualifications for the work, and in other cases men with very little education of a special or even general kind are pitchforked into these positions by friends. But the principal obstruction to rapid progress and the attainment of higher efficiency consists in the limitation of the rate imposed by Parliament. The reasons which existed in 1850 and 1855 for such limitation no longer hold good, and I fail to see that Parliament has any right to dictate to a community how much it may spend on local objects. When corruption or maladministration of any sort creeps into local affairs, which the ratepayers are themselves unable to correct, it will be time enough for the Legislature to step in and stop the abuse. Meanwhile it seems to me that any town or district should have the same power over the development of its Libraries as it has over its schools, workhouses and drains. Many towns are forced by this artificial and arbitrary limitation to rely on the generosity of individuals for the provision of Libraries. In this work no one has been so active as Mr. J. Passmore Edwards, who has done for Cornwall and London what a niggardly legislative provision prevented communities from doing for themselves. The work accomplished by Mr. Edwards has been splendid and fruitful, while much of it has been done in districts which most required such substantial aid. There is yet another field remaining to be worked by philanthropic means, and that is the providing of large district reading-rooms for the juvenile population of London. With all the will in the world, comparatively few of the London Library Boards have been able to provide adequate accommodation for boys and girls, and especially for little waifs between the ages of six and twelve, who most need the shelter and educational influence of such rooms. I have little hesitation in stating that if Mr. Edwards, or some other philanthropist, could get the various Library Authorities and the School Board to join forces and co-operate with him, there would be no difficulty in establishing and maintaining such reading-rooms in every district of London requiring them.

In conclusion, I should like to address a few remarks to Library Authorities who have, as yet, not fully grasped the proper ideal of Library work. There is much need for reforms in many directions in some Libraries, and in none more than in those which simply continue the policy and rules which were adopted to suit the conditions of thirty or forty years ago. The timid and distrustful policy which was natural in the early days of the Library movement is no longer tolerable, although it will be found in many Libraries which are other-wise well managed. I will refer separately to several of these antiquated notions which, in my opinion, are not in harmony with modern ideals, and tend to irritate and annoy the public without being any great advantage or safeguard. The rules and regulations of some Libraries are apparently drafted by some prison governor or police magistrate, so full of suspicion do they seem. Others again are drawn in such a fashion as to suggest that they are made to protect the personal property of the Committee, while others manifestly bear the mark of the over-bearing Jack-in-office or lazy librarian. First, then, by what right does any Library make a charge for a ticket *before* the reader can use the Library? In face of the Act of 1892, a decision in a Sheriff's Court in Scotland, and the opinion of the honorary solicitor of the Library Association, it is clearly illegal to impose any such preliminary charge, and I trust intending readers will not scruple to resist it. Second, what is the object in demanding, as is done in many towns, that every enrolled ratepayer shall be guaranteed by one or two other ratepayers? Surely if a householder's name appears on the register he is entitled to borrow on his own responsibility. At any rate, if this can be allowed in some towns, why not in all? Again, why should intending borrowers have to wait a week, and in some cases a fortnight, while their applications for tickets are being verified? This is a most vexatious regu-lation, and the time of waiting should be reduced to two or three days at most. Some Libraries only lend books, without fine, for seven days, and charge all kinds of imposts from 1d. a day to 1d. a week on borrowers who fail to return their books within the seven days. In my opinion, seven days is just half the time which should be allowed for reading any book, and any fine over 1d. a week, or part of a week, should be declared illegal. A Library has no right to make profit out of the readers who support it while exercising some salutary method of preventing books being retained too long. There are Libraries which refuse to exchange a book on the day of issue, although the borrower explains he has read it before, and others which keep books back for a whole day when returned, before reissuing them. Some Libraries in the country close the lending department for a whole or half day, finding their excuse in a small staff. But surely this provincial plan is not required in the large London Libraries which possess fairly large staffs? Nevertheless certain London Libraries do close, and the practice is found most inconvenient by the readers. There are other petty, little, irritating regulations, which annoy and harass readers, but I have named enough to show that there is still room for improvement. The fewer restrictions put upon readers and the more that is done to interest the people in the work of the Public Libraries, the greater hope there will be of a great improvement in the status and means of those institutions. They were instituted by the people, and by the people they will be used, and judged.

THE EARLY HISTORY OF THE PUBLIC LIBRARY MOVEMENT.

By WILLIAM E. A. AXON.

WHEN the early days of the Public Library Movement come to be fully chronicled, the name of Edward Edwards will be written on almost every page. It is to be regretted that we know so little as to the personal history of the man to whom in a large measure it is due that the British municipalities have been able to make such provision for the study of literature and science as is implied in the establishment and maintenance of public libraries. Of Mr. Edwards's parentage and birthplace nothing is known with certainty. He is believed to have been born in London, in the year 1812, and the fact of his Welsh extraction was evidenced by his temperament no less than by his name and physique. Where he received his education is unknown, but that he was a diligent student is certain from the breadth of his scholarship and the wide variety of his information. When German literature was little studied, he had found the value of it for these literary and bibliographical researches in which he was interested. As early as 1835 he had begun to collect materials for an exhaustive treatise on the history and economy of public libraries. He edited a sumptuous volume on the Napoleon medals; he catalogued the medals in the British Museum relating to that great warrior; he wrote on the great seals of England, and he published several pamphlets and articles relating to educational matters. The affairs of the British Museum were attracting the attention both of literary men and of the general public. He was a witness before the Parliamentary Committee of 1836, which gave a fair warning to the Trustees to set their house in order, and the introduction of Panizzi's energetic personality had been favourable to reform. In 1838 the Trustees decided to print an alphabetical catalogue, and the carrying out of their decision was entrusted to Panizzi, who was now keeper of the printed books. The rules for its compilation were matters of anxious consideration and discussion, in which Mr. Edwards, in common with Mr. Thomas Watts, Mr. J. H. Parry and Mr. Winter Jones, had a share. The plan adopted had never been cordially accepted by Panizzi, and after the letter A had appeared the printing was abandoned.

In 1848 a Royal Commission was appointed to examine into the condition of the British Museum, and the general result was to strengthen the influence of Panizzi. Mr. Edwards was one of the witnesses, and his evidence was of some importance, contrasting as it does, in common with that of Panizzi and De Morgan, in its accuracy and reasonableness with the random assertions and ignorance of the first principles of bibliography shown by those who thought it an easy task to catalogue nearly half a million of volumes, and to do so without either plan or rules. By this time Mr. Edwards had become a warm advocate for the multiplication of public libraries. He had collected with laborious industry a considerable mass of data as to the statistics of Libraries. There is perhaps no branch of statistical inquiry in which it is, even now, so difficult to obtain trustworthy data, and the difficulties were much greater then than they are at present. The results, which he published in the *Athenæum*, were subjected to severe criticism in the same paper by Mr. Thomas Watts, who adopted the signature of "Verificator". Those who were behind the scenes, no doubt, smiled at this conflict of two doughty champions who were both in the service of the British Museum. But Mr. Edwards had taken his place as an authority on educational matters, and especially as one familiar with the history, management and statistics of libraries at home and abroad. When in 1849 Mr. William Ewart, M.P., obtained the appointment of a Select Committee "on the best means of extending the establishment of Libraries freely open to the public, especially in large towns in Great Britain and Ireland," Mr. Edward Edwards was the chief witness, although the others included Guizot, Van de Weyer, George Dawson, Samuel Smiles, Henry Stevens of Vermont, and Guglielmo Libri. The last named was still in the flush of his official reputation as a bibliophile, and had not yet been accused of loving valuable MSS. not wisely for honesty, but too well for the comfort of their proper owners. He was asked: "Do you think that it is safe in a public library to allow persons to see important manuscripts?" And he answered, cautiously and judiciously: "I think it would be inexpedient to allow every person; it would perhaps be dangerous". But whatever may be thought of Libri's character, his evidence was sound and useful.

It was an easy task for Mr. Edwards to show that there was a great lack of public libraries in this country. Abroad, when the monastic houses were disestablished, their books often served as the nucleus for a town library. In England the literary possessions of the monasteries became at the time of the Reformation the prey of ignorance and cupidity. Shiploads of MSS. are said to have been sent to the Netherlands for the use of the bookbinders. Dr. Dee, who urged Queen Mary to take measures for their preservation, mentions the existence of Cicero's "De Republica," which disappeared from view and was only recovered, in part, by Cardinal Mai from a MS. at the Vatican, in which a treatise of St. Augustine had been written over the classic. Not only were the monastic libraries

THE LATE WILLIAM EWART, M.P.

dispersed, but in the few instances where town or parish libraries had been formed, they had, by the carelessness of their custodians, been dispersed or alienated. In Mr. Edwards's statistics, Great Britain made a poor show. The number of volumes to every hundred of the population of the cities containing libraries was in Brunswick 2353, in the Papal States 266, in France 125, in Great Britain 43. The Tuscan town of Siena had 50,000 volumes for its 19,000 inhabitants; the old endowed library founded by Humphrey Chetham at Manchester, which had then a population of 360,000, contained only 19,000. To make the contrast more complete, the Manchester Library was the only one in Great Britain that was absolutely free to the public. Mr. Edwards, who had managed to' offend various people by his evidence, was severely cross-examined by Lord Seymour, who seemed even to take a pleasure in eliciting the fact that his services at the British Museum were remunerated at the rate of only £164 per annum. Panizzi, who was also a witness, energetically defended his own management of the British Museum, and contended that in no other country was the National Library managed so liberally. The British Museum, he declared, was more accessible, and the readers had greater facilities than in other institutions with which it could be compared. And in this he was right. He also roundly declared that the statistical information collected by the Committee was "most fallacious and of no authority whatever". He was asked: "Supposing that libraries were formed, not libraries of research, not recondite libraries, but libraries for general readers, do not you think that persons might be admitted there, as they are admitted in the library at Manchester called Chetham's Library, simply upon writing down their names and addresses?" He answered: "I think there would be bad consequences from it, not merely to the books, but there would be many other disorders; for instance, there are ladies coming to read at the British Museum. Now that alone forms a great objection to admitting everybody indiscriminately to the library. Then we have plenty of pickpockets at the Museum, who would often go to the reading-room if the admission were too free. There are some other objections of this sort which might arise. I am not sufficiently acquainted with the police of London to know how such disorders might be prevented." Panizzi was a great librarian, and he was a true friend of libraries, but neither instinct nor observation had given him the power of prophecy. The experience of the town libraries that have since been established shows that his apprehensions were groundless and his fears chimerical.

The result of the inquiries of the Committee was that the weight of evidence was felt to be on the side represented by Mr. Edwards. It was impossible to contend that there was not a lamentable lack of freely accessible public libraries. The fact was too obvious to be denied or even to be explained away. The most important "finding" is in the following paragraph :—

"Your Committee further recommend that a power be

given by Parliament enabling Town Councils to levy a small
rate for the creation and support of town Libraries.   An Act
was passed in the year 1845 conferring the power on Town
Councils to levy a rate (to the extent of a halfpenny in the
pound) 'for encouraging the establishment of Museums in
large towns,' commonly known under the name of the
'Museums Act'.   Some few towns have availed themselves of
this privilege.   It is probable that more will do so.   A call,
however, has been made upon the Legislature from more than
one quarter, and especially from Limerick, to extend this
power of rating to the case of Libraries.   One town (Warrington), even under the sanction of the existing Museums Act,
has founded an open Public Library as well as a Museum.
The association of the two institutions seems to be a most
obvious and desirable alliance.   In all our chief provincial
towns it is requisite that there should be Topographical
Libraries as well as Topographical Museums, where history
may find a faithful portraiture of local events, local literature,
and local manners; and art and science a collection of all
objects illustrative of the climate, soil, and resources of the
surrounding country.   Special Libraries would, no doubt, form
themselves in appropriate localities.   At Hamburg the Commercial Library has been famous for more than a century.   Its
existence is stated by Dr. Meyer to have had a most beneficial
influence on the character of the merchants of Hamburg.   It
would seem that in our large commercial and manufacturing
towns, as well as in our agricultural districts, such Libraries
would naturally spring up, illustrative of the peculiar trade,
manufactures, and agriculture of the place, and greatly favourable to the practical development of the science of political
economy.   Your Committee are convinced that the first great
step in the formation of Libraries (and of similar institutions)
is to establish a place of deposit, a local habitation for the
books.   That once formed, measures should be taken (as suggested in the valuable evidence of Mr. Brotherton) for securing
the property—the buildings as well as the books—in the Town
Council of the place, or in some fixed and perpetually renew-
able body.   Thus the evils which have befallen so many of our
charitable foundations from the loss of Trustees, and a necessary
appeal to a court of equity, would be avoided.   There can be
no doubt, that these two conditions once fulfilled—a fixed and
proper place of deposit, and due investments of the property
—donation will abundantly supply the books.   Donation has
been the source of the principal Libraries which have ever or
anywhere been formed.   The British Museum (though supplied
from the public revenue with the means of buying books) owes
its principal literary treasures to donation.   So do our Colleges
and almost all our local Libraries.   A large proportion of the
books in foreign Libraries have been contributed by individuals.   It it not easy to conceive that a benevolent and

enlightened citizen can leave a more pleasing or lasting monument behind him than a donation of books to a Public Library; constituting a department on which his name might be inscribed as a benefactor, not only to his own times but to future ages."

The Committee also recommended the application to Public Libraries of the principle of grants in aid that had

MR. WILLIAM E. A. AXON. From photo by M. Guttenberg, Limited, Manchester.

already been recognised in the case of Elementary Schools and Schools of Design. This was part of Mr. Edwards's scheme, but it never came into practical operation, and Public Libraries, except those of a national character, remain exclusively local institutions. The Committee had good reason to be satisfied. Mr. Joseph Brotherton, with the practical good sense that characterised his movements, determined that Salford, which he represented in the House of Commons, should have a library without waiting for fresh legislation. He discussed the matter with the Mayor, and some liberal subscriptions were at once forthcoming.   This was in 1849, and in 1850 the Salford Library had a printed catalogue extending to 236 pages. Mr. Brotherton saw that many of the old foundations had failed because as Trustees died they were not replaced, and hence he felt the advantage there would be in vesting the property in a body like the Town Council, of whose permanent continuance there could be no doubt.   But if Warrington and Salford could thus establish Libraries, why was further legislation.necessary ?   The present writer has always thought that a community had, and has, a right at common law to establish a public library, and it is certain that in the seventeenth century a rate was levied for the benefit of the "English Library" that was then housed in the Collegiate Church of Manchester.   Apart from this a library might be regarded as a department of a museum, and the Museums Act passed in 1845 authorised the levying of a rate.   The legal aspect of the question was not free from doubt, and Mr. William Ewart, the Chairman of the Committee, who was also the author of the Museums Act, brought in a bill, and the result was the passing of the Public Libraries and Museums Act, 1850 (13 and 14 Victoria, cap. 65).   It is perhaps as well that the older volumes of Hansard are not frequently read.   The debates on Ewart's bill were distinguished by some very foolish and illiberal speeches, which were all the more lamentable as they came from men who by their position ought to have had more sympathy with proposals for extending education and diffusing good literature.   The essential point, however, was achieved, the bill passed, but the Act was restricted to towns of more than 10,000 inhabitants, the rate was not to exceed a halfpenny, and none of it was to be spent on books.   The cost of the building and shelves and the payment of salaries could thus be provided for, but for books to go on the shelves the Libraries were to trust entirely to gifts.   This ridiculous restriction remained until 1855, but Manchester had already escaped from its jurisdiction by a clause in a private Act.

The first town to adopt the Act was Manchester.   The poll showed 3962 votes for and 40 against.   The leading spirit in its formation was Sir John Potter.   A public subscription brought in £12,823, of which about £800 was raised by a Committee of working men.   It is a remarkable circumstance that no effort was made to incorporate any existing library in the new institution.   The Committee had received interesting evidence about Chetham's Library, Manchester, which at that time was the only one in England of absolutely unrestricted access.   It was founded in accordance with the will of Humphrey Chetham, a wealthy merchant, who also left money for the endowment of a Blue-coat School.   In the older literature of theology and history it was strong, but was very deficient in modern books. Comparatively little use had been made of it, which was partly due to the fact that it was not open in the evening. This regulation is still in force, and whilst a delightful haunt for the antiquary, it is necessarily little used by those whose days must be given to industry and commerce. An influential Committee was formed, which included the first Bishop of Manchester, that remarkable thinker Prof. A. J. Scott, Mr. James Crossley, Mr. Alexander Ireland, Dr. J. P. Joule, and other representatives of the literature and science of the city. This Committee appointed Mr. Edward Edwards as librarian, and secured his services for the moderate stipend of £200 per year. The building and books were bought under their direction, and they had full control until it was transferred to the Corporation. Although the Act gave power for the Committee of Management to include persons not members of the Town Council, no effort was made to secure the continuance of their services, and the Manchester Free Library has from the first been managed exclusively as a department of the municipality. In Salford the opposite practice prevailed, and for many years the "Auxiliary Committee" furnished a considerable part of the funds for the purchase of books, pictures, and specimens for the Library, Art Gallery and Museum. After the Auxiliary Committee had ceased, honorary members were appointed, but at present the Salford Committee, like that of Manchester, is composed exclusively of members of the Corporation.

The Manchester Free Library was opened 2nd September, 1852, and it was a red letter day. Representatives of literature, science, and philanthropy assembled to bid the new institution godspeed. Amongst those present at the meetings were Dickens, Thackeray, Lytton, John Bright, Monckton Milnes, Peter Cunningham, Sir James Stephen, Lord Shaftesbury, Charles Knight, Joseph Brotherton, Abel Heywood, and other national and local notables. Of all the bright and brilliant company who took an active part in the opening ceremony, one alone, it is believed, remains, Mr. W. J. Paul, who acted as honorary secretary of the working men's Committee. "Nothing," he said, "can be more conducive to the prosperity of a nation than the refined understanding of a moral and intelligent people, ever bearing in remembrance that the sole end and aim of their existence here should be to leave the world better than they found it." It has often been told how Thackeray at the morning meeting sat down in the midst of the unfinished sentence of what had promised to be a remarkable speech. But the failure of the morning had a sequel. He attended the workmen's meeting in the evening, and, after hearing what Lord Shaftesbury had to say, he asked permission to address the gathering, and made a speech that was witty and wise and full of kindly feeling. The audience readily took up his points, and his little speech was punctuated with laughter and cheers. The proceedings were, of course, fully reported, and the new movement thus received a powerful impetus. In another way the example of Manchester was wholly good. For the first time in a town library provision was made by which books could be taken out for home reading. The success of the Free Lending Library was assured from the first. There was thus afforded to many a method of recreation not only harmless but elevating, and to the strenuous few the means of self-education and a preparation for more onerous duties and a different position in the social order. At the beginning of such an institution as the Manchester Public

THE FIRST PUBLIC LIBRARY UNDER THE EWART ACT.

Library the danger of limited views and a low ideal had to be faced. Here Mr. Edwards's influence was on the right side. He did not hesitate to buy for the "People's Library" a copy of the famous Jews' Bible printed in Spanish at Ferrara in 1553, a long set of the Elzevir *Republics*, Walton's *Polyglot*, and many other books that must have been caviare to the general, but gave dignity to the collection and set an example of learning and catholicity that has since been followed with advantage. The value of pamphlet literature was early appreciated, and by the purchase of the bulk of the Magens collection the Library acquired a series of printed documents relating to the history of trade and political economy generally that has been of great service to students and investigators. The principle was thus stamped on the Free Library movement that the town library was to be helpful to the learned as well as the unlearned—an institution for the increase as well as the diffusion of knowledge.

The experiment was watched with great interest and information was eagerly sought, and Mr. Edwards with his strong taste for statistics was ready to supply all the data that could be needed. Whether all the details that, following his example, are commonly given in library reports are necessary or worth the trouble that is involved in their preparation is a question that is fairly matter of argument. But the statistics were useful when free town libraries were still an experiment of which many doubted the success. The great difficulty in the way of the usefulness of the new institutions was the want of preparation of the readers. Men came with a genuine desire for mental improvement, but found that after the fatigues of a day of toil they were too weary to concentrate their attention upon the scenes of history or the problems of philosophy. Even the typography of the last century presented difficulties. The locality of the library proved to be not very convenient or suitable. Notwithstanding these drawbacks, the library was felt to be doing excellent work, and the city of Manchester was proud of the new institution which offered the treasures of literature and science, the teaching of history, and the inspiration of the poet alike to rich and poor. *

The early history of the Public Library movement in Liverpool was on somewhat different lines to those adopted in Manchester. Mr. J. A. Picton was elected a member of the Liverpool Town Council in 1849, and early in the following year he moved for the appointment of a Committee "to consider the practicability of the establishment of a Public Library freely open to all classes". The report made by this Committee was favourable, and an effort, which failed, was made to secure the transfer of the Royal Institution to the Corporation. A public subscription only resulted in £1389. Then came the news that the thirteenth Earl of Derby had left directions that his fine natural history collection should be devoted to the benefit of Liverpool. The plan thought of by the noble donor had been to associate his collection with the Collegiate Institution, but in a building to be provided by the Corporation. Mr. Picton, however, entered into negotiations with the fourteenth earl, and it was decided to make it a part of the new institution. The Corporation obtained a private

---

* Mr. Edwards, whose many excellent qualities were marred by a certain inability to work comfortably with other people, remained at Manchester until 1858, when he resigned and devoted himself to literary pursuits. He died 10th February, 1886.

Act which empowered the levying of a penny rate, and the Liverpool Public Library and Museum was opened 18th October, 1852, a little more than a month later than the opening at Manchester. The Mayor of Liverpool spoke of the library as one "for the poor," but no such notion was in Mr. Picton's mind. He had before him a clear ideal of a great public library that should respond to the intellectual needs of all classes of society. He was not afraid of placing on the shelves books that might not be asked for until years had elapsed. What he was afraid of was that when the man came the books might not be ready for him. From the first he contemplated a Free Lecture Hall as an integral part of the scheme. In no other city has this received so remarkable a development as in Liverpool. In the Manchester Library there was soon after the opening an admirable series of six lectures, but after this pioneer effort in 1852 the lectures ceased, and the next address on books was not delivered until 1874. Curiously enough he was at first rather out of sympathy with the idea of a lending department, though this also was added at a later time, His fine ideal for a great central Library was not shared by all his colleagues. "The opposition he met with in Duke Street" [where the Committee met], says the Rev. H. H. Higgins, "was very strenuous and sometimes amusing. For two years or more I was witness to one of the most splendid struggles ever made by any man against Philistinism and unintelligible opposition." But Picton held his own, took the line of least resistance, and when it was necessary to yield at least in appearance, bided his time for a more favourable opportunity. He laid the foundation, deep and broad, and lived to see rise a magnificent series of institutions of which any city might be proud. The Library given by Sir William Brown, the Art Gallery given by Sir A. B. Walker, the National History Museum bequeathed by the Earl of Derby, and the archæological collection given by Mr. Joseph Mayer are donations which in value and extent are unrivalled in this country. The Picton reading room which forms part of the group is a fitting memorial of the man to whose energy, tact, and influence it is due in so large a degree that Liverpool has this splendid inheritance for the public good. In a happy and honoured old age Sir James Picton could regard with unmingled satisfaction the result of the long years of public spirit he had given to the intellectual and moral advancement of Liverpool.

Here we must draw to a close. Later influences have had their share in the development of the Public Library movement, but its early history is bound up with the names of Ewart, Edwards and Picton. The great library at Birmingham did not take form until 1866, although a lending library was established in 1861. In the formation and experimental stages of the Public Library movement Manchester and Liverpool led the way, and in their great city libraries showed a splendid exemplar, which has happily been followed by many other municipalities, great and small. The founders of the movement had broad views, and to them we owe it that the Public Libraries, which derive their funds from all classes, respond to the needs of all classes, and give aid alike to the artisan, the merchant and the scholar. The pioneers of the movement felt, as Channing has finely expressed it, that "the diffusion of these silent teachers, books, through the whole community, is to work greater effects than artillery, machinery and legislation. Its peaceful agency is to supersede stormy revolutions. The culture which it is to spread, whilst an unspeakable good to the individual, is also to become the stability of nations."

PUBLIC LIBRARY LEGISLATION.

PAST AND PROSPECTIVE.

BY H. W. FOVARGUE, TOWN-CLERK, EASTBOURNE.

THE legislation relating to Public Libraries and Museums commenced in the year 1845 with "an Act for encouraging the establishment of Museums in large towns," and since that year no less than twenty-three Acts of Parliament have been passed in relation to those subjects.

Very few Public Libraries (established by munificent gifts or under Local Acts of Parliament) existed when the Select Committee of the House of Commons (presided over by Mr. W. Ewart) sat in 1849 to inquire into them, but from the year 1850, when the Act "for enabling Town Councils to establish Public Libraries and Museums" was passed, as the fruit of that Committee's labours, their number has steadily increased.

It is unnecessary to deal at length with legislation now repealed. Some of the Acts affected the United Kingdom, some applied to England, some to Scotland, and some to Ireland, while one affected Ireland and Scotland, and others particular towns. One feature marks all the legislation, namely, the limit of the amount to be expended. In the first Act this limit was fixed at a halfpenny rate, but subsequently was increased to a penny, the present maximum rate (though it may be fixed at less), except in a few large towns, where by special provision in local Acts further powers have been obtained, but not in any case so as to enable the levying of a rate exceeding twopence in the pound.

So far as regards England and Wales, the Act passed in the year 1855, though amended in many respects by subsequent legislation, was, until the year 1892, the "principal" Act relating to the establishment and regulation of Public Libraries and Museums; but as the Act passed in the latter year was simply a consolidating Act, it will be sufficient for the purposes of this chapter to summarise briefly its leading provisions and those of any amending Act, to obtain information as to past legislation affecting those parts of the United Kingdom.

ENGLAND AND WALES.—THE EXISTING ACTS.

The Adoption of the Public Libraries Act, 1892.—It is to be observed that the Act only comes into operation in particular districts when adopted in the prescribed manner. The method of adoption has been complicated by the Public Libraries Amendment Act, 1893, and the Local Government Act, 1894, so that different methods now apply to different districts. Thus the Act is adopted (1) in an *urban district* by a resolution passed by the Urban District Council; (2) in a *rural parish* by the Parish Meeting, or (if demanded) a poll of the voters by ballot; (3) in the *city of London*, a *metropolitan parish* or a *metropolitan district*, by a poll of the voters by means of voting papers. It is impossible in the limits of the present chapter to give the various details of these different methods—reference should be made to the recent publication of the Library Association on the adoption of the Public Libraries Acts in England and Wales, published at 6d.

Library Districts.—The Act may be adopted in (1) any urban district (*i.e.*, a municipal borough, Improvement Act district, or local government district); (2) any parish not within an urban district, or any part of a parish outside an urban district; (3) the city of London; or (4) a metropolitan district.

The Maximum Rate.—The rate to be levied for the purposes of the Act must not exceed one penny in the pound, and it may be still further limited on adopting the Act to three farthings or one halfpenny in the pound. This is almost a universal rule, but there are exceptions; thus there is no limit to the rate which may be levied in the city of London, and in certain large towns special power has been obtained under local Acts to levy a higher rate.

The Library Authority.—The administration of the Libraries Act is entrusted (1) in an urban district to the Urban District Council, but that authority may, and usually does, delegate all, or some of its powers, to a Library Committee, the members of which need not necessarily be members of the District Council; (2) in a rural parish having a Parish Council that body is to be the Library Authority, and in a rural parish without a Parish Council the Parish Meeting may appoint Library Commissioners (*i.e.*, not less than three nor more than nine voters), or it may appoint a Committee of its own number; (3) in the city of London the Common Council is to be the Library Authority; (4) in a metropolitan district the District Board, and in a metropolitan parish the Vestry, must appoint Library Commissioners, *i.e.*, not less than three nor more than nine voters in the district or parish, but it should be remembered that the Vestry or District Board, with the sanction of the Local Government Board, may act as the Library Authority. If Commissioners are appointed, the Act contains regulations as to their quorum, election meetings, and duties.

Amalgamation of Districts.—In some cases it may be found beneficial for two or more Library districts to have a common Library or Museum. Provision is therefore made for the Vestries of two or more neighbouring parishes to combine together so as to form one Library district with a common Library or Museum, or a parish adjoining or near to any Library district may be amalgamated with it. Again, the Library Authorities of two or more urban districts may agree to combine together, and lastly the Commissioners (or Parish Council where there is one) separately appointed for any two or more rural parishes may make agreements for the use of a common Library, subject to the consent of the voters (or *query* Parish Meeting). Doubtless these provisions will become more operative in future in view of the recent establishment of Parish Councils.

The Institutions which may be provided.—When once the Public Libraries Act, 1892, is adopted, the Library Authority may not only purchase or hire land and erect or hire buildings and furnish the same for Public Library purposes, but it has power to provide (1) Public Museums, (2) Schools for Science, (3) Art Galleries, and (4) Schools for Art, but always subject to the limited rate.

Regulations and Management.—Libraries and Museums established under the Act are to be "Free," *i.e.*, no charge can be made for the admission of the inhabitants to a Library or Museum or for the use of a Lending Library (this does not apply to Schools for Science, Art Galleries, or Schools for Art provided by a Library Authority). Persons residing outside the district may be allowed to use the Library or Museum either free of charge or on payment of the charges fixed by the Authority. The general management, regulation, and control of every institution provided under the Acts is vested in the Library Authority, which may provide books, newspapers, maps, etc., appoint officers, and make regulations for the safety and use of the institution and the admission of the public. An Urban Authority may delegate all or some of its powers to a Committee, members of which need not be members of the Urban Authority.

Expenses and Accounts.—Subject to the limited rate, the expenses of executing the Act are to be defrayed (1) *in a borough*, out of the borough fund or borough rate or by a separate Library rate; (2) *in any other urban district*, out of a rate levied under the Public Health Act or by a Library rate levied in the like manner; (3) *in a parish*, by a rate raised with and as part of the poor rate; (4) *in a metropolitan district*, out of the funds of the District Board as if they had been incurred for the general purposes of the Metropolitan Management Acts; (5) *in the city of London*, out of the consolidated rate levied by the Commissioners of Sewers or by a separate rate levied in like manner.

In rural parishes it is obligatory to show on the rate demand note the amount required for Library purposes, and it is desirable that this should be done in all cases. The Library Authority may borrow money for the purchase of land or erection of buildings, with the approval of the Local Government Board, but in the case of a parish the additional sanction of the Vestry (*query* Parish Meeting) or District Board is required. Separate accounts of receipts and expenses are to be kept and audited, and these accounts are to be open to the inspection of the ratepayers.

SCOTLAND.—THE EXISTING ACTS.

The legislation affecting Libraries and Museums in Scotland is in several respects in advance of the English law. The Public Libraries Consolidation (Scotland) Act, 1887, not only consolidated but amended the multifarious Acts which previously existed. Excepting the Edinburgh Public Library Assessment Act, 1887, and the Public Libraries (Scotland) Act, 1894, it is the only statute in operation in Scotland affecting Public Libraries. As the following is only a short summary of its provisions the Act itself should be consulted for fuller information.

Adoption of the Act.—The method of adopting the Act for burghs was changed by the Public Libraries (Scotland) Act, 1894, which provides for the adoption of the principal Act in those districts by a resolution of the Council in substitution for the determination of the householders. Due notice of the meeting and of the proposal is to be published, and if the resolution is passed an advertisement thereof must be issued. In a parish the Act can only be adopted by a majority of the householders, whose opinion is to be ascertained either by means of voting papers or at a public meeting to be called and held in the manner prescribed by the Act; the Sheriff may distribute voting papers or call a public meeting. Two years must elapse in the event of the adoption being rejected before the question is submitted again to the householders in a parish, but this limit does not now apply to burghs. Even if the Act is not adopted in a parish, the expenses of determining as to its adoption are to be paid out of the rates, and if the Act is adopted, the Sheriff may borrow the amount on the security of the Library rate to be afterwards levied.

Expenses and Accounts.—If the Act is adopted the expenses for the maintenance and management of the Libraries and Museums, or the purchase of articles, or repayment of loans and interest, are to be paid out of a Library rate to be levied in a burgh by the Magistrates and Council, and in a parish by the Board, but the rate is not to exceed a penny per pound. (Note there is no provision for fixing a lower limit.) True and regular accounts are to be kept and audited, and are to be open to inspection by every person liable to be assessed to the Library rate. The Authority may borrow a capital sum not exceeding one-fourth of the Library rate capitalised at twenty years' purchase, and the amount is to be repaid by a sinking fund into which one-fiftieth part of the money so borrowed shall be paid ; such sinking fund is to be invested as directed by the Act. The Authority is authorised to accept from the Education Department any grant toward the purchase of the site, or the erection, enlargement or repair of any school for science or art, teachers' residence or furnishing.

The Committee and its Powers.—The Library Authority is annually to appoint a Committee of not less than ten nor more than twenty members, half to be chosen from the Magistrates and Council (or Board) and half from the householders. Provision is made for filling vacancies for the appointment of chairman and as to the meetings. The powers of the Committee are specifically enacted ; they may appoint Sub-Committees and salaried officers, purchase books, etc., provide suitable rooms, regulate the lending of books, and not merely to residents, but to the inmates of industrial schools, training ships, etc., and to persons employed in any business in the district, although they may not be householders, and may not reside within the limits. The foregoing powers of the Committee are to be exercised without any control by the Library Authority. They may make bye-laws for the control, management, protection and use of any property, articles or things under their control, subject to a penalty not exceeding five pounds for each offence, but these bye-laws require confirmation and approval, and are to be published, exhibited and printed as specified in the Act.

Institutions.—The following institutions may be provided :— (1) Public Library, (2) Public Museum, (3) School of Science, (4) School for Art, (5) an Art Gallery, but (1), (2), and (5) are to be open to the public free of charge.

The Schedules.—The Act contains in the schedules particular directions as to the procedure to be followed for determining (1) by voting papers, (2) by public meeting as to the adoption of the Act.

Edinburgh.—Special provisions apply to the city of Edinburgh ; *vide* Edinburgh Public Libraries Act, 1887.

IRELAND.—THE EXISTING ACTS.

The legislation affecting Ireland is contained in the Public Libraries and Museums Act, 1855, and other amending Acts, the principal amending Act being the Public Libraries (Ireland) Act, 1894.

Institutions which may be provided.—The Library Authority may provide Public Libraries and Museums, Schools of

Science and Art, and Schools of Music. Libraries and Museums are to be open to the public free of all charge.

Adoption of Act.—The Act may be adopted in any urban district, and the amount of the rate fixed (but not exceeding the maximum rate of one penny in the pound) raised and removed by a resolution of the Urban Authority. A month's notice of the meeting when the resolution is intended to be proposed is to be given to every member of the Authority, and, if passed, the resolution must be published as prescribed by the Act of 1894. If the Urban Authority fails to pass a resolution adopting the Act this is not to prejudice the right given by the Act of 1894 to the voters of expressing their opinion. Any twenty or more voters (or the Urban Authority) may request the Mayor or other Chairman of the Urban Authority to ascertain the opinion of the voters on the question or questions stated in the requisition. The Mayor or Chairman is then to ascertain the opinion by ballot, and a majority of answers on valid ballot papers is to decide every question submitted to them. No further poll is to be taken on any question submitted to the voters until the expiration of one year from the polling day.

Library Districts.—The Act may be adopted only in an urban district, *i.e.*, any incorporated borough, or any town or place in which Commissioners, Trustees, or other persons are elected under 9 Geo. IV., cap. 82, or the Towns' Improvement (Ireland) Act, 1854, or any local or other Act or Acts.

Library Authority.—In an incorporated borough the Council or Board of Municipal Commissioners are to be the Library Authority, and in every other town the Town Commissioners, in whom the institutions are to vest and who are to provide the necessary books, etc., appoint officers and servants, and make rules and regulations for the safety and use of the institutions, but the Authority may appoint a Committee for these purposes, which may consist in part of persons not members of the Council or Board of Commissioners.

Expenses and Accounts.—The expenses are to be raised out of the borough or town fund, as part of the borough or town rate, or by a separate rate, and distinct accounts are to be kept, audited, transmitted to the Lord-Lieutenant, and deposited, and be open to inspection by all householders. The rate must not exceed one penny in the pound, but a lower rate of assessment may be fixed by the Urban Authority or the voters. With the approval of the Commissioners of Her Majesty's Treasury, the Library Authority may borrow such money as may be required on security of a mortgage or bond of the borough fund or the town fund or the Library rate.

If a poll of the voters is taken and the Act is adopted, the Urban Authority must act as the Library Authority. Should they fail, however, in this respect, the Local Government Board are authorised, on the application of ten or more voters,

to appoint five voters as Commissioners to carry the principal
Act into execution in place of the Urban Authority.

Amalgamation.—Provision is made in the Act of 1894, when
the principal Act is adopted, for the Authorities of two or more
neighbouring districts, by agreement, to combine together for
carrying the Act into execution, appointing a Joint Committee
to manage the institutions ; or the Urban Authorities of any
two or more districts (whether neighbouring or not) may agree
to share a common Library, Museum, School for Science, Art
Gallery, or School for Art.

Miscellaneous.—The use of a Lending Library may be
granted by the Authority to persons not being inhabitants of
their district either gratuitously or for payment.

The Authority may let any house or building vested in
them but not required for the purposes of the Act, and the
Local Government Board are authorised to make regulations
for carrying into effect the object of the Act.

Every person who is registered as a Parliamentary voter,
either as owner, occupier, or lodger (or in the case of a borough
as a freeman), is to be a voter under the Act.

PROSPECTIVE LEGISLATION.

A Bill has been prepared, and will doubtless be shortly
introduced into Parliament, to enable the voters in an urban
district to adopt the Act if the Urban District Council fail to
pass the necessary resolution on request. This will make the
English law correspond with the Irish Act of 1894. As
previously stated, the existing diversity of methods for adopting the Acts is most confusing, and the Bill proposes to simplify
the procedure by providing that where the opinion of the
voters is to be ascertained, the poll shall be taken by ballot in
all cases, and not by the distribution of voting papers. Powers
are also suggested to enable the Local Government Board to
appoint Library Commissioners where a Vestry or other
Authority fails to give effect to the resolution adopting the Act ;
and it is proposed to protect Library Authorities against
actions for any libel which may be contained in any book on
their shelves, unless they wilfully. persist in circulating the
libellous book after proper notice.

The power to make regulations contained in the Act of 1892
is insufficient, and the Bill proposes, following the precedent
in the Scotch Act, to give the Library Authority power to make
bye-laws for the regulation of the buildings under its control.

There can be no doubt that a great future lies before the
extension of Library work in rural parishes, and further provisions are proposed by the Bill so as to enable the Library
Authorities of any two or more districts to agree together for
the joint use of a common Library. The question of exempting
Public Libraries from rates is one upon which a very strong

feeling has manifested itself, it being felt to be unjust that literary and scientific institutions are exempt from being rated, while Libraries and Museums have been held by the courts of law not to be so exempt. Doubtless when the Bill comes before Parliament some member or members will be prepared to add a clause so as to extend this exemption to the institutions provided by a Library Authority, and this ought to meet with favour, bearing in mind the fact that the amount of the rate which can be levied is limited in every case. Possibly the recent decision in the Manchester case may be taken to justify the exemption of Public Libraries from rates, and further legislation on the point would therefore be unnecessary.

HOW TO ADOPT THE ACTS.

SINCE the publication of the last edition of Greenwood's *Public Libraries*, Parliament has made some important changes in the mode of adopting the Public Libraries Acts. Up to 1892, when the Public Libraries Acts were consolidated, they could only be adopted in any district by a poll of the ratepayers taken by means of voting papers. By an amending Act of 1893 this was altered to enable any Urban District Authority, without a poll of the ratepayers, to put the Acts in force, on certain conditions as to notice, etc., being complied with. This Act does not extend to the city or county of London. In 1894 this amending Act was extended to burghs in Scotland. When the Local Government Act of 1894 was passed some further modifications affecting rural districts were introduced, so that now the methods of adopting the Acts in different administrative areas are as follows:—

> In London, by a poll of the voters taken by means of voting papers as described in *Public Libraries*, fourth edition, and in Fovargue and Ogle's *Public Library Legislation*.
> In urban districts and municipal boroughs, by a resolution of the Council, after due notice of motion.
> In rural parishes, by a majority vote of the Parish Meeting, or, if duly demanded, by a poll of the voters taken by ballot.

There has been as yet no authoritative opinion given as to whether or not a County Council could adopt the Acts, but it seems doubtful if it could. The same means of educating the public and spreading accurate information concerning the uses and objects of the Libraries must still be used for London as before. Many useful hints will be found in the last edition of Greenwood, previously mentioned. It is difficult to educate Town Councils or District Councils, some of which, through sheer fear of the ratepayers (as at Hornsey), require a special mandate from the constituency; while in other places (as at Glasgow) a hostile ring of financial anti-educationists may rule the Council for years. On the other hand it is easier to bring pressure to bear on the comparatively small number composing a District or Town Council, than on the general body of ratepayers in a large town, and it is possible that in most cases proper representations from the leading men of a locality would receive careful attention at the hands of the Local Authority. The Library Association has a special Library Promotion Committee charged with the duty of helping those who desire to move in the matter of having the Acts adopted in districts where Libraries are not yet established. It has also issued as number 7 of its series of handbooks a very useful pamphlet entitled *Adoption of Public Libraries Act*, by H. W. Fovargue, price 6d. For the purpose of giving information such a Committee would be useful, but it is difficult to see how any body of comparative outsiders could effectively intervene in any matter which concerned them not, such as the question of rating a district for Public Library purposes. Nevertheless, the information possessed by such a Committee may be useful, and inquiries should be addressed to Mr. MacAlister, 20 Hanover Square, London, W., Secretary of the Association; or to Mr. H. W. Fincham, 172 St. John Street, London, E.C., Secretary of the Committee.

Friends of the movement would materially strengthen the hands of the Local Governing Body by aiding in the securing of signatures of leading residents to such a memorial as that suggested below.

To the Mayor, Aldermen, and Members of the Council of the Borough of ....

(or by whatever description the Local Governing Body may be known).

Gentlemen,

We, the undersigned Burgesses of the Borough of ...., desire to remind you that the responsibility of adopting the Public Libraries Acts and of establishing a Public Library in .... now rests with yourselves.

We feel that such an Institution would place within the reach of every one the means of self-improvement and of study, and continuing the education of which the foundation may have been laid at school.

The experience of the numerous other towns where Public Libraries exist also shows that they are immensely valued as places of resort for the intelligent reading of Newspapers, Magazines, and other current Literature.

In fact, it is almost too late in the day to recapitulate their advantages, and we beg you to move in the matter without delay, that we may no longer be at a disadvantage in this respect as compared with other and smaller places in our own neighbourhood.

HEATING, LIGHTING, AND VENTILATING PUBLIC LIBRARIES.

By J. W. HART.

THE art of heating, lighting, and ventilating Public Libraries and other public buildings where large numbers of persons assemble during all seasons of the year, and more particularly after dark when artificial lighting is resorted to, is becoming of increasing importance, not only from a physical but from an intellectual point of view. For whether it is at home or at the Public Library, a low or an extremely high temperature in conjunction with a vitiated atmosphere is not calculated either to aid the enjoyment of the perusal of light literature, or to prepare the mind for the reception of those weightier matters which require close study and a retentive and active brain. To a very large number of persons the subject is regarded as unimportant, because their idea of a Public Library is that it exists principally for the purpose of lending books to be read at home in comfortable and uncrowded sitting rooms, forgetful of the fact that the Public Library is the poor man's college, recreation room, or only literary resort, as the case may be. Many are glad to pass a very large portion of their spare time in these rooms, not only on account of the educational facilities offered, but because they have no means wherewith to provide themselves otherwise with the comfort and convenience which is obtainable at these institutions. There is no reason, therefore, why the Libraries should not be warmed, lighted, and ventilated as well as it is possible under the circumstances, avoiding extravagance and unnecessary complications which some delight to introduce in buildings of this kind. There is one peculiar feature in connection with Libraries which tends to make the matter more difficult to deal with, and which is likely to upset the calculations of those who attempt to reduce the subject of heating and ventilation to an exact science, and work it out to their own satisfaction by an elaborate display of figures. To do this it is necessary to assume that the apartment is occupied by a given number of persons who consume a given quantity of oxygen and give off a corresponding amount of carbonic acid gas. It is also imperative to calculate how much heat is given off by each person in determining the amount of heating power required to keep the rooms at an equable temperature.

In the most important room, however, in a Public Library it would be very difficult if not impossible to regulate matters in this way, because the numbers vary to an unusual extent and make exact calculations rather unreliable. Not that it is my intention to deprecate the working out of problems of this kind in a strictly scientific manner, but it may be well to remark that it requires a very large measure of practical experience to render the various systems successful when applied. With regard to heating, it is difficult to make most people believe that the open fire-place is the most wasteful method possible, as, notwithstanding the undoubted appearance of comfort and cheerfulness which that mode of heating

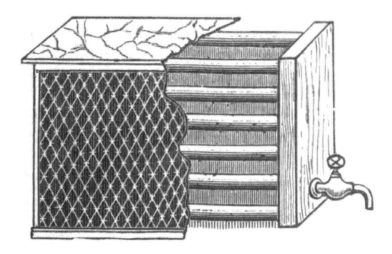

Fig. 1.

always imparts, it is not at all suitable for Public Libraries, on account of its wastefulness, and the tendency of a selfish few to monopolise the whole of the comfort and cheerfulness, and effectually screen others from it. It is therefore advisable to economise the fuel and distribute the heat as equally as possible throughout the apartment by some approved system of hot-water apparatus. And in giving a description of something of the kind in a short article, one must necessarily be brief by pointing out the main features and leaving the details until some future time.

A great advantage both in efficiency and economy is obtained by combining, as much as possible, the heating and ventilating, and in some degree the lighting can be made to assist in the latter purpose. Of late years steam is being used to a very large extent for heating purposes, but as it generally requires apparatus of a special character and a large amount of attention when used for heating apartments only, we shall for the present confine our remarks to a system of heating by low pressure hot water, this being the simplest, requiring least attention and generally giving satisfaction, although in large institutions

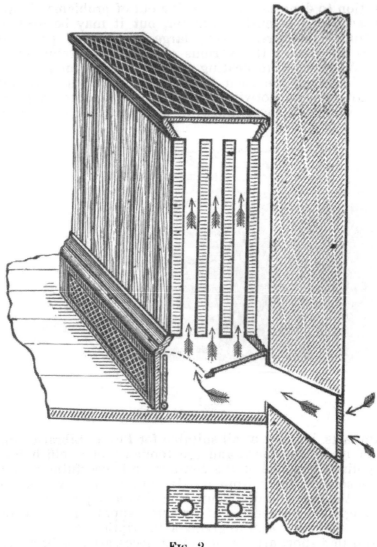

FIG. 2.

where a steam boiler is used for other purposes it is undoubtedly an excellent means for conveying heat over the building. The old style of hot-water coil, like that shown at Fig. 1, is very good in some cases where the question of ventilation is not of much importance, but when it is desired to make the heat-

ing apparatus assist the ventilation, one of the best arrangements to adopt is what is known as the ventilating radiator.
The chief difference was that the old coil warmed and
rewarmed the air in the room continually without assisting, to
any great extent, in causing a renewal of the air by ventilation,
whereas the ventilating coil or radiator is arranged in such
a way that a current of fresh air can be warmed and distributed
about the rooms in a very simple manner. It is important to
remember that air is not warmed by radiation, notwithstanding
the name given to the modern heating coils. The air must
come into actual contact with a heated surface, from which
the heat is conducted to the air. And this may be the radiator
itself, or the walls or furniture in the room which have been
heated in the first place by radiation. A section of the ventilating radiator referred to, together with the tube for the

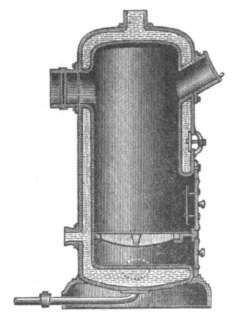

Fig. 3.

admission of fresh air, is shown at Fig. 2. These are made in
various sizes, shapes, and designs, but the principles upon
which they are formed are much the same. They consist of a
series of vertical concentric tubes as shown in the section, the
inner tube being that through which the fresh air passes and
receives the heat from the heated water circulating inside
the outer tube. The base of the radiator is a hollow box
having a grating in the front which can be closed by a flap
valve running the whole length. When it is desired this valve
can be opened for the purpose of allowing the air to pass from
the room through the heated tubes. By this arrangement the
temperature of the room can be rapidly raised without lowering

the heat of the radiator by cold air. In summer time, when no heat is required, the radiator acts as a Tobin tube by admitting fresh air and giving it an upward direction in such a way as to prevent draughts being felt. A convenient form of boiler and furnace, suitable for heating the water for a few radiators, is that known as the independent boiler, similar to that shown at Fig. 3. The special feature of the one shown in the sketch is that the boiler extends below the ash pit, for the purpose of receiving the sediment, which generally produces incrustation, more especially when the boiler is used for a hot water supply. A cleaning door is fitted to this part of the boiler, so that it can be easily cleaned out when it is necessary. But when the heating arrangements are extensive it is better to fix a boiler with greater heating surface, similar to that shown at Fig. 4, which should be set in a furnace and the outside flues formed with fire bricks.

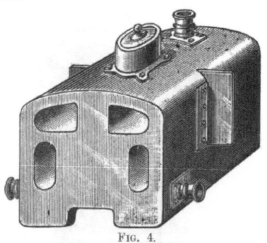

FIG. 4.

In addition to the admission of fresh air through the radiators it is advisable to provide some other means for supplying air, and this can be done at a very small expense by fixing Tobin tubes in the angles of the rooms and communicating with the external air as shown by the section at Fig. 5. Valves should be placed in the tubes so that the current of air can be shut off when it is found necessary.

The next important matter, after providing for the ingress of fresh air, is the outlet of foul air, which, of the two, is generally the more difficult. A mere opening in the ceiling or through the walls is in most cases of little or no use, as these act almost invariably as inlets and allow cold air to pour in like a stream of water on the heads of the occupants of the room, more especially when an open fire-place is made use of, owing to the large extracting power of the chimney, although the latter can be made to serve a useful purpose as an extractor by fixing chimney outlet valves into the flues near the ceiling.

The draught up the chimney induces a current of air from the upper part of the room to pass through the valve and so removes a large amount of the vitiated atmosphere. A better plan, however, is to form air flues by the side of the smoke flues, the

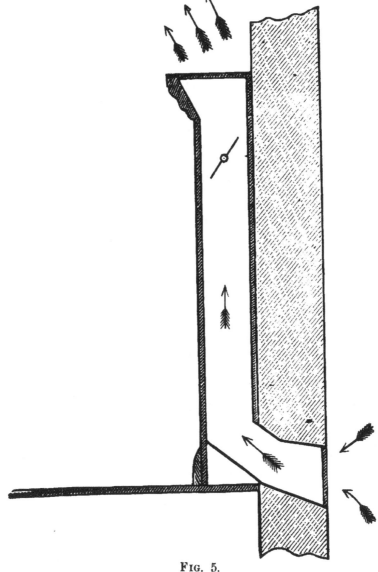

FIG. 5.

upper ends terminating just below the tops of the chimneys, vertical open gratings being fixed at the lower ends of the air flues at the ceiling line. If these are arranged when the building is planned, they form an effectual and economical method of automatically extracting the foul air, the motive power being provided by the warmth from the smoke flues inducing an up-draught. Another simple plan is to arrange the lighting so that it assists in extracting the foul air and products of combustion. The most familiar and in many instances the most satisfactory is the sunlight and some forms of regenerative burners placed at ceiling level having a large flue taken through the roof and fitted with an efficient fixed cowl. It may be remarked that this method is only available during the night when the gas is lighted. But as the rooms of Public Libraries are used more at night than during the day, the difficulty could be overcome by leaving a light burning in the flue just above the sunlight in the daytime; this would give enough heat to produce an up-draught of sufficient velocity to act as an extractor. In the event of the height of the ceiling or open roof being too great for one or more sunlights to give enough light, it would of course be necessary to provide some other additional means of lighting. Where gas has to be used, the incandescent system is the most suitable, because this not only gives a suitable light for reading, but the combustion is more complete and the amount of gas consumed is comparatively small. There can be no doubt, however, that the best system of lighting in the kind of buildings under consideration is by the incandescent electric lamps, of which but little need be said, because it is indisputed that for a comfortable light, cleanliness, and pure atmosphere, there is no lighting at present introduced which can claim so many advantages. But in that case no assistance would be given in extracting the vitiated atmosphere by the heat given off by the lighting arrangements as above described. It would therefore be necessary to provide rotary fans in the extracting flues, which fans could be made to revolve by electric motors fed by the lighting current. This has one advantage of being always available both day and night, and can be regulated without difficulty. Or where the electric current is not available the fans can be worked by a small jet of water which may be arranged in such a way as to render the motive power costless. This is done by discharging the waste water from the fan into a storage cistern which may be used for water closet flushing, or to supply automatic flushing cisterns for urinals, some of which are generally required in public buildings. In any case some provision must be made for the effectual removal of vitiated air, if the ventilating arrangements are to work satisfactorily. Extracting cowls are sometimes used for this purpose, and in some conditions of the atmosphere they will cause an up-draught and do the work required of them, but as they depend upon the wind currents, it often happens that ventilation is most needed when the external atmosphere is calm and still, hence the necessity for mechanical assistance to give the desired effect.

THE RATING AND TAXATION OF PUBLIC LIBRARIES.

By W. R. CREDLAND, of the Manchester Public Libraries.

THE rating of Public Libraries by local Authorities is a subject as vexed as it is vexing. There is no uniformity of procedure with regard to local rating. In some places where several buildings are used as Public Libraries the whole of them are rated, in others some of the institutions are rated and some are not. There are also towns in which the Libraries are totally exempted from local burdens, and still others in which the Authorities have taken a benevolent attitude and reduced the assessment considerably, or even made it merely nominal. All this seems to imply that doubt and hesitancy exist as to the equity of casting a burden upon undertakings intended mainly for the intellectual benefit and educational advancement of those who provide them. This being so no effort need be wasted in attempting to prove that a condition so anomalous is highly undesirable and needs to be abolished at the earliest opportunity. As regards the legal aspect of the question it is impossible to deny that as the law at present stands local Authorities have the right to assess Library buildings if they choose to exercise it. This right has been once or twice contested, but the decision has generally gone against the Library Authorities. But under Act 6 and 7 Vic., cap. 36, many public institutions, including Libraries, have claimed and secured exemption from local rates, while others have claimed and been refused. This Act provides that any society instituted for purposes of Science or Literature exclusively, and occupying for the transaction of its business any lands, houses or buildings, may obtain exemption from rates on certain conditions. These are that the society is supported wholly or in part by annual voluntary contributions, and does not make any dividend, gift, division or bonus of money to its members. It is also required to obtain a certificate of exemption from, in England, the barrister appointed to certify the rules of Friendly Societies, or in Scotland, from the Lord Advocate. Some Public Libraries may be said to be "supported wholly or in part by annual voluntary contributions," for they have, working in connection with them, systems by which those who choose to pay a subscription can obtain a prior use, or a greater facility of use, of the books supplied to the Library. Does this arrangement constitute them Literary Societies within the meaning of the Act? This question has not yet been threshed out in any court of law. Then again arises the question of what constitutes a "contribution". Are books, periodicals, and other gifts contributions within the meaning of the Act? The delay which ever attends attempts to amend the law through the regular channel—the House of Commons—makes it very desirable that those engaged in the management of Public Libraries should not withhold their hands until the next Amendment Act is obtained, but should at once arrange for the bringing into court of a test case. If the case is won, well and good; if not, there is always Parliament to fall back upon. Should any Library Committee deem it desirable to take action in this direction, the process is simple enough. In the first place it must pass a rule showing that the Library is established exclusively for purposes of literature and science, and that no dividend, gift, division, or bonus in money shall be divided among the members of the Library. This done, three copies of the rules, signed by the Chairman, three other officers, and countersigned by the secretary, should be sent to the Registrar of Friendly Societies, together with a fee of one guinea, and a request that he will certify the Library as exempt from local rating.

From these rules it is necessary to exclude those relating to the newsroom, as the Registrar will not certify on them. It is important to show by the rules that the conditions of the Act are complied with, as the certificate is added to a copy of these rules. The Registrar will not accept a separate statement explaining what the rules do not show. Public Libraries have a strong equitable right to this exemption, for they surely ought not to be placed in a worse position than private institutions, since their objects are identical and their usefulness more widespread. Their income, too, is so restricted by law—which has always exhibited a curious frigidity in its encouragement of the Free Library movement—that in many small places the remission of a few pounds of taxation is a matter of serious import and may constitute the difference between something and almost nothing on the book-shelves. The exaction of local imposts falls with peculiar hardship upon these institutions, because every penny deducted from their income is so much actual loss. They cannot like every other department of a Corporation say they must have a certain sum to carry on their work—and if they do not get it in meal they must in malt. Their income is definitely limited, yet they have to stand helplessly by whilst some of it is taken from them and devoted to such purposes as lighting, paving, sewering and so on which have not the remotest relationship to the object for which the money was granted. Parliament in its wisdom has said that you shall spend a penny in the pound and no more on the enlightenment of the community by means of reading, and our local Parliaments in their wisdom, which is necessarily a minor quantity, have said you shall not have even that, but shall hand some of it over for the accomplishing of that more noble purpose—the removal of nightsoil. To transfer money from one pocket to another in this manner would be laughable in its futility were it not that in this case a gross injustice is done, and an institution whose tendency for good is in the direction of rate-saving has its work hampered and its influence lessened by the shortsightedness of the local Authorities.

A few years ago one of the officers of the Income Tax Commissioners made the discovery that the property of the Public Library Committees had till then escaped the lynx eyes of their officials. This was not to be tolerated longer, and accordingly in 1892 such property was in various parts of the country scheduled for payment of income tax. Bristol and Manchester immediately appealed against this imposition. The Bristol case was tried first, and was decided against the Corporation on the ground that the buildings assessed did not belong to a "Literary or Scientific Institution," within the meaning of the Act. This rebuff did not alarm Manchester. The Corporation of that city determined to fight their appeal to the end, and the final result of their efforts was complete victory and the relief of the Public Libraries throughout the country from this additional load sought to be laid upon their already over-burdened shoulders. This case was of such high importance to the institutions concerned and so many novel, debatable and vital points in connection with them were raised and discussed during its progress that a brief account of it should be placed on record.

When the Manchester Public Libraries Committee received in 1892 a demand for income tax from the Commissioners of Inland Revenue they appealed locally, but postponed any further action until the settlement of the Bristol case. At the meeting of the Library Association in Aberdeen in 1893 the Chairman of the Manchester Libraries Committee gave a promise that Manchester would proceed with its appeal. It was thought necessary to endeavour to obtain a reversal of the Bristol judgment in the Queen's Bench Division of the High Court. This meant in effect a request to the judges, Mr. Justice Wright and Mr. Justice Collins, who had decided the Bristol case to review their judgment and come to a totally opposite conclusion. After a careful hearing these gentlemen decided not to stultify themselves, but strongly recommended the appellants to carry the case to the Court of Appeal. This accordingly was done, and the case came on for hearing on January 30th, 1895, before the Master of the Rolls and Lords Justices Lindley and Rigby and once more suffered the misfortune of being dismissed with costs. But the decision was not unanimous. Justices Lindley and Rigby supported the adverse decision, but the Master of the Rolls (Lord Esher) strongly opposed it. In delivering judgment Lord Justice Lindley said he "could not think that a Municipal Corporation or body of ratepayers, who by adopting the Public Libraries Act have become liable to be rated in order to maintain a Public Library, is a Literary Institution within the meaning of that phrase in Schedule A, Part 6 of the Income Tax Act, 1842. A Literary or Scientific Institution supported by rates is not in my opinion such an institution as was contemplated by the Legislature. To call the Corporation of Manchester, even in its character of Library Authority, a Literary Institution is in my opinion to misapply the expression, and to extend the exemption to a class of cases to which it was never intended to apply."

Lord Justice Rigby said he was of the same opinion, and he drew a distinction between the owners of the building and the building itself, and the purposes to which it was devoted. Though these institutions might be said to be Literary Institutions their owners could not be described as a Literary or Scientific Institution.

The Master of the Rolls, in dissenting from the views of his colleagues, made certain observations which may possibly prove of the utmost value in determining the construction to be placed upon the wording and intention of the Public Libraries Acts. "I feel much pressed by this," he said, "that if the law is as has been stated it must have been about as severe a blow to the intention of the Legislature when they passed the Public Libraries Act as can be given, for the case would stand thus: That if any person is willing to give a building or land of his for the purpose of a Public Library he gives up all control of that land, he has no power to take it back, he has no power to sell it, he has no power to interfere with it, he gets nothing from it, but he gives it for the purpose of a Public Library to be enjoyed by other people than himself, and he is left to pay this tax to the Government for the rest of his life or for ever. Well, I should say that anything more absurd than such legislation, if it is the legislation, which was meant to encourage people to give their land or to give their property for these Public Libraries, cannot well be imagined."

Then he proceeded to define the position of a Mayor and Corporation, in their general and ordinary capacity, as regards the ownership of any building devoted to Public Library purposes, and to the expression of views which, if acted upon, may lead to friction and even litigation between Library Committees and the body by whom they may have been appointed. "The first thing in my opinion," he contends, "is this, that they (the Mayor, etc.) are not the owners of this building in that capacity—they are not the owners at all, and if they are not the owners at all, they cannot be made liable to this tax. These buildings did belong to the Corporation of Manchester, but they resolved to give them up—to turn them into Public Libraries." He then argues that the Corporation of Manchester in its capacity. as Urban Authority had delegated these Libraries and the property connected therewith to a "Library Authority" and such property was vested in them. He continues: "Now what are the Library Authority with regard to that land. It is vested in them, they never can receive any benefit from it; they are obliged to deal with it solely for the purposes of the Library. It seems to me that they are nothing but bare Trustees for the people who use the Library. They are the Library Authority— not the Corporation of Manchester, mind. If the Corporation of Manchester attempted to intermeddle with this thing at all, in their capacity of Corporation, I should say they would be doing that which they have no possible right to do. In my opinion the proper inference is that they (the Legislature) in 1892 intended to put these Free Libraries within the exception in the Act of 1842. If they have not done it they have defeated their own object in the greatest measure." This strong dissension on the part of so eminent an authority encouraged the Manchester Committee to continue the combat, but as much expense had been already incurred they appealed to the Free Library Committees throughout the country for assistance in carrying the suit to the highest court in the realm—the House of Lords. Their request was promptly responded to, and a sum of £300 was guaranteed. An action was entered accordingly and the case was heard before the Lord Chancellor (Lord Halsbury), Lord Herschell, Lord Macnaghten, and Lord Morris. After an exhaustive hearing judgment was finally given nearly six months later, in favour of the appellants. Thus after four persevering efforts this important victory was won, and another obstacle in the somewhat thorny path of the Free Library movement was removed.

During the progress of the case some curious and interesting points were debated. One of these was, "Is a Public Library a Literary Institution?" Such a question seems too simple to be serious, but it gave the legal quidnuncs much scope for learned discussion, the gist of it turning however on the meaning attachable to the word "institution". Even the dictionary was called upon for an authoritative pronouncement, but its definitions also got terribly belaboured, until the Lord Chancellor had to admit that "if you begin to apply rigorous rules of verbal accuracy to phrases contained in a statute, I do not know where we shall be". The Lord Chancellor based his disagreement with the view of the majority of the court on the assumption that the Legislature in passing the Income Tax Act of 1842 intended the exemption to apply to institutions then in existence and whose constitutions and objects were well known. Lord Herschell in the course of his judgment said:—

"Apart from any question of the ownership of the buildings

4

and of the maintenance of the Libraries by a rate levied on the occupiers within the city, I do not think it was doubted that a Public Free Library is a Literary Institution. Its object is to spread a knowledge and love of Literature among the people. Such an institution is in my opinion quite aptly termed Literary. The difficulty arises from the other words used. To be exempted the building must be 'the property of a literary institution'. What was meant by this was property appropriated to and applied for its purposes. I think therefore that even though the Corporation of Manchester, in whom the buildings the taxation of which is now in question are vested, cannot be said to be itself a Literary Institution, nevertheless the buildings being appropriated for the purpose of Public Libraries, being devoted exclusively to that use, and incapable of being legally applied to any other purpose, may properly be said to be the property of a Literary Institution."

Lord Macnaghten considered that the Legislature intended that the character of the institution, not the circumstances of its origin or the means by which it was established or supported, should give rise to the claim for exemption. He could not see that it mattered in the very least in whom the legal ownership of Public Library buildings was vested, provided the buildings themselves are legally appropriated to the purposes of the institution.

By this judgment three important points have been definitely settled. We know now that Free Libraries are "Literary Institutions," that Corporations are "Literary Institutions," and that property devoted to Public Library purposes is exempt from income tax.

Now that the Government has been beaten, it naturally follows that efforts will be made to shake off the burden of local taxation. The Act exempting Literary Institutions from these imposts expressly stipulates that they must be supported "wholly or in part by annual voluntary subscriptions". This will form the difficulty to be overcome. But those who may be contemplating a tilt against the Authorities anent this question may well take heart of grace from the words of the Government's own advocate, Mr. Danckwerts, who in the course of his argument made these momentous admissions :—

"The contest here is between imperial and local taxation, and the question is whether, when buildings of this sort become appropriated under the Public Libraries Act, they shall cease to contribute to imperial taxation, although they are still liable to local taxation. I submit that all the reasons which *a priori* would have made in favour of exemption from imperial taxation apply equally to local taxation. I submit that there is no greater reason why they should be exempt from one kind of taxation than from the other kind of taxation."

In these words is encouragement and hope enough. And after all it is merely a legal cobweb that needs be swept away, for on the grounds of equity or reasonableness local taxation of these useful institutions is more indefensible and iniquitous than even the proposed imperial extortion which has been so successfully resisted.   It may be added that under spur of the Manchester decision a number of Libraries have applied to the Registrar of Friendly Societies with every hope of success. It remains to be seen if local rating authorities will contest these certificates before a court of Quarter Sessions.

THE TRAINING OF PUBLIC LIBRARY ASSISTANTS.

By J. J. OGLE, Librarian, Bootle Public Library.

THAT the librarian's craft, occupation, or profession is a highly specialised one, and consequently needs much and prolonged training for its due exercise, too few people are at once ready to admit. Yet a very little reflection will serve to convince any thoughtful person that the mere exchange of books is the least of a librarian's duties. The librarian is or ought to be appointed, not because he has qualities which will enable him to serve the average shop boy, mechanic, or young lady with credit to himself and satisfaction to his clients, but that he may attend with self-respect and credit to the requests of the most refined and intellectual people in the place. The greater requirement should of course include the less, but we have yet to learn of the librarian whose learning prevented him being civil and helpful to a mechanic or obliging to a boarding-school miss. It is bad for any Library when the average or ordinary demands on the institution regulate the maximum abilities of its chief official.

A high level of general education ought to be demanded from every candidate for a responsible Library position. A fair knowledge of Latin and say French or German, some acquaintance with the sciences of number, form, and dimensions (Mathematics), of forces (Mechanics), and of living phenomena (Biology), besides a good grounding in British History and English Grammar, are the minimum to be desired in one who seeks to equip himself for the acquisition of practical Library knowledge. Some of these subjects may be thought to have little bearing on the care of books, but in these days of the study of science they are absolutely necessary to enable a librarian to understand the relations of subjects, a partial bibliography of which he will have to attempt in his first Library catalogue. As to foreign languages, the more are known before commencing work on the staff of a Library the better, as appointment to an active responsible post makes further acquisitions if not impossible at least difficult.

A somewhat shorter programme of general studies may be recommended to those who aim no higher than the charge of a small town Library. For these a good all-round English education may suffice as a basis, though the elements of science may not be neglected with impunity. Scientific and technical knowledge is spreading even in villages and every librarian should command the respect of students by his own intellectual attainments.

Sooner or later, a standard of knowledge represented by that of the matriculation for London University will be regarded as indispensable in pupil-assistants in first-class town Libraries. Nay, there is little doubt such would be a common requirement now but for the crippling limitation on Library finance involved in the "penny rate". One of the first effects of general freedom from the present legal limitation will be a demand for a more highly educated class of assistants; consequently the Library service will improve as to efficiency and also as to remuneration. The latter effect has followed the introduction of higher standards of education in the Library profession in America, where salaries both for men and women are much higher than in similar positions in this country. Even the book-porters in a Boston Library are required to pass a searching examination in Geography and History, Literature and General Information, before receiving an appointment. Recently the competition for three of these posts was so keen that seventy candidates submitted themselves to examination. So far, the requirements of efficiency may be acquired by private study or by attendance on lectures and classes, but we now approach some parts of the mental equipment which cannot wholly be obtained out of books or from the lips of a professor, at least not in any particular part of the United Kingdom that the writer is acquainted with. This is not to say that much help cannot be got from the sources indicated.

The history and criticism of the special literatures of France and Germany, Britain and America, Greece and Rome may on no account be neglected. A librarian without something more than a surface knowledge of these subjects is continually in danger of running the ship of his Library into the shallows and among the rocks instead of out into the deeps of human thought and expression. The knowledge required of these renowned literatures should embrace the peculiarities and excellencies of the best editions of the standard writers, a knowledge only to be acquired by great diligence and alertness when moving about in a world of books, aided by the really useful maps and charts among many which, with shifting sands and currents, have become obsolete. The main facts of the lives and attainments of the highest leaders of human thought and literary progress of whatever nationality should be carefully studied. Passing over French and German, English and Ancient authors, the names of Dante, Petrarch, Boccaccio, Alfieri, Mazzini; of Cervantes, Lopez de Vega, Calderon; of Tegner; of Jokai; of Tourgenieff,

suggest themselves as worthy of attention. The great names
in art should also receive consideration, for literature is full of
allusions to them, and the men themselves were part of the
intellectual product of their times. General history should be
read in association with literary history, and the outlines of
the history of educational method in connection with the
names of Comenius, Froebel, Pestalozzi and others will prove a
useful acquisition. If to these matters be added a fair knowledge of the movement of popular progress in our own century
and country, including the extension of the popular press and
of popular lecturing, and the rise of Mechanics' Institutes and
Workmen's Societies, the librarian will be all the better
equipped for his duties in relation to the majority of his
clients.

The description of a book is not in the popular mind
regarded as a matter of science, yet there is probably no action
of the human mind where more mistakes have been made than
in the describing of books. Hence has arisen the science of
bibliography, which teaches the history of the externals of
book production, and the correct method of book description.
That this science should be carefully and practically studied
by every Library assistant ought not to need saying, but, un-
fortunately, its importance is not sufficiently realised. An
excellent and striking instance of the knowledge of historical
bibliography has recently been furnished in the rescue from
destruction of an extremely rare book from Wynkin de
Worde's press by the librarian of the Birkenhead Free
Libraries. This copy of the *Vita de Christi* would have found
its way into the waste paper bin but for Mr. May's skilled eye
and ready observation, which instantly detected a possible
treasure in the peculiar Caxton-like type, and in other
characteristics of the printed page.

The confusion of editions through the errors of cataloguers
has led to the adoption of specific rules for the description of
books, usually known as cataloguing rules, which must be
studied by every assistant. Those of the British Museum, the
Bodleian Library, and the Library Association are more or less
closely followed by British librarians. The Bodleian and the
Library Association rules are for author-entries only, though
the former adds a table for determining size notation. In Free
Public Libraries in the United Kingdom much use is also made
of Cutter's *Rules for Making a Dictionary Catalogue,* now in the
third edition, and hitherto freely distributed by the United
States Bureau of Education. The principal Cis-Atlantic rules
are published by the Library Association in a sixpenny
pamphlet. The notes in Cutter's book are of the greatest value
for their discussion of difficulties, and for their illustrative
treatment of the rules. The notes on subject headings cannot
be neglected without great loss by any assistant. For study,
the writer would recommend the assistant to ground himself

on the Library Association rules by making for himself a set of illustrations to each rule, transcribing titles from actual books. At the same time the Bodleian size-notation table should be mastered, the various folds being imitated on large sheets of blank paper. Cutter's rules should then be carefully studied and a comparison between the various codes instituted to discover the variations among them. This may be made a very interesting —as it certainly is a very useful and wit-sharpening—exercise.

Cataloguing as applied to fifteenth and sixteenth century books cannot be carried on without a good basis of special knowledge of such books, and this can only be acquired by handling many specimens and a careful study of many special articles and treatises, among which the following may be named :—

Articles: Bibliography, Paper and Typography in the *Encyclopædia Britannica.*

The Caxton Exhibition (1877) Catalogue.
The British Museum *Guide to the Printed Books* exhibited in the King's gallery.

Blades' *Pentateuch of Printing.*
Duff's *Early Printed Books.*
De Vinne's *History of Printing.*
Bernard's *De l'origine et des Débuts de l'Imprimerie en Europe.*

No amount of reading is of much value without frequent contact with the books themselves; and every opportunity of visiting and seeing books from the early presses whether in Public Museums and Libraries or in private collections should be seized and made the most of by the assistant.

Closely connected with the subject of the cataloguing is that of the classification of books. The fundamental principles may be studied in any standard book on Logic, but the practical difficulties in large Libraries are great. Here, more than anywhere else, the librarian's general knowledge is put to the test. A sufficient acquaintance with the *elements* of every department of human knowledge is hard of acquisition, but it must be acquired. At the very least a knowledge deep enough and broad enough to enable the relationships of the divisions and sub-divisions of the chief subjects to be readily understood, and the distinctive terminologies recognised, is imperative. On this foundation ampler experience may build, but the whole foundation must be laid. If the assistant be fortunate enough to have access to a set of the American *Library Journal* he should make himself acquainted with the leading systems of classification proposed by Americans in its pages, and should study the distinctive notations attached to certain of the schemes. In any case, Dewey's *Decimal System of Classification* cannot be overlooked, and a copy of the published system must be obtained, either by loan or purchase, and its main features closely scanned. Neither should the *Transactions* and other official publications of the Library Association of the United Kingdom be forgotten, for they contain many valuable and suggestive papers on this difficult subject. After all, practical experience in a Library can alone make productive the wisdom gathered from books, and practical experience must be had before any one can rightly be fitted to organise a Public Library.

The large subject of Library management yet remains to be treated. How can effective training in this be obtained? As regards the United Kingdom there is only one answer at present, *viz.:* By actual service for a few years in a Library. Let it be remembered that a librarian has to know the leading provisions of the law relating to Libraries; to act as clerk and adviser to his Committee; to investigate the qualifications of candidates for positions on his staff, and to control and regulate the service, to be somewhat of an accountant; to devise a variety of special record books for special needs; to draw up rules and regulations, and occasionally to prosecute persons for breaches thereof; to understand the conditions of effective control and of unhampered and economic use as they affect the design of any proposed Library building or annexe, so as to be capable of giving a prompt and unwavering opinion on the merits of plans and specifications; to be well-informed as to schemes of lighting, heating, ventilating; and to have studied thoroughly the various appliances for facilitating the receipt, storage, and issue of books. Further, he must be a good judge of binding leathers and binders' work, and an economic buyer of books, understanding well his opportunities and knowing how to use them for the public advantage. Moreover, he must know, or early get to know, his neighbourhood, and gather up the materials for its future, as well as the records of its past, history, and be ready to act the part of historiographer to the town or district. He must also know his clients, anticipate their wants, study their temper, pocket their abuse, and recognise that he has to deal with men as well as with books. In short, the librarian is expected to be a good part of a scholar, a greater part of a man of business, and a little of a diplomat.

Surely these requirements have only to be stated to make it clear that book-lore can give little assistance herein. The papers and discussions recorded in the publications of the Library Associations on both sides the Atlantic must be the driest of dry reading to the man or woman who by reading up hopes to be a librarian, if such a person there be; but to the assistant in daily contact with the problems discussed these same papers palpitate with actuality and interest. Latterly one or two manuals of Library economy have been published in France and in the United States, but the writer cannot speak confidently of their merits. Such books generally contain something of good and new or at least of stimulating and suggestive to the thoughtful librarian. A little pleasant fruit even if it lurk amid a sheaf of leaves is worth the gathering.

Up to this point it has been assumed that when out of the region of general knowledge the Library assistant cannot obtain personal help in his studies. This is not entirely so. Early in the Library Association's career a system of examinations was devised for testing the knowledge of assistants, and the syllabuses of subjects drawn up and from time to time modified have had a wholesome influence in directing the studies of those who aim at becoming librarians. True the examinations have not been used to a very great extent, but the cause of this is to be found in the lack of means of systematic instruction. But in 1893 a better day dawned. A Summer School for Students of Librarianship was inaugurated in London, and has been in session for a week in each succeeding June. At the beginning the work of the school consisted chiefly in visits of observation, under proper guidance, to various Libraries, printing offices, binderies, type foundries, paper mills, and other establishments bearing on the making, care, or preservation of books. These visits were regarded by all who took part in them as of great benefit; but an improvement has latterly been effected in the development of the lecturing element, which was never wholly absent from the scheme. At the last (the fourth session) the following items were included in the programme :—

LECTURES.

Mr. T. J. Cobden-Sanderson .	. The Book Beautiful.
Mr. E. Gordon Duff .	. The History of the Development of the Printed Book.
Mr. E. Gordon Duff .	. The Bibliographical Description of a Book.
Mr. E. M. Borrajo . .	. On Catalogues and Cataloguing.
Mr. T. F. Hobhouse .	. English Fiction, History, and Biography of the Last Hundred Years.
Dr. R. Garnett . .	. English Literature of the Last Hundred Years.
Mr. F. J. Burgoyne .	. Library Buildings.

CONFERENCE.

Things Seen and Heard .	. The Students.

PLACES VISITED.

The British Museum.
The Guildhall Library.
Sir Charles Reed & Sons' Type Foundry.
Sion College Library.
The Tate Library, Brixton.

Eighteen London and twenty-five provincial Library assistants attended, and a good account of the work done is to be seen in the *Library* for August, 1896. The aim of the Committee is to make the instruction in the Summer School bear directly on the subjects of the professional examination, giving prominence to successive sides of the syllabus in succeeding years. An examination (not to be confounded with the certificate examination) is held near the close of the Summer School session, and prizes are given on the results, also a special prize is given for the best report of the proceedings.

Additional help has of late been offered to assistants through the "Assistant's Corner" of the *Library*, the monthly organ of the Association. Here are invited questions and answers to questions, and hints and news calculated to be of use and to interest the tyro are printed.

Whether out of the modest Summer School there will ever grow a Training College for Librarians it is perhaps too soon to say. The University of the State of New York has such a College in full operation with a two years' course in Library economy. Here is given a more thorough training in Library work than can be got elsewhere. Candidates for admission must be twenty years of age, and are expected to have passed through the usual four years' High School or College course. Actual service in the Library of the State is given by the students during certain hours of the week, and remuneration reckoned as a set-off against high fees. By this means the cost of the course is reduced to about £20 a year, plus the expense of living. The Library profession is acknowledged by the University as ranking with the legal and medical, and degrees are conferred in Library Science. In eight years 159 persons had taken the course of training, and well-trained and enthusiastic librarians have gone out to important posts all over the States at the conclusion of the successive courses, many of them to a remarkably successful career. The inception and development of the scheme of a Library School was due to the energy and ability of Mr. Melvil Dewey, the present secretary to the Board of Regents of the University, and the deviser of the Dewey Decimal Classification, which has now the largest vogue of any one system in the world. Besides this school there are in the States, following more or less closely the original pattern, Library Schools at the Armour Institute, Chicago; the Pratt Institute, Brooklyn; the Drexel Institute, Philadelphia; and another at Denver. A school was also for a time in vigorous existence at Los Angeles. The existing schools were all founded by pupils of Mr. Dewey's. Summer Schools of Library economy lasting for five or six weeks are established at Albany, at Amherst, and at Wisconsin University.

The character of the training given in the American schools may be judged by the following estimate of a friend and advocate of the movement, Miss Adelaide R. Hasse :—

"As to the nature of training classes, plainly they are nothing more or less than the old-fashioned apprentice system, with a competitive examination before admission and another when the required term of apprenticeship has been completed. The relative standard obtained by the pupil in the second examination determines the pupil's chance for employment."

One can hardly accept this dictum as applying to the Albany school, where the widest possible comparative study of methods is carried out.

As yet no over-production of skilled workers seems to have resulted, or to be likely to result in the near future; for although two or three American States march ahead of Britain in Library matters, most of the States lag far behind her, and there is an immense Continent for future alumni of the Albany and other Colleges to practise upon. The world is, however, indebted to the initiative and enthusiasm of the few American librarians who have put the training of librarians on this high plane, for a move forward, the far-reaching influence of which cannot yet be estimated.

PROCEDURE IN THE FORMATION OF PUBLIC LIBRARIES.

By JAMES D. BROWN, LIBRARIAN, CLERKENWELL PUBLIC LIBRARY.

ONE of the commonest questions asked by newly appointed Committees and inexperienced librarians is: "How should we set about organising our Library?" or, "Is there any book which gives instructions as to how to form a Library?" To both questions even the most willing librarian finds a difficulty in replying, because there is nothing in existence in the way of a Library Primer giving systematic directions in the art of Library formation, while very few librarians will face the task of writing out a series of instructions for the benefit of other people. Nevertheless, a number of the public librarians of the country do an immense amount of this sort of unacknowledged missionary work, finding their reward, it is assumed, in the pleasure of aiding a good cause. In these circumstances it has seemed a wise thing to briefly lay down a few rules for the guidance of inexperienced Committees or librarians.

In drafting these instructions an effort has been made to give the system described as much elasticity as possible, so that it can be adopted by large, or small and growing Libraries, or modified to suit particular needs. Everything recommended has been tried in various Libraries for many years, and the whole combination of methods is as simple as it is possible to have it with security and accuracy of working. Assuming, then, that the Public Libraries Acts have been adopted and a Committee appointed, the next few steps will concern that Committee, which will doubtless proceed to elect a chairman and an honorary secretary. Afterwards the procedure will be to:—

1. Authorise the honorary secretary to order all necessary stationery, such as paper, pens, ink, etc.; Account Books; a Minute Book (18); Order Book (18); Donation Book (4); Inventory Book (18), etc.

The honorary secretary should keep minutes of the proceedings of the Committee and a record of accounts, orders, and donations till a paid librarian or other officer is appointed.

2. Before proceeding to arrange for a site, building, etc., the Committee should, if in a position to do so, appoint a *trained* librarian, or, failing that, procure expert advice. It will be found in the end that there is no economy in trying to save a salary or fee, by proceeding with the preliminary work of organisation without skilled aid. Committees have in the

past made numerous mistakes through neglect to call in experienced advice, and the results are to be seen now in many places in expensive buildings which cripple the work of the Library, unsuitable fittings, bad catalogues and, generally, arrangements which hamper and complicate the administration of the institution at every turn. Whatever else may be done, it is certainly of the utmost importance that the foundation work of a Library should be directed by an expert. The details set out in the following paper are more or less subsidiary to the general scheme of organisation which may be recommended, and can be followed by any one of ordinary intelligence. But for preliminary work there is only one wise course—*get expert advice.*

Having settled foundation lines of procedure as regards buildings, rules, and finance, the actual work of building up the Library can be confronted.

3. Stocking the Library is a first consideration. Books are acquired in various ways—by proposals from the Committee, readers or librarian, and by donations. Of these, the lists prepared by the librarian, assisted by the Committee, are the most important. It is usual to have all books proposed for addition to the Library entered in a PROPOSITION BOOK or on

PROPOSITION BOOK.

Author.	Title.	Vols.	Net Price.			Pub. Price.	Publisher or Vendor.	Remarks.
			£	s.	D.			
Jones	Grammar of Ornament	1	1	10	...	...	Grant	Ordered
Rubric	Christian Church -	20	20	...	...	...	Jones	Not ordered
Corelli	Sorrows of Satan -	1	...	4	...	6/-	Methuen	Ordered

slips similar to specimens annexed, which the Committee can

SUGGESTION SLIP.

BOOKTOWN PUBLIC LIBRARY.

I beg to make the following suggestion (If of a book or periodical, please give publisher and price):—

....

....

....

Name...

Address ....

Date ....

Please fold across and leave in "Suggestions" Box.

consider. But in first forming a Library, the librarian, or other responsible officer, should draw up a list which will form the basis of the collection. In this will be included handy editions of all the great writers of all ages and countries, with works representative of every art, science and topic likely to be in popular demand. Books for the Lending Library should be bought in one volume form whenever possible, while those for the Reference Library should be got in editions most likely to prove useful to students. It is impossible to lay down any rules for guidance in this matter of selection, there being so many differences between places as regards funds and local conditions, but the following works will be found useful to all :—

Sonnenschein. *The Best Books, and Supplement.* 42s.
Reference Catalogue of Current Literature (latest issue). Whitaker.
Greenwood. *Sunday School and Village Libraries.* 1s. 6d. Clarke.
Catalogue of "A. L. A." Library (1893). (To be had on application to the Bureau of Education, Washington, D.C., U.S.A.)
Books for Village Libraries, by Burgoyne, etc. 1s. Library Association.
Guide to the Formation of a Music Library, by Brown. 6d. Library Association.

There are numerous other guides of the same sort, but those mentioned, with perhaps a few catalogues of other Public Libraries, will give ample information regarding all standard works save those of a very recent date. When the list is made out and approved, the next thing is to get the books. It is recommended that all novels, technical books, and recent works of science be purchased new, as late editions are very seldom to be had second-hand in good condition. In the long run, there is no advantage in re-binding such books in leather to begin with, and it is recommended that they be put in circulation as bought in their cloth bindings. All other classes of books may be purchased more advantageously second-hand. Lists of them should be made out, by one of the many manifolding processes (Cyclostyle or Mimeograph), and sent to some of the leading second-hand booksellers, of whom a list will be found in Clegg's *Directory of Second-hand Booksellers.* It is advisable to give local booksellers a chance of estimating, but as a rule it will be found that most of the reports of books will come from London and Edinburgh firms. But it is impossible to single out names from among so many, all equally deserving, so that the Committee must use discretion in sending out lists for report. As a rule, nearly all the books wanted will be got from these second-hand lists, and, of course, the cheapest and soundest copies in the most suitable editions reported will be selected. When the selection is made, orders should be sent and copies of them kept in the Order Book (18).

4. Another source of stock is DONATIONS, which come from private individuals, publishers, learned societies and other

bodies.   Every gift, whether of books, periodicals or prints, should be entered in the Donation Book, with a running number applied to each item, to enable anything not placed in the Library to be easily identified in after years.   This reference to the source or origin of gifts will be found of immense service when numbers of duplicates, etc., have collected.   It is customary to send a printed form of acknowledgment to donors.   Specimens of these may be had from any Public Library.

DONATION BOOK.

Donation Number.	Date of Receipt.	Date of Acknowledgment.	Author.	Title.	Vols.	Donor.	Accession Number.		Remarks.
	1896.	1896.					Len.	Ref.	
1	Oct. 1	Oct. 24	Jamieson	Steam Engine	1	J. E. Passmore 60 Echo Grove	1		
	,,	,,	Hugo	Les Miserables	1		2		
			and	so on					
2	Nov. 6	Nov. 26	Scott	Waverley Novels	25	Alex. Tait 20 North Wall	1001 to 1025		

5. The books being assembled from various sources should next be entered in a Routine Book, which fixes the order in which each lot of books must be dealt with, and gives a handy means of checking the number and cost of books added at any moment.   The following is a suitable ruling with specimen entries:—

ROUTINE BOOK.

Date.	Source: Donor or Vendor.	First Word of Invoice.	Nmbrs applied.		No. of Vols.		Cost.		Remarks.
			Lend.	Ref.	Ld.	Rf.	Lend.	Ref.	
							£ s. D.	£ s. D.	
1896 Oct.									
1	Donation	See Book	1-90	1-20	90	20	... ...	... ...	
5	Sothéran	Robinson	91-800	21-106	710	86	82 16 6	8 17 4 ...	
14	Quaritch	Woods	801-860	..	60	..	7 10 ...	... ...	Also 6 Replacements 15s.

The donations referred to on line 1 are those reported at the last Committee meeting.   It is best to enter them altogether after they have been accepted.   (*See* Donation Book, 4.)

6. The books, being now arranged in strict order of invoice or Donation Book, with the lending and reference ones in a separate sequence, and entered as above in the Routine Book, must next receive accession numbers.   The main object in numbering is to give a simple method of referring to a book without quoting its title or author.   In some systems the number is also the sole method of classification, and affords

the only clue to the place of books on the shelves. In this scheme it is a short symbol for all purposes. It is customary to give an accession number to each *volume*, there being great advantage in having a distinct symbol for each book or part of a book. To avoid confusion, it is recommended that books be numbered straight on, regardless of class or series, as in the following specimen page of an

ACCESSION NUMBER, OR LOCATION BOOK.

Number.	Class.	Author and Title.	Shelf.
1	G	Jamieson. Steam Engine.	30
2	K	Hugo. Les Miserables.	
3	E	Huxley. Physiology.	86
4	B	Malleson. Indian Mutiny, v. 1.	215
5	B	,, ,, ,, 2.	,,
6	B	,, ,, ,, 3.	
7	L	Chambers' Journal, 1895.	,, 431
8	K	Besant. All Sorts and Conditions of Men.	

The numbers, when applied, should be written with the class letter on the title-page of each book, preferably on the back, and carried against the entries on the invoice or in the Donation Book. When the invoice is finished, the first and last numbers of each lot should be entered in the Routine Book as shown. So with a lot of donations. Of course the shelf numbers are entered last, and the class letters will be fixed by the method adopted. (*See* Section 7.)

7. The CLASSIFICATION recommended is that devised by Messrs. Quinn and Brown, and described in the *Library* for March, 1895, page 75. Its main heads are given in the article on "Recent Developments of Library Practice" in this Year Book, but for convenience sake we add the chief sub-divisions.

Class A. 1 Bible, 2 Church, 3 Theology, 4 Philosophy.

B. 1 Universal History and Geography, 2 National History and Geography by great geographical divisions (Africa, Europe, etc.), sub-divided into countries.

C. 1 General Biography, 2 Class Biography (Artists, Authors, etc.), 3 Individual Biography, arranged alphabetically by subjects, as Bacon, Gladstone, Scott, etc.

D. 1 Society, 2 Government and Politics, 3 Law, 4 Political Economy, 5 Education, 6 Commerce.

E. 1 Biology, 2 Zoology, 3 Botany, 4 Geology, 5 Chemistry, 6 Physiography, 7 Astronomy, 8 Physics, 9 Mathematics.

F. 1 Architecture, 2 Painting, 3 Sculpture, 4 Decoration, 5 Engraving, 6 Music, 7 Amusements, 8 Sports.

G. 1 Engineering, 2 Building and Mechanical Arts, 3 Manufactures, 4 Agriculture and Gardening, 5 Sea and Navigation, 6 Health and Medicine, 7 Household Arts.

H. 1 Philology, 2 Literary History, 3 Bibliography, 4 Libraries.

J. 1 Poetry Collections, 2 Single Authors in alphabetical order, 3 Drama.

K. Novels in alphabetical order of authors. Juvenile works the same.

L. 1 Encyclopædias, 2 Miscellanies, 3 Collected Works, 4 Periodicals not in other classes.

General works in each class are simply lettered. Books in other divisions have class letters and class numbers as well. This classification is simply to facilitate arrangement, and the class numbers have nothing whatever to do with the catalogue, charging, or anything else. For classification and arrangement purposes the class letter and *class* (not accession) number should be pencilled on the title-page of each book in addition to the accession number, as noted in section 6. When all the books in Classes A 1, 2, 3, E 1, 2, 3, etc., are brought together according to these class numbers, the Library will be found very fairly classified. Not only will the whole main class science be together, but all the books on botany, chemistry will also be together by themselves. It is well to remember, therefore, that the class numbers are simply to be used by the staff for arrangement purposes. In the case of fiction, individual biography, poetry, essays or other classes arranged in alphabetical order of author or subject names, it is not necessary to pencil the class letters or numbers. To make the foregoing perfectly clear, it may be stated that a book like Jamieson's *Steam and the Steam Engine* would be numbered with the class letter G and accession number 1 on the back of the title-page, while in pencil it would be marked, say at the bottom of the same page, G 1 to show that it was a work on the useful arts, section engineering. Huxley's *Physiology* would be marked E 3, and in pencil E 1. All other necessary sub-division would be easily made by reference to the table in the Quinn-Brown classification already mentioned.

8. Books being now classified and numbered should next have BOOK CARDS written for them, ruled as below. Stout manilla paper or card is the best for the purpose, and 4 × 2 inches will be found good dimensions.

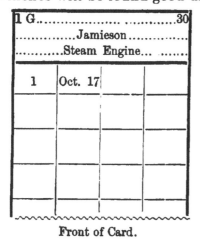

Front of Card.

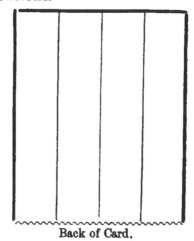

Back of Card.

These cards are used for registering or charging books when loaned to borrowers in the lending department, as described under charging (17). On the top left hand corner appears the class letter and accession number, and on the top right hand corner is the number of the shelf on which the book is located or placed. Then follow the author's name and title of the book in brief. The ruled spaces in the first and third columns are for the numbers of borrowers; those in the second and fourth columns are for dates of issue. The columns on the back are used in a similar fashion. These cards when all written are kept in numerical order in trays of 1000, provided with project-

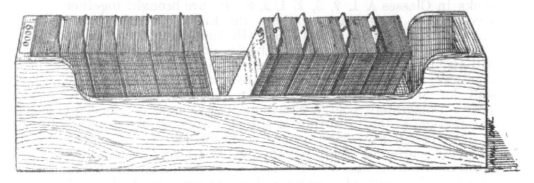

BOOK-CARD TRAY.

ing number guides at every 100, and they act as an indicator to the staff of books out and in. The systems used at Clerkenwell, Bournemouth, Kingston-on-Thames, Worcester, Croydon, Christ Church (Southwark), Hammersmith, Nottingham Mechanics' Institution are all on the same principle and can no doubt be seen if wanted, or particulars furnished. The further use of these cards will be found under the section devoted to charging (17).

9. It is next advisable to enter the books on a SHELF REGISTER, which should consist of ruled sheets as in the following specimen :—

Accession Number.	Author.	Title.	Vols	Aug. 6, '96.							Shelf 30.
5961	Bourne	Steam Engine	1	1							
431	Galloway	Steam Engine	1	1							
1	Jamieson	Steam Engine	1	1							
96	Reynolds	Stationary Engine	1	1							

These shelf registers serve the double purpose of enabling stock to be taken of the contents of the Library at any time, and providing a rough, but handy catalogue in brief of the various classes of books.   The arrangement on the sheets should follow that of the shelves, a little author alphabet, and it is best to keep the sheets loose in boxes, so that any one can be re-written without interfering with the rest.   The register is usually ruled on single sheets, both sides alike, and a handy size is 9½ by 7 inches, similar to those used at Clerkenwell, Bourne-mouth, Kingston and elsewhere.   Several firms keep them ready ruled at a very small charge.   The column headings are not necessary, and are only added to make clear the purpose of the rulings.   The narrow columns represent stock-takings. The date at the top and mark opposite the book between them indicate when it was last accounted for.   If the book is not found on its shelf or its card in the charging system, the space on the register should be left blank.   By using these sheets it is possible to take stock continuously without closing the Library for the purpose.   As regards the actual shelving or location of the books, this must be done in accordance with the system of classification adopted.   To facilitate finding books it is recommended that the shelves be numbered in one numerical series, from top to bottom of the tiers, in the order which seems most natural.   Printed labels numbered consecutively can be had from almost any stationer. These should be pasted on to the fore-edges of the shelves about an inch from one or other of the ends.   The numbers should be not less than ⅜ in. in size.   The books having been all arranged according to main classes and sub-divisions, or by author alphabet, as may be necessary, should have allocated for each sub-division as many shelves as may be required.   It is well to allow a fair amount of space on each shelf for future additions, and if there are plenty of shelves the books should be spread liberally over all the space available.   If room for six to ten books is left on every shelf, it will be long before conges-tion takes place even in a rapidly growing Library.   The books being all properly placed and entered in the shelf register, the shelf numbers should be carried on to the labels inside the books (*see* Labelling, 12), and added to the book cards and Accession Number Book.   They are thus all easily found when required, while the power of shifting any book to any position is given without interference with the catalogue or anything else, by simply altering the shelf numbers wherever they appear, and changing the shelf register.   Though there seems much repetition of the same number, yet the convenience of it all is so great as to make it well worth doing.   If a par-ticular number is wanted, the book card or Accession Number Book directs instantly to the place where the work is located.   If a book is away from its place, the label directs at once to the exact location.   Should a list of all the books on a particular shelf be wanted, the shelf register will give it.   Class or topic labels for pasting on the middle of shelves to indicate the contents of each, as well as main class labels attached to the cornice of each bookcase, are used at many Public Libraries, like Croydon, Clerkenwell, Bournemouth, Darwen, Worcester, Kingston-on-Thames, etc. Most of the shelf labels can be had ready printed for a small sum. The question of further marking the outsides of books for the open access system is dealt with in the chapter on "Recent Developments of Library Practice," and need not be described here.

10. CATALOGUING.—It is not proposed to describe the many ways of cataloguing books in vogue, but simply to give a few hints of a practical character. Reference might be made, however, to the methods mentioned in Greenwood's *Public Libraries*, last edition; Greenwood's *Sunday School and Village Libraries;* the *Library*, vol. vi., p. 45, article on "Mechanical Methods of Displaying Catalogues and Indexes"; and to the remarks on class catalogues in the article on "Recent Developments of Library Practice" in this Year Book.

It is best and most convenient in the long run to catalogue books on separate slips of paper, say 5 × 2 inches. When the catalogue is all written, these slips can be manipulated easily, and arranged in any order. Each book should be thoroughly catalogued as it passes through the librarian's hands, and slips written for every necessary heading under which it comes. From the author-entry slip and the invoices entries can be made in the Stock Book (11) before the slips are distributed in alphabetical order.

11. STOCK BOOK.—This volume contains a complete record of the origin and manner of accession of every book in the Library. It is well to keep the lending and reference stocks apart in separate books. There are all kinds of rulings in use by different Libraries, and certain firms keep ruled books in stock, bound or in sheets, which will serve every useful purpose. The following headings will be found ample for ordinary use :—

BOOKTOWN PUBLIC LIBRARY, STOCK BOOK, LENDING DEPT.

Accession Number.	Author.	Title.	Class.	No. of Vols.	Date of Publication.	Donor or Vendor.	Price if Purchased.	Date of Receipt.	Remarks.
							£ s. d.	1896	
1	Jamieson	Steam Engine	G	1	1894	J. K. Passmore		Oct. 1	
2	Hugo (V.)	Les Miserables	K	1	1889	,,		,,	
3	Huxley (T. H.)	Physiology	E	1	1893	,,		,,	
4-6	Malleson	Indian Mutiny	B	3	1885	,,		,,	

The place of publication is sometimes added, but it is scarcely required in these days of abundant bibliographical lists. As before stated the Stock Book can be written up from the catalogue slips and invoices, or from the books themselves and the invoices, or even in cases of urgency from the Accession

Number Book and the invoices. In any case it is best to write the Stock Book up before the books are put away. It will be seen that, by adding up various columns of the Stock Book, an idea can be gathered as to how the stock stands. The classes can be abstracted on separate ruled sheets, or even better, the whole entries of each complete year can be abstracted on sheets ruled on ordinary foolscap, as follows :—

| Page. | Classes. | | | | | | | | | | | Total. | Bought. | Gifted. |
	A	B	C	D	E	F	G	H	J	K	L			
1	...	7	8	6	2	1	3	4	8	10	1	50	...	50

In this summary the distinction "pamphlet" is omitted. For Public Library purposes "a book's a book although there's nothing in it," and a pamphlet, for enumeration purposes at least, is practically a volume or book. Every separate publication is entitled to complete and special treatment in every department of Library work, and for that reason no distinction is made between books and pamphlets, so called.

12. Although described last in the procedure of preparing books for issue to the public, STAMPING, LABELLING and CUTTING UP should really be going on concurrently with the other work. Every book should be stamped with a mark denoting ownership in certain fixed places in the text, and on every separate plate or map. Ink stamps are cheapest and most used, but they are not so effective as perforating stamps. It is usual to stamp the name of the Library in small letters on the

book, say | BOOKTOWN PUBLIC LIBRARY. | within a square, oval or circular

border, or just the plain name of the institution. Convenient places are the half-title (front), title-page (back), first page of text or prefatory matter, end of text, and at any fixed pages that may be thought best. All separate illustrations, plans or maps should also be stamped back and front. Labels are of various kinds. Lending Library books usually get two, one being a mark of ownership with extracts from the rules (a), and the other being a ruled label for dating purposes (b). The following specimens will make clear the difference, but a third variety (c) can be used by combining the two other kinds in one label :—

A.

No....................   Shelf ....

BOOKTOWN PUBLIC LIBRARY.

LENDING DEPARTMENT.

Open on Week-days from 10·30 A.M. till 9 P.M.   No access to the shelves after 8·45 P.M.

Borrowers' Tickets and Vouchers must be renewed annually from date of issue.   *They are not transferable.*

FIFTEEN DAYS, INCLUDING DAYS OF ISSUE AND RETURN, ARE ALLOWED FOR READING THIS BOOK.   A fine of ONE PENNY per week, or portion of a week, is recoverable for each volume kept beyond that period.

Borrowers desiring to retain books beyond the period of 15 days, must intimate the same to the Librarian either in person or by post-card, when the book will be renewed for a further period of 15 days from the date of intimation. Such renewals will only be made once for each reader if the book is wanted by another reader.

No book will be delivered except in exchange for a Borrower's Ticket.

Messengers should be furnished with a list of numbers and titles of books wanted.

B.

No......... ....
BOOKTOWN PUBLIC LIBRARY.
This Book is returnable within 15 days from the date last marked below.

C.

No...................... Shelf..... ....

BOOKVILLE PUBLIC LIBRARY.

Open on Week-days from 11 till 2 and 6 till 9 ; Wednesdays 11 till 2 only. No access to the shelves after 1·45 and 8·45.

FIFTEEN DAYS, INCLUDING DAYS OF ISSUE AND RETURN, ARE ALLOWED FOR READING THIS BOOK. A fine of ONE PENNY per week, or portion of a week, is recoverable for each volume kept beyond that period.

Messengers should be furnished with a list of numbers and titles of books wanted.

This Book is returnable within 15 days from the date last marked below.

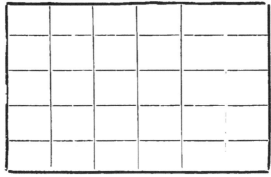

It is usual to paste labels like A on to the inside of the front board. Labels like B and C are usually attached down one edge only with about one-sixteenth of an inch of paste to the same board or to the waste or fly-leaf opposite. This enables them to be removed when full, and fresh ones inserted. Many Libraries use an engraved book plate or book label for their Reference Library books, while others have also a date label to show how often they have been in use, and when. Some Libraries use a variation of label A.

There is only one thing to be said about cutting up books— the leaves should be cut evenly and firmly, right into the back or fold of the section.

The process of preparing books for public use has now been fully described and it only remains to say that Reference Library books do not require book cards (8), as they are not issued for more than a few hours at a time. Of course there is no reason why a somewhat similar system should not be used, but in most cases application slips are used and these are placed in the space vacated by the book on loan till it is returned, when the slip is either returned to the reader or used for statistical or other purposes. Periodicals are dealt with in a similar fashion to books. They are received as donations or bought, and when bound go through the same processes described in sections 5 to 12. In addition it is usual to mark them off as received, number by number, in books or on cards ruled for the purpose.

GOOD WORDS.   Supplied by Mr. Jones.

Year	Jan.	Feb.	Mar.	Apl.	May	June	July	Aug.	Sept.	Oct.	Nov.	Dec.
1896	Dec 26	Jan 27										
1897												

They also require to have their titles displayed on placards so that readers can ascertain whether or not the Library takes certain periodicals.   The adjustable form of placard described in the article on "Recent Developments" seems to be the best for the purpose.   Reading covers or display stands and filing boxes or cases are matters which also require settlement.

In the lending department borrowers are dealt with in a fashion very similar to books, inasmuch as they have to be numbered and registered before they can become, as it were, part of the system.

13. Intending borrowers are required to lodge special APPLICATION forms with vouchers attached in conformity with the rules adopted for the management.   There are dozens of varieties in use in different Libraries and specimens can easily be obtained.   Whatever form may be used, they all agree in having the borrower's full name and addresses, business and residential, whilst a space is provided on the form for a number, by which the borrower is afterwards identified.   It is not proposed to describe the many ways of numbering and registering borrowers, but simply to recommend a plan which has worked successfully for many years.   The intending borrower's application form being found all right, the accession number as it were, is filled in to the space before mentioned.   The borrower may then become :—

"Walter Scott, 10 Abbotsford Place.   Ticket expires 10th Oct., 1897.   No. 1."

The application forms are usually kept in numerical order bound in volumes or stored in boxes.

14. To get over the difficulty of having numbers overlapping, and confusion getting into the numbering after the first year, a NUMBER REGISTER has been introduced which enables each borrower to retain the same number while he remains in the Library, and simplifies the method of enumerating the borrowers at any given time.   It is ruled as follows :—

No.	1896	1897	1898	1899	1900	1901	1902	1903
1	W. Scott ✓ Oct. 10	M. Corelli Aug. 6						
2	A. Tennyson Oct. 10	A. Tennyson Oct. 14						
3	R. Burns Oct. 12	R. Burns Oct. 9						
4	A.C. Doyle ✓ Oct. 12	G. Byron July 6						

The holder of a given current card can be ascertained at once, and the expired or dead ticket holders counted off very rapidly. Of course, the same result can be obtained by always substituting the new for the expired forms in the unbound sequence of vouchers, but it is not so quick a method of getting at the numbers which are available for using again, and it is more difficult to get at the exact number of current borrowers. Should Walter Scott leave the Library before 10th October, 1897, his name is marked with a tick $\sqrt{}$ in blue or red lead and it is thus shown that his number is cancelled and available for a new borrower. By using this register, the borrowers' numbers are always kept accurate and up-to-date.

15. The BORROWER having received his number, it is necessary to write out a ticket or CARD to represent him in his subsequent dealings with the Library, on which is also noted the numbers of the books he takes out. This should be a stout manilla card ruled exactly the same as the book card (8), but only $3\frac{1}{2} \times 2$ inches in size. The following example shows how it is entered up with the borrower's number, date when the ticket expires, name, address, and the number of the book he has out. On the corresponding book card will be found the borrower's number entered in similar fashion.

1.		10th October, 1897.
Walter Scott,		
10 Abbotsford Place.		
1		

When these cards are written, they should be placed in trays in alphabetical order of surnames. There are cheap special trays with alphabetical guides made for the purpose.

16. If these cards remained permanently in this alphabetical sequence there would be no need for an INDEX TO THE NAMES OF BORROWERS, but as they are continually being moved about in the charging system (17), it is best to provide an alphabetical index. This may be kept on cards, or in the adjustable holders described in the article on "Recent Developments". The information on these cards or slips, copied from the vouchers, should comprise, number, name and addresses of the borrower, and when his ticket expires. These cards or slips must, of course, be kept in strict alphabetical order. In many Libraries a similar index of guarantors is kept, showing, in addition to the address, the numbers of the borrowers guaranteed. The books and borrowers being now fully registered and numbered, it is necessary to briefly describe how the registration or charging of issues is accomplished with the apparatus available.

17. CHARGING or registration of issues is the process of keeping a record of books which are out on loan. The method should be simple, yet sufficiently full to supply any information about the transaction which may be required. The system recommended works as follows :—

The book cards (8) and borrowers' cards (15) being all arranged in trays, the former numerically and the latter alphabetically, the procedure in an open-access Library would be this. The borrower having proved his *bona fides* by surrendering his ticket voucher, which is given to readers temporarily withdrawing from the Library, is then admitted

---

BOOKTOWN PUBLIC LIBRARY.

TICKET VOUCHER.

The Bearer is entitled to Ticket No.... ....1...... .. on producing this slip and giving the correct name on the ticket.

....A. B.... ....Librarian.

Date...........Oct. 16, 1896..............

Admission to the Bookshelves will only be allowed to borrowers who hold Ticket Vouchers, or who come to return books. Messengers should be provided with lists of books wanted.

---

among the shelves, and either receives his card to carry round with him, or the assistant deposits it in an open alphabetical rack. The reader having chosen his book, takes it to the exit barrier and hands it with his card to the assistant, or, in the other case, the assistant selects the borrower's card from the rack. Next the book card is taken from its tray and placed with the borrower's card in a loose paper pocket, which then assumes an appearance like this:—

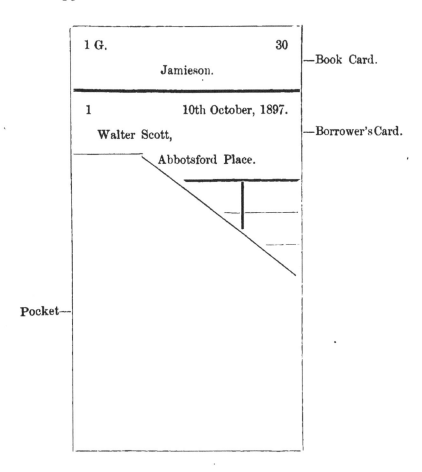

The date is next stamped on the date-label of the book and the borrower takes it away. These conjoined cards are then arranged in the numerical order of the book cards in special trays, and divided up by projections to show where each different thousand begins. The date of issue is put at the beginning on a specially shaped and coloured projecting guide. A tray so arranged then looks like this:—

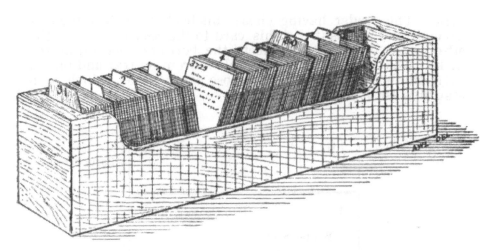

CHARGING TRAY, ARRANGED BY DATES AND NUMBERS.

The statistics of the day's issues can be taken from these cards whenever the Library closes and the staff has leisure. When the borrower returns the book, the date on its label directs the assistant to the tray, and the number to the exact place of the conjoined cards, which are then removed, the book card being restored to its original place and the borrower's card to the rack or the borrower as the case may be. Overdue books by this method declare themselves automatically. The system has other merits which need not be described now. When used without open access, the borrower always retains his card when he has no book out, and, of course, he must supply the assistant with a list of the books he would like, in place of choosing one for himself from the shelves. There are other varieties of this card method in use, and it will be enough to name some of the Libraries using them: *Open Libraries*—Clerkenwell, Bournemouth, Kingston-on-Thames, Croydon, Darwen, Kettering, Cripplegate Institute (London), Worcester, Widnes, etc. *Non-indicator Libraries without open access*—Chelsea, Holborn, Bradford, Penzance, Liverpool, Christchurch (London), Hammersmith, etc. *Indicator Libraries using cards*—Carlisle, Leigh, Lancaster, Hartlepool, Dewsbury, etc.

Having now described various steps necessary in the formation and working of a new Public Library, it only remains to show clearly in one view by means of a graphic recapitulation the processes just noticed for preparing books on the one hand, and readers on the other hand, for their mutual association in the charging system of the Library. The following diagram shows at a glance the sequence of processes :—

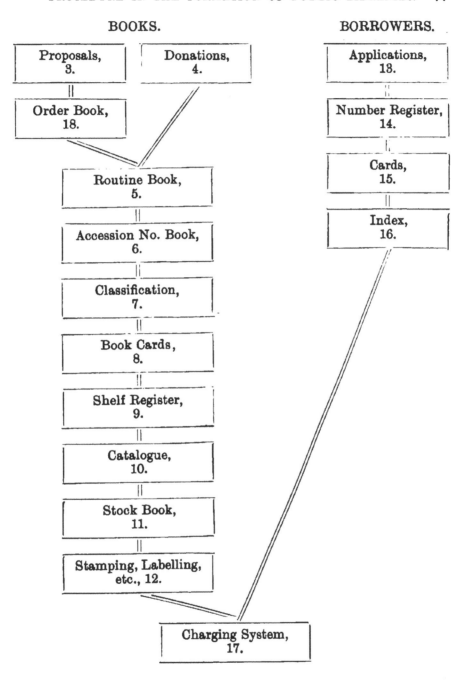

18. Several books of record mentioned previously may now be noticed. The MINUTE BOOK should be a plainly ruled volume with a margin, and should be kept by the honorary secretary or clerk to the Library Committee, in the customary way. The ORDER BOOK is best kept as an ordinary letter copying

book, in which facsimile copies of all orders should be made by the press in the usual way. In large Libraries it is best to keep a special volume for book orders. Usually, special order forms are used, with headings or ruled columns. In such cases care should be taken to have these forms not larger than large-post quarto size. The INVENTORY BOOK should be ruled to show when and at what cost all furniture, fittings, supplies, etc., were procured. A suitable ruling is as follows, and it is recommended that the book be kept in four or more parts, so many pages for "Furniture," so many for "Stationery," etc. This will facilitate reference.

FURNITURE.

Date.	Description.	Price.			Vendor.	Remarks.
		£	s.	d.		
1896 July 6	1 Revolving Book-case	3	10	0	Wallace & Co.	

The financial questions arising out of Library formation and administration are so much bound up with purely Committee work that they need not be considered here. It should be stated, however, that cash receipts from fines, sales and other sources ought to be reported regularly to the treasurer or Committee. Daily issues should be noted in a special book, and all other work requiring record for the use of the Committee or annual report should be regularly done. But these and other matters arising out of the work of a Library after formation may be left for future issues of this Year Book.

RECENT DEVELOPMENTS OF LIBRARY PRACTICE.

ADMINISTRATIVE WORK.

By JAMES D. BROWN, LIBRARIAN, CLERKENWELL PUBLIC LIBRARY.

IN this article it is proposed to notice a few of the more important developments in the administration of Public Libraries which have grown up since 1892. Some of these are not so much innovations as great extensions of older experiments which have sprung into prominence within the past few years ; while others are noticed to supplement what has already been described in the fourth edition of Greenwood's *Public Libraries.* Perhaps the most notable innovation of all has been the adoption of the plan of admitting properly qualified borrowers directly to the shelves of closely classified Lending Libraries, there to make choice of books by actual examination of contents, instead of as formerly by somewhat meagre catalogue descriptions. This method has been conveniently named

OPEN ACCESS,

though a better name would be Safeguarded Access, which describes the system more accurately, and serves to distinguish it from the kind of access allowed in Proprietary and Reference Libraries. The first proposal to apply a safeguarded method of open access to Public Lending Libraries seems to be that advocated in an article which was published in the *Library* of 1892, page 302, entitled, "A Plea for Liberty to Readers to Help Themselves," in which a plan is described closely resembling that now adopted in most of the Libraries using the system. This provides for regulating barriers to ensure that only *bona fide* enrolled borrowers are permitted to enter; close classification of the books on the shelves and the provision of numerous printed shelf and other guides; differential marking of the books by coloured labels or other means, to make permanent misplacements impossible; readjustments in the height, depth, and spacing of bookshelves; and the adoption of a tell-tale card-charging method. On somewhat similar lines the Clerkenwell Public Library Com-

missioners adopted the system in October, 1893, and on
1st May, 1894, they opened their lending department as a
safeguarded open-access Library, and on this method it continues to work with success. One of the immediate results of
this experiment was to call forth a series of adverse comments
from various librarians in different parts of the country, which
were published for the most part in a paper called *London* and
in a few provincial journals. Among the main objections
offered may be mentioned : 1, Likelihood of extensive thefts ;
2, disorder and misplacements among the books ; 3, wear and
tear among books ; 4, crowding and rowdyism among the
borrowers; 5, reduction of storage space for books; 6, practical
uselessness of the system to a large majority of the borrowers,
because they know nothing about books. The experience of
all the Libraries which have adopted safeguarded open access
has proved that numbers 1, 2, 3, 4, and 6 are practically non-
existent, while 5 is a condition which will only be met with in
the older Libraries which have to adapt unsuitable premises
to the system. It might be added that 6 is a very stupid
objection when one considers the sort of catalogue entries
borrowers as a rule have to guide them. About the end of
1894 *London* issued a large table headed " Public Library
Systems of Lending Out and Recording Books," in which are
condensed the opinions of 143 librarians which were delivered
in June, 1894, or about six weeks after the Clerkenwell experiment was commenced. As none of the 143 librarians, favourable or unfavourable, had any experience of safeguarded open
access, and only three or four had at that time seen the
system actually working, it is scarcely surprising to find that
only fifteen out of the whole number expressed themselves in
sympathy with the method. Since then there has been a very
great change of opinion, largely induced by the fact that every
Library which has adopted safeguarded access not only finds
it smooth working and satisfactory to the parties most concerned—the public—but also tending towards the simplifica-
tion of many of the processes which caused trouble by other
methods. Besides this most of the librarians have taken pains
to make themselves acquainted with the system as actually
worked in various open-access Libraries, and this has done
much to modify hastily conceived and erroneous ideas.
Reference might be made here to a few of the articles descriptive of the system which have from time to time been
published : " The Clerkenwell Open Lending Library," in the
Library, 1894, page 344 ; " Classification of Books for Libraries
in which Readers are Allowed Access to the Shelves," in the
Library, 1895, page 75 ; " Open Libraries," in the *Library
Journal* (New York), 1895, page 9 ; circulars and articles in the
local press contributed by the Library authorities of Bournemouth, Darwen, Kingston-on-Thames, Clerkenwell, Croydon,
Kettering, etc. The case against open access is contained in a

tract entitled " The Truth about giving Readers Free Access
to the Books in a Public Lending Library, by One who has
tried the system in two large Libraries," London, 1895. This
is adorned with a frontispiece which may be taken as a graphic
summary of the arguments which have been advanced against
the system. It should be stated, however, that none of the
arguments, pictorial or other, have much bearing on safeguarded open access. Up to the present time the following
Libraries have adopted the safeguarded open-access system in
their lending departments :—

	Adopted.	Opened.
Clerkenwell - - - -	Oct. 1893	May 1, 1894
Bournemouth - - - -	1894	Jan. 1, 1895
Bishopsgate Institute, London	1894	Jan. 1, 1895
Darwen - - - - -	1894	June, 1895
Kingston-on-Thames - -	1895	Aug., 1895
Kettering - - - -	1895	Mar. 2, 1896
Rothwell, Northamptonshire -	1896	Mar. 28, 1896
Croydon - - - - -	1895	June, 1896
Cripplegate Institute, London	1895	Nov. 4, 1896
Worcester - - - -	1895	1896
Widnes - - - - -	1896	1896

At Chester, Middle Claydon, etc., modified forms of the
safeguarded method have been introduced. It is not necessary
at present to mention the other towns which have the adoption
of the system in contemplation. All the places which are
now in operation on the safeguarded method are unanimous
as regards its safety and ease of working, and have found by
experience that thefts, misplacements, crowding, and all the
other objectionable features which were anticipated are
practically non-existent.

A brief description of the system, with plans of its application at different places, will fitly close this article. The main
object sought to be gained by the open-access system is not,
as has been assumed by some, the supersession of existing
mechanical methods, but an earnest endeavour to meet public
needs in the selection of suitable literature by allowing borrowers intimate contact with their own books, as arranged in
classified order on the shelves. To this end, the books are
systematically arranged in classes, and subdivided as may be
necessary, each main class and subdivision being indicated by
means of boldly printed guides fastened to the bookcases and
shelves so as to clearly describe the contents of each. A system
which has been found to work well is that in use at several
open-access Libraries, whereby the literature in the Library
has been divided into the following main classes :—

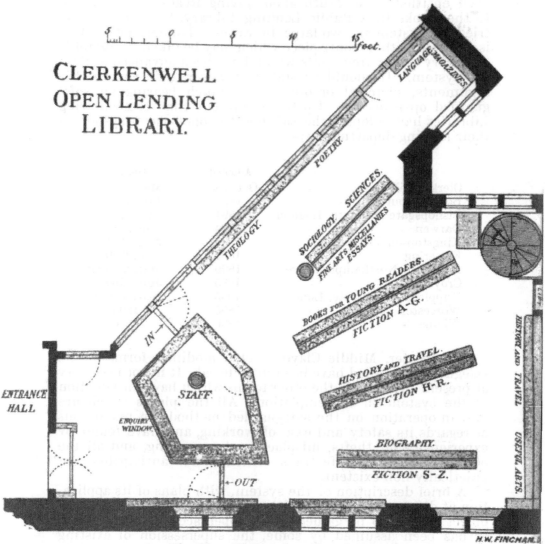

CLERKENWELL OPEN LENDING LIBRARY.

A. Theology, Philosophy, Church History.
B. History and Travel.
C. Biography and Correspondence.
D. Social Science.
E. Natural and Mathematical Sciences.
F. Fine and Useful Arts.
G. Useful Arts.
H. Language and Literature.
J. Poetry and the Drama.
K. Prose Fiction and Juvenile Literature.
L. Miscellaneous.

Classes C, J, K and L (as to Essays), are arranged in alphabetical order of authors' names, or, in the case of C, the subjects
of biography, and ensure the easy finding of all the lives of

Gladstone, or Napoleon I., or Shakespeare, in one place; the various editions of Burns, Swinburne or Tennyson, in one place; the novels of Grant Allen, Brönte, Dickens, Hardy, Clark Russell, Scott, Mrs. Wood, all together; or the essays of Birrell, Carlyle, Lowell, Macaulay and Stevenson, in their proper alphabetical sequence. The other classes are subdivided according to the representation of the sections making up the class in the Library, but all are so arranged as to bring together on one or more adjoining shelves, the various works in, say Class E, on Botany, Chemistry, Geology, Zoology, Astronomy, Mathematics, etc. This is an immense advantage to the student, and has been appreciated and greatly taken advantage of, wherever introduced. The same juxtaposition of related sciences is not obtained by the ordinary methods of dictionary cataloguing, besides which the power of examination and comparison of works is denied to users of Lending Libraries which do not allow open access. Hence, one of the most valuable educational features of Library work is entirely lost in such Libraries, by placing obstacles in the way of a student's desire of determining the *suitability* for his purpose of the various books on the same subject possessed by the Library. This grave defect in the administration of non-open-access Libraries has been so widely recognised that nearly every such Library now possesses a glazed show-case in which are placed for closer examination by the public books which cannot be adequately described by ordinary methods of cataloguing. This fact may be taken as a tacit admission that the catalogue alone, however good, is an insufficient guide to the contents of a Library. When, in addition to open access, catalogues are provided which describe and bring together *all* the books on related subjects, it must be conceded that the borrower who has the use of an open Library is placed at a great advantage as compared with his less fortunate brother who has no such privilege or right.

To prevent books being permanently misplaced, most of the open-access Libraries use a series of specially shaped and coloured labels, which in the most unmistakable manner distinguish class from class and shelf from shelf. Classes are distinguished by having differently *shaped* labels on the backs of the books, and the shelves in a press are distinguished from each other by the books on them being labelled in different *colours*. If a press has four tiers, and each tier eight shelves, the required differentiation is obtained in the simplest possible way by arranging the colours for the shelf labels thus:—

CLASS B.—Oblong shaped label |_____|

First Tier.	Second Tier.	Third Tier.	Fourth Tier.
Shelf 1. Blue Labels.	9. Yellow Labels.	17. Grey Labels.	25. Red Labels.
2. Red ,,	10. Mauve ,,	18. Buff ,,	26. Green ,,
3. Green ,,	11. White ,,	19. Blue ,,	27. Yellow ,,
4. Yellow ,,	12. Grey ,,	20. Red ,,	28. Mauve ,,
5. Mauve ,,	13. Buff ,,	21. Green ,,	29. White ,,
6. White ,,	14. Blue ,,	22. Yellow ,,	30. Grey ,,
7. Grey ,,	15. Red ,,	23. Mauve ,,	31. Buff ,,
8. Buff ,,	16. Green ,,	24. White ,,	32. Blue

It will thus be seen that no colour is repeated in juxtaposition to a shelf having books labelled the same colour; red, for example, occurring only once on Tier 1 and being widely separated from all the repetitions of the colour. But even if a book from shelf 2 is put on shelf 20, by accident or design, a difference in the *altitude* of the label on the book serves to detect the misplacement at once. It is, therefore, advisable to label all the books in Tier 1 about one inch from the foot of the back; Tier 2 about half an inch higher; Tier 3 half an inch higher, and so on, the result being that no matter where in the whole Library a book is wrongly placed, its label will immediately draw attention to the misplacement. It is not desirable to enter into details of the various modifications of the system in use or which have been proposed; enough has been written to show what is done as regards classification and the means taken to preserve it in order. It is, perhaps, hardly needful to add, that with such a method of labelling, the few misplacements which do occur, are very readily and rapidly detected and put right. The labels are all made by simply cutting, in different ways, little square and round discs of thin, coloured paper.

There are a number of methods of arranging for the service of the borrowers and exercising oversight and control, but they have been already described in the papers above mentioned and in the chapter on "Procedure in the Formation of Libraries". The ground plans and pictures incorporated in this article will convey a much better idea of the general arrangements usually made, than is possible by any amount of description. It should be mentioned, however, that the newer open-access Libraries are adopting standard double-faced bookcases, with open wire-work grilles between the backs of shelves, to give light and oversight, and are having the shelves made not more than $6\frac{1}{2}$ or 7 inches wide to prevent books being pushed behind. For wider books special cases must, of course, be provided.

The tell-tale card-charging system usually worked along with the open-access method is fully described in the *Library*, 1894, p. 344, and also in the article on the "Formation of Libraries," so that it is not necessary to go over the same ground again. Since 1894, several improvements have been introduced, chiefly in connection with the mechanical devices attached to the trays, etc., and these may be seen at work in Bournemouth, Darwen, Croydon, and elsewhere. An ingenious form of treadle-latch for regulating the barrier wickets has also been introduced at Kingston, Kettering, Croydon, Clerkenwell, etc., and there are other minor appliances which have been from time to time invented to make the system more perfect in its working. At the Conference of the American Library Association held at Cleveland in September, 1896, a discussion on open access arose out of a paper on "Preparing Books for Issue, and Charging Systems," which showed that the librarians of

CROYDON PUBLIC LIBRARY.   CHARGING SYSTEM.

America are practically unanimous in favour of the principle. According to the report in the *Library Journal*, it was ascertained by actual count that sixty-five Libraries in the States granted open access of one kind or another, to books other than those for reference, while out of 300 delegates present at the meeting, only 12 voted against the practice of giving readers unrestricted access to their own books. Although the safeguarded system has not yet been extended to all the books in any American Lending Library, so far as we know, this expression of opinion on the part of an important public body must be held to possess much weight and significance for the future.

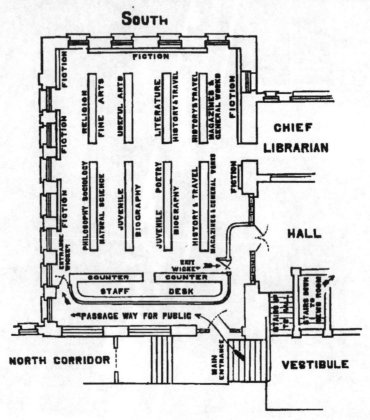

CROYDON PUBLIC LIBRARY. OPEN-ACCESS LIBRARY.

Altogether, the safeguarded open-access system has made wonderful progress since its installation in May, 1894, and its popularity with readers, economy of working, and general simplicity, will probably be the means of further recommending the plan to the attention of librarians and Committees who have new buildings or re-arrangements in contemplation. There are no special features connected with open Reference Libraries as yet, so that it is only needful to refer to the information concerning them given in the notices of Libraries appearing elsewhere in this Year Book.

The constant endeavours made by librarians to meet special requirements on the part of readers have led to various departures from the older practice.   One of these is the introduction of extra

STUDENTS' TICKETS,

available for non-fictional works only, which was originally proposed, it is believed, by Mr. J. Y. W. MacAlister, the honorary secretary of the Library Association, in a paper entitled "How to Keep Down the Issues of Fiction," which was read at Aberdeen in 1893, and published in the *Library*, 1894, p. 236.   This suggestion was adopted at Chelsea for music only, sometime in 1893, and at Clerkenwell in October, 1893, for all classes of literature save fiction.   Other Libraries adopted the method, and now it is working with more or less success at Aberdeen, Ashton-under-Lyne, Birkenhead, Bootle, Bournemouth, Brechin, Darwen, Gosport, Hampstead, Holborn, Kingston-on-Thames, Newington, Reading, St. Giles, Southampton, etc.

The system has also been very extensively applied in the United States since the beginning of 1894.   It need hardly be pointed out that the main object of these extra tickets is not to try and reduce or oust fiction reading, but to meet as effectually as possible the needs of the studious reader who uses books as tools.   There is an endless stream of cross references between works of history and travel; both these and biography; sciences and arts; literary history and biography and art; and, indeed, between every class of literature.   The boy who reads Verne, Henty, Fenn, Ballantyne, Mayne Reid or Kingston, is sooner or later led to study works on the countries in which the scenes of their adventure stories are laid.   A teacher striving to impart a knowledge of English literature will desire to read separate biographies of the greater writers as well as outline text-books, if he has any wish to clothe his teaching in more than the bare bones of dry fact.   The student of Darwin's works can find many valuable side-lights in the biographies of that author; while the young man or woman who writes an essay on Thackeray, Tennyson, Scott, Dickens, or any other celebrity, will find advantage in the parallel study of the author's works as well as his life.   It is, therefore, perfectly manifest that, to a very large section of readers, the extra ticket is a valuable boon, enabling courses of reading or the study of subjects from more than one point of view to be carried on.   So far, no strong objections have been raised to the issue of these extra tickets in the larger Libraries, though it is possible the smaller Libraries would find the practice unadvisable because of smallness of stock.

In several towns and districts where funds are limited, and

it is impossible to provide suitable branch Libraries or reading-rooms, an effort has been made to meet the needs of areas which are situated at a distance from the central or nearest branch Library, by opening

DELIVERY STATIONS,

from which books can be issued or exchanged. These stations are generally shops, and the proprietor undertakes to receive lists of wants from enrolled borrowers, and issue the books when sent from the central Library. The common plan is for a borrower to leave a list of wants at the delivery station on one day, and return for a book on the next or some succeeding day, when the books are sent from the central Library. At Wandsworth, which introduced the plan in 1894, readers were required to wait a week, but the exchanges here and elsewhere are made oftener. There are various economies effected in the work of Libraries in widely scattered districts by means of these stations, but at best they can only be regarded as a makeshift, owing to the fact that book selection becomes reduced very nearly to the level of a lottery, while the delays and disappointments are also certain to cause discontent. The method has been in use at Chicago and other American cities for many years, and, though open to much criticism, is certainly better than no effort at all being made to distribute books in outlying districts. In connection with this subject, which is very important in view of the resemblance between it and the case of book distribution in rural districts, the following papers are recommended to be read:—

Wood, "Yorkshire Village Libraries"; Ogle, "Proposal for the Establishment of District Public Libraries on an Economical Basis"; Brown, "The Village Library Problem"; all in the *Library* for 1894. Baker, "Rural Public Libraries," in the *Library* for July, 1896, p. 298. In Jan., 1895, Mr. Samuel Smith, librarian of Sheffield, read a paper before the Library Association on "Delivery Stations *versus* Branches," but this has not yet been printed.

Delivery stations have been started in connection with the Public Libraries of Sheffield, Enfield, Wandsworth, etc.

Among the many changes which have been rapidly progressing within the past few years perhaps none has been so marked as the altered attitude of many librarians towards the Dictionary

CATALOGUE.

For many years a catalogue in dictionary form was accepted as the high-water mark of book description and the greatest pitch of perfection attainable in the art of cataloguing. Elaborate codes of rules have been issued from time to time, and Libraries have followed each other in the compilation of catalogues according to one or other of them till belief in this particular method has become a fixed dogma. Of late years a reaction against dictionary catalogues has set in among a section of librarians, and doubts are beginning to be expressed, not only as regards the *form* of these catalogues, but also as regards the methods adopted in compilation. The dictum of the late Mr. Crestadoro of Manchester, that the title-page of a book is the only description which any one has a right to regard, has probably done more than anything else to reduce the whole art of cataloguing to a mere mechanical operation, and has called into existence more bald, colourless, unreliable and imperfect inventories of books than even the aforesaid codes of rules. Because of Crestadoro's opinion and the number of catalogues issued in imitation of his example, most of the Public Library catalogues are nothing more or less than bare lists of titles utterly devoid of notes, marks or suggestions of any kind to serve as guides to the borrower who has to make his choice of literature through this medium. It is considered quite enough if all the books by a given author are brought together in these inventories, and if, further, they are placed under such subject-words as occur on the title-pages. The standpoint adopted is that of assuming considerable book-knowledge on the part of the reader, and providing him with a list of the titles of books in the Library, leaving him to ascertain for himself the question of their suitability, antiquity, period and scope. One of the most monumental specimens of this sort of futile cataloguing is the " Catalogue of the Books in the Central Lending Department " at New-castle-upon-Tyne issued in 1880, which was lauded to the skies on its original appearance, and has been responsible for more than half of the thoroughly bad catalogues issued since that time. From the reader's point of view, this is undoubtedly the most colossal piece of pretentious ineptitude ever produced. In all its 300 and odd closely printed pages there is hardly an entry which is in any great measure helpful to the reader. Not only are both dates of publication and origin deliberately omitted, but the entries under main subject heads are positively misleading and useless. Under " Man " for example, where one would naturally expect to find books more or less of an anthropological character, are grouped such ludicrous contrasts in subject matter as " Man, a Story of Light and Darkness, by Greene "; " Man as He is not, a romance, by Bage "; " Man, First, and His Place in Creation, by Moore "; " Man, Rights of, by Paine "; " Man who was like Shakespeare, a tale, by Black," etc., etc., the whole cemented together by the most exasperating and unmeaning array of dashes possible to conceive. Books on the history, topography, social life, language, etc., of England are entered in confused masses according to the leading words of the titles, under such heads as England, English, Britain, British, Great Britain, Anglo-Saxons, etc., so that the poor reader must wade through the whole catalogue before he can obtain the faintest idea of what books on England the Library has. Then as regards subject matter or period of individual books he must puzzle out as best he can such entries as these under England: "— — — — by May "; "— — — — — the Four Georges, *see* Georgian Era "; "— — — — — —- to Victoria, by Knight "; "— — — — — — — to Victoria, by White "; "— -- — — — — — — second series ". As a piece of mental discipline such entries have value, of course, because it must be interesting to finally discover the difference between a six dash history of England and a seven dash one, but whether the ratepayers' money was legitimately spent on such pretty arithmetical conundrums is quite another question. We have devoted all this space to a thoroughly bad specimen of cataloguing because it is the type of many similar inventories being issued even now, as well as being just the antipodes of the more recent style of catalogue mentioned at the end of this section. Luckily only a very small number of the catalogues issued during the past three or four years are guilty of such an abuse of the dash as we have endeavoured above to show, while many of them are distinguished by the care which has been taken to ascertain the subject of which books treat, without regard to the statements on the title-pages. Again, subject headings are more strictly treated, and one need not now expect to find under such headings as Africa, English, Man, Music, War, etc., books which merely have such words on their title-pages without in any degree treating of the subjects indicated by the words. It may, therefore, be assumed that the old form of dictionary catalogue, the author and loose title-form, has been very largely supplanted by the author and strict subject-form. But even with all this great improvement, modern catalogues are still defective in withholding from the intending borrower just the very sort of information which is essential in all Libraries where the books cannot be seen and handled ; and even in those which grant open access, owing to so many borrowers having to send messengers. A bare transcript of a title-page, with the date of publication added, is not sufficient for that complete edification of the reader which most earnest librarians have at heart. To illustrate this, we print a few extracts from catalogues issued during the past few years, adding the assumption that the reader is an ordinary Library user with no special knowledge of books :—

Bates (H. W.), Naturalist on the River Amazons. 1891.   C 938
Cook (Capt. J.), Three Voyages round the World. 1892.   C 997
English History, Green (J. R.), History of the English People,
    4 v. 1877-86.   109
Kinglake (A. W.), Eothen [travel in the East]. 1896.   H 516
London, Hunt (L.), The Town.   14310
White (Gilbert), Natural History of Selborne. 1891.   G 246

These extracts may be taken as fairly typical examples of the

sort of entries considered full enough and instructive enough
for ordinary readers, and no doubt to the man who knows his
Bates, Leigh Hunt, Kinglake or White, they are all sufficient.
But for the vast majority of Public Library users such entries
are not only useless, but misleading. Suppose a reader takes
out Bates' *Amazons* expecting to find an account of Brazil in
1891, and on reaching home discovering that he has got a book
treating of that country as it was in 1848-59! Or some one
interested in the Eastern question withdrawing Kinglake for
information concerning some of the recent misdeeds of Turkey!
We are unable to say if the natural history of the Hampshire
Selborne has changed greatly since 1789, but imagine the
modern cycling naturalist or antiquary would find old Gilbert
White an exceedingly inefficient if, to certain minds, interesting guide. A voyage round the world in a luxurious steamer
in 1892 is a very different affair from a similar voyage in 1768,
as any one would speedily discover who took Cook's book, or
abridgment thereof, as a standard. While Leigh Hunt's *The
Town* is so very far from being a description of modern
London, or even a considerable part of it, that intending
tourists from provincial centres should be warned against it!

The object of the reaction from dictionary cataloguing is
therefore to correct the deficiencies above noted, as well as to
obtain a more economical method of publication. For this
reason the plan of issuing comparatively small class lists
susceptible of frequent and easy revision has been adopted in
many Libraries, including Nottingham, Liverpool, Clerkenwell,
Chelsea, Peterborough, etc., and though all of them are not
successful from the descriptive point of view, they nearly all
succeed in giving a connected and comprehensive view of the
literature of the particular main class to which they are
devoted. Some of them also succeed in giving just the amount
of information concerning books which makes catalogue entries
really useful to all kinds of readers, as the following extracts
will show :—

Bates (H. W.), Naturalist, on the River Amazons, a record of adven-
    tures, habits of animals, sketches of Brazilian and Indian life, and
    aspects of nature under the Equator, during eleven years of travel
    [1848-59]. 1891. Illust.   5523
Kinglake (A. W.), Eothen. 1885.   3114
    Travel Sketches (in 1835) in Constantinople, Cyprus, Palestine, and Egypt.

Without making entries so full as the foregoing, there is no
reason why dates or descriptive words should not be briefly
added to all entries in catalogues which are misleading or
imperfect. The additional space occupied would not be great,
while the extra trouble involved would scarcely be felt by the
true librarian. An example of the use which can be made of
the "daylight" or "fat" spaces left in all short entry catalogues
is furnished by the Clerkenwell Public Library "Class Guide

to Fiction and Juvenile Literature," 1895, wherein all such spaces are as far as possible occupied by brief notes giving a rough idea of the period, country, or motive of every novel or tale capable of being characterised. The catalogues of Holborn, Kettering, and Peterborough also use these notes.   In similar fashion there is no reason why any catalogue should not be supplied with brief indications to aid readers, and prevent them from taking out such books as Buchan's eighteenth century *Domestic Medicine* instead of more modern works. The case as between dictionary catalogues in condensed form and class lists in classified or other order is not far enough advanced for further discussion here, and may be dismissed in the meantime.

Another departure from the older order of things has been the displacement in many Libraries of the bulletin or supplement of additions by the

MAGAZINE OR GUIDE,

appearing periodically as a kind of Library magazine.   These are now issued with items of news of interest to the Library readers, illustrations, annotated lists of recent additions, etc., and seem to be a very effective substitute for the old-fashioned and dry supplement or bulletin.   The following among other Libraries now publish such magazines:—Clerkenwell (since July, 1894); Brentford (since March, 1895); Bournemouth (May, 1895); West Ham (June, 1895); Hampstead (November, 1895); Newington, Surrey (April, 1896), the first monthly; Nottingham, Willesden Green, etc.   Most of these little magazines are issued quarterly.   They are also a feature in many American Libraries.

For some years past many Libraries have been trying by means of lectures and

BOOK EXHIBITIONS

to arouse greater public interest on behalf of their reference collections.   Lectures on the books have been delivered, and periodical exhibitions of the more valuable and interesting works have been given, and in most cases the result has been to permanently direct the attention of readers to the value and uses of the department.   These displays when well advertised and not confined to a few special book rarities seldom fail to attract readers and stimulate their interest in the Library. The older practice of showing a few curiosities in glazed cases after the Museum plan has been found to attract but few readers ; while the more liberal method of laying out all sorts of illustrated, curious, and valuable works which can be examined has been successful in making readers and keeping them. The work in this connection at St. Helen's and Chelsea, St. Martin's, and elsewhere is well worth imitation.   A paper entitled " On the Advantage of Occasional Exhibitions of the more Rare and Valuable Books in Public Libraries " was read by Mr. Alfred Lancaster of St. Helen's at Aberdeen in 1893, and is published in the *Library*, 1894, page 19.   In some Lending Libraries a variety of this same sort of open access has been adopted, though as yet it has been confined to the mere exhibition of the backs or title pages of books in glazed or other bookcases.   The showcase has been alluded to before as a device to aid in overcoming the weakness of the ordinary method of cataloguing.   At Birkenhead the Library authorities have gone further by exhibiting a whole Library at one of the branches on similar lines.   Cases with wire-mesh fronts are displayed on counters, in which the books are arranged so that their backs can be examined by readers.   When the borrower has made up his mind which book he fancies best, either by its title or binding, he pushes it back with his finger so that the assistant can see it from the inside, and duly charge and issue it.   This method of selection by touch has very little to recommend it beyond its seeming novelty, as it is notorious that the description which a book bears on its back is so abbreviated as to be absolutely no guide.   A similar plan was suggested by Mr. Mullins of Birmingham many years ago, and at Aberdeen, in 1893, Mr. Thomas Mason of St. Martin's read a paper advocating the same plan, entitled " A New Method of Arranging a Lending Library," which was printed in the *Library*, 1894, page 263, with an illustration at page 361.   The Birkenhead method is described in a paper entitled " An Improved Form of Book Shelving for Branch Lending Libraries," by Mr. May, the librarian, which was printed in the *Library*, 1896, page 255.

The plan of giving courses of lectures in connection with Public Libraries which was described in Greenwood's *Public Libraries*, last edition, page 470, has spread with great rapidity, and now a very large number of places have organised courses. There has been no new development of any consequence, so that the reference to Greenwood will suffice, as that work gives very full particulars of the practice in all the principal centres.

SALARIES, AND WOMEN LIBRARIANS.

This section may fitly be closed by a brief reference to the position of librarians and assistants in Britain.   Since the publication of the fourth edition of *Public Libraries* little, if any, change has occurred in the status and emoluments of librarians.   The hundreds of persons, male and female, who are striving to enter the Public Library service under the impression that they will become possessed of a highly paid sinecure, may as well salve their sanguine, if often disappointed, hopes, with the consolatory reflection that they have been pursuing an *ignis fatuus*.   The work of a careful and earnest librarian is anything but a sinecure, and in a great number of cases the amount of knowledge and ability brought to bear on the duties is out of all proportion to the meagre reward paid. Speaking broadly, the salaries paid to librarians range from £50 to £550 per annum, but on the average about £80 to £100 represents the maximum salary paid to the British public librarian. Of those who receive from £400 to £550 per annum the number can be counted on one hand; while of those ranging between £300 and £400 the number is about the same. Outside of London, salaries of £200 and over are very seldom paid, while in the smaller towns £50 to £80 is often considered ample. Of course the limitation of the rate makes it difficult to amend this state of affairs, but these remarks may guide those who are fighting for positions in this genteel and ill-paid profession, and will, perhaps, enable some of them to understand that, till a great extension of the Library movement takes place, other sources of livelihood are preferable. Most librarians in the larger towns are overwhelmed with applications from intelligent but inexperienced persons for positions on the Library staff, and it is becoming daily more difficult for such aspirants to gain a footing. This is especially so as regards women, against whom a dead set is made by many librarians on various ridiculous grounds. Saving Manchester, Bristol, Bradford, Aberdeen, and a few other places, there are hardly any of the larger towns which employ women in any capacity. London is practically closed to women librarians, and in small towns local candidates at very small salaries are as a rule appointed. Altogether the outlook is not very promising for women who desire to become public librarians earning a living wage, and until a radical change occurs, it is not worth an intelligent girl's trouble to train herself for work which can hardly be said to exist.

LIBRARY APPLIANCES.

Since the publication of the last edition of Greenwood's *Public Libraries* considerable activity has been displayed in the production of improved forms of bookshelving and charging or registering systems. The tendency as regards

BOOKSHELVES

has been chiefly in the direction of securing absolute adjustment in the height of individual shelves. Nearly a dozen patents have been issued to inventors in England, Germany and the United States for bookcases fitted with mechanical devices, for enabling shelves to be moved up and down to any extent, without the use of fixed points or catches. Most of these inventions are operated by means of set screws, but at the Worcester Public Library there has been adopted a variety of fitting which gives absolute adjustment to any degree by simple automatic means.   As shown in the illustration the shelves are supported on brackets which slide up and down the grooved uprights, and are controlled by means of a small lever which automatically locks the bracket in place wherever released. This enables shelves to be adjusted with great nicety, and is a vast improvement on the fixed point methods which supply adjustments only at about one inch apart. Another method, one of those mentioned above as of American origin, is to be seen at the Publishers' Book Exhibition in London. In this system the adjustment is also absolute but not auto-

STEEL BOOKCASE WITH AUTOMATIC ADJUSTING BRACKETS.

matic, the sliding brackets being controlled by means of a screw turned with a separate key. The other methods, being chiefly foreign, and not likely to be much used in this country, are in the meantime passed over.

INDICATORS.

Among the recently introduced mechanical charging methods is the indicator which has been adopted at Leigh, Lancaster, Carlisle, Dewsbury, Workington, St. Helen's and Wigan. This consists of a wooden frame "on which is displayed in plain gilt figures the number of every book in the Lending Library". Under each number is a longitudinal slot in which is placed a small card bearing the book number and class letter, which underlines the gilt number above it. The presence of this card represents a book *in;* when the slot is blank the book is out. The *withdrawal* of the book card is the method of indicating books out, and it is the union of this card with the borrower's card which forms the basis of the subsequent registration.

"When a book is issued the assistant withdraws the card from the recorder and places it in the reader's ticket, which is formed like a pocket, fetches the book, stamps it with the date of issue, and so completes the transaction at the moment of service.

" Afterwards, when there is time, or when the day's work is being cleared up, the readers' pocket tickets containing the book cards are assembled and arranged according to classes in numerical order. They are then posted, by book and reader numbers only, on to a daily issue sheet or register, and the date of issue is stamped on each book card, if this has not already been done at the moment of service.

BOOK-ISSUE INDICATOR.

"The conjoined book and reader cards are then placed in a tray bearing the date of issue, in the order of classes and book numbers or in one series of book numbers as may be needful.

"The work of finding any given book number is simplified very considerably by arranging the alternate thousands of book numbers in the readers' pocket tickets to the left and right, but of course in one row behind one another. Whatever arrangement of book numbers be adopted in the dated trays the result is the same when the book is returned. The date label directs to the tray and the book card, and the assistant simply looks out the book card and accompanying pocket ticket, then removes them and restores the card to its correct place in the recorder and the ticket to the borrower."

Other indicators have been introduced, and, at least, two have been patented or provisionally protected, but, as none have as yet been used, it is needless to describe them. Refer-

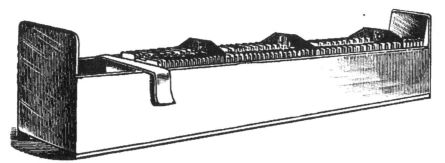

CHARGING-TRAY FOR BOOK-ISSUE INDICATOR.

ence might be made, however, to a paper describing a modified indicating apparatus which appeared in the *Library* for 1896, page 96.

CATALOGUING AND INDEXING METHODS.

Of these the most novel is the adjustable catalogue holders in the form of little sheaves or slip books used at the Public

ADJUSTABLE CATALOGUE HOLDER.

Libraries of Chelsea, Richmond, Hammersmith, Brentford, Darlington, Aberdeen University, Bradford, Reading, etc. As shown in the illustration these holders are really screw binders containing slotted slips which can be arranged in any order and always maintained in strict alphabetical sequence.

"The slips are uniformly punched with slots which hook on to adjustable screws, so that no threading is required, as in all other card indexing systems. A few turns of the key will release the contents so that insertions or withdrawals can be made instantly. When screwed up the slips are clamped so firmly that it is impossible for any one to remove or tear out an entry without leaving a counterfoil to show what has been taken."

DUPLEX CARD CATALOGUE.

Another variety of adjustable catalogue holder invented to overcome the inconveniences and difficulties of card catalogues is that known as the duplex card catalogue used at Wigan and elsewhere. The illustration shows the general appearance of this contrivance, which enables cards or thick paper slips to be used on both sides and turned over like a book. The boxes have falling ends to facilitate the display of the contents, and the slips are secured by a locking rod on which they are threaded.

Various forms of card catalogue trays have recently been introduced, but possess no features of general interest or novelty.

OTHER APPLIANCES

of recent introduction are the following, which are perhaps best described by the illustrations.

Book holders with sliding uprights and carriers with hooks for hanging to shelves as illustrated are in use in the Public Libraries of Brighton, Clerkenwell, Hereford, Kingston-on-Thames, Stoke Newington, Warrington, Wigan, and elsewhere. They are useful for holding and classifying returned books in the Lending Library, and for holding and carrying books during the processes of cataloguing, cutting, stamping, etc.

To avoid the nuisance of having to frequently reprint the public list of periodicals supplied to Reading-rooms, owing to alterations, additions, or discontinuance of magazines, an adjustable magazine list holder has been devised. It consists

ADJUSTABLE BOOK HOLDER.

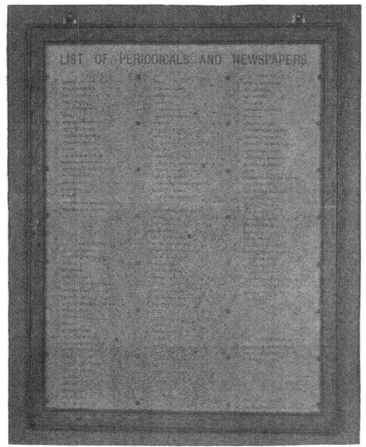

ADJUSTABLE MAGAZINE LIST HOLDER.

SCREW NEWSPAPER CLIP.

READING STAND WITH REVOLVING BAR AND CLIPS.

of a frame with a moveable back to which are attached a series of clips which retain the printed titles of magazines in place, and enable them to be arranged in any order and to be added to or taken from at pleasure.

This appliance has been adopted at Gateshead, Nottingham, Carlisle, Chelsea, Clerkenwell, Hammersmith, Derby, Leicester. Bournemouth, and many other Libraries.

Another useful recent invention is a screw clip for holding newspapers on the reading stands. This is commonly used in pairs, and has the advantage of being adjustable to any size of newspaper or periodical. This is now used in place of the old-fashioned rods at Hammersmith, Leicester, Kingston-on-Thames, Derby, St. Giles, Nottingham, and other Libraries. At Clerkenwell this clip has been used to secure illustrated journals, having vertical and transverse pictures, to the revolving rod of a special reading stand. As shown in the illustration, this stand, by means of the revolving bar, enables pictures to be turned round so as to be viewed easily without change of position on the part of the reader.

It is only necessary to add that in many of the newer Libraries, especially in London, some of the best modern appliances are to be seen, and organising Committees are strongly advised to visit some of them, as the devices noticed above by no means exhaust the number of those recently introduced.

ON SUNDAY LABOUR IN NATIONAL PUBLIC LIBRARIES, MUSEUMS AND ART GALLERIES.

By the Rev. CANON BARNETT, President of the Sunday Society.

AFTER a victory the question is: What is to be done with the victory? On the one side, the opening of Public Libraries, Museums, Picture Galleries, Gardens and Libraries is not sufficient if it is not also made lawful to use public halls for music and lectures. On the other side, Sunday must be protected from the demon of greed which would fill its hours with the noise of strife and strain, substitute for the weekday competition of work a competition of pleasure, and drive for ever from life the feeling of quiet.

Out of twenty-four years' experience in East London, I set myself to answer this question: How the Sabbath may be used for man for whom it was made? If I may put my conclusion before giving my reasons, I would say that Sunday opening should be allowed for all places of recreation or culture which are under National or Municipal control; that private places for the same objects at which money is taken should be opened under licence from the local authority, or when they are under the control of a society either incorporated to trade without profits (30 and 31 Vict. cap. 131), or registered with like limitations under the Act 6 and 7 Vict. cap. 36; that a law considerately framed should be rigorously enforced to prevent unnecessary trading; that contracts for weekly labour should be for six days, and that a certain number of the rest-days so secured should be Sundays.

I have come to this conclusion:—

1. Because one of the chief needs of our time is knowledge.
2. Because only the community is able to meet this need.

I. One of the chief needs of our time is knowledge. The reflection is continually forced on the student of East London life that the people have more brain power than brain food. They feel the stimulus of the intellectual atmosphere, but have few thoughts or facts on which their minds can feed. The keen debater at the clubs, whose points are eagerly taken up, needs the knowledge of history and training in scientific methods of thinking. The few who by ability or success attract notice need to be made aware of what they don't know, so that they may be humble and lowly. A glimpse of the infinite is the best cure for the vanity which is the stumbling-block of ability. Those active spirits who more and more force their way into the country on bank holidays, seeking other interests, need to know how to look for beauty, how to understand the language of birds, beasts and flowers, and how to read the history of the nation from its buildings. Lastly, the many who remain outside church or chapel, neither owning nor disowning their Bibles, need to know how to read those Bibles with understanding, how to separate poetry from fact, and how to judge of acts and words by the times in which they were done or said.

It is largely for want of knowledge that so many of the working-classes take to drink and gambling, defile the country with vulgar pleasures, become fitful followers of any opinion, and stand aloof from religion. They have—what members of other classes often miss—the discipline which comes of work and the sympathy which comes of common suffering, but they want the knowledge which would give them the "life and fuller life of which their nerves are scant". They err in their hearts because they do not know God's ways.

The chief anxiety of our time is as to the use the new inheritors of power will make of their inheritance. Other classes have had power; they have done good or ill. It is the fashion to lay stress on the ill. Courtiers always flatter the new king by abusing the old. But it is certain that without more knowledge the working-classes will not be able to wield the resources of the Empire in the interests of our trade or for the well-being of the mysterious millions toiling under an Indian sun. Power without knowledge will do mischief.

If, therefore, some one were to offer me the choice of one among the many reforms suggested for the remedy of modern ill, I would choose a larger educational policy. The social question is at bottom an educational question.

Better conditions of living—houses, open spaces, higher wages, shorter hours of labour, technical teaching, means of recreation—will surely come, but the means of knowledge must be pushed on the people. Libraries within the reach of all, with quiet rooms in which the boys just out of school will be welcome; museums where the mind will be stimulated to inquire and to admire; teachers and lecturers whose words will give life to the books on the shelves and make the dead bones of the Museums live and move; Picture Galleries where the eye will become familiar with the scenes of past and be taught to find beauty in the common; music, of a sort to train the imagination, freely given in parks and halls; these, as well as schools with a higher reach, represent the wants which my experience of twenty-four years compels me to recognise as most pressing if the majority of the people are to be useful and happy citizens, if they are to be good governors of the nation and find satisfaction in living—if, in one word, they are to know man and to enjoy God.

II. Thus I come to the second conclusion to which I have been forced—that the community must provide the means for this extension of knowledge. The reasons may be shortly stated :—

1. The common purse is that which is deep enough to provide sufficient means in sufficient places.

2. The common will is that which is strong enough to secure the necessary quiet.

3. The common opinion is that which has the authority to decide between what is useful and what is harmful.

(1) It is obvious that the means of knowledge such as have been mentioned—Museums, Libraries, Picture Galleries, Concerts, Lectures—cannot be provided by casual charity. That expense must be met by the contribution of the whole community and not, as in London, by those members of the community who chance to live within the chance boundaries of Whitechapel or Kensington. The common purse must meet the common need.

(2) It is equally obvious that these means of knowledge will not be available unless the people have quiet and leisure. A real holiday must be a common holiday. I cannot rest amid the sound of others' toil. I cannot study when I am tired. I find it hard to read when I am tempted by the chance of earning. I cannot so well worship when my neighbours are working. If, therefore, the community—*i.e.*, the common purse—provides pictures, books, and music, the community— *i.e.*, the common will—must secure a day when, as far as possible, all labour shall cease, when quiet shall be enforced and temptation to trading removed.

No voluntary organisation, no trades union can achieve this result. The community can easily achieve it when a law is made and enforced to forbid Sunday work, and allow the use of public resources for public education and recreation.

(3) But lastly, if the common purse provides sufficient means of knowledge, and if the common will secures the quiet of a day for their use, the question further remains whether private ventures having the same objects, but charging for admission, are to be permitted. Are Sunday popular concerts to be allowed? Is the University Extension Society to give its lectures? May the Royal Academy be opened? This is a matter which only the common opinion, represented by the national and local authority, can decide. The common opinion represents the highest average thought of our time. If some of us do not think it high enough, it is in our power to raise it—a State Church is established for the purpose. Common opinion expressed by its legitimate voice is the only successor of the Pope. It alone has authority to say what shall be and what shall not be done on Sundays. It must license the private

ventures whose aim, apart from any pecuniary profit, is the culture or recreation of the people.

Because this sort of knowledge seems to be one of the chief needs of our time, and because only the community can provide the means of such knowledge, I hold that the law affecting Sunday should be so changed as to permit the giving of lectures, classes, and musical performances, the opening of Museums, Libraries and Galleries, while it rigorously prevents trading and working which interferes with these objects.

The argument is frequently urged : "There is no demand for the Sunday opening of Museums ". "The people do not care for the pictures, and comparatively small numbers have taken advantage of the opportunities lately offered." This argument used by Sabbatarians is the greatest indictment against their methods.

1. Because existing public institutions which might give this knowledge are closed on Sunday, there is therefore little demand on the part of the people to know about the beautiful world in which they have been placed, or about the laws under which they live, or to have more things which are honourable, virtuous and of good report about which to meditate. The people have not developed the taste which raises the cry for more. They go on seeking for bread as if man could live on bread alone. Many fail to recognise any value of the Sunday except as a day for sleep.

2. Because on Sunday the opening minds of boys and girls have not been fed with thoughts about great deeds and great facts, therefore they are filled with thoughts of sport and with desires for exciting pleasures. Men and women spend Sunday in reading about matches or murders, in gossiping over the last race, or in eating and drinking. They hang about the streets hoping to get interest from a quarrel or from the antagonism of rival corner orators. They go out in swarms to country public-houses.

There is, I know, another side to this description. There are many workpeople who spend a quiet Sunday with their friends, and there are many educated people who dissipate Sunday in parties and games ; but of the latter it may be said they have not had the education which comes of contact with the poor or suffering, and of the former it is, I am sure, true to say that the tendency in working-class homes is towards more Sunday excitement, although they may not yet have yielded to it. The people have not that in their minds which would compel them to keep the day holy. They have not been allowed on Sundays to learn about God's gifts, and so on Sundays they often ignorantly spoil those gifts.

3. Lastly, because Sabbatarians have tried to enforce a law whose day is past—the law is rapidly becoming a dead letter. Sunday trading in East London increases every year. Markets which were once confined to a back street now extend to wide

GREENWOOD'S LIBRARY YEAR BOOK.

thoroughfares and are carried on far into the day. All sorts of merchandise are offered for sale; cheap Jacks and thimble-riggers cry and shout their wares, their offers attracting thousands of people to their neighbourhood. It has, too, become the custom for many shops to be open. If there were available Lecture Rooms, Picture Shows and Libraries, there is no longer the quiet which provokes to study; the hush in the world's noise in which men are led to listen to the voices which speak from the unseen.

The Sabbatarians are the enemies of the Sabbath. We members of the Sunday Society, and kindred bodies, claim to be the true Sabbatarians, the true children of those who recognise man's need for a day of rest and a day of worship. If it be that people are careless about the good and perfect gifts of God and that they prefer sleep and noise and rowdiness to visits to Museums, then are we doubly bound to strive so that by open doors and all honest temptations they may be drawn to places where they may learn the joy of admiration, hope and love.

THE GREAT FICTION QUESTION.

DURING the past thirty years two stock arguments against the establishment of Public Libraries have been used by opponents of education and others. These are, Rates and Fiction. It is not the purpose of this article to deal with other arguments based on the spread of fleas and infectious diseases by means of Libraries, because it might do an injustice to bookselling, newsvending, commercial libraries, banking, church- and theatre-going, and other businesses conducted gregariously. It is our object mainly to defend fiction reading as exhibited in the municipal libraries of the country, and incidentally to show that it has been deliberately misrepresented and derided as a hateful practice by persons chiefly qualified for such censorship by bigotry and ignorance. The two cries, "More rates" and "Fiction," are somewhat closely connected, inasmuch as it is generally sought to be shown that, for the additional payment, too much of an undesirable article is circulated. What a pity it is these strenuous advocates of municipal economy will not direct attention to the much more serious questions of increases in poor and police rates, which yield neither visible return nor adequate advantage of any sort to a vast majority of the rate-payers. On the other hand, rates which are levied for the purpose of promoting health of mind and body, such as educational and sanitary rates, are eternally being protested against by all sorts of fanatics, who seem to imagine that the best interests of a community are served by a ceaseless and munificent care of thieves, drunkards and shiftless wastrels. The well-being of the morally dead is preferred by such advocates to that of the active, living majority of the nation, who ought to claim most consideration. If the rates of a district amount to 5s. per pound of rental, it will generally be found that more than one-half is devoted to covering up social sores, while a mere tithe is spent in administering to the intellectual and moral needs of the deserving well-doers. The actual amount of visible good which is accomplished by any ordinary municipal Library, when compared with the workhouse or the jail, bearing in mind the disproportionate expenditure, is so manifest that it is hard to believe there are persons endowed with so much perversity as to miss observing it for themselves. Yet so it is, and as with the Fiction bogey, so the Rate bogey is always being dragged forth to frighten ignorant ratepayers. Happily, the good sense of nearly every large community in the country has risen superior to such sordid considerations, and there remains but the Fiction question, which it is the purpose of this article to discuss.

Fiction may be roughly defined as a kind of imaginative history, in which prominence is given to the actions of individuals rather than to those of nations. In this respect it resembles biography, though differentiated again by the number of *dramatis personæ* brought into play. It has formed, in all periods and among every nation and class of the people, the chief literary means whereby history, tradition, law, custom, humour, and even morality, have been cultivated and disseminated. The story-teller of all ages has been the recorder of incident and the historian of manners. His influence in the spread of information has been enormous, and it is doubtful if instruction by parable has not been of more general value than all the dry matter-of-fact teaching imparted since culture became a recognised part of civilised life. Among the thousands of works of fiction, in prose and verse, which have been issued from the press, whether consisting of nursery and folk tales, allegories or novels of sentiment, of action, or of description, we doubt if among all the large number of such works circulated by Public Libraries, a score of thoroughly bad and worthless books could be picked out of any catalogue. The meaning attached to the word "Fiction," by the busy-bodies who write so much about its pernicious influences, is, we assume, novels published since *Robinson Crusoe* first saw the light, or, at any rate, the books which have appeared during the last hundred and fifty years. Well, then, among all this enormous mass of literature there is a wide latitude for choice, and Public Library Committees have, as a rule, exercised their power of selection with so much care and catholicity, that the most eager carper will find the utmost difficulty in detecting any novel which can be fitly described either as "trashy" or unwholesome. To read some of the articles condemning fiction reading, one would gather that only the weakest and silliest three-volume novels were stocked by Public Libraries; that a very great proportion of such works were selected because they had an immoral tendency, or were written by male and female libertines whose part in life was to act as devil's advocates of sins against every canon of social purity and good taste. Of course, the object of such wholesale denunciation is to frighten the unwary and the indifferent citizen into the belief that he is paying too much for a bad thing; and consequently sweeping statements of the most exaggerated kind are constantly creeping into the press, while much misunderstanding and harm are caused by this industrious circulation of baseless calumnies. It perhaps occurs that some member of the public reads *Adam Bede*, and is shocked to find in such a respectable work some mention of a seduction. He or she, forgetful of the fact that such cases are chronicled in every shape and form by newspapers, as being settled in the various law courts of the land, writes in feverish haste to the press pointing out that a certain Library contains nothing else but novels of a distinctly immoral tendency! Then follows a regular hue and cry all over the country. Journal after journal makes comments on the statement in every variety of attack and defence, till finally it comes back to its author as a sort of gigantic indictment of Public Libraries and popular education! Long after the clamour has settled down, wiseacres in all parts of the country remember to cite the horrible case whenever arguments against Libraries are wanted; and so the play continues. We shall not stop to discuss what constitutes immoral teaching in a novel. No doubt to some minds Mrs. Ward's *Robert Elsmere* or Mrs. Linton's *Under which Lord* are blasphemous works, which should be burned in the shadow of a gallows tree; while others will object to Wallace's *Ben Hur* and Ingraham's *Prince of the House of David* on the ground that they are irreverent towards biblical history. It is very little to the point what view of particular books differently organised minds will take, our concern is entirely with the sweeping statements made to the effect that Public Libraries are purveyors of nothing but trashy novels. A very wide and extensive knowledge of the Public Libraries of the country, derived from long observation, catalogues and personal communication, enables us to state that not one Public Library in Britain deliberately buys novels which are either trashy or immoral, while Committees positively fight to keep the Libraries under their care free from offensive literature of all sorts, and for positive proof of this we need only refer to the catalogues. Not only is this the case, but the amount of the incomes spent on novels bears but a very small proportion to that spent on the other departments of literature represented on the shelves. If a Library possesses more fiction than seems a fair proportion of its stock, it will be found on examination that a very high percentage of the total consists of additional copies of works by authors like Scott, Dickens, Thackeray, Charles Reade, Lytton, Cooper, Eliot, Marryat, and other standard writers, who are in constant demand for educational as well as recreative purposes. Then it must be pointed out that the opponents of Public Libraries very unfairly take the work of a lending department alone to represent the entire annual operations of the institution, as if reference departments, special reading-rooms, news-rooms, etc., did not exist. In this way it is simple enough to show that the annual expenditure is largely devoted to securing the issue of a high percentage of novels. But this is very much the same as arguing that an hospital spends its whole annual receipts on the provision of beef-tea, and is therefore undeserving of support. Again, it is not recognised that novels are much more rapidly read than solid literature, and in consequence are changed very frequently, so that the turnover is certain to be greater. If, however, two novels be reckoned as equal to one solid work, like Green's *Short History*, or Darwin's *Descent of Man*, the excess disappears, and fiction, so far from dominating even the Lending Library, will be found to assume very minor proportions. But it is so manifestly wrong and unfair to state that the whole income of a Public Library is spent on the supply of novels, and especially of trashy novels, that we must point out in more detail the relation between the expenditure and total work accomplished by the average Library. A Public Library with an income of £2000 per annum will spend about £50 to £100 annually on novels, of which a large number will be new copies of worn-out books. In books for the Reference Library and in non-fictional classes of literature from £400 to £500 may be spent annually. The remainder of the income will be spent in redemption of loans, rent, rates and taxes, gas and water, salaries and general administration expenses, newspapers and periodicals, bookbinding, repairs to structure and fittings, etc. It is therefore obvious that the amount spent on novels is only about 5 per cent. to 7 per cent. of the total annual income of any Public Library; surely a very small proportion considering the popularity of the class. The alleged excess of fiction reading is another bogey which has been reared with much gravity and frequency. Some have gone so far as to state that there are hundreds of persons afflicted with a kind of novel-reading disease, somewhat akin to the drink habit, who neglect their daily duties and bring ruin on themselves by perpetual indulgence in the vice of excessive fiction reading! The truth of this may be easily measured by the fact that the annual issues from Public Lending Libraries amount to about two volumes per head of population, or about one book a fortnight to every enrolled borrower in such Libraries. When the number of borrowers and stock of books in Public Libraries are taken into account, it will be seen that only a very small number of persons, if any, get habitually intoxicated with novels and neglect the serious affairs of life. That there are persons in Public Libraries, and out of them, who read too much is undeniable, but there is nothing more abnormal in this than in excessive indulgence in cycling, angling, billiard-playing, cricket, theatre-going, or any other pleasure or sport common to the human family. But such excess is an exceptional and not a ruling condition. The intoxication of public life is not an unknown condition, and there are many cases on record of persons who have devoted so much time to the work of Town Councils, Boards of Guardians and other public bodies that it has resulted in the ruin of personal business. It has yet to be proved that anything remotely approaching this has been caused by persons reading the works of fiction provided by Public Libraries.

We come now to another aspect of the question, and it must be admitted that the resource and ingenuity of the opposition have left nothing unnoticed. This is the common and constantly repeated assertion that novels are so cheap that every working man in the country can buy all he needs for less than the annual Library rate. This statement was first made some years ago when publishers commenced to issue cheap reprints of non-copyright novels at 1s. and 6d. each. Previous to this the halfpenny evening paper had been relied upon as affording sufficient literary entertainment for the working man, but when it was found to work out at 13s. per annum, as against a Library rate of 10d. to 1s. 4d., the cheap newspaper argument was dropped like a hot cinder. We doubt if the cheap paper-covered novel is any better. Suppose a workman pays £20 per annum for his house, and is rated at £16, he will pay 1s. 4d. as Library rate, or not much more than 1¼d. per month for an unlimited choice of books, newspapers and magazines. But suppose he has to depend on cheap literature. The lowest price at which he can purchase a complete novel of high quality by an author of repute is 3d., but more likely 4½d. or 6d. However, we will take 3d. as an average rate, and assume that our man has leisure to read one book every fortnight. Well, at the end of one year he will have paid 6s. 6d. for a small library by a restricted number of authors, and it will cost him an additional 4s. or 5s. if he contemplates binding his tattered array of books for future preservation. Besides this, he will be practically shut off from all the current literature on topics of the day, as his 3d. a fortnight will hardly enable him to get copyright books by the best living authors. With a Public Library at command he can get all these, and still afford to buy an occasional poet, or essayist, or novel, or technical book, well bound and printed on good paper, such as his friend who would protect him against an iniquitous Library rate would not blush to see on his own shelves. It seems hard that the working men of the country should be condemned to the mental entertainment afforded by an accumulation of pamphlets. Literature clothed in such a dress as gaudy paper covers is not very inspiring or elevating, and even the most contented mind would revolt against the possession of mere reading matter in its cheapest and least durable form. The amount of variety and interest existing among cheap reprints of novels is not enough, even if the form of such books were better. It is well known to readers of wide scope that something more than mere pastime can be had out of novels. Take, for example, the splendid array of historical novels which have been written during the present century. No one can read a few of these books without consciously or unconsciously acquiring historical and political knowledge of much value. The amount of pains taken by authors in the preparation of historical novels is enormous, and their researches extend not only to the political movements of the period, but to the geography, social state, costume, language and contemporary biography of the time. Thus it is utterly impossible for even a careless reader to escape noticing facts when presented in an environment which fixes them in the memory. For example, the average school history gives a digest of the Peninsular War, but in such brief and matter of fact terms as to scarcely leave any impression. On the other hand, certain novels of Lever and Grant, slipshod and inaccurate as they may be in many respects, give the dates and sequence of events and battles in the Peninsula in such a picturesque and *detailed* manner, that a better general idea is given of the history of the period than could possibly be acquired without hard study of a heavy work like Napier's *History*. It is hardly necessary to do more than name Scott, James, Cooper, Kingsley, Hugo, Lytton, Dumas, Ainsworth, Reade, G. Eliot, Shorthouse, Blackmore, Doyle, Crockett and Weyman in support of this claim. Again, no stranger can gain an inkling of the many-sided characteristics of the Scot, without reading the works of Scott, Ferrier, Galt, Moir, Macdonald, Black, Oliphant, Stevenson, Barrie, Crockett, Annie Swan and Ian Maclaren. And how many works by these authors can be had for 3d. each? The only way in which a stay-at-home Briton can hope to acquire a knowledge of the people and scenery of India is by reading the works of Kipling, Mrs. Steel, Cunningham, Meadows Taylor and others. Probably a more vivid and memory-haunting picture of Indian life and Indian scenery can be obtained by reading these authors than by reading laboriously through Hunter's huge gazetteer. In short, novels are to the teaching of general knowledge what illustrations are to books, or diagrams to engineers, they show things as they are and give information about all things which are beyond the reach of ordinary experience or means. It is just the same with juvenile literature, which is usually classed with fiction, and gives to that much maligned class a very large percentage of its turnover. The adventure stories of Ballantyne, Fenn, Mayne Reid, Henty, Kingston, Verne and others of the same class are positive mines of topographical and scientific information. Such works represent more than paste and scissors industry in connection with gazetteers, books of travel and historical works; they represent actual observation on the part of the authors. A better idea of Northern Canada can be derived from some of Ballantyne's works than from formal topographical works; while the same may be said of Mexico and South America as portrayed by Captain Mayne Reid, and the West Indies by Michael Scott. The volume of *Personal Reminiscences* written by R. M. Ballantyne before he died will give some idea of the labour spent in the preparation of books for the young. The life of the navy at various periods can only be learned from the novels of Smollett, Marryat and James Hannay, as that of the modern army is only to be got in the works of Lever, Grant, Kipling, Jephson, "John Strange Winter" and Robert Blatchford. There is scarcely an aspect of life which is not well presented in the fictional literature of the country, and we can imagine no more instructive and valuable piece of work, than a complete classification of fiction under appropriate heads or subjects. A very suggestive, but apparently jocular, effort in this direction appeared in the *Library* of January, 1896, as an article entitled "Fiction Classification" by Jas. D. Brown, with examples, and it is strange that a serious effort has not yet been made to prove that novels have a secondary value as agents for the communication of instruction as well as a primary value as recreative agents. It may be as well to specify here some attempts which have been made to show the real educational value of novels. These are:—

Bowen: *Historical Novels and Tales.* London, 1882.
Cotgreave: *Analytical Index to English Prose Fiction.* 1890.
Sargant and Whishaw: *Guide Book to Books.* 1891.
San Francisco Public Library: *Classified English Prose Fiction.* 1891.
Russell: *Guide to British and American Novels.* London, 1894.
Los Angeles Public Library: *List of Novels and Tales.* 1894.
Brookline (Mass.) Public Library: *English Prose Fiction.* 1895.
Clerkenwell Public Library: *Class Guide to Fiction.* 1895.
Salem (Mass.) Public Library: *Class List No. 1, Fiction.* 1895.
Leypoldt and Iles: *Books for Girls and Women.* Boston, 1895.
Peterborough Public Library: *Class List No. 2, Literature.* 1896.

This does not exhaust the attempts made to deal with the subject, but it shows how the importance and necessity of the work have occurred to different minds in various parts of the world, and is, perhaps, a good augury for the future, when novels will be strictly classified and take their place among the educational machinery of literature.

A plea may be entered here for the recreative value of fiction-reading. Those who condemn novels on the ground that they are trashy or unwholesome, probably have something else in mind than the average type of work supplied to the public through the municipal Libraries. They must be thinking of novelettes and "penny bloods," or the stuff which gives an odour to Holywell Street in London. That there is a great mass of low literature in pamphlet form circulated is undeniable, but surely this, like the circulation of indecent photographs, is a matter for the police and in no way concerns municipal Libraries. Yet to read some of the articles which have been written against novel-reading in Libraries one would imagine that it was just this class of stuff which was meant, while readers are solemnly warned against books which no

Public Library possesses, and are exhorted to avoid the evil teaching and waste of time connected therewith, though such gutter literature is unknown in the institutions which get the blame of circulating it broadcast. To the worker who labours ten or twelve hours a day at some soul- and body-wearing task, such as filing, metal-engraving, mining, office routine, weaving, shoemaking, shop-keeping, machine-tending, or hod-carrying, complete rest and change are absolutely necessary. Some find them in the music hall, some in the public house, while very many find them in the Public Library, from which books can be withdrawn for home reading, or magazines can be taken up in the reading-room. When librarians imbued with the mission-ary spirit approach the average working man and suggest that for entertainment he might take out something which will reduce the issues of fiction, they are reminded that history, science, philosophy, biography and travel do not possess sufficient attractions for an untrained mind, nor do they induce *forgetfulness of the past day's labours*. A complete change from the deadly monotony of everyday toil is absolutely necessary to such workers, hence it is that so many of them choose novels by Dumas, Haggard, Doyle, Lever, Ainsworth, and so forth. Women who are practically domestic drudges, and have no variety in life save the occasional episode of new babies, who from one year's end to another are engaged in an endless turmoil of dish-washing, floor-scrubbing, clothes-washing, bed-making, clothes-mending and general house-clean-ing duties, are just the very class to whom the novel comes as absolutely the sole intellectual amusement. There are thou-sands of such women in every large town, and it is they who read more than one-half of the novels which are circulated by Public Libraries. And he is a boor who would deny them such a cheap, helpful and stimulating pleasure. Far from being critical and censorious, we ought to be thankful that working women find solace and forget the steam of the wash-tub in following the heroines of Miss Braddon, Mrs. Wood, Miss Yonge, Mrs. Worboise, Edna Lyall, Rosa Carey, and others, through their varied experiences. Of what earthly use to such women are the works of Mr. Herbert Spencer or the late Adam Smith? Of what value is any abstruse work to people who are occupied daily in laborious tasks, or those who are mentally exhausted at the close of the day's work? The greatest minds of the age find their recreation and rest in fictional literature, and that alone is a reason why all classes should be allowed to partake of similar mental refreshment and stimulus whenever so disposed. We are assured that Prince Bismarck's favourite reading consists of the sensational detective romances of Emile Gaboriau; Beethoven, the greatest musical thinker the world has known, found Scott's novels his best companions in the dusk of life; and men with elevated intellectual endowments, like Mr. Gladstone, are not ashamed to publicly announce their appreciation of novels, and point out the value of their teaching. Is it then anything short of the thinnest kind of cant, to say to workers, "You shall not read novels because they are bad for you, nor shall you have Libraries because they only circulate novels," when it is the fact that fiction-reading is as much a habit and necessity of the age as church-going or money-making? The mere fact that there are more novels published annually than any other two or three classes of literature is enough to show that the public demand for works in fictional form is greatly in excess of the call for anything else, and that there is nothing abnormal in the Public Library circulation of books which are issued from the press in the largest numbers.

We will conclude with a brief reference to some remarks which were made on this subject of fiction-reading by Mr. Charles Welch of the Guildhall Library, London, as they have been frequently used by opponents of Public Libraries, apparently on the assumption that their author was, by reason of his office, an authority. Mr. Welch contended in a paper entitled "The Public Library Movement in London" that the student had "been ousted from his rightful place by the inordinate favour afforded to the demands of the general reader, and the devourer of fiction". In support of his statement he produced the usual series of manipulated statistics, and the curious will find them, together with a crushing rejoinder and exposure by Mr. E. Foskett, in the *Library* for April, 1895, p. 97, etc. Notwithstanding this exposure, it was asserted in newspapers from Land's End to John o' Groat's that Mr. Welch, an "eminent authority," etc., had proved that Public Libraries issued 75 per cent. of novels, from stocks which bore the inordinate proportion of about 70 per cent. to that of the whole Libraries. A brief reference to the articles and table in another part of this "Year Book" will show that Mr. Welch's figures are inverted. As a matter of fact the percentage of fiction issued from the *lending departments alone* of British Public Libraries is on the average about 60 to 65, and this issue is made from a stock of novels forming not more than 30 per cent. of the total lending stock. We have already shown how little is spent on novels compared with other classes of literature, and we now show that the supply of fiction is kept short, more out of dread of pharisaical objections than because the demand is slight. Library Committees should proceed supplying, as copiously as possible, the demand for healthy fiction in proportion to its popularity and to the importance of other strictly educational classes of literature, without regard to the outcry of more or less ignorant opponents. Mr. Welch's outcry was more or less pharisaical, as any one may judge by comparing the annual expenditure on the Guildhall Library with the work accomplished. Public Libraries spending one-half and even one-quarter of what is spent on the Guildhall Library, do more actual work of every kind, without reckoning the fiction issues at all ! The moral of which is, that people living in glass houses should not throw stones.

The conclusion we have arrived at, after careful examination and consideration of the whole question, is that not half enough of fiction is circulated by Public Libraries, nor anything like enough spent on it annually. When the whole work of a thriving Public Library is taken into account—its reference- and reading-rooms, news-rooms and lending libraries—it seems that only about a beggarly 25 per cent. of fiction is all that is read. So far from ousting more solid literature, it is being itself ousted by trade and scientific journals, magazines, music, technical works and sensational theology. The refining, stimulating and refreshing influences of the novel are being positively swallowed in the feverish anxiety of young people to equip themselves in technical and other subjects to enable them to fight competing Germans, and it looks as if imaginative literature, whether in poetry or prose, would lose its hold in the face of urgent commercial needs. May the day never come when the British love for pure literature is superseded by adoration of ready reckoners and trade directories.

LIST OF BRITISH RATE-SUPPORTED LIBRARIES ESTABLISHED UNDER THE VARIOUS PUBLIC LIBRARIES OR OTHER ACTS, GIVING PARTICULARS OF ESTABLISHMENT, ORGANISATION, STAFF, METHODS AND LIBRARIANS.

ABERDEEN, Scotland.—Population, 121,905. Acts adopted in 1884. Reading-room opened, 1885; lending department, 1886; reference department, 1892. Has one small branch reading-room. Contains 47,632 vols., of which 23,412 are for lending, 24,183 for reference, and 37 in the branch. Borrowers, 8673. Staff, 17: librarian and 11 assistants; 5 attendants and caretakers. Books loaned for 14 days. Printed catalogue in dictionary form. Reference catalogue on cards and in guard books. Classification: numerical in main classes in lending department: Dewey system in reference department. Charging system for lending, indicator and borrowers' ledger. Open access allowed for new books. Reference charging done on application forms, but open access allowed to 700 reference books and all new additions. A local collection is forming and students' extra tickets are issued in the lending department. From £100 to £150 annually received from excise duties for purchase of technical books.

. LIBRARIAN: Alexander Webster Robertson, M.A., born at Aberdeen in 1847. Trained in Aberdeen University Library from 1880 to 1884. Librarian of Aberdeen Public Library from 1884. Member of Council of Library Association. Author of papers on the "Art of Describing Books," 1886-90; "Handlist of Bibliography of the Shires of Aberdeen, Banff and Kincardine," 1893; paper on "The Board School in relation to the Public Library," 1896, etc. Inventor of the duplex indicator, and of a contrivance for keeping books upright on the shelves, etc.

ABERYSTWITH, Wales.—Population, 6696. Acts adopted and Library opened in 1874. Contains about 4000 vols.

AIRDRIE, Lanarkshire, Scotland.—Population, 19,135. Acts adopted in 1853. Library first opened, 1856. New building opened in 1894. Contains about 10,000 vols., of which 9000 are for lending and 1000 for reference. Borrowers, 2310. Staff, 2: librarian and 1 assistant. Books loaned for 15 days. Printed catalogue in classified form. MS. catalogue kept in numerical order. Classification, numerical in main classes. Charging for lending, indicator; reference, signature book. Has a museum founded in 1894; photography classes; lectures in connection with photographic, naturalists', literary, and other societies.

LIBRARIAN: John Gardiner, born near Airdrie, 26th September, 1863. Commercially trained, but became librarian at Airdrie in 1892. Author of a novel, *Harry Rutherford*, and many poems and short stories contributed to periodicals.

ALLOA, Clackmannan, Scotland.—Population, 10,754. Act adopted, 1885. Library opened, 1888. Contains 9636 vols., of which 8836 are for lending and 800 for reference. Borrowers, 1400. Staff, 3: librarian, 1 assistant, 1 caretaker. Books loaned for 14 days (non-fiction), and 7 days (fiction). Printed catalogue in dictionary form. Classification, numerical in main classes. Charging: lending, indicator; reference, application forms.

LIBRARIAN: John Simpson, who was trained in the publishing firm of Messrs. Jas. Maclehose & Sons, Glasgow.

ALTRINCHAM, Cheshire. — Population, 12,424. Acts adopted and library opened in 1892. Contains 6786 vols., of which 6354 are for lending, 292 for reference, and 140 for the reading-room. Borrowers, 2512, and 203 subscribers. Staff, 4: librarian, 2 assistants, 1 caretaker. Books loaned for 14 days. Printed catalogue in dictionary form. Classification, numerical in main classes. Charging for lending, indicator and ledger; reference, open access. Has lectures and separate accommodation for ladies and juveniles.

LIBRARIAN: Florence Beckett, who was trained in the Literary Institution and Public Library of Altrincham.

ANDOVER, Hampshire.—Population, 5900. Acts adopted in April, 1896.

ARBROATH, Scotland.—Population, 22,960. Acts adopted in October, 1896.

ARLECDON AND FRIZINGTON, Cumberland.—Population, 5697. Acts adopted in August, 1891. Library opened in June, 1892. Has a branch reading-room. Contains 2200 vols., of which 2000 are for lending and 200 in the branch. Borrowers, 304. Staff, 1: librarian. Books loaned for 14 days. Printed catalogue under authors and titles. Classification, numerical. Charging for lending, ledger.

LIBRARIAN: Wilson Johnston, born in Frizington, Parish of Arlecdon, Cumberland.

ASHTON-UNDER-LYNE, Lancashire.—Population, 40,463. Heginbottom Free Library. Acts adopted, 1880. Newsroom

PUBLIC LIBRARY TECHNICAL SCHOOL, ASHTON-UNDER-LYNE.

opened in August, 1881, and Library opened in March, 1882; both in Town Hall. Heginbottom Technical School and Free Library Building opened formally in July, 1893, but actual work of newsroom recommenced in January, 1894, and lending department in March, 1894. Contains 13,663 vols., of which 9369 are for lending and 4294 for reference. Borrowers, 3313. Staff, 5: librarian, 3 assistants, 1 caretaker. Books loaned for 15 days. Printed catalogue in dictionary form; MS. catalogue in slip books. Classification, numerical in main classes. Charging for lending, indicator; reference, application forms. Students' extra tickets are issued. Magazine covers in reading-room are chained to racks on the tables in a numerical order.

LIBRARIAN: D. H. Wade, born at Oldham, 2nd July, 1865. Has devised the method of displaying magazines above mentioned.

ASHTON-ON-MERSEY, Cheshire.—Population, 4500. Acts adopted in June, 1896.

ASTON MANOR, Warwickshire.—Population, 69,523. Acts adopted in May, 1877. Rooms opened in February, 1878. Has a branch reading-room. Contains 15,733 vols., of which 9146 are for lending and 6587 for reference. Borrowers, 3200. Staff, 4: librarian and 3 assistants. Caretakers of public buildings look after Library. Books loaned for 7 days; music for 10 days. Printed catalogue of Lending Library in classified form, also issued as class lists. Printed reference catalogue in diction-ary form. MS. catalogue kept in guard books. Classification by subjects in Reference Library, numerical in main classes in Lending Library. Charging for lending, indicator; reference, application forms, but open access allowed to some standard works, such as dictionaries, encyclopædias, etc. Special features are free lectures, instituted in 1883; the blacking out of betting news in newspapers; and a local collection. Technical instruc-tion Acts have been adopted under a special Committee.

LIBRARIAN: Robert Kirkup Dent, born at Tamworth, 6th December, 1851. Was trained in Library work in the Birming-ham Public Libraries. Member of Council of the Library Association, to whose *Transactions* he has contributed papers on "Free Libraries of the Birmingham District," 1887; "Gnats, or the Little Worries of a Librarian's Life," 1891; "Free Lectures," 1892; "On the Blacking Out of Betting and Sporting News," 1893. Also a work entitled *Old and New Birmingham*, 1880, and other works on local and Midland topography and history.

ATHERSTONE, Warwickshire.—Population, 5000. Acts adopted in December, 1895.

AYR, Scotland.—Population, 24,791. Carnegie Public Library. Acts adopted, August, 1890. Library building, given by Mr. Andrew Carnegie, opened 2nd September, 1893. Contains 17,015 vols., of which 12,282 are for lending and 4733 for reference. Borrowers, 5557. Staff, 5 : librarian and 4 assistants; also cleaners. Books loaned for 14 days. Printed catalogue in dictionary form. Classification, subject and alphabetical by authors. Charging system for lending, indicator; reference, application forms. Provision is made for a museum and art gallery.

LIBRARIAN : George Bayne Phillips.

BANBRIDGE, Ireland.—Population, 5600. Acts adopted, 1890.

BANGOR, Wales.—Population, 9892. Acts adopted in November, 1870. Library opened in January, 1873. Contains 1500 vols. Borrowers, 386. Staff, 2 : librarian, 1 assistant. Books loaned for 7 days. Printed catalogue in classified form. Classification, numerical. Charging for lending, ledger. There is a museum connected with the Library.

LIBRARIAN : Peter Williams.

BARKING, Essex.—Population, 14,301. Acts adopted, November, 1888. Reading-room and Lending Library opened in 1889. Contains 5210 vols., of which 4700 are for lending and 510 for reference. Borrowers, 1100. Staff, 2 : librarian and caretaker. Books loaned for 14 days. Printed catalogue in dictionary form.

LIBRARIAN : George Jackson.

BARNSLEY, Yorkshire.—Population, 35,437. Acts adopted in 1890. Temporary newsroom opened in April, 1890 ; Library opened 7th December, 1890. Contains 5442 vols., of which 4447 are for lending and 995 for reference. Borrowers, 1500. Staff, 3 : librarian, 1 assistant and 1 caretaker. Books loaned for 10 days. Printed catalogue in dictionary form. MS. catalogue displayed on cards. Classification by subject. Charging for lending, indicator; reference, application forms. Has classes and a special ladies' room. The Technical Instruction Acts have been adopted, but are under a special Committee.

LIBRARIAN : John Blennerhassett Kane, born at Ripon, 25th December, 1865.

BARROW-IN-FURNESS, Lancashire.—Population, 52,000. Acts adopted, 1881; Library opened, 1882. Contains 20,173 vols., of which 17,033 are for lending and 3140 for reference. Borrowers, 3634. Staff, 6 : librarian and 5 assistants. Books loaned for 14 days. Printed catalogue in dictionary form. Classification, numerical in main classes. Charging system for lending, indicator; reference, application forms. Has two varieties of delivery stations, a collection of local literature and a reading-room for ladies. The Technical Instruction Act has been adopted by the town, under a special Committee, and £50 worth of technical works have been given by the Committee to the Library.

LIBRARIAN: Thomas Aldred, born at Manchester in 1866. He was trained at Salford Public Library from 1881 to 1889, and held the appointment of librarian at Stalybridge Public Library from March, 1889, to June, 1891. Librarian at Barrow since 1891.

BARRY, Glamorganshire, Wales.—Population, 12,665. Acts adopted in 1891. Has two branch reading-rooms. Contains 2657 vols. for lending. Staff, 5: librarian, 1 assistant, and 3 caretakers. Books loaned for 14 days. Printed catalogue in dictionary form. Classification, numerical in main classes. Charging for lending, indicator.

LIBRARIAN: Edwin F. Blackmore, born at Bristol in 1848. Had no previous training in Library work.

BATTERSEA, London (Lavender Hill, S.W).—Population (1896), 165,115. Acts adopted, 16th March, 1887. Reading-rooms first opened, 27th September, 1887. Has branches at Lurline Gardens and Lammas Hall. Central Library building at Lavender Hill, near Clapham Junction. Contains 35,860 vols., of which 13,865 are in the central lending department; 10,520 are for reference; and 11,475 are in the branches. Borrowers, 10,626. Staff, 22: librarian, 17 assistants, 4 caretakers and attendants. Books loaned for 14 days. Printed catalogues in dictionary form, with one supplement in classified form. Reference catalogue on cards. Classification, numerical in main classes. Charging for lending, indicator; reference, application forms.

LIBRARIAN: Lawrence Inkster, born at Shetland in 1854. Trained in South Shields Public Library as an assistant, from November, 1872. Succeeded as principal librarian, 24th June, 1879. Librarian at Battersea since July, 1887. Member of Council of Library Association, and author of papers contributed to its *Transactions*.

BEBINGTON, Cheshire.—Population, 41,013. Acts adopted in January, 1894, with the view of taking over and working the Meyer Free Library. See " List of Public Libraries not Rate-supported ".

BEDFORD, Bedfordshire.—Population, 28,023. Acts adopted in 1889.

BELFAST, Ireland.—Population, 255,950. Acts adopted in 1882. Newsroom and Lending Library opened in 1888. Has a handsome permanent building. Contains 32,969 vols., of which 16,584 are for lending and 16,385 for reference. Borrowers,

6954. Staff, 18: 1 librarian, 11 assistants, 6 caretakers and attendants. Books loaned for 14 days. Printed catalogue in dictionary form. Classification, numerical in main classes. Charging for lending, ledger and indicator; reference, application forms. Special features are a museum and art gallery, opened in 1890; and a ladies' room, opened in the same year.

LIBRARIAN: George Hall Elliott, born at Newcastle-on-Tyne in 1856. Trained in the Library of the Literary and Philosophical Society, Newcastle, 1875-1883. Afterwards librarian of Gateshead Public Library, 1883-88; and first librarian of Belfast Public Library from 1888. Member of Council of Library Association.

BERMONDSEY, London (Spa Road, S.E.).—Population (1896), 85,475. Acts adopted in 1887. Reading-rooms opened in November, 1891; Lending and Reference Libraries in new building in January, 1892. Contains 12,107 vols. Borrowers, 2900. Staff, 7: 1 librarian, 5 assistants, 1 caretaker. Books loaned for 14 days. Printed catalogue in dictionary form. Classification, numerical in main classes. Charging for lending, indicator; reference, application forms. Special features are a ladies' room and a collection of local literature.

LIBRARIAN: John Frowde, born at Liverpool in 1856. Trained in the Liverpool Public Libraries as an assistant from 1871 to 1882. Librarian of Barrow-in-Furness Public Library, 1882-1891. Librarian of Bermondsey Public Library since 1891. First President of Society of Public Librarians for London and the Home Counties.

BEXLEY, Kent.—Population, 10,605. Acts adopted in July, 1896.

BIDEFORD, Devonshire.—Population, 7908. Acts adopted and Library opened, 1877.

BILSTON, Staffordshire.—Population, 22,730. Acts adopted in 1870. Library opened in 1873. Contains 7500 vols., of which 7000 are for lending and 500 for reference. Staff, 2: librarian and caretaker. Books loaned for 10 days.

BINGLEY, Yorkshire.—Population, 21,418. Acts adopted in 1890.

BIRKENHEAD, Cheshire. — Population, 99,857. Acts adopted in February, 1856; rooms first opened in December, 1856. Has two branch Libraries. Contains 61,966 vols., of which 36,647 are for lending, 14,389 for reference, and 10,930 are in the branches. Borrowers, 8698. Staff, 12: 1 librarian and 11 assistants. Books loaned for 7, 10 and 14 days, according to class of work. Printed catalogue in dictionary form; reference catalogue on cards and in guard book. Classification by subjects. Charging for lending by cards; reference, application forms. Special features are: a ladies' room (1890); juvenile library (1865); annual bulletin of additions; local collection, also special Shakespeare, dialect and topographical collections; and students' tickets (1887). The Technical Instruction Acts have been adopted, and £200 per annum is granted from the excise duties for purchase of technical books.

LIBRARIAN: William May, born at Liverpool in 1856. He was trained in the Liverpool Public Libraries. Member of Council of the Library Association, and author of papers on "The Printing of Library Catalogues"; "Plea for a Classification Scheme"; "What the People Read"; "New System of Shelving for Branch Lending Libraries"; "Account of Caxton's Speculum".

BIRMINGHAM, Warwickshire.—Population, 478,113. Acts adopted in 1860. Has a fine central Library erected in place of the building which was burned in 1879. There are 9 branch Libraries. Contains 209,497 vols., of which 26,033 are in the central Lending Library, 129,600 in the Reference Library, and 53,864 in the branches. Borrowers, 27,710. Staff, 77: 1 librarian, 55 assistants, 21 caretakers, etc.; also 5 Jewish assistants for Sundays. Books loaned for 7 days. Printed catalogues of Lending Libraries are classified; of Reference Library, in dictionary form. MS. catalogue kept in guard books. Classification, numerical in main classes in Lending Library; subject in Reference Library. Charging for lending, ledgers; reference, application forms, with open access to 48 shelves of the principal reference books. Has large special collections of literature relating to Shakespeare, Birmingham, Warwickshire; and on a smaller scale, collections relating to Byron, Cervantes and Milton.

LIBRARIAN: John D. Mullins, born at London in 1832. He was librarian of the Birmingham Proprietary Library from 1858 to 1865, and of the Public Libraries since 1865. He is a vice-president of the Library Association, and has written a work entitled *Free Libraries and Newsrooms*, and contributed papers to magazines and to the *Transactions* of the Library Association.

BLACKBURN, Lancashire. — Population, 120,064. Acts adopted in 1860. Rooms opened in 1862. Contains 50,117 vols., of which 26,315 are for lending and 23,802 for reference. Borrowers, 3745. Staff, 7: 1 librarian, 4 assistants, 2 caretakers. Books loaned for 7 days (fiction) and 14 days (other classes). Printed catalogue in dictionary form. Slip books also used. Classification, numerical in main classes. Charging for lending, indicator; reference, application forms. Special features: a museum of Lancashire birds (1874); art gallery (1894);

MR. JOHN D. MULLINS, BIRMINGHAM. From a photograph by
McLucas, Birmingham.

sculpture gallery (1896); ladies' room (1894). Collection of over 500 vols. of local literature.

LIBRARIAN: Richard Ashton, born at Blackburn in 1863. Assistant in Blackburn Public Library, March, 1880, to October, 1889. Appointed librarian and curator at Blackburn in October, 1889.

BLACKPOOL, Lancashire. — Population, 23,846. Acts adopted in 1879. Rooms first opened in 1880. There are two branches or delivery stations. Contains 10,237 vols., of which 9425 are for lending and 812 for reference. Borrowers, 3127. Staff, 8: librarian, 4 assistants, 3 caretakers. Books loaned for 14 days. Printed catalogue in dictionary form. MS. catalogue in guard books. Classification, numerical in main classes. Charging for lending, ledger; reference, application forms. The Technical Instruction Acts have been adopted.

LIBRARIAN: Kate Lewtas.

BLAENAU FESTINIOG, Wales.—Population, 7700. Acts adopted in 1894.

BODMIN, Cornwall.—Population, 5200. Acts adopted in March, 1895.

BOLTON, Lancashire.—Population, 115,000. Acts adopted in 1852, and Library first opened in 1853. There are 4 branch Libraries. Contains 75,000 vols., of which 16,000 are for lending, 43,000 for reference, and 16,000 are in the branches. Borrowers, 5000. Staff, 20: librarian and 17 assistants, 2 caretakers. Books loaned for 7 days. Printed catalogue in dictionary form. Classification, Edwards' fixed location by press, shelf and number. Charging for lending, indicator; reference, signature book and application forms. Technical Instruction Acts have been adopted under a special Committee.

LIBRARIAN: James K. Waite, born at Preston in 1829. He has been librarian at Bolton since 1870. Author of papers in the *Transactions of the Library Association*, etc.

BOLTON PERCY, Yorkshire. — Population, 842. Acts adopted in 1895.

BOOTLE, Lancashire.—Population, 49,217. Acts adopted in 1884. Buildings opened in 1887. Contains 15,000 vols., of which 10,750 are for lending and 4250 for reference. Borrowers, 2500. Staff, 7: librarian, 5 assistants, 1 janitor. Books loaned from 7 to 14 days. Printed catalogue in dictionary form; author list of children's books. MS. catalogue on cards. Classification by subjects on special system. Charging for lending, indicator; reference, application forms. Special features: museum, art gallery, classes, lectures, local collection, students' extra tickets. £50 annually received from the excise duties for purchase of technical works.

LIBRARIAN: John J. Ogle, born at Lincoln, 4th February, 1858. Trained in the Nottingham Public Libraries from 1881 to 1887. Librarian and curator at Bootle since June, 1887. Member of Council of Library Association, and virtually the founder of the Summer School for Assistants held in connection with that body. Joint author, with Mr. H. W. Fovargue, of *Public Library Legislation*, London, 1895; numerous papers in the *Transactions of the Library Association* and contributions of a literary and scientific character to other books and journals.

BOURNEMOUTH, Hampshire.—Population, 37,781. Acts adopted in March, 1893. Library opened on 1st January, 1895. Has a branch reading-room. Contains 8492 vols., of which 7692 are for lending and 800 for reference. Borrowers, 6101. Staff, 7: librarian, 4 assistants, 2 caretakers. Books loaned for 15 days. Printed catalogue in form of author list with subject index. MS. catalogue of Reference Library in slip books. Classification by subjects, on the Quinn-Brown method. Charging for lending, open access and cards; reference, application forms. Students' extra tickets issued since March, 1895.

LIBRARIAN: Charles Riddle, born at North Shields, 8th February, 1869. Trained in Tynemouth Public Library. Sub-librarian at Clerkenwell Public Library, December, 1888, to June, 1894. Librarian at Bournemouth from June, 1894.

BOW, London.—Population, 41,687 Acts adopted in April, 1896.

BRADFORD, Yorkshire.—Population, 216,361. Acts adopted, 1871. Library first opened, 15th June, 1872. Has 9 branch Libraries. Contains 79,703 vols., of which 19,181 are in the central Lending Library; 22,863 in the Reference Library; and 37,659 in the branches. Borrowers, 10,756. Staff, 34: librarian, 23 assistants and 10 caretakers and attendants. Books loaned for 7 and 14 days. Printed catalogues in dictionary form; MS. catalogues in slip books. Classification, numerical in main classes. Charging for lending, cards; reference, application forms. Special features: museum (under Act adopted in 1892); art gallery (1879); ladies' room. Grants from the excise duties have been made for the purchase of technical books, amounting to £1000 in 1892 and £300 in each of the succeeding years.

LIBRARIAN: Butler Wood. Member of the Council of the Library Association, and author of papers on "Special Features of Free Library Work—Open Shelves, Women's Reading Rooms, and Juvenile Departments"; "Yorkshire Village Libraries," contributed to the *Transactions* of that body.

BRECHIN, Forfar, Scotland.—Population, 10,500. Acts adopted in March, 1890. Library building opened in 1893. Contains 7383 vols., of which 5800 are for lending and 1583 (including bequest of 1000 vols. from Rev. Alex. Gardiner) for reference. Borrowers, 1583. Staff, 1: librarian, and cleaner. Books loaned for 14 days. Printed catalogue in dictionary form. Classification by subjects. Charging for lending, indicator; reference, application forms and verbal request. Students' extra tickets available for technical works, issued since September, 1894. Juveniles between 11 and 14 years of age are restricted to one book each per week. Grant of £29 for purchase of technical books from excise duties made in 1893.

LIBRARIAN: James Craigie, born at Meigle, Forfarshire, in 1854. Trained as a bookseller, and has travelled in Australia. Author of articles in Gaelic, etc.

BRENTFORD, Middlesex.—Population, 13,918. Acts adopted in 1889. Library opened in January, 1890. Contains 5431 vols., of which 4131 are for lending and 1300 for reference. Borrowers, 1700. Staff, 3: librarian, 1 assistant, 1 caretaker. Books loaned for 7 days. Printed catalogue in dictionary form. Classification, numerical in main classes. Charging for lending, indicator; reference, application forms. Has a collection of local literature, and issues a quarterly magazine entitled *The Brentonian*, first published in March, 1895.

LIBRARIAN: Fred. Turner, born on 8th September, 1864. Trained in Library work in Wolverhampton Public Library, 1879-89. Librarian at Brentford since September, 1889. Author of "The Place of Public Libraries and their Relationship to Higher Education," read before the Library Association. Editor of a series of tracts on "Famous Old MSS. and Books," No. 1 of which was entitled "Beowulf". Also author of various papers on historical topics.

BRIDGWATER, Somerset. — Population, 12,436. Acts adopted and Library opened in 1860. Has one branch. Contains 2761 vols., of which 2000 are for lending, 50 for reference, and 711 are in the branch. Borrowers, 550. Staff, 5: librarian, 3 assistants, 1 caretaker. Books loaned for 7 days. Printed catalogue in dictionary form. Classification, numerical. Charging for lending, and reference, open access. Has a room for ladies.

LIBRARIAN: Mrs. Baker.

BRIERLEY HILL, Staffordshire. — Population, 11,184. Acts adopted in 1875. Reading-room opened in 1876; Library opened in 1877. Contains 2170 vols., of which 2146 are for lending and 24 for reference. Borrowers, 1170. Staff, 3: librarian, 1 assistant, 1 caretaker. Books loaned for 14 days. Printed catalogue issued in class-list form. Classification, numerical and author alphabetical in main classes. Charging for lending, indicator; reference, application forms. Has courses of lectures. The Technical Instruction Acts have been adopted by the town.

LIBRARIAN: Joseph Henry Dudley, born at Dudley, 7th December, 1851. Trained in the Dudley Institute. Librarian at Brierley Hill since 1884.

BRIGHTON, Sussex.—Population, 142,129. Acts adopted 1850. Library opened in 1873. Contains 43,012 vols., of which 28,181 are for lending and 14,831 for reference. Borrowers, 9309. Staff, 11: librarian, 8 assistants, 2 attendants. Books loaned for 14 days. Printed catalogue in author and classified form. MS. catalogue kept in guard books. Classification, by subjects. Charging for lending, ledger; reference, application forms. Special features are a museum and art gallery (distinct from Library); lectures on contents of the museum; and various local and other special collections of literature.

LIBRARIAN: Frederic William Madden, who was born at the British Museum, London, and trained there. He is author of a work on the coins of the Jews, etc.

BRISTOL, Gloucestershire. — Population, 221,665. Acts adopted in 1874. Library first opened in 1876. Has 5 branch Libraries. Contains 84,250 vols., of which 13,250 are in the central Lending Library, 16,000 in the central Reference Library, and 55,000 in the branches. This is exclusive of the Museum Library noticed elsewhere. Borrowers, 16,381. Staff, 44: librarian, 34 assistants, 3 binders and 6 caretakers. Printed catalogues in dictionary form. Classification, numerical and alphabetical in main classes. Charging for lending, indicator; reference, application forms. Has a valuable collection of local literature. Museum Act has been adopted.

LIBRARIAN: Edward Robert Norris Mathews, born at Bristol, 11th November, 1851. Trained in Birmingham Public Libraries, 1876-1883. Librarian of Bristol Museum and Library, 1883-1893. Librarian of Bristol Public Libraries since 1893. Author of papers read before the Library Association; *Guide to Bristol and Clifton*, 1886; *Black's Guide to Gloucestershire*, 1892 (edited), etc. He has also lectured on musical and literary subjects.

BROMLEY, Kent.—Population, 21,700. Acts adopted in May, 1892. Library building opened, 8th December, 1894. Contains 6379 vols., of which 5191 are for lending and 1188 for reference. Borrowers, 2963. Staff, 4: librarian, 2 assistants, 1 caretaker. Books loaned for 14 days. Printed catalogue in dictionary form. Also a "classified hand-list of additions". Classification, numerical in main classes. Charging for lending, indicator; reference, application forms. A grant of £25 for the purchase of technical books has been made from the excise duties.

LIBRARIAN: John Harrison, born at South Shields, 18th

October, 1868. Trained in South Shields Public Library, 1887-91. Sub-librarian in Lewisham Public Library, 1891-94. Librarian of Bromley since 1894.

BROMLEY-BY-BOW, London.—Population, 69,821. Acts adopted in 1891.

BROUGHTON, Wales (near Wrexham).—Population, 5000. Acts adopted in November, 1895.

BURSLEM, Staffordshire.—Population, 32,251. Acts adopted in 1863. Library opened in 1870. Contains 7546 vols., of which 6714 are for lending and 832 for reference. Borrowers, 1839. Staff, 2: librarian and caretaker. Books loaned for 7 days. Printed catalogue in dictionary form. Classification, numerical in main classes. Charging for lending, ledger; reference, application forms. Has a museum, opened in 1879, and classes, started in 1870. The Technical Instruction and Museum Acts have been adopted.

LIBRARIAN: James Rigby.

BURTON-UPON-TRENT, Staffordshire. — Population, 46,000. Acts adopted in October, 1894. Library not yet established.

BURWELL, Cambridgeshire.—Population, 2000. Acts adopted in March, 1895.

BURY ST. EDMUNDS, Suffolk.—Population, 16,630. Acts adopted in 1895.

BUXTON, Derbyshire.—Population, 9000. Acts adopted, 1886. Library opened in Town Hall, 1889. Contains 3743 vols., of which 3372 are for lending and 371 for reference. Borrowers, 2421. Staff, 3: librarian, 1 honorary assistant, 1 caretaker. Books loaned for 7 and 14 days. Printed catalogue in dictionary form. Classification, numerical in main classes. Charging for lending, indicator; reference, application forms and open access. Has small collection for a museum. The Museum and Gymnasium Act has been adopted.

LIBRARIAN: Thomas Alan Sarjant, born at Halesworth, Suffolk, in 1858. Was for 16 years with Messrs. Bemrose & Sons, Ltd., of Derby, in which town he acted as hon. librarian (1883-86) to the Telegraph Messengers' Library. Librarian at Buxton since 1892.

CAMBERWELL, London (High Street, Peckham, S.E.).—Population, 235,076. Acts adopted in 1889. Temporary premises opened in March, 1890. Has now a permanent central Library, and 4 branches. Contains 53,134 vols., of which 14,103 are in the central lending, 6531 in the reference, and 32,500 in the branches. Borrowers, 18,000. Staff, 21: librarian, 16 assistants,

4 caretakers. Books loaned for 14 days. Printed catalogues in dictionary form, with alphabetical and numerical subject lists. Classification, alphabetical by authors under subjects. Charging for lending, indicator; reference, application forms, open

CAMBERWELL PUBLIC LIBRARY. CENTRAL REFERENCE LIBRARY.

access to directories, etc. There is a fine art gallery and museum, and a technical art school.

LIBRARIAN AND CURATOR: Edward Foskett, F.R.S.L., born at London, 25th November, 1848. Appointed to Camberwell in January, 1890. Author of *Unveiled: a Vision*, 1875; *A Nation's*

Fame, 1876; *Harold Glynde*, 1881; *Poems*, 1886; *The Window in the Rock, a Cornish Tale, in verse*, and other poetical and literary works.   He is also author of a paper on "The Educational Value of the Public Library Movement," read before the Library Association.

CAMBORNE, Cornwall.—Population, 15,000.   Acts adopted in 1893.   Library building, presented by Mr. Passmore Edwards, opened in May, 1895.   Contains 4700 vols., of which 4600 are for lending and 100 for reference.   Borrowers, 2340.   Staff, 3: librarian, 1 assistant, 1 caretaker.   Books loaned for 15 days.

CAMBORNE PUBLIC LIBRARY.

Printed catalogue in dictionary form.   Classification, numerical in main classes.   Charging for lending, special indicator and cards; reference, application forms.

LIBRARIAN: Jacob Laity, born at Camborne in 1866.

CAMBRIDGE, Cambridgeshire.—Population, 36,983.   Acts adopted in March, 1853.   Library first opened in June, 1855. Has one branch Library.   Contains 41,844 vols., of which 24,917 are in the central Lending Library, 10,822 in the Reference Library, and 6105 in the branch.   Borrowers, 3134.   Staff, 6: librarian, 4 assistants, 1 attendant.   Books loaned for 14 days. Printed catalogue in dictionary form.   MS. catalogue in slip book. Classification, by subjects and numbers. Charging for lending, ledger; reference, application forms and open access since 1856. Has large local, Shakespeare (1874) and dramatic (1880) collections.

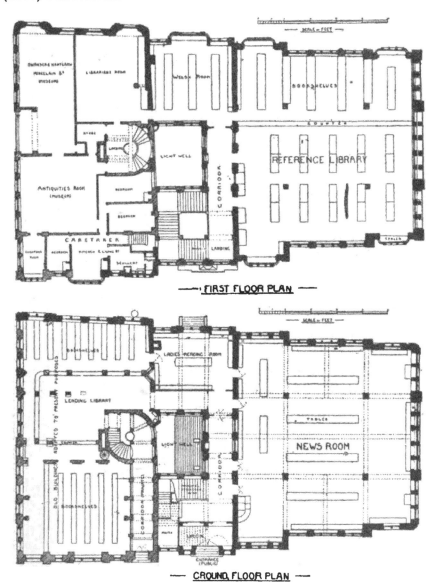

— FIRST FLOOR PLAN —

— GROUND FLOOR PLAN —

CARDIFF PUBLIC LIBRARY. Edwin Seward, Architect, Cardiff

LIBRARIAN: John Pink, born at Cambridge in 1833. He was originally a bookseller's assistant, but was appointed librarian of the Public Library at Cambridge in April, 1855, being therefore the oldest public librarian now living. He is author of *The Cambridge Free Library, Its Rise and Progress,* 1882; and introduced, in 1860, oak reading cases for magazines.

CARDIFF PUBLIC LIBRARY.

CAMPBELTOWN, Argyleshire, Scotland.—Population, 5500. Acts adopted in 1896.

CANTERBURY, Kent.—Population, 23,026. Acts adopted in 1858, when an older Library of 1825 was handed over to the town.   Contains 11,000 vols., of which 8000 are for lending and 3000 for reference. Borrowers, 4519.   Staff, 2: librarian and assistant.   Books loaned for 14 days.   Printed catalogue in author form.   Charging for lending, and reference, open access. Has a museum, art gallery, juvenile room and a local collection.

LIBRARIAN: A. D. Blaxland, librarian since 1883.

CARDIFF, Wales.—Population, 128,849. Acts adopted in 1862.   Has 6 reading-rooms with small Reference Libraries attached.   Contains 62,095 vols., of which 26,962 are for lending, 31,118 for reference, and 4015 are in the branches.   Borrowers, 7200.   Staff, 19: librarian, 8 assistants, 10 caretakers and attendants.   Books loaned for 14 days.   Printed catalogue in dictionary form.   MS. catalogue on cards.   Classification, numerical in main classes.   Charging for lending, indicator; reference, application forms.   Has a ladies' room, large Welsh collection and other special collections.   The Technical Instruction and Museum Acts have been adopted.

LIBRARIAN: John Ballinger, born at Portnewynydd in Monmouthshire.   Assistant librarian at Cardiff, 1875.   Librarian at Doncaster, 1880-84.   Librarian at Cardiff since 1884.   Member of Council of the Library Association, and author of papers contributed to its *Transactions.*

CARLISLE, Cumberland.—Population, 39,176. Acts adopted in 1890.   Library opened in Tullie House in November, 1893. Contains over 20,000 vols., of which 8220 are for lending, 2000 for reference, and 10,000, not yet dealt with, which have been received from the old Carlisle Library. Borrowers, 4378. Staff, 7: librarian, 4 assistants and 2 attendants.   Books loaned for 14 days.   Printed catalogue in dictionary form. MS. catalogue in slip books.   Classification, Dewey system.   Charging for lending, indicator; reference, application forms and open access.   Has a museum, art gallery, lectures, and extensive collection of Cumberland books.   The Technical Instruction Act and Museum Act have been adopted.

LIBRARIAN: Robert Bateman, born at Rochdale in 1863. Trained in Rochdale Public Library from 1877-1885.   Sublibrarian and assistant curator at Oldham from August, 1885, to October, 1893.   Librarian at Carlisle since September, 1893.

CARLTON, Nottinghamshire.— Population, 6627.   Acts adopted in 1888.

CARNARVON, Carnarvonshire, Wales.—Population, 9800. Acts adopted in 1886.   Library opened in 1887. Contains 2300 vols., of which 1550 are for lending and 750 for reference.

Borrowers, 535. Staff, 2: librarian and 1 caretaker. Books loaned for 10 days. Printed catalogue in classified form. Classification, alphabetical by authors. Charging for lending, ledger; reference, application forms.

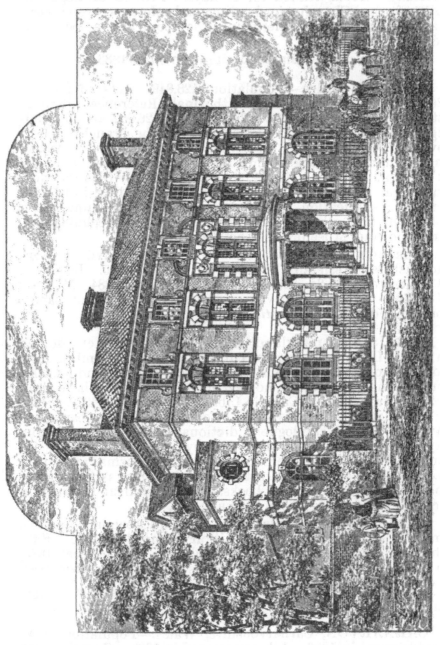

CHELSEA PUBLIC LIBRARY.

LIBRARIAN: Mrs. G. K. A. Thomas, who was a native of Hayle, Cornwall.

CHELSEA, London (Manresa Road, S.W.). — Population (1896), 96,646. Acts adopted in June, 1887. Temporary rooms opened in November, 1887. Permanent buildings opened— Kensal Town branch, January, 1890; Central Library, January, 1891. Contains 28,561 vols., of which 13,652 are in the central lending, 7996 in the central reference, and 6913 in the Kensal Town branch Library. Borrowers, 8344. Staff, 14: librarian, 4 assistants, 9 caretakers and attendants. Books loaned for 14 days. Printed catalogues in dictionary form, also classified supplements and a class list of technical and scientific books. MS. catalogue of Reference Library in slip books. Classification, numerical in main classes of Dewey system. Charging for lending, cards and indicator; reference, application forms. Special features: ladies' room, boys' room; collection of local literature, prints, etc.; students' extra tickets and special ticket for music in addition. The central Library forms the Library of the South-west London Polytechnic Institute, which is in an adjoining building.

LIBRARIAN: John Henry Quinn, born at Liverpool in September, 1860. Trained in the Liverpool Public Libraries from November, 1873, till December, 1887, where he latterly held the position of principal cataloguing assistant. Librarian at Chelsea since December, 1887. Member of Council of the Library Association and of several of its standing Committees. Author of papers on "Card Charging" and "Classification for Open-access Libraries," and of articles, etc., which have appeared in the *Library* and other journals.

CHELTENHAM, Gloucestershire.—Population, 47,514. Acts adopted in July, 1883. Library first opened in October, 1884. One branch reading-room. Contains 23,588 vols., of which 13,626 are for lending and 9962 for reference. Borrowers, 4600. Staff, 6: librarian, 4 assistants, 1 caretaker. Books loaned for 14 days. Printed catalogue in dictionary form. MS. catalogue in guard books. Classification, numerical in main classes. Charging for lending, indicator; reference, application forms. Has local collection and the Day Library of natural history (fish and fish culture). Receives about £113 per annum from excise duties for technical books.

LIBRARIAN: William Jones, born at Leeds, 25th January, 1860. Trained in Leeds Public Libraries, 1875-1884. Librarian of Cheltenham since 1884.

CHESTER, Cheshire.—Population, 37,105. Acts adopted in 1874. Library first opened in 1877. Contains 16,155 vols., of which 8523 are for lending and 7632 for reference. Borrowers, 1839. Staff, 4: librarian, 2 assistants, 1 caretaker. Books loaned for 14 days. Printed catalogue in dictionary form. Classification of Lending Library, numerical in main classes; of Reference Library, Dewey system. Charging for lending, indicator and partial open access; reference, open access. Has a ladies' reading-room and free lectures. Grants from the excise duties have been received for the purchase of technical books.

LIBRARIAN: Stephen Bickley, a native of Chester, where he was trained in the Public Library. Appointed librarian in January, 1896.

CHESTERFIELD, Derbyshire.—Population, 13,242. Acts adopted in 1875. Library opened in 1879. Contains 10,811 vols., of which 9111 are for lending and 1700 for reference. There is also a subscription department with a stock of 2159 vols. Borrowers, 1875. Staff, 2: librarian, 1 assistant. Books loaned for 7 or 14 days. Printed catalogue in dictionary form. Classification, numerical. Charging for lending, indicator; reference, signature book. The Technical Instruction Act has been adopted.

LIBRARIAN: Denis Gorman, born at Kilkenny, 17th December, 1835. He was in the Civil Service before being appointed to Chesterfield in 1878.

CHISWICK, Middlesex.—Population, 21,965. Acts adopted in March, 1890. Temporary newsroom opened in November, 1890; Library opened in temporary premises, November, 1891. Contains 5253 vols., of which 4327 are for lending and 926 for reference. Borrowers, 3448. Staff, 2: librarian and assistant. Books loaned for 7 days. Printed catalogue in dictionary form. Classification, numerical in main classes. Charging for lending, indicator; reference, application forms.

LIBRARIAN: Henry J. Hewitt, who was successively sub-librarian at Wandsworth and Fulham before being appointed to Chiswick.

CHRIST CHURCH, Southwark, London (Charles Street, Blackfriars Road, S.E.).—Population, 13,064. Acts adopted, 22nd February, 1888. Library opened, 1st October, 1889. Contains 4320 vols., of which 3603 are for lending and 717 for reference. Borrowers, 695. Staff, 3: librarian, 1 assistant, 1 caretaker. Books loaned for 7 days. Printed catalogue in dictionary form. MS. catalogue on cards. Classification, numerical in main classes. Charging for lending, cards; reference, signature sheet. Has a local collection.

LIBRARIAN: Roland Austin.

CLAPHAM, London (near Orlando Road, Clapham Common, S.W.).—Population, 46,953. Acts adopted in July, 1887. Library opened, 31st October, 1889. Contains 8000 vols., of which 7200 are for lending and 800 for reference. Borrowers, 4500. Staff, 4: librarian, 2 assistants, 1 caretaker. Books loaned for 14 days. Printed catalogues issued in dictionary form and as class lists. Classification, numerical in 8 main classes. Charging for lending, indicator; reference, application forms and open access to 200 books most in request.

LIBRARIAN: Joseph Reed Welch, born at South Shields, 28th October, 1860. Assistant in South Shields Public Library, 1874-1882. Librarian at Halifax Public Library, 1882-1889. Librarian at Clapham since March, 1889.

CLEATOR MOOR, Cumberland.—Acts adopted in October, 1892.

MR. JAS. D. BROWN, CLERKENWELL.

CLERKENWELL, London (Skinner Street, E.C.).—Population, 66,202. Acts adopted 13th December, 1887. Temporary newsroom opened 20th November, 1888; temporary Lending Library opened 31st March, 1889; permanent building opened 10th October, 1890. Contains 15,557 vols., of which 10,857 are for lending and 4700 for reference. Borrowers, 3858. Staff, 7: librarian, 5 assistants, 1 caretaker. Books loaned for 15 days. Printed catalogue issued as class lists in classified and author index form. MS. catalogue of Reference Library in slip books. Classification, by subjects on Quinn-Brown method. Charging for lending, open access and cards; reference, application forms with open access to dictionaries, directories, etc. Issues a *Quarterly Guide for Readers* in magazine form (1894). Has students' extra tickets (1893) and a local collection.

LIBRARIAN: James D. Brown, born at Edinburgh in 1862. Trained in Mitchell Library, Glasgow, 1878-1888. Librarian of Clerkenwell since October, 1888. Member of Council of Library Association. Author of *Biographical Dictionary of Musicians* (1886); *British Musical Biography* (with S. S. Stratton, 1897); *Handbook of Library Appliances* (L.A. Series, 1892); *Guide to the Formation of a Music Library* (L.A. Series, 1893); numerous papers on Library management, etc., contributed to the *Library* and read before the Library Association. Inventor of the sheaf or slip cataloguing method; various methods of indicator and card charging, etc. In 1893 he attended the International Conference of Librarians at Chicago, for which he collected a series of British library appliances, etc.

CLITHEROE, Lancashire.— Population, 10,815. Acts adopted in October, 1878. Library opened, April, 1879. Contains 5981 vols. Borrowers, 1010. Staff, 2: librarian and 1 assistant. Books loaned for 14 days. Printed catalogue in classified and author form. Classification, numerical in main classes. Charging for lending, ledger; reference, application forms and signature book. The Technical Instruction Act has been adopted, but is worked by a special Committee.

LIBRARIAN: James Robinson.

COLCHESTER, Essex.—Population, 34,459. Acts adopted in October, 1891. Library opened in October, 1894. Has 4 branch reading-rooms. Contains 7475 vols., of which 5150 are for lending and 2325 for reference. Borrowers, 2864. Staff, 2: librarian and assistant. Books loaned for 14 days. Printed catalogue in dictionary form. MS. catalogue in guard books. Classification, numerical in main classes. Charging for lending, indicator; reference, application forms. Has a collection of local works. The Museum Act has been adopted.

LIBRARIAN: George Rickward, born at Colchester in 1856. Member of Colchester Library Committee from 1891, and librarian since March, 1896. Author of *Historical Sketch of Parish of S. Martin, Colchester*, etc.

COLERAINE, Ireland.—Population, 11,000. Acts adopted in 1881.

COLNE, Lancashire.—Population, 17,775. Acts adopted in 1894. Library opened in 1895. Contains 2955 vols. Borrowers, 1300. Staff, 2: librarian and caretaker. Books loaned for 14 days. Printed catalogue in dictionary form. Classification, numerical in main classes. Charging for lending, indicator. The Technical Instruction Act has been adopted.

LIBRARIAN : Ernest Crowther, born at Nelson, Lancashire, in 1868.

CORK, Ireland.—Population, 75,345. Acts adopted in 1855. First put in operation in 1892, when Library was opened in December. Contains 6600 vols., of which 5000 are lending and 1600 reference. Staff, 4 : librarian and 3 assistants. Books loaned for 14 days. Printed catalogue in dictionary form. MS. catalogue on cards. Classification, numerical in main classes. Charging for lending, indicator ; reference, application forms. Has issued students' extra tickets since May, 1895.

LIBRARIAN : James Wilkinson, born at Leeds in 1868. Trained in Leeds Public Library to 1892. Librarian at Cork since October, 1892.

CORWEN, Wales.—Population, 3000. Acts adopted in February, 1896.

COVENTRY, Warwickshire. — Population, 52,720. Acts adopted in 1867. Library opened in 1868. Contains about 33,000 vols.

CROYDON, Surrey.—Population, 102,697. Acts adopted, 21st November, 1888. Temporary central Library opened in 1890. Permanent building in Town Hall opened in 1896. Has 3 branch Libraries. Contains 32,353 vols., of which 11,761 are in the central Lending Library ; 4900 in the central Reference ; and 15,692 in the branches. Borrowers, 8324. Staff, 16 : librarian, 14 assistants and 1 caretaker. Books loaned for 14 days. Printed catalogues in dictionary form and also as class lists. Classification, numerical in main classes at branches, Dewey method at central Library. Charging for lending, open access at central, indicator and ledger at branches ; reference, application forms. Has a collection of local literature.

LIBRARIAN : Thomas Johnston, born at Newcastle-on-Tyne, 27th August, 1868. Trained in the Newcastle Public Library, 1884-1890. Sub-librarian at Croydon, 1890. Librarian at Croydon since April, 1895.

DALKEY, Ireland.—Acts adopted in 1894. Library not yet in operation.

DARLASTON, Staffordshire. — Population, 14,422. Acts adopted in 1876. Library first opened in 1876. Contains 4353 vols. Borrowers, 900. Staff, 2 : librarian and caretaker. Books loaned for 14 days. Charging for lending, indicator. There

CROYDON PUBLIC LIBRARY. | BRAITHWAITE HALL.

are technical instruction classes in connection with the Library, the Technical Instruction Act having been adopted.

LIBRARIAN: Annie Simkin, born on 19th July, 1873. Had no previous training in Library work.

DARLINGTON, Durham.—Population, 38,060. Acts adopted in 1883. Library building opened in 1885. Contains 21,739 vols., of which 15,674 are for lending and 6065 for reference. Borrowers, 3000. Staff, 4: librarian, 2 assistants, 1 caretaker. Books loaned for 14 days. Printed catalogue in dictionary form. MS. catalogue in guard and slip books. Classification, numerical in main classes. Charging for lending, indicator; reference, signature book and application forms. Has a special ladies' room, and a collection of local literature. The Technical Instruction Act has been adopted.

LIBRARIAN: W. J. Arrowsmith.

DARWEN, Lancashire.—Population, 34,192. Acts adopted in 1871, and Library opened. Re-opened in new building in 1895. Has 20 small branches in the public schools. Contains 20,282 vols., of which 9000 are in the central lending, 3000 in the reference, and 2700 in the branches. Borrowers, 3000. Staff, 4: librarian, 2 assistants, 1 caretaker. Books loaned for 14 days. Printed catalogues in dictionary form, issued in 3 sections. Classification, by subjects, with movable location. Charging for lending, open access and cards; reference, open access. Has a ladies' room, and issues students' extra tickets. The Technical Instruction Acts have been adopted.

LIBRARIAN: Albert Cawthorne, a native of Liverpool. Trained in Liverpool Public Libraries, 1883-86. Afterwards assistant at Bootle Public Library, 1886-92; Birmingham Central Reference Library, 1892-94. Librarian at Darwen since 1894.

DENTON, Lancashire.—Population, 13,993. Acts adopted in 1887. Library opened in 1889. Contains 2418 vols., of which 2360 are for lending and 58 for reference. Borrowers, 1200. Staff, 1: librarian. Books loaned for 14 days. Printed catalogue in dictionary form. Classification, numerical in main classes. Charging for lending, ledger; reference, verbal application. The Technical Instruction Act has been adopted, and there have been classes and a juvenile room since the formation of the Library.

LIBRARIAN: David Smith, born at Ashton-under-Lyne in 1861. Appointed to Denton in 1892.

DERBY, Derbyshire.—Population, 94,600. Acts adopted in May, 1870. Temporary Library opened in March, 1871; present building, in June, 1879. Has a branch reading-room opened in 1895. Contains 29,173 vols., of which 18,754 are for lending and 10,419 for reference. Borrowers, 7500. Staff, 9 : librarian, 5 assistants, 3 caretakers and attendants. Books loaned for 7 and 14 days. Printed catalogues issued in dictionary form and as class lists. Classification, numerical in main classes. Charging for lending, indicator ; reference, application forms. Has a museum and art gallery, and a juvenile Library opened 1st July, 1895. Technical Instruction Act has been adopted.

LIBRARIAN : William Crowther. Trained as a teacher, and appointed to Derby in November, 1885. He is a member of Council of the Library Association.

DEVONPORT, Devon.—Population, 54,848. Acts adopted in 1881. Library opened, 6th February, 1882. Has one branch. Contains 13,300 vols., of which 12,000 are for lending, 1000 for reference, and 300 are in the branch. Borrowers, 1200. Staff, 4 : librarian, 2 assistants, 1 caretaker. Books loaned for 7 and 10 days. Printed catalogue in dictionary form. Classification, numerical in main classes. Charging for lending, indicator ; reference, application forms. Has a museum and a ladies' room.

LIBRARIAN : Frederick William Hunt, born at Poole, Dorset, 8th October, 1863. He was appointed librarian at Devonport in 1892. Previously he was engaged on a daily newspaper.

DEWSBURY, Yorkshire.—Population, 29,847. Acts adopted in 1887. Temporary premises opened, 1889. Permanent building opened, 3rd June, 1896. Contains 12,748 vols., of which 10,001 are for lending and 2747 for reference. Borrowers, 2272. Staff, 3 : librarian and 2 assistants. Books loaned for 14 days. Printed catalogue in dictionary form. MS. catalogue in slip books. Classification, numerical in main classes. Charging for lending, indicator.

LIBRARIAN : William Henry Smith, born at Manchester. Trained in the Public Libraries of Manchester and Bradford. Librarian of the Constitution Hill Branch Library, Birmingham, and librarian at Dewsbury since the commencement.

DONCASTER, Yorkshire.—Population, 25,933. Acts adopted in 1868. Library opened in 1869. Contains 17,542 vols., of which 14,719 are for lending and 2823 for reference. Borrowers, 2175. Staff, 4 : librarian, 2 assistants, 1 caretaker. Books loaned for 14 days. Printed catalogue in dictionary form. MS. catalogue on cards. Classification, numerical in main classes. Charging for lending, indicator ; reference, application forms. Has a ladies' room, opened in 1889.

LIBRARIAN : Miss Mary Cordelia Scott, born at Boston in June, 1856. Trained at Doncaster, to which she was appointed librarian in November, 1893.

DOUGLAS, Isle of Man.—Population, 19,525. Acts adopted

in 1886 and Library opened in 1886. Local Act passed in 1895 and adopted in 1896, when new building was opened. Contains 11,251 vols., of which 9157 are for lending and 2094 for reference. Borrowers, 1953. Staff, 3; librarian and 2 assistants. Books loaned for 14 days. Printed catalogue in dictionary form. Classification, numerical in main classes. Charging for lending, cards; reference, application forms. Has a local collection.

LIBRARIAN: John Taylor.

DRUMOAK, Aberdeenshire, Scotland.—Population, 1000. Acts adopted in 1893.

DUBLIN, Ireland.—Population, 273,282. Acts adopted in 1884. Has a branch Library. The Capel Street Library contains 6000 vols. Borrowers, 1800. Staff, 5: librarian, 3 assistants, 1 caretaker. Books loaned for 14 days. Printed catalogue in dictionary form. MS. catalogue on cards. Classification, numerical in main classes; fiction, arranged by authors. Charging for lending, ledger; reference, application forms. Has a ladies' reading-room, opened in 1895.

LIBRARIAN: Patrick Grogan, who was educated at Maynooth College.

DUDLEY, Worcestershire. — Population, 45,740. Acts adopted in 1878. Building opened in 1884. Has branches at Netherton and Woodside. Contains 11,519 vols., of which 9212 are in the central Lending Library, 184 for reference, and 2123 in the branches. Borrowers, 1896. Staff, 4: librarian, 2 assistants, 1 caretaker. Books loaned for 10 and 14 days. Printed catalogue issued as class lists. Classification, numerical in main classes. Charging for lending, indicator; reference, application forms. Has an art gallery, and £100 per annum are received from the excise duties.

LIBRARIAN: William Southall, born at Dudley, 18th September, 1839. Was for 4 years an assistant at Dudley previous to being appointed librarian.

DUKINFIELD, Cheshire.—Population, 17,408. Acts adopted on 6th August, 1894. Reading-room opened, 1st January, 1895; Lending Library opened, 16th December, 1895. Contains 6165 vols., including those transferred from the Village Library. Borrowers, 605. Staff, 2: librarian and 1 caretaker. Books loaned for 15 days. No printed catalogue yet. Classification, alphabetical by authors. Charging for lending, cards; reference, application forms. Has technical classes, and students attending them are allowed to borrow from the Library.

LIBRARIAN: Edwin Bennett Broadrick, born at Dukinfield, 11th October, 1839. He was hon. secretary of the Dukinfield Village Library from 1869 to 1874 and from 1884 to 1895.

10

DUMBARTON, Scotland.—Population, 16,908. Acts adopted in 1881. Newsroom opened in 1883; Lending Library in 1884. The Library was removed to the Denny Institute in 1892. Contains 5400 vols. Borrowers, 1479. Staff, 2: librarian and 1 assistant. Books loaned for 7 and 14 days. Printed catalogue in dictionary form. MS. catalogue on cards. Classification, by subjects. Charging for lending, ledger; reference, application forms.

LIBRARIAN: Archibald Macdonald, who was formerly an assistant in the Hawick Public Library. Appointed to Dumbarton in January, 1896.

DUNDALK, Ireland.—Population, 12,449. Acts adopted in 1856. Library opened in 1858. Contains about 7000 vols. Borrowers, 200. Staff, 1: librarian. Books loaned for 21 days. Printed dictionary catalogue. Classification, numerical in main classes. Charging for lending, ledger; reference, signature book.

LIBRARIAN: T. Comerford.

DUNDEE, Forfar, Scotland. — Population, 155,640. Acts adopted in 1866. Library opened in 1869. Has a branch at Lochee. Contains 65,209 vols., of which 45,236 are for lending and 19,973 for reference. The newly opened branch at Lochee also has about 5000 vols. Printed catalogues in dictionary form. Charging for lending, indicator. Has art gallery, museum, etc.

LIBRARIAN: John Maclauchlan.

DUNFERMLINE, Fife, Scotland.—Population, 22,500. Acts adopted, 29th August, 1883. Building presented by Mr. Andrew Carnegie. Contains 15,357 vols., of which 12,620 are for lending and 2737 for reference. Staff, 3: librarian, 1 assistant, 1 caretaker. Books loaned for 14 days. Printed catalogue in dictionary form. Classification, numerical in main classes. Charging for lending, indicator; reference, application forms. Has a local museum in course of formation.

LIBRARIAN: Alexander Peebles, who is a native of Dunfermline.

EALING, Middlesex.—Population, 23,978. Acts adopted in January, 1883, and Library opened. New building opened in 1893. Contains 11,263 vols., of which 10,222 are for lending and 1038 for reference. Borrowers, 5284. Staff, 6: librarian, 4 assistants, 1 caretaker. Books issued for 7 and 14 days. Printed catalogue in classified form. Classification, numerical and alphabetical by authors in certain classes. Charging for lending, indicator; reference, application forms.

LIBRARIAN: Thomas Bonner, formerly of Birmingham. He has invented a special form of indicator.

EAST HAM, Essex.—Population, 28,700. Acts adopted in June, 1895.

EASTBOURNE, Sussex.—Population, 34,969. Acts adopted, 3rd February, 1896; Library opened 7th July, 1896. Contains 1772 vols., of which 1362 are for lending and 410 for reference. Staff, 2: librarian and 1 assistant. Books loaned for 14 days. Printed catalogue in classified form. Classification, numerical in main classes. Charging for lending, indicator; reference, application forms.

LIBRARIAN: John Henry Hardcastle, born at Wolverhampton, 4th August, 1873. Trained in the Wolverhampton Public Library, 1889-96. Librarian at Eastbourne since 1896.

MR. HEW MORRISON, LIBRARIAN, PUBLIC LIBRARY, EDINBURGH.

EDINBURGH, Scotland.—Population, 263,646. Acts adopted in February, 1887. Library opened in June, 1890. Branches in process of formation. Contains over 98,528 vols., of which 53,619 are for lending, 36,906 for reference, and 8000 for the branch. Borrowers, 47,470. Staff, 30: librarian 1, assistants 16, attendants, etc., 13. Books loaned for 7 and 14 days. Printed catalogues in dictionary form. Charging for lending, indicator; reference, application forms. Has juvenile Library and local collection.

LIBRARIAN: Hew Morrison, a native of Tongue, Sutherland. Was previously a schoolmaster for 20 years.

EDMONTON, Middlesex.--Population, 25,381. Acts adopted in 1892; library opened, January, 1893. Contains 2050 vols., of which 1800 are for lending and 250 for reference. Borrowers, 1000. Staff, 2: librarian and 1 assistant. Books loaned for 14 days. Printed catalogue in dictionary form. Classification, numerical in main classes. Charging for lending, indicator. New building to be presented by Mr. Passmore Edwards in contemplation.

LIBRARIAN: Percy Wellington Farmborough, F.Z.S., trained in the Shoreditch Public Libraries.

ELGIN, Scotland.—Population, 7797. Acts adopted in April, 1891. Library opened in May, 1892. Contains 4713 vols., of which 4356 are for lending and 357 for reference. Borrowers, 2019. Staff, 3: librarian, 1 assistant, 1 caretaker. Books loaned for 14 days. Printed catalogue issued as author list. MS. catalogue in slip books. Classification, alphabetical by authors. Charging for lending, indicator; reference, application forms and open access. Has a subscription department in connection with the Lending Library.

LIBRARIAN: Miss Isabella Mitchell, born at Spynie, Elgin. Appointed librarian at Elgin in 1891.

ENFIELD, Middlesex.—Population, 34,000. Acts adopted November, 1893. Library opened in July, 1894. Has two branches. Contains 6200 vols. Borrowers, 3207. Staff, 2: librarian and assistant. Printed catalogue in dictionary form. Classification, numerical. Charging for lending, indicator. Has a small local collection.

LIBRARIAN: Charles Frederic Harrison, born at Plymouth in 1868. Trained in Halifax Public Library, and afterwards successively librarian of Harrogate, Stoke Newington, and Enfield Public Libraries.

ENNIS, Ireland.—Population, 6300. Acts adopted in 1860.

EXETER, Devon.--Population, 37,608. Acts adopted in May, 1869. Contains 15,767 vols., of which 7166 are for lending and 8601 for reference. Borrowers, 1600. Staff, 5: librarian, 2 assistants, 2 attendants. Books loaned for 14 days. Printed catalogue in dictionary form. Reference catalogue on cards and in MS. book. Charging for lending, indicator; reference, application forms. Has a museum, art gallery, classes, lectures and a local collection.

LIBRARIAN: James Dallas, F.L.S., formerly of the Geological Society of London. Author of various papers on scientific and antiquarian subjects, and editor of *Notes and Gleanings: a magazine devoted chiefly to matters connected with the counties of Devon and Cornwall.*

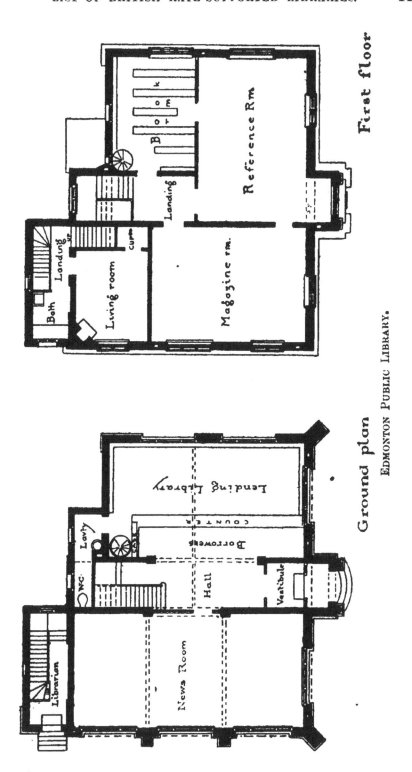

First floor

Ground plan

EDMONTON PUBLIC LIBRARY.

FALKIRK, Scotland.—Population, 17,300. Acts adopted in January, 1896.

FALMOUTH, Cornwall.—Population, 11,047. Acts adopted in 1893. Library open in April, 1894. Building presented by Mr. Passmore Edwards opened in 1896. Contains 2950 vols., of which 2300 are for lending and 650 for reference. Borrowers, 580. Staff, 1: librarian, with honorary assistance. Books loaned for 7, 14 and 21 days. Catalogues in course of preparation. Classification, numerical in main classes. Charging for lending, ledger; reference, signature book.

LIBRARIAN: Richard H. Brenton, with whom are associated 2 honorary librarians who are also members of the Committee.

FLEETWOOD, Lancashire. — Population, 9274. Acts adopted, 1887. Library opened in 1888.

FOLKESTONE, Kent.—Population, 23,905. Acts adopted in May, 1878. Library opened in January, 1879. Contains 8591 vols., of which 7231 are for lending and 1360 for reference. Borrowers, 2681. Staff, 3: librarian, 1 assistant, 1 caretaker. Books loaned for 7 days. Printed catalogue in dictionary form. MS. catalogue on cards. Classification, numerical in main classes. Charging for lending, indicator; reference, signature book and open access. There is a museum, opened in 1888, supported under Museum and Gymnasium Act.

LIBRARIAN: Stuart G. Hills.

FORFAR, Scotland.—Population, 12,057. Acts adopted in 1870. Library opened in 1871. Contains about 7000 vols.

FULHAM, London.—Population, 113,781. Acts adopted in 1887. Library first opened in 1887. Has one branch opened in 1896. Contains 12,045 vols., of which 9015 are for lending and 3030 for reference. Borrowers, 4376. Staff, 8: librarian, 5 assistants, 2 caretakers. Books loaned for 14 days. Printed catalogue in dictionary form. MS. catalogue in guard books. Classification, numerical with author alphabet in certain classes. Charging for lending, indicator; reference, application forms.

LIBRARIAN: Franklin T. Barrett. Trained in the Mitchell Library, Glasgow. Appointed to Fulham in 1894.

GALASHIELS, Selkirkshire, Scotland.—Population, 17,000. Acts adopted in 1872. Library opened in 1874. Contains 6967 vols., of which 6600 are for lending and 367 for reference. Borrowers, 1188. Staff, 1: librarian. Books loaned from 12 to 18 days. Printed catalogue in dictionary form. Charging for lending, indicator; reference, signature book.

LIBRARIAN: Mrs. Margaret Marshall Pretsell Dick, appointed librarian in 1876.

GATESHEAD, Durham.—Population, 85,692. Acts adopted in 1880. Library opened in 1885. Contains 10,119 vols., of which 9239 are for lending and 880 for reference. Borrowers, 3068. Staff, 5: librarian, 3 assistants, 1 caretaker. Books loaned for 14 days. Printed catalogue in dictionary form. MS. catalogue on cards. Classification, numerical in main classes. Charging for lending, indicator; reference, application forms. There is an art school in connection with the Library, and it has also a ladies' room. During the past 3 years £200 have been received from the excise duties for the purchase of technical books.

LIBRARIAN: Henry Edward Johnston, born at Newcastle-on-Tyne in 1866. Trained at Gateshead Public Library, 1885. Appointed librarian in 1888.

GLOSSOP, Derbyshire.—Population, 22,414. Acts adopted in 1888. Library opened in 1889. Has a branch at Hadfield. Contains 3316 vols. Borrowers, 3000. Staff, 3: librarian, 1 assistant, 1 caretaker. Books loaned for 14 days. Printed catalogue in dictionary form. Classification, numerical. Charging for lending, cards.

LIBRARIAN: Mary Hannah Warhurst, a native of Glossop.

GLOUCESTER, Gloucestershire.—Population, 39,444. Acts adopted in May, 1894, but Library not yet established.

GOSPORT AND ALVERSTOKE, Hampshire.—Population, 25,457. Acts adopted in 1886. Temporary building opened in 1891. Contains 5853 vols., of which 5270 are for lending and 583 for reference. Borrowers, 2450. Staff, 4: librarian, 2 assistants, 1 caretaker. Books loaned for 14 days. Printed catalogue in dictionary form. MS. catalogue in guard books. Classification, numerical in main classes; fiction, alphabetical by authors. Charging for lending, indicator; reference, application forms. Has a local collection and issues students' extra tickets (July, 1894).

LIBRARIAN: Albert Gray, born at Gosport in 1877. Trained in Gosport Public Library and appointed librarian in Feb., 1895.

GRANDBOROUGH, Bucks.—Population, 500. Acts adopted on Sept. 25, 1896.

GRANGEMOUTH, Stirlingshire, Scotland. — Population, 5833. Acts adopted in March, 1887. Rooms first opened in September, 1887; Library building, "Victoria Public Library," opened, 31st January, 1889. Contains 2665 vols. Staff, 1: librarian. Books loaned for 14 days. Printed catalogue in classified form. Classification, numerical in main classes. Charging for lending, indicator. There is a ladies' room.

LIBRARIAN: William C. Dibbs, born at Grangemouth, 24th October, 1862.

GRAVESEND, Kent.—Population, 24,076. Acts adopted in 1892; Library opened in 1893. Contains 5029 vols., of which 3829 are for lending and 1200 for reference. Borrowers, 1491. Staff, 3: librarian, 1 assistant, 1 caretaker. Books loaned for 14 days. Printed catalogue in dictionary form. MS. catalogue on cards. Classification, numerical in main classes. Charging for lending, indicator for fiction, cards for other classes. Reference, application forms, but more frequently open access. The Technical Instruction Act has been adopted, and £50 have been granted from the excise duties for the purchase of technical books.

LIBRARIAN: Alfred Watkinson, who was trained in the Maidstone Museum and Public Library, 1890-95.

GRAYS, Essex.—Population, 13,000. Acts adopted in 1893. Reading-room opened in 1894; Lending Library in February, 1896. Contains about 1000 vols. Borrowers, 80. Staff, 1: librarian. Books loaned for 14 days. Printed catalogue in classified form. Classification, by subjects with authors in alphabetical order. Charging for lending, ledger.

LIBRARIAN: Annie George, born at Edinburgh in 1855.

HALIFAX, Yorkshire.—Population, 83,109. Acts adopted in 1881. Library opened in 1882. There is one branch Library and four delivery stations in connection with schools. Contains 46,214 vols., of which 28,788 are in the central Lending Library, and 17,426 in the branches. Borrowers, 10,249. Staff, 9: librarian, 6 assistants, 2 caretakers. Also 4 teachers in charge of the school delivery stations. Books loaned for 14 days. Printed catalogue in dictionary form. MS. catalogue on cards. Classification, numerical in main classes. Charging for lending, indicator; reference, application forms. Has an industrial museum and ladies' reading-rooms. A grant of £100 from the excise duties was made in 1895-96.

LIBRARIAN: Joe Whiteley, born at Halifax in 1842. He was a bookseller in Halifax previous to becoming librarian.

HALKIN, Flintshire, Wales.—Population, 1500. Acts adopted in October, 1896.

HALTON, Yorkshire.—Acts adopted in July, 1895.

HAMMERSMITH, London (Ravenscourt Park).—Population, 104,199. Acts adopted in 1887. Library opened in 1889. A branch at Shepherd's Bush, presented by Mr. Passmore Edwards, was recently opened. Contains 21,566 vols., of which 10,300 are in the central Lending Library, 2766 in the Reference Library, and 8500 in the branch. Borrowers, 3500. Staff, 10: librarian, 7 assistants, 2 caretakers. Books loaned for 14 days. Printed catalogue in dictionary form. MS. catalogue in slip books. Classification, numerical in main classes at central Library, alphabetical by authors in main classes at branch. Charging for lending, cards, with indicator for fiction only; reference, application forms. Has a local collection of books, prints, etc., and has issued extra tickets available for music, since 1893.

LIBRARIAN: Samuel Martin, author of a paper read before the Library Association.

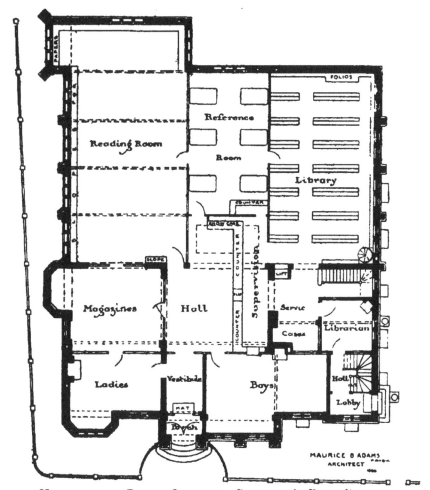

HAMMERSMITH PUBLIC LIBRARY. SHEPHERD'S BUSH BUILDING.

HAMPSTEAD, London (Priory Road, N.W.).—Population, 75,449. Acts adopted in February, 1893. Library opened in 1894. Has 2 branches in operation and another being built. Contains 8550 vols., of which 6500 are for lending and 2050 for reference. Borrowers, 3814. Staff, 8: librarian, 6 assistants, 1 caretaker. Books loaned 7 and 14 days. Printed catalogue in dictionary form. MS. catalogue on cards. Classification, by subjects and alphabetical by authors. Charging for lending, indicator; reference, application forms. Has a local collection; students' extra tickets; and recently purchased the Library (8000 vols.) of the late Prof. Henry Morley.

LIBRARIAN: William E. Doubleday, trained at Nottingham Public Library, 1882-89. Librarian of Marylebone Free Library (voluntary), 1889-94. Librarian of Hampstead since 1894. Member of Council of Library Association and a contributor to its *Transactions*. Late Secretary of the Summer School of the Library Association. Author of novels, etc.

HANDSWORTH, Staffordshire.—Population, 32,756. Acts adopted, 26th December, 1876. Library opened, 1st May, 1880. Has a branch at Birchfield. Contains 12,982 vols., of which 11,309 are for lending and 1673 for reference. Borrowers, 2185. Staff, 3: librarian, 1 assistant, 1 caretaker. Books loaned for 7 and 14 days. Printed catalogue in dictionary form. Classification, numerical. Charging for lending, indicator; reference, application forms. Issues extra tickets for music.

LIBRARIAN: John William Roberts. Was trained in Swansea Public Library. Librarian at Handsworth since 1883.

HANLEY, Staffordshire.—Population, 54,946. Acts adopted in June, 1884. Reading-room opened, 1886; Library opened, 1887. Contains 12,093 vols., of which 7737 are for lending, 2681 for reference, and 1675 in boys' reading-room. Borrowers, 1608. Staff, 4: librarian, 2 assistants, 1 attendant. Books loaned for 7 and 10 days. Printed catalogue in dictionary form. Classification, numerical in main classes. Charging for lending, ledger; reference, application forms. Has a ladies' room (1886), science classes (1887), and boys' reading-room (1893). Grants have been received from the excise duties.

LIBRARIAN: Arthur J. Milward, born at Manchester, 12th October, 1863. Trained in Manchester Public Libraries, 1881-88. Librarian at Hanley since May, 1888.

HARROGATE, Yorkshire. — Population, 13,917. Acts adopted in June, 1887. Reading-room opened in December, 1887; Lending Library opened in April, 1888. Contains 8791 vols., of which 8425 are for lending and 366 for reference. Staff, 2: librarian and 1 assistant. Books loaned for 14 days. Printed catalogue in dictionary form. MS. catalogue in slip books. Classification, numerical in main classes. Charging for lending, indicator; reference, application forms. Has a local collection.

LIBRARIAN: George William Byers, born at Carrick-on-Shannon, 18th August, 1872. Chief assistant at Harrogate, 1888-92. Chief librarian from June, 1892.

HARTLEPOOL, EAST, Durham.—Population, 21,271. Acts adopted in 1891. Library not yet formed.

HARTLEPOOL, WEST, Durham.—Population, 42,476. Acts adopted in 1891. Building opened, 23rd October, 1895. Contains 9600 vols., of which 8300 are for lending and 1300 for reference. Borrowers, 5300. Staff, 4: librarian and 3 assistants. Books loaned for 14 days. Printed catalogue in dictionary form. MS. catalogue on cards. Classification, numerical in main classes. Charging for lending, indicator; reference, application forms. Has a local collection. The Technical Instruction Act has been adopted.

LIBRARIAN: Albert Watkins, born at Great Yarmouth in April, 1871. Trained in Public Library of Great Yarmouth, 1886-90. Sub-librarian in Minet Public Library, Lambeth, 1890-94. Librarian at West Hartlepool since 1894.

HAWICK, Roxburghshire, Scotland.—Population, 19,204. Acts adopted in April, 1878. Newsroom opened in November, 1878; Library opened in March, 1879. Contains 11,421 vols., of which 9763 are for lending and 1658 for reference. Borrowers, 2026. Staff, 2: librarian and caretaker. Books loaned for 14 days. Printed catalogue in dictionary form. Classification, numerical in main classes. Charging for lending, indicator; reference, application forms.

LIBRARIAN: George S. S. McNairn, born at Edinburgh, 1st June, 1870. Assistant librarian in a private Library, 1889-94, and also had some training in the Edinburgh Public Library. Librarian at Hawick since July, 1894.

HAYLE, Cornwall.—Population, 1673. Acts adopted in 1896.

HEREFORD, Herefordshire. — Population, 20,267. Acts adopted in July, 1871. Library opened in temporary premises, 4th December, 1871. New building opened, 8th October, 1874. Contains 10,000 vols., of which 7000 are for lending and 3000 for reference. Borrowers, 1350. Staff, 4: librarian, 2 assistants, 1 caretaker. Books loaned for 8 days. Printed catalogue in dictionary form. MS. catalogue in guard books. Classification, numerical in main classes. Charging for lending, ledger; reference, application forms. Has a museum; also lectures, and a local collection.

LIBRARIAN: James Cockcroft, born at Salford in 1863. Assistant in Salford Museum and Library, 1877-83. Librarian of Manchester Royal Exchange Library, 1883-88. Librarian at Hereford from 1888.

HERTFORD, Hertfordshire. — Population, 7232. Acts adopted in 1855. Library opened in 1856. Contains over 12,000 vols.

LIBRARIAN: E. Lawrence.

HEYWOOD, Lancashire.—Population, 23,286. Acts adopted in 1874. Library opened in October, 1874. Contains 11,160 vols., of which 9360 are for lending and 1800 for reference. Borrowers, 850. Staff, 2: librarian and 1 assistant. Books loaned for 14 days. Printed catalogue in dictionary form. MS. catalogue on cards. Classification, alphabetical by authors. Charging for lending, cards; reference, application forms. Has a special juvenile reading room.

LIBRARIAN: George Grundy Chiswell.

HINCKLEY, Leicestershire. — Population, 9638. Acts adopted, 1888. Library opened, 1888. Contains 3135 vols., of which 2950 are for lending and 185 for reference. Borrowers, 450. Staff, 2: librarian and 1 assistant. Books loaned for 7 days. Printed catalogue in dictionary form. Classification, numerical. Charging for lending, indicator; reference, signature book.

LIBRARIAN: Peter Payne, born at Hinckley in 1845. He was previously librarian of a subscription Library in Hinckley, which was established in 1874.

HINDLEY, Lancashire.—Population, 18,973. Acts adopted, May, 1887. Library opened in June, 1887. Contains 4447 vols. Borrowers, 1596. Staff, 2: librarian and caretaker. Books loaned for 14 days. Printed catalogue in dictionary form. Classification, numerical. Charging for lending, indicator.

LIBRARIAN: John Smith, born at Wigan, 30th June, 1833. Trained at Wigan Mechanics' Institution, 1866-89. Librarian at Hindley since 1889.

HOLBORN, London (10 John Street, Bedford Row, W.C.).—Population, 31,208. Acts adopted, 13th May, 1891; Library opened, 16th January, 1893. Contains 7213 vols., of which 6259 are for lending and 954 for reference. Borrowers, 1464. Staff, 4: librarian, 2 assistants, 1 caretaker. Books loaned for 14 days. Printed catalogue in dictionary form; also supplements issued as author lists. Classification, numerical in main classes. Charging for lending, cards; reference, application forms. Students' extra tickets for non-fictional works issued since December, 1895.

LIBRARIAN: Harry Hawkes, born at Ampthill, Beds, 2nd May, 1865. Trained at Cambridge Public Library from 1881 to 1887. Assistant librarian in charge of the Barnwell branch at Cambridge, 1887-92. Librarian at Holborn since July, 1892.

HOLYHEAD, Anglesea, Wales.—Population, 9700. Acts adopted, 23rd January, 1896. Library opened, 25th April, 1896. Contains 500 vols., all gifts. Had not been opened to the public when return was made.

LIBRARIAN: Mair Griffith, born at Holyhead in 1872.

HORNSEY, Middlesex.—Population, 61,097. Acts adopted, 7th December, 1896.

HOVE, Sussex.—Population, 28,335. Acts adopted in April, 1891. Newsroom opened, December, 1891; Lending Library, October, 1892; Reference Library, 1894. Contains 8669 vols., of which 6612 are for lending and 2057 for reference. Borrowers, 3050. Staff, 5: librarian, 3 assistants, 1 caretaker. Books loaned for 14 days. Printed catalogue in classified form. MS. catalogue on cards. Classification, numerical. Charging for lending, ledger; reference, application forms. The Technical Instruction Act has been adopted.

LIBRARIAN: John William Lister, born at Batley, Yorks, 31st March, 1870. Trained in the Sheffield Public Libraries, 1884-92. Librarian at Hove since January, 1892.

HUCKNALL TORKARD, Nottinghamshire. — Population, 13,094. Acts adopted in April, 1884; Library opened, 14th January, 1887. Contains 4230 vols., of which 3980 are for lending and 250 for reference. Borrowers, 611. Staff: librarian. Books loaned for 7 and 10 days. Printed catalogue in dictionary form. Classification, numerical in main classes. Charging for lending, indicator; reference, application forms. Adopted plan of giving half-hour talks on books in the Library, etc., in 1892.

LIBRARIAN: Henry Dennis, born at Hucknall Torkard, 18th March, 1862. Librarian since 1886.

HULL, Yorkshire.—Population, 200,041. Acts adopted, 10th December, 1892. Central Library opened, October, 1894. Has 3 branches, of which the Eastern was originally the James Reckitt Library, opened in 1889, and handed over to the Public Libraries Committee in 1893. West branch opened, January, 1895; North branch opened, June, 1895. Contains 52,588 vols., of which 12,549 are in the central lending, 12,830 in the central reference, and 27,209 in the branches. Borrowers, 17,418. Staff, 24: librarian, 19 assistants, 4 caretakers. Books loaned for 14 days. Printed catalogue in dictionary form. MS. catalogue in guard and slip books. Classification, numerical in main classes. Charging for lending, indicator; reference, application forms.

LIBRARIAN: William Frederick Lawton, born at Leeds in 1861. Trained in the Leeds Public Libraries from 1875 to 1893. He was sub-librarian at Leeds for 4 years previous to his appointment as librarian at Hull in October, 1893.

HYDE, Cheshire.—Population, 30,670. Acts adopted in 1893. Reading-room opened, 18th September, 1893; Library opened, 8th December, 1894. Contains 5530 vols., of which 5170 are for lending and 360 for reference. Borrowers, 1760. Staff, 3: librarian, 1 assistant, 1 caretaker. Books loaned for 10 days. Printed catalogue in dictionary form. Classification, numerical in main classes. Charging for lending, cards; reference, application forms. Lectures have been given in connection with the Library, and the Technical Instruction Act has been adopted.

LIBRARIAN: John Chorton, born at Woodley, Cheshire, 26th October, 1855. Trained in Hyde Mechanics' Institution and became librarian of the Public Library in 1893.

IBSTOCK, Leicestershire.—Population, 3000. Acts adopted in November, 1895.

ILFORD, Essex.—Population, 10,900. Acts adopted in 1892, but owing to opposition no further action has been taken.

INVERNESS, Scotland.—Population, 19,211. Acts adopted, 4th July, 1877. Library opened in June, 1883. Contains 7677 vols., of which 5871 are for lending and 1806 for reference. Borrowers, 1700. Staff, 2: librarian and assistant. Books loaned for 14 days. Printed catalogue in dictionary form. Classification, numerical in main classes. Charging for lending, ledger; reference, signature book and application forms. There are a museum, and technical and art schools in connection with the Library.

LIBRARIAN: Simon Fraser Donaldson, who is a native of Inverness.

IPSWICH, Suffolk.—Population, 57,260. Acts adopted in 1853. New building opened in 1887. Contains over 15,000 vols. Charging for lending, ledger.

LIBRARIAN: Wm. Fenton.

JEDBURGH, Scotland.—Population, 2500. Acts adopted in May, 1892.

KENDAL, Westmoreland. — Population, 14,430. Acts adopted in April, 1891. Library opened in 1892. Contains 9329 vols., of which 8599 are for lending and 730 for reference. Borrowers, 3225. Staff, 2: librarian and 1 assistant. Books loaned for 14 days. Printed catalogue in dictionary form. Classification, numerical. Charging for lending, indicator; reference, application forms. Has a ladies' room and a local collection. Grants have been made by the Westmoreland County Council from the excise duties.

LIBRARIAN: Robert Clarkson Garner, born at St. Helen's, 8th June, 1873. Assistant in Atkinson Free Library, Southport, 1888-94. Librarian at Kendal since October, 1894.

KENSINGTON, London (Central Library, High Street, Kensington).—Population, 170,465. Acts adopted in June, 1887. Notting Hill Library opened in temporary premises, 2nd January, 1888. Central Library opened, November, 1889;

Brompton branch opened, November, 1888; North Kensington branch opened in October, 1891. Contains 36,065 vols., of which 9325 are in the central Lending Library, 10,285 in the Reference Library, and 16,455 in the 2 branches. Borrowers, 9830. Staff, 19: librarian, 15 assistants, and 3 caretakers. Books loaned for 14 days. Printed catalogue in dictionary form. MS. reference catalogue on cards. Classification, numerical in main classes. Charging for lending, indicator; reference, signature book and application forms. Has a special collection of English topographical works.

LIBRARIAN: Herbert Jones, who is a native of Ireland. He was trained in the Heywood (now North Kensington) Public Library from 1874-87, and became chief librarian at Kensington in 1887. He is a member of Council of the Library Association, and has distinguished himself as an amateur etcher of book plates and other works.

KETTERING, Northamptonshire.—Population, 19,000. Acts adopted in 1895. Library opened on 2nd March, 1896. Contains 1743 vols., of which 1489 are for lending and 254 for reference. Borrowers, 1130. Staff, 2: librarian and 1 caretaker. Books loaned for 15 days. Printed catalogue, author entry with subject index. MS. catalogue in slip book. Classification, by subjects on Quinn-Brown system. Charging for lending, open access and cards; reference, application forms.

LIBRARIAN: Miss Kate E. Pierce, born at Kettering in November, 1873. Was originally a teacher, but had some training in Library work in the Clerkenwell Public Library.

KIDDERMINSTER, Worcestershire.—Population, 24,803. Acts adopted in 1854. Lending Library opened in 1881. Contains 6000 vols., of which 5000 are for lending and 1000 for reference. Borrowers, 2500. Staff, 4: librarian, 1 assistant, and 2 caretakers. Books loaned for 14 days. Printed catalogue in dictionary form. MS. catalogue on cards. Classification, numerical in main classes. Charging for lending, indicator; reference, application forms and open shelves. Has a museum, art gallery, lectures and a local collection. The Technical Instruction Act has been adopted.

LIBRARIAN: George Archibald Sparke, born at Cardiff, 19th July, 1871. Assistant in Cardiff Public Libraries from 1884-94. Librarian at Kidderminster from 1894. Author of *The Uses of Public Libraries*, a pamphlet, and numerous papers on fiction contributed to newspapers. He has also written several short stories.

KILMARNOCK, Ayrshire, Scotland.—Population, 28,438. Acts adopted, 12th June, 1893. Library opened, 16th February, 1895. Contains 14,950 vols., of which 14,000 are for lending and 950 for reference. Borrowers, 4714. Staff, 4: librarian, 2 assistants, 1 janitor.   Books loaned for 14 days.   Printed catalogue in dictionary form.   Classification, numerical.

KIDDERMINSTER PUBLIC LIBRARY.

Charging for lending, indicator; reference, application forms. Has a museum and a ladies' room.

LIBRARIAN: Henry Young Simpson, born at Arbroath, 7th April, 1868. Assistant in the Mitchell Library, Glasgow, from 1883-94. Librarian at Kilmarnock since 1894.

KINGSTON-UPON-THAMES, Surrey.—Population, 27,059. Acts adopted, 1st March. 1881. Library opened, 1st May, 1882. Contains 8078 vols., of which 6100 are for lending and 1978 for reference. Borrowers, 1951. Staff, 5: librarian, 1 assistant, 2 attendants and 1 caretaker. Books loaned for 14 days. Printed catalogue in dictionary form; classified lists in preparation. MS. catalogue in slip books. Classification, by subjects, on Quinn-Brown system. Charging for lending, open access and cards; reference, application forms. Has a local collection, and issues students' extra tickets (Aug., 1895).

LIBRARIAN: Benjamin Carter, who was trained in the Portsmouth Public Library, and became librarian of the Gosport and Alverstoke Public Library on its foundation. Librarian of Kingston since 1895.

KINGSTOWN, Ireland.—Population, 17,340. Acts adopted in 1884.

KIRKCALDY, Scotland.—Population, 27,200. Acts adopted in 1895.

KIRKMICHAEL, Banffshire, Scotland.—Population, 1500. Acts adopted in December, 1895.

KIRKWALL, Scotland.—Population, 3895. Acts adopted in 1890. Library opened in 1891. Contains about 4000 vols.

LAMBETH, London (Tate Central Library, Brixton Oval, S.W.).—Population, 295,033. Acts adopted in December, 1886. First Library opened in temporary premises, July, 1887. Has 5 branches, the buildings having been all presented. One of them, the Minet, is held jointly with Camberwell, but is under the management of the Lambeth librarian. Contains 69,907 vols., of which 14,225 are in the central Lending Library, 10,250 in the Reference Library, and 45,432 in the branches. Borrowers, 19,669. Staff, 37: librarian, 30 assistants and 6 caretakers. Books loaned for 14 days. Printed catalogues in dictionary form. MS. reference catalogue on cards. Classification, numerical in main classes for Lending Libraries; Dewey system for Reference. Charging for lending, indicator; reference, application forms. Has ladies' rooms at the central Library and 2 of the branches; a special reading-room for children under 12 at the Minet joint-branch; and special collections of books relating to Surrey and Francis Bacon.

LIBRARIAN: Frank James Burgoyne. Trained for 4 years in the Birmingham Public Libraries; afterwards, for 5 years, sub-librarian at Newcastle-on-Tyne. Librarian at Darlington for 3 years, and chief librarian at Lambeth since 1887. Member of the Council of the Library Association and a contributor to its *Transactions*. Joint author of *Books for Village Libraries*.

LAMBETH. TATE CENTRAL LIBRARY, BRIXTON.

LANCASTER, Lancashire. — Population, 31,000. Acts adopted in December, 1892. Library opened in July, 1893, in the Storey Institute. Contains 8218 vols., of which 7655 are for lending and 563 for reference. Borrowers, 2000. Staff, 2: librarian, 1 assistant. Printed catalogue in dictionary form. MS. catalogue on cards. Classification, numerical and size. Charging for lending, indicator.

LIBRARIAN : James M. Dowbiggin.

LEADGATE, Durham.—Population, 5000. Acts adopted in November, 1896.

LEAMINGTON, Warwickshire.—Population, 26,074. Acts adopted in 1857, and Library opened in the same year. Contains 18,528 vols., of which 12,045 are for lending and 6483 for reference. Borrowers, 5187. Staff, 3: librarian and 2 assistants. Books loaned for 7, 10 and 14 days. Printed catalogue in dictionary form. Classification, numerical. Charging for lending, ledger ; reference, application forms.

LIBRARIAN : David B. Grant.

LEEDS, Yorkshire.—Population, 367,506. Acts adopted in 1868. Central Library opened in 1871. Has 21 branches, and 37 juvenile Libraries established in schools. Contains 191,096 vols., of which 48,100 are in the central Lending Library, 50,990 in the Reference Library, and 92,006 in the branches. Borrowers, 28,040. Staff, 68: librarian and 67 assistants and caretakers. Books loaned for 14 days. Printed catalogue in classified form. MS. catalogue on cards. Classification, by subjects. Charging for lending, indicators ; reference, application forms. Has an art gallery (1888), and has received grants from the excise duties.

LIBRARIAN : James Yates, born at Bolton-le-Moors, where he had 13 years' experience. Librarian at Leeds since 1870.

LEEK, Staffordshire.—Population, 14,628. Acts adopted in 1888. Nicholson Institute, opened in 1884. Contains 9825 vols., of which 6496 are for lending and 3329 for reference. Borrowers, 765. Staff, 4: librarian, 2 assistants, 1 caretaker. Books loaned for 14 days. Printed catalogues issued in dictionary form and as classified hand-lists. Classification, by subjects. Charging for lending, ledger; reference, application forms. Has a museum (1884); art gallery (1884); University extension lectures (1884); popular lectures (1891); students' extra tickets (1895). There is a school of art (1884), and science and technology (1891). The Technical Instruction Act has been adopted, and grants of books have been made from the excise duties.

LIBRARIAN : Kineton Parkes, born at Aston Manor in 1865 Educated at King Edward Grammar School and Mason College, Birmingham. Principal of the Nicholson Institute in 1891. Editor of *The Library Review*, 1892-93, and author of numerous papers, articles, etc.

LEICESTER, Leicestershire.—Population, 174,624. Acts
adopted in 1870. Library first opened, 10th April, 1871. Has
5 branch Libraries. Contains 52,807 vols., of which 20,804 are

in the central Lending; 16,994 for reference; and 15,009 are in
the branches. Borrowers, 13,009. Staff, 27: librarian, 20

assistants, 6 caretakers. Books loaned for 7 days. Printed catalogue in classified form. MS. catalogue in slip books. Classification, alphabetical by authors. Charging for lending, indicator; reference, application forms. Has a local collection.

LIBRARIAN: Charles Vernon Kirkby, born at Leeds. Trained as an assistant in the Leeds Public Library in 1872. Librarian at Leicester since 1st May, 1888. He is a member of Council of the Library Association, and has invented a slip book for MS. catalogues.

LEIGH, Lancaster.—Population, 30,815. Acts adopted in October, 1892. Library opened in September, 1894. Contains 5500 vols., of which 4500 are for lending and 1000 for reference. Borrowers, 2200. Staff, 5: librarian, 3 assistants, 1 caretaker. Books loaned for 14 days. Printed catalogue in dictionary form. Classification, numerical. Charging for lending, indicator; reference, application forms. There is a technical school.

LIBRARIAN: James Ward, born at Leigh in 1858. Librarian of the Literary Society Library, Leigh, 1884-92.

LEOMINSTER, Herefordshire. — Population, 5675. Acts adopted in January, 1891. Library opened, December, 1895. Contains 5020 vols., of which 4900 are for lending and 120 for reference. Borrowers, 326. Staff, 3: librarian, 1 deputy, 1 caretaker. Books loaned for 7 and 14 days. Printed catalogue in dictionary form. Classification, by subjects. Charging for lending, ledger. Has science and art classes.

LIBRARIAN: John Benjamin Dowding, born 24th February, 1860. Had no previous training.

LEWISHAM, London (Perry Hill, Catford, S.E.).—Population, 82,313. Acts adopted in June, 1890. Newsroom opened, July, 1891. Library opened, 26th November, 1891. Has 3 branches, but no central Library. Contains 12,703 vols., of which 7109 are for lending at Perry Hill, 1908 for reference, and 3686 in the other branches. Borrowers, 5306. Staff, 9: librarian, 5 assistants, 3 caretakers. Books loaned for 14 days. Printed catalogues in dictionary form. Classification, numerical in main classes. Charging for lending, indicator; reference, application forms.

LIBRARIAN: Charles Wm. Frederick Goss, born at London in April, 1864. Trained at Birkenhead Public Library from 1880-87 and Newcastle-on-Tyne, 1887-91. Librarian at Lewisham since 1891. Has contributed various articles to newspapers.

LEYTON, Essex. — Population, 77,000. Acts adopted in 1892. Library opened in 1893. Contains 12,250 vols., of which 10,000 are for lending and 2250 for reference. Borrowers, 4500.

Staff, 4: librarian, 2 assistants, 1 caretaker. Books loaned for 7 days. Printed catalogue in dictionary form. MS. catalogue on cards. Classification, numerical in main classes. Charging for lending, indicator; reference, application forms. Has a local collection. The Technical Instruction and Museum Acts have been adopted.

LIBRARIAN: Zebedee Moon, formerly librarian of Loughborough Public Library. Author of *Leicestershire Worthies*, a pamphlet, and translator from the French of *La Dégénération* and other short stories.

LICHFIELD, Staffordshire.—Population, 7864. Acts adopted in 1856. Library opened in 1859.

LIMERICK, Ireland.—Population, 37,072. Acts adopted, 1889. Library opened in December, 1893. Contains 3030 vols. Staff, 1: librarian. Classification, numerical in subjects.

LIBRARIAN: John Hogan, born at Newcastle West, Limerick, 9th April, 1843. Received no training in Library work.

LINCOLN, Lincolnshire.—Population, 41,491. Acts adopted in January, 1892. Library opened in 1895. Contains 7140 vols., of which 6250 are for lending and 890 for reference. Borrowers, 2442. Staff, 4: librarian, 2 assistants, 1 Sunday attendant. Books loaned for 14 days. Printed catalogue in dictionary form. MS. catalogue on cards. Classification, numerical in main classes. Charging for lending, indicator; reference, application forms. Has a ladies' room and a local collection. The Technical Instruction Act has been adopted. A grant of £200 has been given from the excise duties for the purchase of technical books.

LIBRARIAN: Henry Bond, born at Barrow-in-Furness, 23rd November, 1871. Trained in the Barrow Public Library, 1887-92. Librarian at Kendal Public Library, January, 1892, to November, 1894. Librarian of Lincoln Public Library since November, 1894.

LISKEARD, Cornwall.—Population, 4000. Acts adopted in April, 1895.

LIVERPOOL, Lancashire. — Population, 517,951. Established under a special Act in 1852. First opened to the public, 18th October, 1852. Has 4 branch Libraries and 4 evening reading-rooms. Contains 179,442 vols., of which 71,163 are for lending and 108,279 for reference. Borrowers, 14,652. Staff, 55: librarian, 47 assistants, 7 attendants and janitors. Books loaned for 10 days. Printed catalogues in classified and dictionary forms. MS. reference catalogue on cards. Special classification, numerical in classes. Charging for lending, special card system; reference, application forms.

LIVERPOOL PUBLIC LIBRARY, ART GALLERY, ETC.

Has a museum, art gallery, lectures and a local and other collections. Music introduced in 1859; books for the blind introduced in 1857. The Museum Act was adopted in 1896, and grants have been received from the excise duties.

LIBRARIAN: Peter Cowell, who has been in the Library service at Liverpool since he was sixteen years old. He is a vice-president of the Library Association and a contributor to its *Transactions.* Author of *Library Staffs* (Library Association Series, No. 3). In 1893 he attended the International Conference of Librarians at Chicago, and printed a report on his visit to American libraries.

LLANUWCHLLYN, Merioneth, Wales.—Population, 1500. Acts adopted in March, 1895.

LONGTON, Staffordshire.—Population, 34,327. Acts adopted in May, 1891. Library opened, January, 1892. Contains 5850 vols., of which 5200 are for lending and 650 for reference. Borrowers, 1000. Staff, 3: librarian, 1 assistant, 1 caretaker. Books loaned for 7 days. Printed catalogue in dictionary form. Classification, numerical by classes; fiction, alphabetical by authors. Charging for lending, ledger; reference, application forms. The Technical Instruction Act has been adopted.

LIBRARIAN: Herbert Walker, born at Hanley in 1872. Trained in Hanley Public Library from 1886-93. Librarian at Longton since 1893.

LOUGHBOROUGH, Leicestershire. — Population, 18,196. Acts adopted in 1885. Library opened in January, 1886. Contains 7250 vols., of which 5500 are for lending and 1750 for reference. Borrowers, 1400. Staff, 2: librarian and 1 assistant. Books loaned for 7 days. Printed catalogue in dictionary form. Classification, numerical in main classes. Charging for lending, indicator; reference, application forms. Has a small museum (1896) and a local collection.

LIBRARIAN: George H. Andrews, born at Anstey, near Leicester, in 1873. Trained in the Loughborough Public Library.

LOWESTOFT, Suffolk.—Population, 23,347. Acts adopted in 1891, but no action taken towards establishing a Library.

LURGAN, Armagh, Ireland.—Population, 11,500. Acts adopted in 1891. Rooms opened in October, 1895. Contains 800 vols. which have not yet been catalogued. Has a collection of natural history objects.

Mr. William White is the present hon. secretary.

LUTON, Bedfordshire.—Population, 30,000. Acts adopted

and rooms opened in 1894. Contains 1800 vols., of which 1650 are for lending and 150 for reference. Staff, 2: librarian and caretaker. Books loaned for 14 days. Printed catalogue in classified form. Classification, alphabetical. Charging for lending, ledger; reference, application forms.

LIBRARIAN: David Wootton, born at Renhold, Bedfordshire, 11th December, 1857. He was previous to 1894, for about 12 years, librarian of the Luton Subscripton Library.

MACCLESFIELD, Cheshire. — Population, 36,007. Acts adopted in July, 1874. Building opened in May, 1876. Contains 17,020 vols., of which 12,366 are for lending and 4654 for reference. Borrowers, 1576. Staff, 3: librarian, 1 assistant, 1 caretaker. Books loaned for 14 days. Printed catalogue in classified form. MS. catalogue in guard books. Classification, alphabetical by authors. Charging for lending, ledger; reference, application forms.

LIBRARIAN: Atherton Brunt, born at Lambeth, London, 21st August, 1866.

MAIDSTONE, Kent.—Population, 32,140. Acts adopted in 1855. Library opened in 1858. Has 17,595 vols., of which 2595 are for lending and 15,000 for reference. Borrowers, 852. Staff, 2: librarian, 1 assistant. Books loaned for 14 days. Printed catalogue in dictionary form. MS. catalogue on cards. Classification, alphabetical by authors in subjects. Charging for lending, indicator; reference, application forms. Has a museum and art gallery.

LIBRARIAN: Frederick V. James.

MANCHESTER, Lancashire.—Population, 505,368. Acts adopted in 1852, and Library first opened, 6th September, 1852. It has 15 branch Libraries. Contains 257,459 vols., of which 152,767 are for lending, etc., at the branches, and 104,692 for reference. Borrowers, 49,516. Staff, 138: librarian, 101 assistants, 34 caretakers, attendants and cleaners, and 2 bookbinders. Books loaned for 7 (fiction) and 14 (other classes) days. No fines. Printed catalogues in dictionary form. MS. catalogue in guard books. Classification of Lending Libraries, numerical in main classes; Reference Library is being classified on the Dewey method. Charging for lending, ledgers; reference, application forms, and has a considerable number of books on open shelves. Has juvenile reading-rooms at all the branches, first started in January, 1878, and ladies' rooms at 2 of the branches. Special collections of Chinese books; on cotton trade; English dialects; gipsies; Lancashire; shorthand, etc., of which separate catalogues have been issued or are in the course of preparation. The Technical Instruction Act has been adopted.

MANCHESTER CENTRAL PUBLIC LIBRARY. By permission of *Publishers' Circular.*

LIBRARIAN: Charles William Sutton, born at Manchester in 1848. He was appointed an assistant in the Manchester Public Libraries in 1865, and succeeded to the chief librarianship in 1879. Vice-president of the Library Association, and a contributor to its *Transactions*. He is author of a *List of Lancashire Authors*, 1876, and contributes articles to the *Dictionary of National Biography*, etc.

MR. C. W. SUTTON, LIBRARIAN, PUBLIC LIBRARIES, MANCHESTER. From photo by Mr. W. H. Fischer, Withington.

MANSFIELD, Nottinghamshire.—Population, 15,925. Acts adopted in March, 1890. Library opened in 1891. Contains 3609 vols., of which 2378 are for lending and 1231 for reference. Borrowers, 1340. Staff, 1: librarian. Books loaned for 14, 21, and 28 days. Printed catalogue in dictionary form. Classification, numerical in main classes. Charging for lending, indicator; reference, signature book and application forms.

LIBRARIAN: William Gouk, born at Southampton, 12th

November, 1827.   Was employed in the bookselling trade from
1840.   Librarian at Mansfield since 1891.   Author of "The

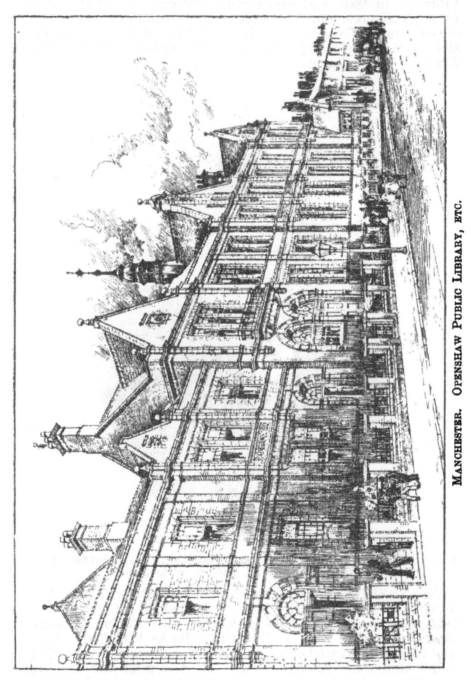

MANCHESTER.   OPENSHAW PUBLIC LIBRARY, ETC.

Libraries of Mansfield, Old and New," a paper read before the
North Midland Library Association.

MIDDLE CLAYDON, Buckinghamshire.—Population, 205. Acts adopted in September, 1893. Library opened, 13th October, 1893. Contains 1100 vols. There is an hon. librarian and 1 hon. assistant. Books loaned for 14 days. Printed catalogue in classified form. MS. catalogues in guard book. Classification, numerical in subjects. Charging system, open access. A special feature in this, the smallest village which has adopted the Acts, has been talks on the books in the Library.

LIBRARIAN: Miss Ellin Verney, born at London in 1873. Daughter of Sir Edmund and Lady Verney. Author of "The Public Libraries Act of 1892 in a Small Country Parish," read at the Cardiff meeting of the Library Association and printed in the *Library*, 1895, p. 353.

MIDDLESBROUGH, Yorkshire.—Population, 75,532. Acts adopted, 23rd November, 1870. Reading-room and Library opened in 1871. Contains 18,168 vols., of which 13,862 are for lending and 4306 for reference. Borrowers, 3925. Staff, 4: librarian, 2 assistants, 1 caretaker. Books loaned for 14 days. Printed catalogue in dictionary form. MS. catalogue in slip books. Classification, by size and numerical. Charging for lending, indicator; reference, application forms. Has a museum and a ladies' room.

LIBRARIAN: Baker Hudson, appointed in October, 1889. He was previously an accountant at Redcar.

MIDDLETON, Lancashire. — Population, 21,310. Acts adopted in 1887. Library opened in 1889. Contains over 5000 vols.

MIDDLEWICH, Cheshire.—Population, 3704. Acts adopted in February, 1889. Library opened in March, 1890. Contains about 3000 vols. Borrowers, 372. Staff, 3: librarian, 1 assistant, 1 caretaker. Books loaned for 14 days. Printed catalogue in classified form. Classification, subjects and numerical. Charging for lending, indicator. There is a Workman's Institute in connection with the Library, in which is a public recreation room, supported out of the rate. The Technical Instruction Acts have been adopted.

LIBRARIAN: Thomas Lawrence Drinkwater, born at Middlewich, 4th June, 1862. Not trained in Library work, and only devotes a small portion of his time to the Library.

MILE END, London.—Population, 111,060. Acts adopted in January, 1896.

MILLOM, Cumberland.—Population, 8895. Acts adopted in February, 1887. Library opened in October, 1887. Contains 7000 vols. Borrowers, 905. Staff, 3: librarian, 1 assistant, 1 caretaker. Books loaned for 14 days. Printed catalogue in classified dictionary form. Classification, numerical by subjects. Charging for lending, cards; reference, application forms. Students' extra tickets are issued, and the Technical Instruction Acts have been adopted.

LIBRARIAN: Alfred J. Hutchinson, born at the Whinns, Cumberland, 28th February, 1873. Trained in Library work at the Barrow-in-Furness Public Library. Librarian at Millom since the opening.

MORLEY, Yorkshire.—Population, 21,100. Acts adopted in 1892.

MOSS SIDE, Lancashire.—Population, 23,833. Acts adopted in 1887. Foundation stone of Library building laid, 5th September, 1896.

NANTWICH, Cheshire.—Population, 7412. Acts adopted in August, 1887. Library opened in December, 1888. Contains 3642 vols., of which 2649 are for lending and 993 for reference. Borrowers, 310. Staff, 2: librarian and 1 assistant. Books loaned for 14 days. Printed catalogue in dictionary form. Classification, alphabetical by authors. Charging for lending, indicator; reference, application forms. The Technical Instruction Acts have been adopted.

LIBRARIAN: Annie Jackson, who is a native of Nantwich.

NELSON, Lancashire.—Population, 22,700. Acts adopted in 1889. Newsroom opened in November, 1889; Lending Library in April, 1890. Contains 6914 vols., of which 6186 are for lending and 728 for reference. Borrowers, 1500. Staff, 2: librarian and 1 caretaker. Books loaned for 14 days. Printed catalogue in dictionary form. Classification, numerical in main classes. Charging for lending, indicator; reference, application forms. Has a ladies' room, and lectures. The Technical Instruction Acts were adopted in 1890.

LIBRARIAN: David Rushton, born at Barrowford, Lancs, in 1848. He was previously connected with the Nelson Liberal Club, 1881-86, and Nelson Co-operative Society, 1885-89, and compiled their catalogues.

NENAGH, Tipperary, Ireland.—Population, 5000. Acts adopted in March, 1895.

NEWARK-ON-TRENT, Nottinghamshire. — Population, 14,457. Acts adopted in 1881. Library opened in 1883. Contains about 7000 vols.

NEWBURGH, Fife, Scotland.—Population, 2000. Acts adopted in 1895. Has a collection of books, etc., bequeathed by Dr. Alex. Laing.

NEWCASTLE-UNDER-LYME, Staffordshire.—Population, 18,452. Acts adopted in 1884. Library opened in 1891. Contains 4248 vols., of which 3930 are for lending and 318 for reference. Borrowers, 830. Staff, 2: librarian, 1 caretaker. Books loaned for 10 days. Printed catalogue in dictionary form. Classification, numerical in main classes. Charging for lending, ledger; reference, application forms.

LIBRARIAN: Miss Alice Peacock, appointed in 1891.

NEWCASTLE-UPON-TYNE, Northumberland. — Population, 186,300. Acts adopted in 1874. Lending Library opened in 1880; Reference Library in 1884. Has a branch reading-room. Contains 84,000 vols. Borrowers about 13,000. Staff, 22: librarian, 18 assistants, 3 caretakers. Books loaned for 14 days. Printed catalogues in dictionary and classified forms, with occasional class lists. MS. catalogues on cards and in slip books. Classification, numerical in main classes. Charging for lending, indicator; reference, application forms. Has a local collection, a ladies' room at the branch, and a juvenile Library (1880). The Technical Instruction Acts have been adopted, and grants have been received from the excise duties.

LIBRARIAN: Basil Anderton, B.A. of London University. He was sub-librarian at Newcastle, and succeeded Mr. Haggerston as chief in 1894.

NEW MILLS, Derbyshire.—Population, 6700. Acts adopted in 1893.

NEWINGTON, London (Walworth Road, S.E.).—Population, 120,939. Acts adopted in October, 1890. Building opened, 28th November, 1893. Contains 13,696 vols., of which 11,556 are for lending, 2050 for reference, and 90 for the boys' room. Borrowers, 5290. Staff, 9: librarian, 7 assistants, 1 caretaker. Books loaned for 7 days. Printed catalogue, alphabetical in single-entry, chiefly subjects. MS. catalogue in guard books. Classification, numerical in main subjects in Lending Library; subjects in Reference Library. Charging for lending, cards; reference, application forms, with open access to directories, etc. Has lectures, boys' room, a monthly magazine (April, 1896), local collection, students' extra tickets, etc.

LIBRARIAN: Richard William Mould, born at Birmingham, 22nd April, 1862. Trained in the Birmingham Public Libraries, 1881-1893. Librarian at Newington since 1893. Author of prize essay on "How to make a Library known in its District," and "How to get the Acts adopted". Also papers on "How to make the Library assist the Work of Teachers," etc. Inventor of a special form of indicator and a newspaper holder.

NEWPORT, Monmouthshire. — Population, 54,707. Acts

adopted, 1870. Library opened in 1871. Has 2 branch reading-rooms. Contains 21,204 vols., of which 15,096 are for lending and 6108 for reference. Borrowers, 5524. Staff, 5: librarian, 3 assistants, 1 caretaker. Books loaned for 10 days. Printed catalogue in dictionary form. Classification, numerical in main classes. Charging for lending, indicator; reference, application forms.

LIBRARIAN: James Matthews, born at Kidderminster, 20th August, 1846. Assistant in the Birkenhead Public Library, 1868-1875. First librarian of Newport from April, 1875. Author of papers on "Book-Size Classification," "Abolishment of Classification," "Branch Libraries," etc. Inventor of a card-rack indicator, etc.

NEWRY, Ireland.—Population, 13,000. Acts adopted in July, 1895.

NEWTOWNARDS, County Down, Ireland. — Population, 9197. Acts adopted in 1895. No further steps have been taken, pending arrangements being made for housing the Library when formed.

NORTHAMPTON, Northamptonshire.—Population, 61,016. Acts adopted in 1860. Library opened in 1876. Contains 15,000 vols., of which 10,000 are for lending and 5000 for reference. Staff, 5: librarian, 3 assistants, 1 caretaker. Printed catalogue in dictionary form. Classification, numerical in main classes. Charging for lending, indicator; reference, application forms.

LIBRARIAN: T. J. George.

NORTHWICH, Cheshire.—Population, 14,914. Acts adopted in 1885. Library opened in 1885. Has a book delivery station. Contains 7778 vols., of which 6763 are for lending and 1015 for reference. Borrowers, 1450. Staff, 3: librarian, 1 assistant, 1 caretaker. Books loaned for 7 and 14 days. Printed catalogues issued in dictionary and classified forms. MS. catalogue in slip books. Classification, numerical in main classes. Charging for lending, indicator; reference, application forms. Has a museum and art gallery; lectures; and a separate collection of works on the manufacture, etc., of salt, and an exposition (in museum style) of salt manufacture. The Technical Instruction Acts and Museum Acts have been adopted.

LIBRARIAN: Thomas J. Yarwood, born at Northwich in 1872. Assistant at Northwich from 1885 to 1893. Librarian from 1893.

NORWICH, Norfolk.—Population, 100,970. Acts adopted in 1850. Library first opened in 1857. Supplies 24 elementary schools with books. Contains 31,251 vols., of which 16,764 are for lending, 11,437 are for reference, and 3000 are in the schools. Borrowers, 3519.   Staff, 6 : librarian, 3 assistants, 2 caretakers. Books loaned for 14 days.   Printed catalogue in dictionary form.   Classification, numerical in main classes.   Charging for lending, ledger.   Has a local collection, a ladies' room, and National Home Reading Circles.   The Technical Instruction Acts, under a separate committee, have been adopted.

LIBRARIAN : George Easter.   Appointed librarian at Norwich in 1877.

NOTTINGHAM, Nottinghamshire. — Population, 213,877. Acts adopted in 1867.   Library first opened in 1868.   Now housed in a building along with the University College Museum, etc.   Has 13 branch Libraries.   Contains 81,416 vols., of which 29,186 are in the central Lending Library, 28,966 in the central Reference Library, and 23,284 in the branches.   Staff, 29 : librarian, 11 assistants, and 17 caretakers and attendants.   Books loaned for 7, 8, 9, 10, 12 and 14 days. Printed catalogues issued in dictionary form and as class lists. Classification, numerical in main classes, and subject and author.   Charging for lending, indicator; reference, application forms.   Has a local collection, a ladies' room, children's Library, Library Bulletin (July, 1896), and also collections of books on lace and hosiery, hymnology, Byron, Kirke White and Robin Hood.

LIBRARIAN : John Potter Briscoe, born at Lever Bridge, Bolton, 20th July, 1848.   Trained in the Bolton Public Libraries, where he was sub-librarian from 1866-69.   Librarian at Nottingham since 1869.   He is a F.R.H.S., vice-president of the Library Association, and has read papers on practical subjects at its meetings.   Author of *The Literature of Tim Bobbin*, 1872 ; *Nottinghamshire Facts and Fictions*, 1876-77, 2 series; *Nottinghamshire Anecdote*, 1879; *Old Nottinghamshire*, 1881-84, 2 series; *Curiosities of the Belfry*, 1883; *Gleanings from God's Acre*, 1883; guides to Nottingham, Nottingham Castle, etc.   Editor of *Midland Notes*, 1879-82, 4 series; *Sonnets and Songs of Robert Millhouse*, 1883.

OLDBURY, Worcestershire. — Population, 20,348.   Acts adopted in July, 1888.   Library opened, 9th September, 1891. Contains 4097 vols., of which 3985 are for lending and 112 for reference.   Borrowers, 1171.   Staff, 3 : librarian, 1 assistant, 1 caretaker.   Books loaned for 7 days.   Printed catalogue in author and classified order.   Classification, numerical and author alphabetical.   Charging for lending, ledger; reference, application forms.   The Technical Instruction Acts have been adopted.

LIBRARIAN : George Henry Burton, born at Birmingham in 1860.   Trained in the Birmingham Public Libraries.   First librarian at Oldbury.

OLDHAM, Lancashire.—Population, 131,463. Established under a special Act in 1865. New Library opened in 1885. Has 1 branch and 3 delivery stations. Contains 43,427 vols., of which 18,854 are for lending, 17,000 for reference, and 7573 are in the branch. Borrowers, 4918. Staff, 11: librarian, 6 assistants, and 4 caretakers. Books loaned for 8 and 14 days. Printed catalogue in dictionary form. MS. catalogue on cards. Classification on the Dewey system. Charging for lending, cards and indicator for fiction; reference, application forms. Has a museum, art gallery, lectures, a ladies' room and a local collection.

LIBRARIAN: Thomas W. Hand, trained in the Manchester Public Libraries from 1866, and in 1875 appointed librarian of the chief Lending Library of that city. In 1885 he was appointed librarian and curator at Oldham. Member of Council of the Library Association.

OSWESTRY, Shropshire.—Population, 8496. Acts adopted in May, 1890. Temporary building opened in April, 1891. Present building opened, 19th January, 1895. Contains 9800 vols., of which 9200 are for lending and 600 for reference. Borrowers, 720. Staff, 3: librarian, 1 assistant, 1 caretaker. Books loaned for 14 days. Printed catalogue in dictionary form. Classification, numerical. Charging for lending, indicator; reference, open access.

LIBRARIAN: Thomas Pomeroy Diamond, born at Devonport in 1838. Was for 2 years in a Library, but afterwards connected with the press. Librarian at Oswestry since May, 1894.

OXFORD, Oxfordshire.—Population, 45,741. Acts adopted in 1852. Library first opened in 1854. New building opened in 1896. Has a branch Library at Summertown. Contains over 10,000 vols. Borrowers, 845. Staff, 5: librarian and 4 assistants. Books loaned for 15 days. Printed catalogue in dictionary form. MS. catalogue on cards. Classification, numerical in main classes. Charging for lending, indicator; reference, application forms. Has a ladies' room opened in February, 1896.

LIBRARIAN: Thomas Harwood, born at Oxford in 1832. Was trained as a publisher.

PAISLEY, Scotland.—Population, 66,427. Acts adopted in 1867. Library opened in 1871. Contains about 30,000 vols. Charging for lending, indicator.

PENARTH, Wales.—Acts adopted in April, 1894.

PENGE, London (Anerley, S.E.).—Population, 21,308. Acts adopted in 1891. Library opened in 1892. Contains 5500 vols., of which 5000 are for lending and 500 for reference. Borrowers, 3400. Staff, 4: librarian, 2 assistants, 1 caretaker. Books loaned for 14 days. Printed catalogue in dictionary form. Classification, numerical in main classes. Charging for lending, indicator; reference, application forms.

LIBRARIAN; William Bridle. Trained at Cardiff Public Library, 1879-88. Sub-librarian at Battersea Public Library, 1888-92. Librarian at Penge since 11th May, 1892.

PENRITH, Cumberland.—Population, 8981. Acts adopted in 1882. Library opened, January, 1883. Contains 7501 vols., of which 6822 are for lending and 679 for reference. Borrowers, 1018. Staff, 2: librarian and 1 assistant. Books loaned for 14 days. Printed catalogue in dictionary form. Classification, numerical. Charging for lending, ledger; reference, open access.

LIBRARIAN: John George Dixon Stuart, a native of Carlisle. He was formerly secretary and librarian of the Penrith Working Men's Reading-Room.

PENZANCE, Cornwall.—Population, 12,432. Acts adopted in February, 1893. Library opened, 14th October, 1893. Contains 7500 vols., of which 7000 are for lending and 500 for reference. Borrowers, 2350. Staff, 3: librarian, 1 assistant, 1 caretaker. Books loaned for 15 days. Printed catalogue in dictionary form. Classification by subjects. Charging for lending, cards; reference, application forms. Has a collection of 130 vols. of books for the blind.

LIBRARIAN: Charles Henry Benn, born at London, 18th November, 1872. Trained in Clerkenwell Public Library, 1888-93. Librarian at Penzance since June, 1893.

PERTH, Perthshire, Scotland.—Population, 29,919. Acts adopted in 1896. Building being erected from bequest of the late Mr. Sandeman. Library not formed.

LIBRARIAN: John Minto, M.A., formerly of Aberdeen Public Library.

PETERBOROUGH, Northamptonshire.—Population, 25,171. Acts adopted in 1891. Reading-room opened in September, 1892; Library opened, 10th April, 1893. Contains 4100 vols., of which 3300 are for lending and 800 for reference. Borrowers, 2625. Staff, 4: librarian, 2 assistants, 1 caretaker. Books issued for 14 days. Printed catalogue issued as annotated class lists. MS. catalogue on cards. Classification on the Dewey system. Charging for lending, indicator; reference, open access and application forms. Half-hour talks to readers on the books in the Library are given in the winter time.

LIBRARIAN: Louis Stanley Jast, born at Halifax in 1868. Trained in the Halifax Public Libraries, where he was chief assistant for several years, and librarian of the Akroyd Park branch, 1888-92. Librarian at Peterborough since 1892. Author of papers, read before the Library Association, on "Classification in Public Libraries, with special reference to the Dewey Decimal System" (printed in the *Library*, June, 1895); "The Dewey Classification in the Reference Library and in an Open Lending Library" (printed in the *Library*, August, 1896); "Revival of the Class List," 1896, etc.

PETERHEAD, Aberdeenshire, Scotland. — Population, 12,195. Acts adopted in 1890.

PLEASLEY, Derbyshire.—Population, 1500. Acts adopted in 1895.

PLYMOUTH, Devon.—Population, 89,686. Acts adopted in 1871. Library first opened in August, 1876. The building underwent extensive alterations in 1895-96. Has 2 evening reading-rooms and about 20 Lending Libraries attached to board and other schools. Contains 40,161 vols., of which 22,594 are for lending and 17,567 for reference. Borrowers, 2500. Staff, 13: librarian, 6 assistants, 6 caretakers and attendants. Books loaned for 7 days. Printed catalogue in dictionary form and class lists. MS. catalogues in guard and slip books. Classification, numerical in main classes. Charging for lending, cards and special indicator; reference, application forms, readers' medals, and partial open access. Has a special collection (about 8000 vols.) of books relating to Devon and Cornwall, and a ladies' department. The Technical Instruction, and Museum Acts have been adopted by the town.

LIBRARIAN: William Henry Kearley Wright, born at Plymouth, 15th September, 1844. Has been librarian at Plymouth since March, 1876. Vice-president of the Library Association, Secretary of the Ex-Libris Society, and a contributor of papers to the *Transactions* of both. Editor of *The Western Antiquary* and *The Ex-Libris Journal*. Author of *West Country Poets*, numerous guide books, poems, papers on antiquarian and local subjects, etc., etc.

PONTYPRIDD, Glamorgan, Wales. — Population, 19,971. Acts adopted in 1887 and Library opened in same year. Contains 4150 vols., of which 4000 are for lending and 150 for reference. Borrowers, 1000. Staff, 2: librarian and 1 caretaker. Books loaned for 14 days. Printed catalogue in dictionary form. MS. catalogue in guard books. Classification by subjects. Charging for lending, ledger; reference, application forms. Has a ladies' room.

LIBRARIAN: George Hughes, born at Merthyr in 1842. Was for 16 years a bookseller.

POOLE, Dorset.—Population, 15,405. Acts adopted in 1885. Library opened in 1886. Contains about 7000 vols. Charging for lending, indicator.

POPLAR, London (High Street, Poplar, E.).—Population, 57,759. Acts adopted in December, 1890. Temporary reading-rooms opened in December, 1892. Permanent building opened, October, 1894. Has 1 evening branch Library. Contains 10,755 vols., of which 7174 are in the central Lending Library; 1081 in the Reference Library; and 2500 at the branch. Staff, 8: librarian, 6 assistants, 1 caretaker. Books loaned for 14 days. Printed catalogue in dictionary form. Classification, numerical in main classes. Charging for lending, indicator; reference, application forms.

LIBRARIAN: Harry Rowlatt, born at Leeds. Assistant in the Leeds Library (Proprietary), February, 1877, to January, 1888. Sub-librarian of Kensington Public Library, January, 1888, to November, 1891. Librarian at Poplar since November, 1891. Joint inventor, with Mr. Herbert Jones, of the periodical rack shown on page 397 of Greenwood's *Public Libraries*, 1891.

PORTSMOUTH, Hampshire.—Population, 159,251. Acts adopted in 1876. Library opened in 1883. Has 2 branch Libraries. Contains 48,802 vols., of which 31,971 are in the central Lending Library, 6411 in the Reference Library, and 10,420 in the branches. Borrowers, 19,213. Staff, 19: librarian, 13 assistants, 1 caretaker, 4 bookbinders. Books loaned for 7 and 14 days. Printed catalogues in dictionary form. MS. catalogues in album and on cards. Classification, numerical in main classes. Charging for lending, indicator; reference, application forms. Has a ladies' room, local collections, etc. The Technical Instruction Acts have been adopted.

LIBRARIAN: Tweed Daniel Abraham Jewers, born at Great Bentley, near Colchester, in 1841. Had some training in Dale's Library, Farnham, in 1856, and under Mr. A. Cotgreave. Librarian in the army for a time. Librarian at Portsmouth since 1883. Inventor of a catalogue slip tray; finding list of new books; magazine reading cases, etc.

PRESTON, Lancashire.—Population, 111,000. Acts adopted in 1878. First opened in January, 1879. Contains 39,000 vols., of which 20,000 are for lending and 19,000 for reference. Staff, 13: librarian, 5 assistants, 7 caretakers and attendants. Books loaned for 14 days. Printed catalogue in dictionary form. MS. catalogue on cards. Classification, numerical in main classes. Charging for lending, ledger; reference, signature book and application forms. There are a museum, art gallery, and ladies' room contained in the fine Harris building. The Technical Instruction Act has been adopted but is not worked by the Library Committee.

LIBRARIAN: William Storey Bramwell, formerly librarian

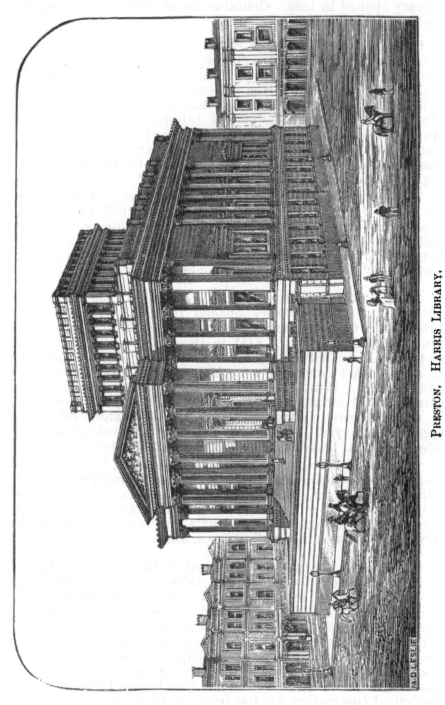

PRESTON, HARRIS LIBRARY.

of the Preston Literary and Philosophical Institution, which became merged in the Public Library on the adoption of the Acts. Mr. Bramwell has been librarian and superintendent since 1879.

PUTNEY, London.—Population, 20,566. Acts adopted in 1887. Library opened in 1888. Contains about 6000 vols.

LIBRARIAN: C. F. Tweney.

QUEENBOROUGH, Kent.—Population, 1153. Acts adopted and Library opened in 1887. Contains 875 vols. Books loaned for 14 days. No catalogue yet. Charging system, open access.

LIBRARIAN: Alfred Hall, born at Queenborough in 1836. Had no previous training.

RAMSGATE, Kent.—Population, 24,700. Acts adopted in July, 1894.

RATHMINES AND RATHGAR Township, Ireland.—Population, 27,796. Acts adopted and rooms opened in 1887. Contains 8000 vols., of which 5000 are for lending and 3000 for reference. Borrowers, 2043. Staff, 3: librarian, 2 assistants. Books loaned for 14 days. Printed catalogue, classified, with author index. Classification, numerical and alphabetical by authors. Charging for lending, open access and ledger; reference, application forms.

LIBRARIAN: John J. Loton, born at Rathmines, Dublin, 19th October, 1853. Educated at Diocesan College, Dublin, and Catholic University of Ireland.

RAWMARSH, Yorkshire. — Population, 12,000. Acts adopted in December, 1892.

READING, Berkshire.—Population, 60,054. Acts adopted in May, 1877. Library opened in February, 1883. Contains 26,590 vols., of which 15,700 are for lending, 3400 are in the juvenile Library, and 7490 are for reference. Borrowers, 6748, of whom 1477 are juveniles. Staff, 7: librarian, 5 assistants, 1 caretaker. Books loaned for 14 days. Printed catalogue in dictionary form. MS. catalogue on placards and in guard books. Classification, by subjects. Charging for lending, indicator; reference, application forms. Has a museum and art gallery, juvenile Library, students' extra tickets, special students' room. The Museum Act has been adopted, and grants of £100 have been received from the excise duties.

LIBRARIAN: William Henry Greenhough, born at Manchester. Trained in Library work at Salford. Librarian at Stockport from 1876 to 1882. Librarian of Reading since 1882. Author of a paper on the "Ventilation, Heating and Lighting of Libraries," read before the Library Association.

REDRUTH, Cornwall.—Population, 10,324. Acts adopted

in 1891.   Library opened, 24th May, 1895.   Contains 1700 vols.,

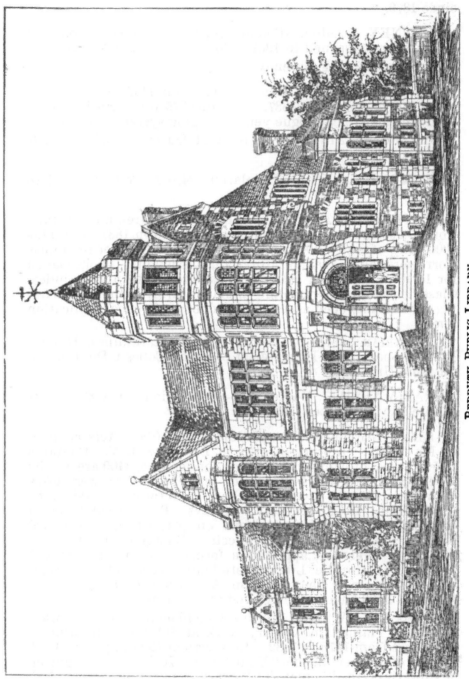

REDRUTH PUBLIC LIBRARY.

of which 1600 are for lending and 100 for reference.   Borrowers,

950. Staff, 1: librarian. Books loaned for 14 days. Printed catalogue in dictionary form. Classification, numerical in one series. Charging for lending, ledger; reference, application forms. Local collection forming.

LIBRARIAN: William Gifford Hale, born at Grafton, near Marlborough, 21st November, 1866. Evening assistant in Rochdale Public Library. Librarian at Redruth since 1895.

RICHMOND, Surrey.—Population, 26,859. Acts adopted, 18th March, 1879. Library opened, 18th June, 1881. Has branch reading-rooms and delivery stations at Kew and Petersham. Contains 22,050 vols., of which 11,673 are for lending, 9921 for reference, and 456 in branches. Borrowers, 3244. Staff, 6: librarian, 4 assistants, 1 porter. Books loaned for 7 days. Printed catalogue in dictionary form. MS. reference catalogue in slip books (sheaf system). Classification, numerical in Lending; author, alphabetical under classes in Reference Library. Charging for lending, indicator; reference, application forms. Has a ladies' room, and a special collection.

LIBRARIAN: Albert A. Barkas, born in Jersey, 26th August, 1861. Trained in Birmingham Public Library for 10 years. Librarian at Richmond since 1890.

ROCHDALE, Lancashire.—Population, 71,401. Acts adopted 25th May, 1870. Library opened in 1872. Contains 49,407 vols., of which 35,309 are for lending, 12,838 for reference, and 1260 in special boys' reference room. Borrowers, 6000. Staff, 5: librarian, 3 assistants, 1 caretaker. Books loaned for 14 days. Printed catalogues in dictionary form. Classification, numerical in main classes. Charging for lending, special ledger; reference, application forms. Has a ladies' room, juvenile room and local collections, including all but complete set of "Tim Bobbin's" works, works on wool, etc.

LIBRARIAN: George Hanson, born at Rochdale, 20th June, 1845. Trained as a bookseller. Librarian of Rochdale Equitable Pioneers' Society, 1866-71, and of Public Library from 1871.

ROCHESTER, Kent.—Population, 26,290. Acts adopted in February, 1894. Library opened, 10th October, 1894. Contains 2969 vols., of which 2903 are for lending and 66 for reference. Borrowers, 1232. Staff, 1: librarian. Books loaned for 14 days. Printed catalogue in numerical order. Classification, numerical. Charging for lending, indicator. There is a museum, and the Technical Instruction Acts have been adopted.

LIBRARIAN: William Richard Bartley, born at Chatham, 16th June, 1861. He was in the Garrison Military Library at Chatham, from 1874-88. Librarian of Jubilee Free Library, Rochester, from 1888 till appointed to the Public Library in 1894.

ROTHERHAM, Yorkshire. — Population, 42,050. Acts adopted in 1876. Library opened in 1879. Contains 13,000 vols., of which 12,000 are for lending and 1000 for reference. Borrowers, 2000. Staff, 3: librarian, 1 assistant, 1 caretaker. Books loaned for 7 and 14 days. Printed catalogue in dictionary form. Classification by size, numerical. Charging for lending, indicator; reference, signature book, etc. Has a Reading Circle, of which an account is published in *A Series of Letters and Papers on Books*, 1895-96.

LIBRARIAN: John Ridal.

ROTHERHITHE, London (Lower Road, S.E.).—Population, 40,379. Acts adopted in November, 1887. Reading-rooms opened in October, 1890. Library opened, May, 1891. Delivery station opened in March, 1896. Contains 5227 vols., of which 4167 are for lending and 1060 for reference. Borrowers, 2565. Staff, 6: librarian, 4 assistants, 1 caretaker. Books loaned for 7 and 14 days. Printed catalogue in dictionary form. MS. catalogue in guard book. Classification, numerical in main classes and author alphabetical. Charging for lending, indicator; reference, application forms. Has a ladies' room (1890) and a collection of local books, prints, etc.

LIBRARIAN: Herbert Archer Shuttleworth, born at Perry Barr, Staffordshire, 26th August, 1865. Trained in Birmingham Public Libraries and was branch librarian at Harborne, 1892-93, and Deritend, 1893-95. Librarian at Rotherhithe since October, 1895. Inventor of an adjustable hanging reading-stand for newspapers.

ROTHWELL, Northamptonshire.—Acts adopted in March, 1894. Library opened in 1896 in old Market House of Sir Thos. Tresham. Contains about 1800 vols. Charging for lending, and reference, open access.

LIBRARIAN: Miss E. Tebbutt.

RUGBY, Warwickshire.—Population, 11,262. Acts adopted in June, 1890. Building opened, 8th February, 1891. Contains 3356 vols., of which 2777 are for lending and 579 for reference. Borrowers, 750. Staff, 2: librarian and 1 attendant. Books loaned for 14 days. Printed catalogue in dictionary form. Classification, numerical in main classes. Charging for lending, indicator; reference, application forms.

LIBRARIAN: James William Kenning.

RUNCORN, Cheshire.—Population, 20,050. Acts adopted in 1881. Library opened in 1882. Contains 7859 vols., of which 6940 are for lending and 919 for reference. Borrowers, 777. Staff, 2: librarian, 1 caretaker. Books loaned for 14 days. Printed catalogue in dictionary form, also classified hand-lists. Classification, numerical in main classes. Charging for lending, indicator for fiction, cards for other classes; reference, application forms. Has lectures, and the Technical Instruction Acts have been adopted under a special Committee.

LIBRARIAN : John Daniel Jones, born at Runcorn, 18th March, 1850. Not trained in Library work. Author of *Half Hours in the Runcorn Free Library, a Guide to Readers*, 1893.

ST. ALBANS, Hertfordshire. — Population, 12,895. Acts adopted in 1878. Library opened in 1883.

ROTHWELL, NORTHAMPTONSHIRE, PUBLIC LIBRARY.

ST. AUSTELL, Cornwall.—Population, 4500. Acts adopted in 1895.

ST. GEORGE, HANOVER SQUARE, London (Buckingham Palace Road, S.W.). — Population, 79,967. Acts adopted in June, 1890. Central Library opened in July, 1894. Branch in South Audley Street opened in July, 1895. Contains 26,325 vols., of which 19,000 are for lending and 7325 for reference. Borrowers, 7398. Staff, 17 : librarian, 12 assistants, 4 hall-keepers, etc. Books loaned for 14 days. Printed catalogues in dictionary form. MS. catalogues of Reference Libraries on cards and in slip books. Classification, numerical in main classes in Lending; chief divisions of Dewey system in Reference Libraries. Charging for lending, indicator, with a supplementary posting against the borrowers on separate series of cards; reference, application forms. Has a natural

St. George, Hanover Square, Public Library, Central Building.   From photo by Bedford Lemere Co.

history museum, ladies' rooms and children's Lending Libraries; extra tickets allowed for the borrowing of music.

St. George, Hanover Square, Central Reference Library. From photo by Bedford Lemere Co.

LIBRARIAN: Frank Pacy. Trained in the Public Libraries of Birmingham and Wigan, and for many years librarian of Richmond Public Library. Librarian at St. George since 1890. Member of Council of the Library Association and a contributor to its *Transactions*.

ST. GEORGE-IN-THE-EAST, London.—Population, 47,506. Acts adopted in March, 1896.

ST. GEORGE-THE-MARTYR, London. — Population, 60,278. Acts adopted in March, 1896.

ST. GILES AND ST. GEORGE, London (Holborn, W.C.).—Population, 38,237. Acts adopted in 1891. Temporary premises opened in 1892. Permanent building opened in 1896. Contains 6558 vols., of which 5788 are for lending and 770 for reference. Borrowers, 1300. Staff, 8: librarian, 5 assistants, 2 caretakers. Books loaned for 10 and 14 days. MS. catalogue in guard books. Classification, numerical in main classes with fiction in author alphabet. Charging for lending, cards; reference, application forms. Students' extra tickets issued.

LIBRARIAN: William Arthur Taylor, born at Macclesfield in 1864. Trained in the Macclesfield Public Library, 1876-81, and Manchester Public Library, 1881-86. Librarian of Hanley Public Library, 1886-88; of Medical Library, Owens College, Manchester, 1888-93. Librarian of St. Giles since 1893.

ST. HELEN'S, Lancashire.—Population, 71,288. Established under the "St. Helen's Improvement Act" of 1869, and incorporated with a Mechanics' Institution founded in 1854. Present Library building opened in August, 1877. Has 3 branch Libraries, at Sutton, Thatto Heath and Parr. Contains 26,716 vols., of which 15,647 are in the central lending, 5141 for reference, and 5928 in the branches. Borrowers, 4000. Staff, 8: librarian and 7 assistants. Books loaned for 7 days. Printed catalogue in dictionary form. Classification, numerical in main classes with fiction in author alphabet. Charging for lending, indicator; reference, application forms. Has a museum, lectures, ladies and boys' reading-rooms, and has given book exhibitions.

LIBRARIAN: Alfred Lancaster, born at Bolton, 9th September, 1855. Trained in Bolton Public Library, 1874-82. Librarian at St. Helen's from February, 1882. Author of papers on "Free Libraries and Technical Education"; "On the Advantages of Occasional Exhibition of the more Rare and Valuable Books in Public Libraries," contributed to the Library Association; a book entitled *Dr. Adam Clarke's Residence at Millbrook, Eccleston*, and various papers on literary and other topics.

ST. IVES, Cornwall.—Population, 6100. Acts adopted in 1895. Building being erected by Mr. Passmore Edwards.

ST. MARTIN-IN-THE-FIELDS, London (St. Martin's Lane, W.C.).—Population, 16,716, including St. Paul, Covent Garden, which adopted the Acts in 1893 and is served by St. Martin.

Acts adopted for St. Martin, 10th February, 1887. Temporary premises opened, 1st January, 1889. Permanent building opened, 12th February, 1891. Contains 27,628 vols., of which

12,101 are for lending and 15,527 for reference. Borrowers, 1817. Staff, 9: librarian, 6 assistants, 2 commissionaires. Books loaned for 15 days. Printed catalogue in dictionary form. MS. catalogue on cards. Classification, numerical. Charging for lending, indicator; reference, open access. Has a fine collection of local prints, etc.

LIBRARIAN: Thomas Mason, born at Aberdeen in 1857. Educated at Arbroath. In 1877 he became senior assistant in the Mitchell Library, Glasgow, and in 1881 librarian of Stirling's Library, Glasgow. Afterwards, in 1886, he was also appointed librarian of Baillie's Institution, Glasgow. Librarian of St. Martin-in-the-Fields since 1888. Member of Council of the Library Association and contributor of many papers to its *Transactions.* Author of *Free Libraries of Scotland,* Glasgow, 1880; *Public and Private Libraries of Glasgow,* 1885; *Adam Dickson* (a novel), Glasgow, 1888; *Royal Guide to the City of Glasgow,* 1888, etc. He also edited several selections from Dickens and other popular writers. Mr. Mason is also librarian of the Royal Historical Society, and honorary librarian of the Savage Club.

ST. PAUL, Covent Garden, London.—Acts adopted in 1893. Now comprised in St. Martin-in-the-Fields.

ST. SAVIOUR, Southwark, London (Southwark Bridge Road, S.E.).—Population, 12,301. Acts adopted in November, 1891. Library building opened, November, 1894. Contains 9484 vols., of which 8912 are for lending and 572 for reference. Borrowers, 1474. Staff, 6: librarian, 3 assistants, 2 caretakers. Books loaned for 14 days. Printed catalogue in dictionary form. MS. catalogue on placards and in slip books (sheaf system). Classification, numerical by subjects. Charging for lending, indicator with card register of borrowers' reading; reference, application forms. Has a special ladies' room, and issues students' extra tickets (1894).

LIBRARIAN: Henry David Roberts, born at Worcester, 6th February, 1870. Trained in the Public Library, Newcastle-on-Tyne, 1885-93. Librarian of St. Saviour since October, 1893. Secretary of the Summer School Committee of the Library Association, and author of papers on "The Library Assistant, Criticisms and Suggestions"; "Training of Library Assistants," etc.

SALE, Cheshire.—Population, 9644. Acts adopted in February, 1890. Library opened in March. 1891. Contains 6142 vols., of which 5606 are for lending and 536 for reference. Borrowers, 1860. Staff, 5: librarian, 3 assistants, 1 caretaker. Books loaned for 7 and 10 days. Printed catalogue in dictionary form. MS. catalogue in guard books. Classification, by subjects and authors in alphabetical order. Charging for lending, ledger; reference, application forms. Has classes, a juvenile room, students' extra tickets (Aug., 1895). The Technical Instruction Act has been adopted.

LIBRARIAN: George Bethell, born at Manchester, 5th September, 1869. Trained in Manchester Public Libraries, and was senior assistant in the reference department, 1889-91. Librarian at Sale since February, 1891. Appointed organising secretary for Technical Instruction in May, 1893.

SALFORD, Lancashire.—Population, 198,139. Acts adopted in 1850. Central Reference Library founded, 1849; opened, 1850. Has 6 branches, of which 2 are reading-rooms only. Contains 81,556 vols., of which 11,089 are in the central Lending, 32,186 are in the Reference Library, and 38,281 are in the branches. Borrowers, 9587. Staff, 30: librarian, 24 assistants, 5 caretakers and attendants. Books loaned for 10 days. Printed catalogue in dictionary form. MS. catalogue in guard books. Classification, by subject and alphabetical by authors. Charging for lending, ledger; reference, application forms. Has a museum, art gallery, lectures, and ladies' rooms. In 1 branch Library and 2 reading-rooms, chess and draughts are provided, while in one of the reading-rooms a smoking-room is provided. The Museum Act has been adopted.

LIBRARIAN: Benjamin Henry Mullen, born at Dublin in January, 1862. Assistant in the Science and Art Museum, Dublin, 1883-92. Curator and librarian at Salford since 1892. He is a M.A. and F.R.S.A. Author of papers on antiquarian and other subjects, contributed to periodicals, etc., and of "A Plan for the Constant Supervision of Expenditure in Public Libraries," read before the Library Association and printed in the *Library*, June, 1896.

SALISBURY, Wiltshire.—Population, 15,980. Acts adopted in 1890. Library opened in 1890. Contains 3200 vols., of which 3000 are for lending and 200 for reference. Borrowers, 2500. Staff, 2: librarian and 1 caretaker. Books loaned for 7 and 14 days. Printed catalogue in dictionary form. Classification, by size and numbers. Charging for lending, indicator; reference, application forms. The Technical Instruction and Museum Acts have been adopted.

LIBRARIAN: Oliver Langmead, born at Newport, Monmouth, 9th November, 1871. Trained in the Newport Public Library, 1888-94. Librarian at Salisbury since August, 1894. Author of a *Guide to Salisbury*, etc.

SELKIRK, Selkirkshire, Scotland.—Population, 5788. Acts adopted in October, 1888. Library opened in 1889. Contains 5480 vols., of which 5060 are for lending and 420 for reference. Borrowers, 966. Staff, 1: librarian. Books loaned for 7, 14 and 21 days. Printed catalogue in dictionary form. Classifica-

tion, by subjects and author alphabetical. Charging for lending, indicator; reference, open access.

LIBRARIAN: Mrs. Agnes Scott, who has been librarian since
1889.

SHEEPSHED, Leicestershire.—Population, 4500. Acts
adopted in January, 1896.

SHEFFIELD, Yorkshire. — Population, 324,241. Acts
adopted in October, 1853. Library first opened in 1856. Has
4 branch Libraries and a delivery station. Contains 104,952
vols., of which 32,675 are in the central Lending Library, 16,062
in the Reference Library, and 56,215 in the branches. Borrowers, 15,754. Staff, 29: librarian, 20 assistants, 5 caretakers, 3
binders. Books loaned for 7 and 14 days. Printed catalogues
issued in dictionary form and as class lists. MS. catalogue on
cards. Classification, numerical in main classes. Charging
for lending, ledger at central Library, indicator at branches;
reference, application forms. There are museums and art
galleries separately administered. Has a ladies' room; local
collection, and issues a bulletin.

LIBRARIAN: Samuel Smith, born in Yorkshire in 1855.
Trained in the Leeds Public Libraries, 1871-79. Librarian at
Worcester, 1879-94. Librarian at Sheffield since 1894. Member
of Council of the Library Association and a contributor to its
Transactions. Author of papers, etc., in numerous newspapers
and periodicals.

SHOREDITCH, London (Kingsland Road, E.).—Population,
122,348. Acts adopted in March, 1891. Newsroom at Haggerston opened in November, 1892; Library opened in May, 1893.
Hoxton premises opened in 1893-94. New buildings are being
erected at the expense of Mr. Passmore Edwards. Contains
17,081 vols., of which 12,485 are for lending and 4596 for reference. Borrowers, 3048. Staff, 11: librarian, 8 assistants, 2
caretakers. Books loaned for 14 days. Printed catalogue in
dictionary form. MS. reference catalogue on cards. Classification, by subjects, numerically. Charging for lending, indicator;
reference, application forms. At Haggerston there is an open-
air reading-room, in a large garden behind the Library, where
a covered shelter has been provided. There is a museum in
process of formation.

LIBRARIAN: William Charles Plant, a native of Leek.
Trained at Leek Public Library, 1880-88; librarian at Buxton,
1888-92; librarian at Shoreditch from January, 1892.

SHOULDHAM, Norfolk.—Population, 750. Acts adopted
in April, 1895.

SHREWSBURY, Shropshire. — Population, 26,967. Acts

adopted in 1883. Library opened in 1885. Contains about 8000 vols.

SITTINGBOURNE, Kent.—Population, 8302. Acts adopted in 1887. Library opened in 1888.

SLIGO, County Sligo, Ireland.—Population, 10,110. Acts adopted and Library opened in 1880. Contains 1600 vols. Borrowers, 50. Staff, 1: librarian. Books loaned for 7 days. Printed catalogue in numerical order, with index. Classification, alphabetical.

LIBRARIAN: David Saultey, born at Dervin House, Tyrawley, County Mayo. Had no previous training.

SMETHWICK, Staffordshire.—Population, 36,170. Acts adopted in September, 1876. Library opened in 1877. Has 2 reading-rooms. Contains 8607 vols., of which 8024 are for lending and 583 for reference. Borrowers, 1155. Staff, 3: librarian, 1 assistant, 1 caretaker. Books loaned for 7 days. Printed catalogue in dictionary form. Classification, by subjects and numbers. Charging for lending, indicator; reference, application forms. The Technical Instruction Act has been adopted.

LIBRARIAN: Joseph Bailey, born at Handsworth, 20th December, 1841. Trained at Smethwick. Died in 1896.

. SOUTHAMPTON, Hampshire.—Population (1895), 94,093. Acts adopted in June, 1887. Temporary premises opened, January, 1889. Permanent building opened in July, 1893. Branches at Northam (1895) and Shirley (1896). Contains 15,440 vols., of which 13,170 are for lending and 2270 for reference. Borrowers, 8562. Staff, 9: librarian, 6 assistants, 2 caretakers, etc. Books loaned for 14 days. Printed catalogues in dictionary form. MS. catalogue on cards. Classification, numerical in main classes. Charging for lending, indicator for fiction, cards for other classes; reference, application forms. Has a local collection, and issues students' extra tickets. The Technical Instruction Acts have been adopted by the town.

LIBRARIAN: Oswald Tatton Hopwood, born at Liverpool, 20th May, 1860. Trained at Southport Public Library from 1876, and was sub-librarian there till 1888. Librarian at Southampton since 1888. Inventor of an improved card-charging system.

SOUTHPORT, Lancashire. — Population, 43,026. Acts adopted and Library opened in 1875. Has 2 branch Libraries. Contains 26,096 vols., of which 18,834 are in the central Lending Library, 4083 in the Reference Library, and 3179 in the branches. Borrowers, 4850. Staff, 6: librarian, 3 assistants, 2 caretakers. Books loaned for 7 and 14 days. Printed catalogue in dictionary form. Classification, numerical. Charging for lending, ledger; reference, open access. Has an art gallery.

LIBRARIAN: Thomas Newman.

SOUTH SHIELDS, Durham.—Population, 78,391. Acts adopted in 1871. Library opened in 1873. Has 2 branch news-rooms. Contains 22,104 vols., of which 14,353 are for lending and 7751 for reference. Staff, 9: librarian, 5 assistants, and 3 caretakers. Books loaned for 15 days. Printed catalogue in dictionary form. Classification, numerical in main classes and alphabetical by authors. Charging for lending, indicator; reference, application forms. Has a museum, art and science classes, and a local collection. The Technical Instruction Acts have been adopted and grants have been received from the excise duties.

LIBRARIAN: Thomas Pyke, born at South Shields. For 15 years he was secretary of the first Working Men's Institute established in England, which was opened at South Shields in March, 1850. Member of the Public Library Committee from 1871; chairman, 1886-87; librarian in succession to L. Inkster] August, 1887.

SOWERBY BRIDGE, Yorkshire.—Population, 10,408. Acts adopted in April, 1893. Library opened in December, 1893. Contains 3282 vols., of which 3200 are for lending and 82 for reference. Borrowers, 1679. Staff, 2: librarian and 1 caretaker. Books loaned for 14 days. Printed catalogue in classified form. Classification, alphabetical by authors. Charging for lending, indicator; reference, application forms. The Technical Instruction Acts have been adopted.

LIBRARIAN: J. Edward Ball, born at Burwell, Cambridge-shire. Had no previous training.

STAFFORD, Staffordshire. — Population, 20,270. Acts adopted and Library opened in 1882. Contains 8143 vols., of which 6143 are for lending and 2000 for reference. Borrowers, 2300. Staff, 3: librarian, 1 assistant, 1 caretaker. Books loaned for 14 days. Printed catalogue in classified form. Classification, numerical in main classes. Charging for lending, indicator; reference, application forms. Has a museum (the Wragge), etc. The Technical Instruction Acts have been adopted.

LIBRARIAN: Thomas Jackson, a native of Stafford. He was trained to be a schoolmaster.

STALYBRIDGE, Cheshire. — Population, 26,783. Acts adopted in 1888. Library opened in 1889. Contains 11,500 vols. Borrowers, 2300. Staff, 3: librarian and 2 assistants. Books loaned for 14 days. Printed catalogue in dictionary form. MS. catalogue in guard books. Classification, numerical in main classes; fiction, author alphabetical. Charging for lending, ledger; reference, application forms. Contains collections of works on cotton manufacture and music.

LIBRARIAN: Thomas Swaine, born at Manchester, 11th November, 1864. Trained in the Manchester Athenæum. Librarian at Stalybridge since 1891.

STOCKPORT, Cheshire.—Population, 70,253. Acts adopted in 1860. Library building opened in 1875. Contains about 25,000 vols.

LIBRARIAN: J. D. Buckland.

STOCKTON-ON-TEES, Durham.—Population, 49,708. Acts adopted in 1874. Library opened in 1877. Contains 8300 vols. Borrowers, 2039. Staff, 3: librarian, 1 assistant, 1 caretaker. Books loaned for 14 days. Printed catalogue, author and classified. Classification, numerical in main classes. Charging for lending, indicator and open access; reference, open access. Has a ladies' room.

LIBRARIAN: T. H. Wright.

STOKE NEWINGTON, London (Church Street, N.).—Population ,33,485. Acts adopted, February, 1890. Temporary reading-room opened in October, 1890; permanent building opened in July, 1892. Contains 10,753 vols., of which 7282 are for lending and 3471 for reference. Borrowers, 3080. Staff, 5: librarian, 3 assistants, 1 caretaker. Books loaned for 14 days. Printed catalogue in dictionary form. Classification, numerical in main classes. Charging for lending, indicator; reference, application forms. Has a local collection.

STOKE NEWINGTON.

LIBRARIAN: George Preece, born at Minsterley, Shropshire, in 1866. Trained in Barrow-in-Furness Public Library, 1882-88. Branch librarian of Kensal Town, Chelsea, 1888-93. Librarian at Stoke Newington from 1893.

STOKE-UPON-TRENT, Staffordshire.—Population, 24,027. Acts adopted in 1875. Library opened, 7th November, 1878. Has one branch. Contains 10,900 vols., of which 8000 are for lending, 1900 for reference, and 1000 are in the branch. Borrowers, 4000. Staff, 4: librarian, 2 assistants, 1 caretaker. Books loaned for 14 days. Printed catalogue in dictionary form. Classification, numerical and author alphabetical. Charging for lending, ledger and open access; reference, application forms. Has a museum and a local collection.

LIBRARIAN: Alfred James Caddie, trained at Stoke-upon-Trent, and chief librarian there from 1888. Hon. librarian of the North Staffordshire Naturalists' Field Club and Archæological Society since 1894. Author of various historical and other papers.

STREATHAM, London (Streatham, S.W.). — Population (1896), 54,338. Acts adopted in December, 1889. Library building, presented by Henry Tate, opened, April, 1891. Contains 15,340 vols., of which 15,026 are for lending and 314 for reference. Borrowers, 5646. Staff, 6: librarian, 4 assistants, 1 caretaker. Books loaned for 14 days. Printed catalogue in dictionary form. Classification, numerical in main classes. Charging for lending, indicator.

LIBRARIAN: Thomas Everatt. Trained in the Newcastle-upon-Tyne Public Libraries, 1879-87. Librarian of Darlington Public Library, 1887-90. Librarian at Streatham since January, 1891.

STRETFORD, Lancashire.—Population, 21,800. Acts adopted in July, 1893.

SUNDERLAND, Durham. — Population, 130,921. Acts adopted in 1866, and Library opened in 1866. Contains about 20,000 vols.

LIBRARIAN: Benjamin Rowland Hill, born at Dudley Port, 21st September, 1865. Trained at Birmingham and Newcastle-upon-Tyne. Appointed to Darlington in March, 1891. Made librarian of Sunderland in 1896.

SWANSEA, Glamorganshire, Wales.—Population, 90,349. Acts adopted in 1870. Buildings opened, 1874-75. Has 6 branch Libraries, of which 4 are reading-rooms only. Contains 36,400 vols., of which 9500 are in the central Lending Library, 24,150 in the Reference Library, and 2750 in the branches. Borrowers, 2550. Staff, 12: librarian, 4 assistants, 7 caretakers and attendants. Books loaned for 7 and 14 days. Printed catalogue in dictionary form. MS. catalogue on cards. Classification, numerical in main classes. Charging for lending, indicator in central, ledger in branches; reference, application forms. Has an art gallery (1876), science and art classes (1887), free lectures (1892), Swansea Cymmrodorion (1893), and various local and other collections. The Technical Instruction Acts have been adopted.

LIBRARIAN: Samuel Edward Thompson, born at Liverpool. Trained in the Liverpool Public Libraries. Sub-librarian of the Leeds Public Libraries, 1871-80. Librarian at Swansea since 1880.

TAMWORTH, Staffordshire. — Population, 6614. Acts adopted in 1881. Library opened in 1882. Contains over 3000 vols.

TARVES, Aberdeenshire, Scotland.—Population, 2196. Acts adopted in 1883, and old Subscription Library of 1878 taken over and carried on. Contains 3250 vols., of which 2800 are for lending and 450 are in a branch. Borrowers, 252. Staff, 1: librarian. Books loaned for 4 weeks. Printed catalogue in dictionary form. Classification, alphabetical by authors. Charging for lending, ledger.

LIBRARIAN: John Young, born at Sheffield, 7th December, 1827. He was formerly librarian of the Tarves Subscription Library.

TEDDINGTON, Middlesex.—Population, 10,100. Acts adopted in 1896.

THORNABY-ON-TEES (formerly South Stockton), Yorkshire.—Population, 15,637. Acts adopted in 1890. Library building, presented by Alderman Thos. Wrighton, opened 9th November, 1893. Contains 3283 vols., of which 2573 are for lending and 710 for reference. Borrowers, 1436. Staff, 3: librarian, 1 assistant, 1 caretaker. Books loaned for 14 days. Printed catalogue in dictionary form. Classification, numerical. Charging for lending, indicator; reference, application forms and open access.

LIBRARIAN: John Thomas Williams.

THURSO, Caithness, Scotland.—Population, 3930. Acts adopted in 1872. Library opened in 1875. Contains 5620 vols., of which 5370 are for lending and 250 for reference. Borrowers, 760. Books loaned for 14 days. Printed catalogue, author and classified. MS. catalogue in guard books. Classification, by subject and author. Charging for lending, ledger; reference, open access. Has a museum and a local collection.

LIBRARIAN: Henry Manson, born at Thurso, 27th July, 1837. Had no previous training.

TIPTON, Staffordshire.—Population, 29,314. Acts adopted in 1883. Library opened in 1890.

TODMORDEN, Lancashire. — Population, 24,700. Acts adopted in May, 1896. The local Co-operative Society is going to erect a Library building and hand it over with its books to the town.

TONBRIDGE, Kent.—Population, 10,500. Acts adopted in 1881. Library opened in July, 1882. Contains 6000 vols. Borrowers, 650. Staff, 1: librarian. Books loaned for 7 and 14 days. Printed catalogue in dictionary form. Charging for lending, indicator; reference, application.

LIBRARIAN: George Pressnell, librarian of Tonbridge since June, 1884.

TOTTENHAM, Middlesex. — Population, 70,278. Acts adopted, November, 1891. Library opened in December, 1892. New building presented by Mr. Passmore Edwards. Contains 5858 vols., of which 4730 are for lending and 1128 for reference. Borrowers, 2214. Staff, 4: librarian, 2 assistants, 1 caretaker. Books loaned for 15 days. Printed catalogue in dictionary form. MS. catalogue on cards. Classification, alphabetical by authors in 8 main classes. Charging for lending, indicator; reference, application forms. Has a ladies' room, juvenile room, and a local collection.

LIBRARIAN: Frederick John West. Formerly an assistant in the Shoreditch Public Library.

TRIMDON, Durham.—Population, 4500. Acts adopted in July, 1895.

TRURO, Cornwall.—Population, 12,000. Acts adopted in February, 1886. New building presented by Mr. Passmore Edwards opened in April, 1896. Contains 4000 vols., of which 3500 are for lending and 500 for reference. Borrowers, 400. Staff, 2: librarian and 1 caretaker. Books loaned for 14 days. No printed catalogue. Charging for lending, indicator; reference, open access. Has a ladies' room and a boys' room.

LIBRARIAN: W. J. Martin, born at Truro in 1864. Had no previous training.

TUNBRIDGE WELLS, Kent.—Population, 27,900. Acts adopted in December, 1895.

TUNSTALL, Staffordshire. — Population, 15,730. Acts adopted and Library opened in 1885. Contains about 4000 vols.

TWICKENHAM, Middlesex.—Population, 16,026. Acts adopted in February, 1882. Newsroom opened in October, 1882; Library opened in February, 1883. Contains 11,600 vols., of which 9200 are for lending and 2400 for reference. Borrowers, 1250. Staff, 3: librarian and 2 assistants. Books loaned for 15 days. Printed catalogue in dictionary form. MS. catalogue on cards. Classification, numerical in main classes. Charging for lending, indicator; reference, application forms. Has a collection of the works of Pope, the poet, commenced in 1888.

LIBRARIAN: Edwin Maynard, born at Whittlesford, Cambridge, in 1840. Was for some time in the Mechanics' Institute of Newport, Monmouth, and afterwards a bookseller in London and the provinces. Librarian at Twickenham since 1887.

TYNEMOUTH, Northumberland.—Population, 46,588. Acts adopted in July, 1868. Library opened in November, 1869. Has 1 branch newsroom. Contains 28,011 vols., of which 23,716 are for lending and 4295 for reference. Borrowers, 4357. Staff, 5: librarian, 3 assistants, 1 attendant. Books loaned for 10 days. Printed catalogue in dictionary form. Classification, numerical in main classes. Charging for lending, ledger; reference, verbal application. Grants have been received from the excise duties.

LIBRARIAN: George Tidey, born at Nutfield, Surrey, 4th September, 1836. Librarian of Royal Artillery Library, Dover, 1864-68. Librarian at Tynemouth since February, 1876.

WALSALL, Staffordshire.—Population, 71,791. Acts adopted in 1857. Library opened in April, 1859. Has 1 branch. Contains 17,020 vols., of which 15,144 are for lending and 1876 for reference. Borrowers, 3500. Staff, 3: librarian, 1 assistant, 1 caretaker. Books loaned for 7 days. Printed catalogue in classified form. Charging for lending, indicator for fiction, ledger for other classes; reference, application forms. Has an art gallery, a ladies' room, and a collection of local books.

LIBRARIAN: Alfred Morgan, born at Birmingham, 23rd March, 1850. Trained in the Birmingham Library (Union St.). Librarian at Walsall since 1871.

WALTHAMSTOW, Essex. — Population, 46,346. Acts adopted in February, 1892. Buildings opened in September, 1894. Has 2 branches, supplied from central Library. Contains 7700 vols., of which 7000 are for lending and 700 for reference. Borrowers, 2500. Staff, 3: librarian, 1 assistant, 1 caretaker. Books loaned for 14 days. Printed catalogue in dictionary form. Classification, numerical in main classes. Charging for lending, indicator; reference, application forms.

LIBRARIAN: George Walter Armstrong, born at Rotherham, 23rd August, 1866. Trained in Rotherham Public Library, 1882-90. Librarian at Salisbury, December, 1890, to August, 1894; at Colchester, August, 1894, to June, 1896. Librarian at Walthamstow since June, 1896.

WANDSWORTH, London (near High Street, S.W.).—Population, 58,101. Acts adopted in July, 1883. Library opened in 1885. Has a delivery station at Earlsfield. Contains over 15,000 vols. Borrowers, 4225. Staff, 7: librarian, 5 assistants, 1 caretaker. Books loaned for 14 days. Printed catalogue in dictionary form. MS. catalogue in guard books. Classification, numerical in main classes. Charging for lending, indicator; reference, application forms and open access. Has a ladies' room, and collections of local books and views.

LIBRARIAN: Cecil T. Davis. Formerly in the Birmingham Public Libraries. Appointed to Wandsworth, 1st December, 1886. Member of Council of the Library Association and a contributor to its *Transactions.*

WARRINGTON, Lancashire.—Population, 52,742. Established under the Museum Act in 1848, and Library opened in the same year. Contains 29,650 vols., of which 13,000 are for lending and 16,650 for reference. Borrowers, 3437. Staff, 9: librarian, 6 assistants, 2 caretakers. Books loaned for 14 days. Printed catalogue in dictionary form. MS. catalogue of pamphlets on cards. Classification, numerical in main classes. Charging for lending, cards; reference, verbal application and partial open access. Has a museum (1848); art gallery (1877); classes (1891); and a large local collection, including many MSS. and Charters.

LIBRARIAN: Charles Madeley, born at Derby in 1849. Assistant in the Birmingham Public Libraries, 1872-74. Librarian and curator at Warrington since 1874. Member of Council of the Library Association, and a contributor to its *Transactions.*

WARWICK, Warwickshire. — Population, 11,903. Acts adopted in 1865. Library opened in 1866. Contains 10,434 vols., of which 9507 are for lending and 927 for reference. Borrowers, 1398. Staff, 1: librarian. Books loaned for 14 days. Printed catalogue in dictionary form. Classification, numerical. Charging for lending, ledger; reference, verbal application.

LIBRARIAN: Thomas Haynes.

WATER EATON, Bucks.—Population, 250. Acts adopted in 1896.

WATERFORD, Ireland.—Population, 20,900. Acts adopted in March, 1894. Library is working in temporary premises.

WATERLOO-WITH-SEAFORTH, Lancashire. — Population, 17,200. Acts adopted in September, 1892.

WATFORD, Hertfordshire. — Population, 16,819. Acts adopted in 1871. Library opened in 1874. Contains 13,039 vols., of which 8769 are for lending and 4270 for reference. Borrowers, 1445. Staff, 5: librarian, 3 assistants, 1 caretaker. Books loaned for 7 and 14 days. Printed catalogue in dictionary form. MS. reference catalogue on cards. Classification, numerical in main classes. Charging for lending, indicator; reference, application forms. The Library is worked in connection with a school of science and art. It has also a school of music (1880), and university extension lecture courses (1885). The Technical Instruction Acts were adopted in August, 1893, and grants hàve been received from the excise duties.

LIBRARIAN: John Woolman, born at Leicester, 13th December, 1863. Educated at the Wyggeston and Queen Elizabeth's Grammar School, Leicester, and privately trained for Library work. Librarian at Watford since July, 1885.

WEDNESBURY, Staffordshire.—Population, 25,311. Acts adopted in 1876. Library opened, 20th March, 1878. Contains 10,264 vols., of which 7937 are for lending and 2327 for reference. Borrowers, 2300. Staff, 3: librarian, 2 assistants. Books loaned for 7 and 14 days. Printed catalogue in dictionary form. Classification, numerical in main classes. Charging for lending, indicator; reference, application forms.

LIBRARIAN: Thomas Stanley, F.L.C.S., F.S.S. Trained in the Birmingham Public Libraries.

WELSHPOOL, Wales.—Population, 6489. Acts adopted in 1887. Library opened in 1888. Contains about 6000 vols.

WEST BROMWICH, Staffordshire.—Population, 59,489. Acts adopted in 1873. Library opened in 1874. Has 3 branches. Contains 15,225 vols., of which 11,347 are in the Lending Library, 3061 in the Reference Library, and 817 in the branches. Borrowers, 2190. Staff, 3: librarian and 2 assistants. Books loaned for 7 days. Printed catalogue in dictionary form. MS. catalogue in guard books and on cards. Classification, numerical in main classes. Charging for lending, ledger; reference, application forms. The Technical Instruction Acts have been adopted.

LIBRARIAN: David Dickinson, born at Bolton in 1852. Trained in the Bolton Public Library, 1866-74. Librarian at West Bromwich since January, 1874.

WEST HAM, Essex.—Population, 204,902. Acts adopted in 1890. Temporary central Library opened in July, 1892. Canning Town branch opened in September, 1893. Contains 38,743 vols., of which 13,000 are in the central Lending Library, 6552 in the Reference Library, and 19,191 in the branch Library. Borrowers, 8103. Staff, 17: librarian, 14 assistants, 2 caretakers. Books loaned for 7 and 14 days. Printed catalogues in dictionary and classified form. MS. catalogues on cards. Classification, numerical and author alphabetical. Charging for lending, indicator; reference, application forms. Has classes, lectures, a quarterly journal, and a local collection. Extra tickets granted for the exclusive borrowing of music on payment of 6d. per annum. Has received a grant from the excise duties.

LIBRARIAN: Alfred Cotgreave, born at Eccleston, Cheshire, 2nd June, 1849. Trained in Manchester Royal Exchange Library and the Birmingham Public Libraries. Librarian successively at Wednesbury; Richmond; Wandsworth; Guille-Allès Library, Guernsey; and West Ham since 1891. Author of *Brief Notes on Free Public Libraries*, and articles in magazines. Inventor of several indicators, magazine racks, automatic shelf-steps, magazine covers, etc.

WESTMINSTER, London (Great Smith Street, S.W.).— Population, 53,234. Acts adopted in 1856. Library opened in 1857. New building opened in 1895. Has a branch at Knightsbridge. Contains 25,361 vols., of which 19,253 are lending, 2600 reference, and 3508 are at Knightsbridge. Borrowers, 4532. Staff, 7: librarian, 5 assistants, 1 caretaker. Books loaned for 14 days. Classification, author alphabetical. Charging for lending, ledger.

LIBRARIAN: H. E. Poole, born and trained at Westminster. Librarian there since 1881.

WESTON-SUPER-MARE, Somerset.—Population, 15,529. Acts adopted in 1886. Newsroom and Reference Library opened in May, 1890. Lending Library opened in August, 1893. Has a branch newsroom. Contains 3759 vols., of which 2736 are for lending and 1023 for reference. Borrowers, 2019. Staff, 3: librarian, 1 assistant, 1 caretaker. Books loaned for 14 days. Printed catalogue in dictionary form; supplements, classified. Classification, numerical. Charging for lending, indicator; reference, application forms and open access.

LIRRARIAN: Frank Wm. Coleman, born in London. He was second master at Chigwell Grammar School and Eastbourne College. Librarian at Weston-super-Mare since 1892.

WHITECHAPEL, London (High Street, E.).—Population, 77,717. Acts adopted in December, 1889. Newsrooms opened in May, 1892. Housed in building presented by Mr. Passmore Edwards. Contains 13,401 vols., of which 10,401 are for lending and 3000 for reference. Borrowers, 2161. Staff, 9: librarian, 5 assistants, 3 caretakers. Books loaned for 15 days. Printed catalogue in dictionary form. MS. catalogue in slip books, sheaf system. Classification, numerical in main classes in Lending; subject, in Reference Library. Charging for lending, indicator; reference, application forms. Has a museum, ladies' room, boys' room and lectures.

LIBRARIAN: W. E. Williams, a native of Cardiff. Trained in the Cardiff Public Libraries, where he was sub-librarian from 1880-84. Librarian at Doncaster, 1884-91. Librarian at Whitechapel since 1891.

WHITEHAVEN, Cumberland.—Population, 19,236. Acts adopted in February, 1887. Reading-room opened in May, 1888. Library opened in June, 1888. Contains 6037 vols., of which 4800 are for lending and 1237 for reference. Borrowers, 760. Staff, 1: librarian. Books loaned for 14 days. Printed catalogue in dictionary form. Classification, numerical in main classes. Charging for lending, ledger; reference, application forms. Has classes under the Technical Instruction Committee.

LIBRARIAN: John Simpson, who was trained in the Whitehaven Mechanics' Institute.

WICK, Caithness, Scotland. — Population, 13,105. Acts adopted in May, 1887. Library opened in November, 1888. Contains 6666 vols., of which 5472 are for lending and 1194 for reference. Borrowers, 1983. Staff, 1: librarian. Books loaned for 10 and 14 days. Printed catalogue in dictionary form. Classification, numerical in main classes. Charging for lending, indicator and partial open access; reference, application forms.

LIBRARIAN: George Bain, born at Wick in 1836. Had no special training as a librarian. Appointed to Wick in 1888.

WIDNES, Lancashire.—Population, 30,011. Acts adopted in December, 1885. Library opened in 1887. New building opened in 1896. Contains 7748 vols., of which 6861 are for lending and 887 for reference. Staff, 3: librarian and 2 assistants. Books loaned for 7 days. Printed catalogue in dictionary form. Charging for lending, open access.

LIBRARIAN: Miss Anne J. Proctor.

WIGAN, Lancashire.—Population, 53,013. Acts adopted in 1876. Library opened in May, 1878. Has 1 branch, the Powell Branch Boys' Reading-room and Library. Contains 47,120 vols., of which 13,200 are for lending, 33,000 for reference, 520 are in the boys' branch and 400 in the newsroom. Borrowers, 6000. Staff, 7: librarian, 4 assistants, 2 caretakers. Books loaned for 7 and 14 days. Printed catalogues in dictionary form. MS. catalogue on slips. Classification, modification of the Dewey system. Charging for lending, indicator; reference, application forms. Has occasional lectures.

LIBRARIAN: Henry Tennyson Folkard, F.S.A., born in London, 11th December, 1850. Trained in the London Library. Sub-librarian at the Royal Academy, Burlington House, 1875-77. Librarian at Wigan since November, 1877. Member of Council of the Library Association. Author of *Journey round the Wigan Reference Library*, 1884-86; *Industries of Wigan*; catalogues of various private Libraries, etc.

WIGAN PUBLIC LIBRARY.   READING ROOM.   From Photo by A. E. Douglas, Wigan.

WILLENHALL, Staffordshire.—Population, 16,852.   Acts adopted in 1877. Library opened in 1878. Contains about 5000 vols.

WILLESDEN, Middlesex.—Population, 61,266. Acts adopted in 1891.   Has Libraries under separate committees, at Harlesden, Kilburn, and Willesden Green.   Contains 16,816 vols., of which 14,201 are for lending and 2615 for reference.   Charging for lending, indicator.

WIMBLEDON, Surrey.—Population, 25,758.   Acts adopted in 1883.   Library opened in 1887.   Contains 10,044 vols., of which 7225 are for lending and 2819 for reference.   Classification, numerical in main classes.   Charging for lending, indicator.

LIBRARIAN: Henry William Bull, born at Watlington, Oxon., 12th July, 1870.   Was an undergraduate of London University.   Sub-librarian of Reading Public Library, 1885-89. Librarian of Christ Church, 1889-96.   Appointed to Wimbledon in 1896.

WINCHESTER, Hampshire.—Population, 19,073.   Acts adopted on 6th February, 1851.   Library opened, November, 1851.   Has one branch.   Contains 5600 vols., of which 4300 are for lending and 1300 for reference.   Borrowers, 1000.   Staff, 2: librarian and assistant.   Books loaned for 14 days.   Printed catalogue in classified form.   Charging for lending, indicator; reference, application.

LIBRARIAN: John Thomas Burchett.   For 24 years previous to his appointment at Winchester, he was with Messrs. W. H. Smith & Son, the booksellers.

WINSFORD, Cheshire.—Population, 10,440.   Acts adopted in 1887.   Library opened in 1888.   Contains about 4000 vols.

WOLVERHAMPTON, Staffordshire.—Population, 82,622. Acts adopted, 8th February, 1869.   Library opened, 30th September, 1869.   Contains 34,900 vols., of which 27,900 are for lending and 7000 for reference.   Borrowers, 2590.   Staff, 6: librarian, 4 assistants and 1 hall-keeper.   Books loaned for 14 days.   Printed catalogues in dictionary and classified form. MS. catalogue in guard and slip books.   Classification, by subject, numerical. Charging for lending, indicator; reference, application forms.   Has a museum (1874); classes (1873); lectures (1874); juvenile reading-room; and a local collection. Grants have been received from the excise duties for technical classes.

LIBRARIAN: John Elliot, born at Wolverhampton. Appointed librarian in September, 1869.   Indicator invented, 1869-70.

Reading-stands introduced, 1880. Magazine indicator invented in 1888. He is author of historical and other papers read at meetings of the local naturalist and archæological associations.

WOOD GREEN, Middlesex.—Population, 28,000. Acts adopted in November, 1891. Reading-room opened, 1st March, 1892. Library opened, 28th January, 1893. There is a branch reading-room. Contains 5000 vols. Borrowers, 2000. Staff, 2: librarian and assistant. Books loaned for 14 days. Printed catalogue in classified form. Classification, numerical in main classes. Charging for lending, indicator. The Technical Instruction Acts have been adoped by a separate Committee.

LIBRARIAN: Arthur Douthwaite, born at Sledmere, Yorks, 15th July, 1855. Appointed to Wood Green in 1892. Previously a schoolmaster.

WOOLTON, Lancashire.—Population, 4545. Acts adopted and Library opened in 1890. Contains about 2000 vols.

WOOLWICH, London.—Population, 41,314. Acts adopted in 1895.

WORCESTER, Worcestershire.—Population, 42,908. Acts adopted in April, 1879. Library opened in March, 1881. New building will be opened soon. Contains 32,000 vols., of which 20,000 are for lending and 12,000 for reference. Borrowers, 4700. Staff, 6: librarian, 4 assistants, 1 caretaker. Books loaned for 14 days. Printed catalogue in dictionary form. Classification, by subjects and authors. Charging for lending, open access and cards; reference, application forms. Has a museum with 40,000 specimens; art gallery; science, art, and technical classes; local collection, etc. The Technical Instruction Acts have been adopted.

LIBRARIAN: Thomas Duckworth, born at Blackburn in 1866, trained in the Blackburn Public Libraries, and became sub-librarian there in 1889. Librarian at Worcester since 1894. Introduced the open access system in 1896.

WORKINGTON, Cumberland.—Population, 23,490. Acts adopted in December, 1889. Newsroom opened in June, 1890. Lending Library opened, 2nd November, 1891. Contains 4995 vols., of which 3995 are for lending and 1000 for reference. Borrowers, 1257. Staff, 3: librarian and 2 caretakers. Books loaned for 15 days. Printed catalogue in dictionary form. Classification, on the Dewey system. Charging for lending, indicator; reference, open access.

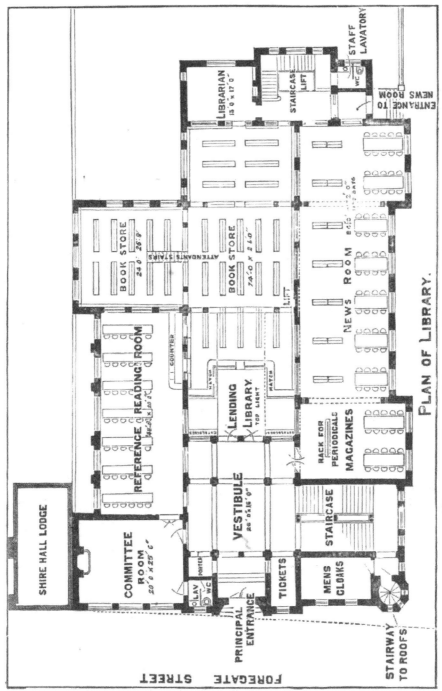

WORCESTER PUBLIC LIBRARY.   ORIGINAL ARRANGEMENT.

PLAN OF LIBRARY.

14

LIBRARIAN: John William Cummings Purves, born at Birtley, Durham, 10th May, 1873. Trained in the Newcastle-upon-Tyne Public Library. Librarian at Workington since November, 1895.

WORKSOP, Nottinghamshire.—Population, 12,734. Acts adopted in December, 1895. Reading-room opened, 26th March, 1896; Library, on 1st July, 1896. Contains 2000 vols. Staff, 1: librarian. Books loaned for 7 and 14 days. Printed catalogue in dictionary form. Charging for lending, ledger.

LIBRARIAN: H. Wortley Latham.

WORTHING, Sussex.—Population, 16,600. Acts adopted in December, 1892.

WREXHAM, Denbigh, Wales.—Population, 12,552. Acts adopted in 1878. Library opened, 10th December, 1879. Contains 4792 vols., of which 3595 are for lending, 1134 for reference, and 63 are in the local collection. Borrowers, 916. Staff, 2: librarian and 1 assistant. Books loaned for 10 days. Printed catalogue in classified form. Classification, alphabetical by authors. Charging for lending, indicator; reference, application forms. Lectures are given occasionally, and books are lent to students of the adjoining art school. The Technical Instruction Acts have been adopted.

LIBRARIAN: Richard Gough, born at Coton Hall, Shrewsbury, 6th August, 1844.

YARMOUTH, GREAT, Norfolk.—Population, 49,318. Acts adopted in August, 1885. Library opened, May, 1886. Has one branch. Contains 14,760 vols., of which 10,643 are for lending, 3278 for reference, and 839 are in the branch. Borrowers, 3284. Staff, 6: librarian, 4 assistants, 1 caretaker. Books loaned for 7, 10, and 14 days. Printed catalogue in dictionary form. MS. catalogue in guard books. Classification, numerical by subjects. Charging for lending, indicator; reference, application forms. Has a museum (1895). The Technical Instruction Acts have been adopted.

LIBRARIAN: William Carter, born 1st September, 1858. Trained in the Manchester Public Libraries, 1872-86. Librarian at Yarmouth since 1886.

YORK, Yorkshire.—Population, 67,004. Acts adopted in October, 1891. Newsroom opened in August, 1892. Library opened in October, 1893. Contains 16,529 vols., of which 12,819 are for lending and 3710 for reference.   Borrowers, 5289. Staff, 8: librarian, 6 assistants, 1 caretaker.   Books loaned for 14 days.   Printed catalogue in dictionary form.   MS. catalogue on cards.   Classification of Lending Library, numerical in main classes; Reference Library on the Dewey system. Charging for lending, indicator; reference, application forms. The Technical Instruction Acts have been adopted, and there is an art gallery, 2 schools of science and art, and technical classes.

LIBRARIAN: Arthur H. Furnish.

TABLE SHOWING THE RATE, INCOME, WORK, AND HOURS OF THE RATE-SUPPORTED LIBRARIES.

Places marked with an asterisk (*) have special rating powers or are under special local Acts.
Places marked ... have not yet had the Acts put in operation, or no information has been given.

ENGLAND.

Place.	Rate in £.	Annual Income.		Annual Issues.			Annual Attendances.			Hours open per week.			
		From Rate. £	From Fines, etc. £	Lending.	Reference.	Percent. of Fiction.	Newsroom.	Reading Rooms.	Other Depts.	Lending.	Reference.	Newsroom.	Sundays.
BEDFORDSHIRE.													
Bedford	...	...	...	...	...	...	...	...	...	...	...	...	...
Luton	1d.	420	28	15,000	...	70	100,000	...	...	42	78	78	...
BERKSHIRE.													
Reading	1d.	1110	260	119,581	5,827	...	600,000	...	64,896	58	72	81	...
BUCKINGHAMSHIRE.													
Grandborough ...	...	...	...	...	...	...	...	...	...	...	...	...	...
Middle Claydon ...	1d.	10	5	1,648	...	...	...	...	...	3½	21	...	...
Water Eaton	...	...	...	...	...	...	...	...	...	...	...	...	...
CAMBRIDGESHIRE.													
Burwell	...	...	...	...	...	...	...	...	...	...	...	...	...
Cambridge	1d.	909	138	107,592	...	68	...	...	...	36	69	69	...

Place	Rate											
CHESHIRE.												
Altrincham	1d.	245	425	72,500		86	100,000		63	63	78	
Ashton-on-Mersey												
Bebington	1d.	1845	300	226,453	102,296	63	80,000		69	71½	71½	
Birkenhead	1d.	777	29	52,000	2,000	89			54½	21	81	
Chester	1d.	215	10						37	37	78	
Dukinfield	1d.	460		38,542		75	87,951		56	56	72	
Hyde	1d.	357	51	50,933	4,833		123,008		36	36	78	
Macclesfield	1d.	62	14						6			
Middlewich	1d.	72	28	9,313	1,633	75			69	69	72	
Nantwich	1d.	283	92	31,093	875	80	36,000		58	58	75	
Northwich	1d.	198	25	22,582	485	75			14	14	72	
Runcorn	1d.	233	100	54,823	2460	80		2,500	66	66		3
Sale	1d.	379	40	60,799		70	98,744		55			
Stalybridge	1d.											
Stockport	1d.											
Winsford	1d.											
CORNWALL.												
Bodmin												
Camborne			76	57,000	500				40	40		
Falmouth	1d.	142	16	12,347		78			24	36	72	
Hayle												
Liskeard	1d.	190	50						48	48		
Penzance	1d.	100	65	69,082	824	83			27½	27½	78	
Redruth	1d.			28,000		92					78	
St. Austell												
St. Ives												
Truro	1d.	117	43						39	39		
CUMBERLAND.												
Arlecdon	1d.	93	3	6,323					12			

TABLE SHOWING THE RATE, INCOME, WORK, AND HOURS OF THE RATE-SUPPORTED LIBRARIES—cont.

Place.	Rate in £	Annual Income.		Annual Issues.			Annual Attendances.			Hours open per week.			
		From Rate. (£)	From Fines, etc. (£)	Lending.	Reference.	Percent. of Fiction.	Newsroom.	Reading Rooms.	Other Depts.	Lending.	Reference.	Newsroom.	Sundays.
CUMBERLAND—continued.													
Carlisle	1d.	740	1300	...	...	...	400,000	...	...	46	75	75	...
Cleator Moor	1d.	...	...	...	311	...	120,000	...	...	...	...	...	...
Millom	1d.	330	16	25,000	...	...	...	...	...	60	60	78	...
Penrith	1d.	141	7	12,169	...	...	...	...	...	24	78	81	...
Whitehaven	1d.	275	60	24,731	829	76	...	...	...	42	42	81	...
Workington	1d.	250	20	26,677	...	50	...	...	...	37	37	...	...
DERBYSHIRE.													
Buxton	1d.	238	36	28,520	62	...	...	...	...	38	38	69	...
Chesterfield	1d.	332	30	39,052	14,157	50	...	...	...	58	58	78	...
Derby	1d.	1640	84	157,879	14,383	78	600,000	...	...	58	66	75	...
Glossop	1d.	252	6	21,865	...	...	...	...	...	36	...	78	...
New Mills	...	...	...	...	...	...	...	...	...	...	...	...	...
Pleasley	...	...	...	...	...	...	...	...	...	...	...	...	...
DEVONSHIRE.													
Bideford	1d.	...	...	...	...	40	...	...	...	...	...	...	...
Devonport	1d.	750	50	54,428	...	60	...	...	...	66	66	78	...
Exeter	1d.	720	72	30,573	9,551	...	...	...	...	66	66	72	...
Plymouth	1d.	1350	60	284,288	58,366	...	...	...	...	60	64	78	...

DORSETSHIRE.												
Poole	1d.	200		5,000	1,800					50			
DURHAM.												
Darlington	1d.	685	80	113,408	4,993	84	300,000			58	60	81	7
Gateshead	1d.	1095	108	82,051	814	78	50,000				58	75	6
Hartlepool													
Hartlepool, West	1d.	710	55							66	69	69	6
Leadgate		1052		99,860	15,521	62	629,200	16,140	14,000	58	58	84	
South Shields	1d.	650	84	65,352						50	78	78	6
Stockton	1d.	1900	21										
Sunderland	1d.		90										
Trimdon													
ESSEX.													
Barking	1d.	350	17	15,107		83	180,000			10		72	
Colchester	1d.	580	40	65,005	550	85		900		42	42	66	6
East Ham							29,400						
Grays	1d.	138								12		69	
Ilford				125,000									
Leyton	1d.	880	60							24	69		
Walthamstow	1d.	650	20							25	66	72	
West Ham	1d.	3500	124	138,687	38,358	60	898,140			55	72	78	7
GLOUCESTERSHIRE.													
Bristol	1d.	4412	448	385,122	109,461	63	2,000,000	130,000	140,000	59	60	78	
Cheltenham	1d.	1126	361	127,859	9,876	65	160,000			60		69	
Gloucester													
HAMPSHIRE.													
Andover													

TABLE SHOWING THE RATE, INCOME, WORK, AND HOURS OF THE RATE-SUPPORTED LIBRARIES—*cont.*

Place.	Rate in £.	Annual Income.		Annual Issues.			Annual Attendances.			Hours open per week.			
		From Rate.	From Fines, etc.	Lending.	Reference.	Percent. of Fiction.	Newsroom.	Reading Rooms.	Other Depts.	Lending.	Reference.	Newsroom.	Sundays.
		£	£										
HAMPSHIRE—*continued.*													
Bournemouth ...	1d.	1230	78	137,788	2,300	76	...	...	...	60	60	78	...
Gosport ...	1d.	300	26	43,271	589	88	86,520	...	...	63	69	72	...
Portsmouth ...	1d.	2691	92	178,020	23,445	65	818,382	...	30,170	57	72	72	...
Southampton ...	1d.	1433	...	100,586	11,238	74	296,000	290,084	...	45	72	72	...
Winchester ...	1d.	380	20	32,922	...	75	...	...	...	45½	45½	69	...
HEREFORDSHIRE.													
Hereford ...	1d.	440	76	46,345	...	...	198,000	...	...	...	...	...	...
Leominster ...	1d.	140	...	10,000	...	...	...	...	...	24	24	72	...
HERTFORDSHIRE.													
Hertford ...	1d.	130	...	...	...	...	...	...	...	...	...	...	...
St. Albans ...	1d.	160	...	...	...	...	...	15,000	...	...	...	...	...
Watford ...	1d.	400	465	44,470	1,413	81	80,000	...	...	30	59	78	...
KENT.													
Bexley ...	...	...	...	...	...	...	...	...	...	...	...	...	...
Bromley ...	1d.	590	180	67,042	1,820	52	90,600	...	...	53	53	72	...
Canterbury ...	1d.	430	...	22,272	...	...	...	...	24,000	30	72	72	...
Folkestone ...	1d.	685	39	47,853	...	...	...	...	...	48	48	72	...

Kent—continued.

Town													
Gravesend	1d.	410	23	34,876	1,500	80	150,000	…	…	38½	41	84	…
Maidstone	1d.	610	20	21,452	…	76	…	…	…	66	42	42	…
Queenborough	½d.	20	…	1,560	…	…	3,220	…	…	3	…	24	…
Ramsgate	…	…	…	…	…	…	…	…	…	…	…	…	…
Rochester	¾d.	225	12	19,314	…	84	…	…	…	14	14	14	…
Sittingbourne	1d.	110	…	…	…	…	…	…	…	…	…	…	…
Tonbridge	1d.	170	…	13,000	…	…	…	…	…	48	48	78	…
Tunbridge Wells	…	…	…	…	…	…	…	…	…	…	…	…	…

LANCASHIRE.

Town													
Ashton-under-Lyne *	1¾d.	1020	58	55,284	6,316	88	…	…	…	55	55	72	…
Barrow-in-Furness	1d.	820	71	121,667	23,910	68	…	…	…	72	78	78	…
Blackburn	1d.	1850	60	78,000	23,000	…	600,000	…	66,000	58	70½	70½	…
Blackpool	1d.	950	64	55,245	2,011	…	93,517	…	…	60	60	78	…
Bolton	1d.	1850	100	443,909	…	79	…	…	…	72	72	72	…
Bootle *	1d.	1709	566	75,646	13,152	…	175,000	…	15,000	66	66	75	…
Clitheroe	1d.	130	10	22,590	…	…	…	…	…	8	8	…	…
Colne	1d.	250	…	28,850	…	80	…	…	…	20	…	…	…
Darwen	1d.	500	…	40,485	3,800	54	52,348	…	9,782	66	66	78	…
Denton	1d.	…	…	18,366	…	…	38,000	…	…	18	…	81	…
Fleetwood	1d.	150	70	…	…	…	…	…	…	59	75	75	6
Heywood	1d.	360	12	10,740	…	…	…	…	…	53	48	58	…
Hindley	1d.	220	43	81,037	…	85	…	…	…	48	78	84	…
Lancaster	1d.	500	…	44,335	487	…	…	…	…	61½	78	78	…
Leigh	1d.	446	40	579,243	438,857	…	402,886	667,839	53,453	71	78	81	…
Liverpool *	1d.	13527	…	1,677,000	416,100	…	4,484,914	862,890	…	…	78	…	7
Manchester *	2d.	20000	300	…	…	…	…	…	…	…	…	81	…
Middleton	1d.	300	…	36,218	…	84	30,000	500	5,000	37	37	37	…
Moss Side	1d.	…	…	130,003	17,120	72	…	…	…	62	66	75	…
Nelson	1d.	403	32	142,535	…	70	556,000	81,640	82,941	37	57	78	…
Oldham *	2·098d.	5178	834	…	…	…	…	…	…	62	66	78	4
Preston	1d.	2000	…	…	…	…	…	…	…	66	57	78	…

TABLE SHOWING THE RATE, INCOME, WORK, AND HOURS OF THE RATE-SUPPORTED LIBRARIES—cont.

Place.	Rate in £.	Annual Income		Annual Issues			Annual Attendances			Hours open per week.			
		From Rate.	From Fines, etc.	Lending.	Reference.	Percent. of Fiction.	Newsroom.	Reading Rooms.	Other Depts.	Lending.	Reference.	Newsroom.	Sundays.
		£	£										
LANCASHIRE—continued.													
Rochdale	1d.	1066	118	138,179	89,376	72	223,314	...	...	60	75	75	6
St. Helen's *	1d.	1044	66	164,503	5,718	83	436,152	...	...	66	66	78	7
Salford *	1¾d.	4700	210	268,112	163,956	55	152,555	947,424	...	63	63	72	7
Southport	1d.	1145	30	114,820	2,113	...	...	...	...	52	69½	69½	...
Stretford	...	...	...	...	...	...	...	...	...	...	...	...	...
Todmorden	...	...	...	...	...	...	...	...	...	...	...	...	...
Warrington *	1½d.	1000	130	72,425	...	82	...	...	...	60½	69	69	...
Waterloo-with-Seaforth	...	...	...	...	...	...	...	...	...	...	...	...	...
Widnes	1d.	550	36	73,132	3,912	...	175,313	...	...	66	66	69	...
Wigan *	2d.	1600	44	91,688	29,880	...	300,000	44,910	...	58	53	65½	7
Woolton	1d.	80	...	...	...	...	...	...	...	...	...	...	...
LEICESTERSHIRE.													
Hinckley	1d.	80	76	15,130	320	70	95,000	...	...	10	72	72	...
Ibstock	...	...	...	...	...	...	...	...	...	...	...	...	...
Leicester *	1¾d.	2847	355	379,119	27,936	79	...	...	...	61½	69	75	3
Loughborough	1d.	280	20	41,385	2,738	60	...	...	...	39	72	72	...
Sheepshed	...	...	...	...	...	...	...	...	...	...	...	...	...
LINCOLNSHIRE.													
Lincoln	1d.	550	45	86,500	5,100	69	182,500	17,300	31,000	66	66	72	5

LONDON, COUNTY OF.													
Battersea, S.W.	1d.	3128	257	264,360	21,769	79	750,000	50,000	250,000	58	72	84	6
Bermondsey, S.E.	1d.	1622	100	96,873	10,846	74	450,000	...	...	58	58	75	6
Bow, E.	1d.	...	...	...	...	...	...	...	...	...	...	...	...
Bromley, E.	...	...	...	544,562	69,508	65	2,000,000	...	...	63	72	78	...
Camberwell, S.E.	1d.	4500	270	191,586	71,172	66	559,553	...	...	59	66	72	6
Chelsea, S.W.	1d.	2880	184	15,332	6,447	73	185,555	...	21,779	60	72	78	6
Christ Church, S.E.	1d.	490	45	87,422	3,515	80	...	...	...	50	66	78	...
Clapham, S.W.	1d.	1060	40	110,611	29,947	64	417,827	...	...	63	78	81	6
Clerkenwell, E.C.	1d.	1550	95	122,193	...	72	563,040	199,242	...	55	72	84	6
Fulham, W.	1d.	1900	60	174,945	2,615	70	190,000	...	160,000	55	61½	84	...
Hammersmith, W.	1d.	2080	160	59,179	2,809	...	...	15,000	...	52½	63	72	3
Hampstead, N.W.	1d.	3000	150	48,776	5,099	70	150,000	...	...	35	72	78	6
Holborn, W.C.	½d.	800	55	190,248	29,777	67	859,386	83,032	...	55	68½	78	...
Kensington, W.	½d.	3953	168	673,101	57,997	78	278,751	...	...	52½	69	78	5
Lambeth, S.E.	1d.	6200	500	107,591	5,000	68	...	4,600	...	63	63	81	6
Lewisham, S.E.	½d.	1024	90	...	...	...	...	...	...	...	...	...	...
Mile End, E.	...	...	...	153,242	15,294	74	80,000	...	...	52½	69	78	6
Newington, S.E.	1d.	1830	178	65,227	...	80	321,023	...	...	33	...	78	3
Penge, S.E.	1d.	550	50	67,874	13,681	67	...	...	...	66	72	78	...
Poplar, E.	1d.	1360	65	...	...	...	270,000	...	...	...	...	...	...
Putney, S.W.	...	...	...	25,767	3,704	65	580,000	...	60,000	52½	72	81	...
Rotherhithe, S.E.	1d.	820	50	164,044	27,540	68	...	120	10,000	63	72	78	6
St. George, Hanover Sq., W.	½d.	3900	150	...	...	...	356,186	75,000	...	...	72	78	...
St. George-in-East, E.	...	...	...	38,729	2,473	78	1,102,919	...	...	69	...	...	...
St. George the Martyr, S.E.	...	...	...	69,122	85,206	32½	...	...	...	44	69	...	...
St. Giles, W.C.	1d.	1600	30	...	...	...	409,000	...	...	...	72	78	...
St. Martin-in-Fields, W.C.	1d.	2658	74	51,031	1,113	80	604,430	...	...	58	...	78	...
St. Paul, Covent Garden, W.C.	1d.	...	...	99,554	18,257	70	328,000	...	...	69	58	...	...
St. Saviour, S.E.	1d.	900	40	92,241	9,883	71	600,000	...	...	52	75	66	6
Shoreditch, E.	½d.	1972	...	169,814	...	69	...	...	...	52½	72	75	3
Stoke Newington, N.	1d.	840	140	...	...	...	...	...	...	...	...	75	...
Streatham, S.W.	1d.	1600	150	...	...	...	...	...	...	...	...	72	6

TABLE SHOWING THE RATE, INCOME, WORK, AND HOURS OF THE RATE-SUPPORTED LIBRARIES—cont.

Place.	Rate in £.	Annual Income.		Annual Issues.			Annual Attendances.			Hours open per week.			
		From Rate.	From Fines, etc.	Lending.	Reference.	Percent. of Fiction.	Newsroom.	Reading Rooms.	Other Depts.	Lending.	Reference.	Newsroom.	Sundays.
LONDON, COUNTY OF—cont.		£	£										
Wandsworth, S.W.	1d.	1190	...	106,818	...	...	686,840	...	...	55	55	78	...
Westminster, S.W.	1d.	3310	230	81,580	64,561	...	929,933	64,000	...	72	72	72	...
Whitechapel, E.	1d.	1700	54	74,537	32,867	...	...	...	...	66	78	78	10½
Woolwich, S.E.	...	...	...	...	...	...	...	...	...	...	...	...	...
MAN, ISLE OF													
Douglas	1d.	481	30	45,007	13,339	45	85,963	...	...	55	69	72	...
MIDDLESEX.													
Brentford	1d.	277	38	19,365	...	...	30,000	...	...	55	55	68	...
Chiswick	1d.	428	...	67,216	1,086	75	30,000	...	...	85	...	68	...
Ealing	1d.	716	122	132,173	1,067	83	296,400	...	133,240	53	57½	78	6
Edmonton	1d.	310	25	30,000	...	...	30,000	...	...	21	...	60	...
Enfield	1d.	420	40	51,000	...	75	...	...	...	36	36	36	...
Hornsey	...	...	...	...	...	...	...	...	...	...	...	...	...
Teddington	...	...	...	...	...	...	...	...	...	...	...	...	...
Tottenham	1d.	885	45	26,245 (5 mths.)	2,804	85	225,000	...	...	33	66	78	...
Twickenham	1d.	360	30	56,698	3,542	80	...	...	...	62	62	78	...
Willesden	1d.	1355	233	116,075	10,335	...	...	...	...	...	...	...	...
Wood Green	1d.	400	20	54,000	...	90	125,000	...	...	23	...	78	...

Place													
MONMOUTHSHIRE.													
Newport	1d.	1100	66	76,017	26,115					44		78	
NORFOLKSHIRE.													
Norwich	1d.	1245	150	90,440	48,000	82				50	60	60	6
Shouldham													
Yarmouth	1d.	700		147,467	23,000		196,762	43,500		57	57	72	
NORTHAMPTONSHIRE.													
Kettering	1d.	190								33	33	78	
Northampton	1d.	1015		89,652									
Peterborough	1d.	440	25	44,078	532	87				44	66	75	
Rothwell	1d.												
NORTHUMBERLAND.													
Newcastle-on-Tyne	1d.	4000	305	167,454	67,716	52	872,000			58	66	75	7
Tynemouth	1d.	760	44	102,159	3,399	72	634,000	210,000	130,000	64	64	78	
NOTTINGHAMSHIRE.													
Carlton													
Hucknall Torkard	1d.	108	43	18,654	203	88	53,523	48,475	44,133	10	10	78	
Mansfield	1d.	185	13	28,041						54	54	72	
Newark-on-Trent	1d.	230											
Nottingham	1d.	3225	2000	427,786			2,181,381			69	69	69	
Worksop	1d.	170								36	36	78	
OXFORDSHIRE.													
Oxford *	1d.						470,000			78	66	66	
SHROPSHIRE.													
Oswestry	1d.	170	35	26,250		82				24	24	74	
Shrewsbury	1d.	475											

TABLE SHOWING THE RATE, INCOME, WORK, AND HOURS OF THE RATE-SUPPORTED LIBRARIES—cont.

Place.	Rate in £	Annual Income.		Annual Issues.			Annual Attendances.			Hours open per week.			
		From Rate.	From Fines, etc.	Lending.	Reference.	Percent. of Fiction.	Newsroom.	Reading Rooms.	Other Depts.	Lending.	Reference.	Newsroom.	Sundays.
		£	£										
SOMERSETSHIRE.													
Bridgwater	1d.	150	.15	12,500	...	...	...	...	...	32	32	75	...
Weston-super-Mare	1d.	320	30	28,461	155	84	...	...	...	21	21	69	...
STAFFORDSHIRE.													
Bilston	1d.	200	.10	...	...	...	...	...	...	...	...	...	...
Brierley Hill	1d.	120	...	...	...	...	...	...	...	4	...	74½	...
Burslem	1d.	456	44	27,925	162	78	120,416	...	...	48	...	78	...
Burton-on-Trent	1d.	100	.12	...	...	...	...	...	...	...	...	...	...
Darlaston	1d.	604	63	10,772	...	87	...	...	...	25	78	78	...
Handsworth	1d.	680	30	63,969	2,103	80	...	...	...	55	55	78	...
Hanley	1d.	170	880	56,985	16,756	60	413,432	33,000	...	53	59	75	...
Leek	1d.	100	...	29,573	5,755	...	...	...	...	44	66	78	...
Lichfield	1d.	401	44	...	...	80	...	...	...	...	61	72	...
Longton	1d.	216	9	32,661	1,108	85	240,000	1,000	...	61	45	75	...
Newcastle-under-Lyme	1d.	460	70	25,794	211	83	135,000	...	...	45	55	78	...
Smethwick	1d.	250	30	61,888	117	...	272,700	146,000	...	55	...	75	...
Stafford	1d.	330	80	...	...	72	150,000	...	...	18	75	...	...
Stoke-upon-Trent	1d.	60	...	42,874	14,382	...	...	...	...	66	...	75	...
Tamworth	1d.	...	...	...	...	...	...	...	...	...	...	...	...
Tipton	1d.	...	...	...	...	...	...	...	...	...	...	...	...

STAFFORDSHIRE—*continued.*													
Tunstall	1d.	180	...	...	...	...	...	...	...	...	...	...	...
Walsall *	1½d.	990	51	84,959	601	...	480,000	...	35,615	50	50	78	7
Wednesbury	1d.	320	10	58,333	8,463	...	250,400	8,354	...	55	55	78	...
West Bromwich	1d.	810	41	95,500	109	81	186,000	...	...	55	55	75	...
Willenhall	1d.	120	...	...	...	...	...	...	...	...	...	...	...
Wolverhampton *	1⅝d.	1180	1221	80,901	9,533	78	312,000	26,000	51,000	55	60	78	...
SUFFOLK.													
Bury St. Edmunds	...	...	...	...	...	...	...	...	...	...	...	...	...
Ipswich	1d.	1200	35	71,098	...	...	...	...	...	...	...	...	...
Lowestoft	...	...	...	...	...	...	...	...	...	...	...	...	...
SURREY.													
Croydon	1d.	2600	250	247,932	2,664	84	500,000	...	...	58	78	78	3
Kingston-on-Thames	1d.	500	59	47,195	808	73	281,000	...	47,000	60	72	81	3
Richmond	1d.	937	169	96,184	9,215	69	295,200	...	...	66	66	78	...
Wimbledon	1d.	759	70	80,706	6,362	...	...	...	...	...	...	...	...
SUSSEX.													
Brighton *	1½d.	4280	68	117,865	44,702	54	...	31,699	...	66	72	72	...
Eastbourne	⅜d.	540	...	...	...	...	...	...	...	59	59	...	...
Hove	1d.	1030	100	84,914	5,453	76	130,921	...	...	59	59	78	...
Worthing	...	...	...	...	...	...	...	...	...	...	...	...	...
WARWICKSHIRE.													
Aston Manor	1d.	680	65	87,100	12,409	68	...	...	...	66	72	78	...
Atherstone	...	...	...	...	...	...	...	...	...	...	...	...	...
Birmingham *	1·50d.	13722	947	818,312	394,982	56	2,000,000	...	3,315,600	66	72	66	6
Coventry	1d.	656	...	...	...	...	...	...	...	...	...	...	...
Leamington	1d.	228	28	72,388	7,741	80	...	...	...	30	66	78	4½
Rugby	1d.	220	13	22,632	...	...	...	...	...	49	49	66	...
Warwick	1d.	...	...	24,384	41	72	...	...	...	30	30	78	...

TABLE SHOWING THE RATE, INCOME, WORK, AND HOURS OF THE RATE-SUPPORTED LIBRARIES—cont.

Place.	Rate in £.	Annual Income.		Annual Issues.			Annual Attendances.			Hours open per week.			
		From Rate.	From Fines, etc.	Lending.	Reference.	Percent. of Fiction.	Newsroom.	Reading Rooms.	Other Depts.	Lending.	Reference.	Newsroom.	Sundays.
		£	£										
WESTMORELAND.													
Kendal	1d.	198	100	74,575	2,527	65	...	...	...	54	72	72	...
WILTSHIRE.													
Salisbury	1d.	235	66	28,562	1,170	89	...	...	...	54	54	54	...
WORCESTERSHIRE.													
Dudley	1d.	496	41	...	...	...	192,712	...	...	51	51	...	...
Kidderminster	1d.	350	...	30,550	2,975	50	...	...	...	54	72	78	...
Oldbury	1d.	256	55	35,200	...	77	...	...	...	37½	37½	54	...
Worcester	1d.	675	40	62,000	13,000	65	240,000	30,000	...	53	72	78	...
YORKSHIRE.													
Barnsley	1d.	454	64	38,079	4,488	79	249,981	...	...	58¼	58½	81	...
Bingley	...	...	...	...	...	...	...	...	...	...	...	...	...
Bolton Percy	...	...	...	...	...	...	...	...	...	...	...	...	...
Bradford	1d.	4062	722	501,731	79,609	60	150,000	...	332,478	60	72	78	3
Dewsbury	1d.	450	60	68,401	...	60	...	...	...	61	...	81	4
Doncaster	1d.	517	89	73,732	...	78	...	...	...	66	66	78	...
Halifax	1d.	1366	129	286,531	15,376	80	...	...	...	60	60	75	...
Halton	...	...	...	...	...	...	...	...	...	...	...	...	...

YORKSHIRE—continued.														
Harrogate	...	1d.	435	26	107,823	1,097	71	646,065	...	...	60	60	78	...
Hull	...	1d.	3250	660	506,907	7,101	84	1,678,029	...	...	66	69	81	...
Leeds	...	1d.	5918	589	848,128	142,884	...	...	...	...	63	69	81	...
Middlesbrough	...	1d.	1040	...	92,625	9,535	74	...	...	...	65	65	65	10
Morley	...	...	...	...	...	...	...	...	...	...	...	...	...	...
Rawmarsh	...	1d.	560	32	46,000	...	86	...	...	...	66	66	66	...
Rotherham	...	1d.	4689	845	447,938	48,511	50	...	...	...	59	69	69	...
Sheffield *	...	1d.	160	55	27,860	24	...	...	...	...	30	30	81	...
Sowerby Bridge	...	1d.	180	3	25,287	657	...	8,000	...	...	9	18	78	...
Thornaby-on-Tees	...	1d.	...	...	...	...	...	...	...	...	...	...	...	...
York	...	1d.	1017	...	166,563	1,975	...	309,332	67,906	...	60	69	78	...
IRELAND.														
Banbridge	...	...	...	...	...	...	...	...	...	...	...	...	...	...
Belfast	...	1d.	3283	240	201,433	50,508	63	927,079	21,540	448,000	60	60	65	...
Coleraine	...	¾d.	...	...	...	...	...	...	...	...	...	...	...	...
Cork	...	...	440	50	74,251	3,111	87	174,952	...	...	55	72	78	...
Dalkey, near Dublin	...	1d.	...	...	...	...	...	...	...	...	...	...	...	...
Dublin	...	...	100	25	36,148	11,235	66	348,831	...	...	66	66	75	8
Dundalk	...	1d.	...	...	...	...	...	...	...	...	24	24	...	...
Ennis	...	...	...	...	...	...	...	...	...	...	...	...	...	...
Kingstown	...	...	...	...	7,978	...	...	79,899	...	...	72	72	72	...
Limerick	...	½d.	264	...	...	...	...	45,000	...	...	...	...	78	5
Lurgan	...	1d.	86	...	...	...	...	...	...	...	...	...	...	...
Nenagh	...	1d.	...	...	...	...	...	...	...	...	...	...	...	...
Newry	...	...	...	...	...	...	...	...	...	...	...	...	...	...
Newtownards	...	1d.	60	...	...	...	...	...	...	...	...	...	...	...
Rathmines	...	¾d.	400	...	43,276	7,413	75	156,644	31,214	...	42	42	78	...
Sligo	...	...	70	...	...	...	...	16,800	...	...	72	72	72	...
Waterford	...	1d.	...	...	...	...	...	...	...	...	...	...	...	5

15

TABLE SHOWING THE RATE, INCOME, WORK, AND HOURS OF THE RATE-SUPPORTED LIBRARIES—cont.

SCOTLAND.

Place.	Rate in £.	Annual Income		Annual Issues			Annual Attendances			Hours open per week.			
		From Rate. £	From Fines, etc. £	Lending.	Reference.	Percent. of Fiction.	Newsroom.	Reading Rooms.	Other Depts.	Lending.	Reference.	Newsroom.	Sundays.
Aberdeen	1d.	2100	400	221,925	Not kept	…	…	No record	…	47	64	78	…
Airdrie	1d.	199	47	44,386	284	66	77.150	…	40,000	42	42	60	…
Alloa	1d.	187	46	…	…	…	…	…	…	…	…	…	…
Arbroath	…	…	…	…	…	…	…	…	…	36	42	78	…
Ayr	1d.	500	40	90,073	1,800	76	231,863	…	2,000	60	60	72	…
Brechin	1d.	120	65	33,769	…	73	…	…	…	…	…	…	…
Campbeltown	…	…	…	…	…	…	…	…	…	…	…	…	…
Drumoak	…	…	…	…	…	…	…	…	…	…	…	54	…
Dumbarton	1d.	228	20	18,832	…	79	…	…	…	30	54	…	…
Dundee	1d.	3000	200	232,692	58,449	41	120,000	…	…	…	…	78	…
Dunfermline	1d.	320	…	62,430	5,972	50	…	…	…	36	72	78	…
Edinburgh	¾d.	6520	259	580,231	91,171	…	…	…	…	72	72	54	…
Elgin	1d.	130	40	4,018	595	…	…	…	…	54	54	54	…
Falkirk	…	…	…	…	…	…	…	…	…	…	…	…	…
Forfar	1d.	…	…	…	…	…	…	…	…	…	…	…	…
Galashiels	1d.	263	19	18,788	720	…	…	…	…	18	54	78	…
Grangemouth	1d.	160	20	11,075	…	72	…	…	…	12	…	78	…
Hawick	1d.	275	3	42,837	…	73	…	…	…	26	26	78	…
Inverness	1d.	300	10	18,000	700	75	…	…	…	78	78	78	…

Place	Rate	2	3	4	5	6	7	8	9	10	11	12	13
Jedburgh	…												
Kilmarnock	1d.	434	190	66,572			186,304		39,875	42	45	75	
Kirkcaldy	…												
Kirkmichael	…												
Kirkwall	…												
Newburgh	…												
Paisley	1d.												
Perth	1d.				75								
Peterhead	1d.	95								8	78	78	
Selkirk	1d.	29	26	13,025		109	31,000			3			
Tarves	⅓d.	38	30s.	2,431	64					6	84	84	
Thurso	1d.	150	7	14,695	75	1,400		19,000	15,000	48	72	72	
Wick	1d.												

WALES.

Place	Rate	2	3	4	5	6	7	8	9	10	11	12	13
Aberystwith	1d.	100											
Bangor	1d.		21	1,966			21,000		3,000	10		72	
Barry	1d.	457		15,353	80					12		14	
Broughton	…	3600											
Cardiff	1d.	100		164,781	48	101,605	1,560,000	156,000	726,388	61	72	78	
Carnarvon	1d.	100								24	72	72	
Corwen	…												
Halkin	…												
Holyhead	1d.	78								80		72	
Llanuwchllyn	…												
Penarth	1d.		5	10,000		600	190,000		14,000	72		78	
Pontypridd	1d.	430			80								
Swansea *	1d.	1350	1055	65,799	30	140,244	588,725	105,700	22,650	39	67½	75	
Welshpool	⅓d.												
Wrexham	1d.	228	22	28,691	85	746	105,885			33	63	78	

LIST OF BRITISH LIBRARIES, ENDOWED, COLLE-
GIATE, PROPRIETARY AND OTHER, SHOWING
DATE OF ESTABLISHMENT, NUMBER OF
VOLUMES AND PARTICULARS OF ADMIN-
ISTRATION.

THIS is the largest list ever published of the more important British Libraries not under the Public Libraries
Acts, and yet it is imperfect. It is a matter of much
difficulty obtaining information of any sort concerning the
proprietary and kindred Libraries of the country, but it is
hoped in future to compile a fuller and more perfect list. Commercial Libraries are entirely excluded, as are those connected
with banks, insurance offices, business houses, etc., while the
semi-public Libraries connected with barracks, the navy,
prisons, lighthouses, and rate-supported asylums and schools,
are in the meantime omitted for lack of complete information. The Church and Sunday-school Libraries have also been
excluded for reasons of space, while many parochial and
similar Libraries have had to be ignored because of the lack
of particulars concerning them. The whole question of the
existing Libraries of the country is one of intense interest, as
it must be evident that whatever means are adopted to control
the Library system, which must sooner or later be established
for rural communities, the collections which exist must be taken
into account. Whether the management of rural Libraries is
entrusted to County Councils, as has been proposed, or School
Boards, or a special Library Authority, the foundation of very
many of the necessary Libraries, fixed or travelling, will have
to be based on the parochial and other collections already
established and now existing in a moribund condition. The
system of travelling Libraries which has been proposed for
counties, in order to overcome the difficulties created by inadequate legislative provisions, seems to have attracted much
attention recently. Several attempts have been made to
establish travelling Libraries in connection with institutions
or on general lines. Among the latter may be mentioned the
travelling Libraries started by Mr. W. T. Stead, of the *Review of
Reviews*, while among the former may be named the Yorkshire
Village Library, Leeds ; National Liberal Club Libraries ; Working Men's Club and Institute Union ; Fabian Society, etc. The
idea of travelling or itinerating Libraries was not, as has been

stated, of recent American origin, but seems to date from the early years of this century, when Mr. Samuel Brown established Libraries on this principle in Haddingtonshire in Scotland.

Aberavon. Victoria Institute.

Aberayron, Wales. Aberayron Library.

Abercarne. Library, Reading and Recreation Rooms (1888). 1000 vols.

Aberdeen. Advocates' Library (1788). About 8000 vols. Has a printed catalogue.

Aberdeen. Diocesan Library of the Episcopal Church of Scotland.

Aberdeen. Free Church College Library (1844). 17,000 vols. Has a printed catalogue.

Aberdeen. Medico-Chirurgical Society (1789). 6500 vols. Staff, 2. Printed author catalogue. Members, 70. Hours, 10 to dusk.

Aberdeen. Robert Gordon's College.

Aberdeen. University Library (1495). Over 100,000 vols. Printed catalogue of 1873-74, with supplements. Librarian, P. J. Anderson.

Aberdovey, Wales. Literary Institute.

Abererch, Wales. Village Library (1895).

Aberford, Yorkshire. Parish Lending Library. 1000 vols.

Aberfoyle, Perthshire. Library and Reading-room. Has a special building and a small collection of books.

Aberystwith. University College (1872). 12,000 vols.

Abingdon, Berkshire. Free Library (1895). Has a special building. 4000 vols. (lending, 3400 ; reference, 600). Annual income, £150, derived from the borough funds. Staff, 2. Printed catalogue in dictionary form. Classification, numerical. Card charging. Membership confined to burgesses. Open from 9 A.M. to 10 P.M., save Wednesdays when it is open from 1 to 6 only.

Accrington. Free Library (1858). 1000 vols.

Accrington. Industrial Society Library (1865). 5000 vols.

Accrington. Mechanics' Institute.

Adwalton, Yorkshire. Mechanics' Institute. 400 vols.

Airlie, N.B. Public Library.

Aldershot. Prince Consort's Library (1860). 4000 vols.

Alexandria, N.B. Ewing-Gilmour Institute (1884). 1200 vols.

Alexandria, N.B. S.G.F.S. Institute (1891). 2500 vols.

Alexandria, N.B. Mechanics' Institute (1834). 4000 vols.

Alnwick. Scientific and Mechanics' Institution.

Alton. Mechanics' Institute.

Altrincham. Literary Institution.

Alyth, N.B. Loyal Public Library (1870, building opened in 1895). Gifted by Capt. the Hon. Wm. Ogilvy of Loyal. Librarian, J. R. Mitchell.

Ambleside. Ruskin Library and Book Club. About 500 vols.

Amlwch.   Literary and Scientific Hall.

Andower.   School of Science and Art Institute.

Annan.   Mechanics' Institute (1838). 2000 vols. Printed catalogue of 1889.

Appleton-le-Moors, Yorkshire. Library. 400 vols.

Arbroath.   Public Library (1797, extended in 1875). 16,500 vols. Printed catalogue of 1892. Will be handed over to the Public Library under the Acts, 1896.

Armagh.   Public Library (1771). 19,000 vols. Has a printed catalogue.

Armagh.   Library of the Cathedral Church of St. Patrick.

Armagh.   Natural History and Philosophical Society.

Arncliffe.   Hammond Reading-room (1895).

Arthington, Yorkshire. Village Library. 400 vols.

Arundel.   Reading Society.

Ascot.   Durning Library (1890). 3500 vols.

Ashburton.   Subscription Library.

Ashbury.   Public Reading-room and Library.

Ashford.   South-Eastern Railway Mechanics' Institute.

Ashton-under-Lyne.   Co-operative Society Library. Has 3000 members.

Ashton-under-Lyne.   Mechanics' Institution (1825). Has over 7000 vols. and a printed catalogue.

Ashurst Wood.   Reading-room and Institute. About 500 vols. 117 members.

Aspatria.   Agricultural College.

Auchinleck, N.B.   Public Library.

Auchterarder, N.B.   Smeaton Library and Institute (1896). Founded on an older Library first started in 1884. Re-opened by Mr. Andrew Carnegie in October, 1896, in a new building. Open to subscribers only.

Aylesbury.   Kingsbury Mechanics' Institute.

Aylesbury.   Architectural and Archæological Society.

Bacup.   Co-operative Library (1865). 13,400 vols.

Bacup.   Mechanics' Institute.

Bala.   Welsh Calvinistic College Library.

Ballater, N.B.   Albert Memorial Hall Library (1887). About 1500 vols. Has a printed catalogue.

Banbury.   Mechanics' Institute.

Banchory, N.B.   Public Library.

Bangor, Wales.   Cathedral Library. About 1000 vols.

Bangor, Wales.   Science and Art Institute.

Bardon Mill.   Reading-room (1893). 60 members. Income, £45.

Barmouth.   Barmouth Library. About 600 vols. Hours, 5 to 6.

Barnet.   Hyde Institute (1889). 3700 vols. (3120 lending; 580 reference). Issues, 11,039. Income, £256. Staff, 2. Printed dictionary catalogue. Charging, indicator. Members, 453. Hours, 10 to 9. Librarian, J. H. Vinson.

Barnoldswick. Mechanics' Institute.
Barnsley. British Co-operative Society Library. 9075 vols.
Barnsley. Harvey Institute.
Barnstaple. North-Devon Athenæum, founded by Mr. Rock, and in 1895 greatly enriched by the bequest of Mr. Henry H. Sharland.
Basingstoke. Mechanics' Institute (1843). Over 3000 vols. . Printed catalogue of 1886.
Bath. Guildhall Library.
Bath. People's Club and Institute.
Bath. Royal Literary and Scientific Institution (1825). Over 24,000 vols. Income, £381. Has a printed catalogue.
Bathgate, N.B. Bathgate Institute (1875).
Batley. Co-operative Library. 3820 vols.
Bebington. Mayer Free Library (1866). 15,000 vols. (12,000 lending; 3000 reference). Issues, 15,518. Printed classified catalogue. 600 readers. Hours, 6 to 8·30, etc. Public Libraries Acts have been adopted, and the Mayer Library will be transferred.
Beccles. Subscription Library (1835). About 9000 vols. Income, £100.
Bedford. Literary and Scientific Institute (1830). 16,000 vols. Printed catalogue of 1891. Income, £879. Hours, 11 to 9·30.
Bedford. Working Men's Institute.
Belfast. Belfast Library and Society for Promoting Knowledge, Linen Hall (1788). 40,000 vols. Issues, 90,000. Income, £1600. Staff, 7. Printed dictionary catalogue. MS. catalogue in slip books. Charging, cards. Open access allowed. Members and subscribers, 1120. Special collection of Belfast books. Hours, 9 to 9, etc. Librarian, George Smith.
Belfast. Northern Law Club.
Belfast. Queen's College Library (1849). About 45,000 vols. Hours, 10 to 3. Librarian, A. L. Meissner.
Belfast. Theological Library, Rosemary Street.
Belfast. Working Men's Institute (1873). 5000. Has printed catalogues.
Berkhampstead. Mechanics' Institute.
Berkhampstead. Working Men's College.
Biggar, N.B. Public Library (1800). About 2500 vols. Has printed catalogues.
Biggleswade. Biggleswade Institute.
Birkenhead. Literary and Scientific Society (1857; Library founded, 1874). About 4000 vols. Has a printed catalogue.
Birmingham. Birmingham Library (1779). About 70,000 vols. Has printed catalogues. Librarian, C. E. Scarse.
Birmingham. Friends' Reading-room (1829). About 4000 vols. Has printed catalogues.
Birmingham. King Edward Grammar School.

Birmingham. Law Society (1818; incorporated, 1870). About 11,000 vols. Has printed catalogues.

Birmingham. Mason College (1880). 25,000 vols. Income, £230. Staff, 1. Printed dictionary catalogue. MS. catalogue in guard books. Charging, ledger. Open access allowed. Contains the Hensleigh Wedgwood collection. Hours, 9 to 6. Librarian, Wm. H. Cope.

Birmingham. Medical Institute (1874). About 12,000 vols.

Birmingham. Midland Institute.

Birmingham. Queen's College Library (1828). 3000 vols.

Birnam, Perth. Library for the village.

Blackburn. Stonyhurst College Library (1794). About 60,000 vols.

Blackley. Co-operative Library (1863).

Blackpool. Industrial Co-operative Society Library. 2200 members.

Blaenavon, Wales. Library and Institute (1883). New building opened in 1893. 1600 vols.

Blaina, Wales. Reading-room and Institute (1884). 500 vols. New building, 1893.

Blairgowrie, N.B. Mechanics' Institute.

Blaydon, Durham. Co-operative Library (1847). 3000 vols.

Blyth. Mechanics' Institute.

Bodmin. Literary Institute.

Bolton. Equitable Society Library (1866). 12,000 vols.

Bolton. Mechanics' Institute.

Bolton Abbey, Yorkshire. Parish Library. 800 vols.

Bradford. Bradford Library and Literary Society (1774). 26,000 vols. Income, £1058. Staff, 3. Printed dictionary catalogue. MS. catalogue on cards. Charging, ledger. Open access allowed. Shareholders, 457. Hours, 9 to 6·30; Saturdays, 9 to 2. Librarian, Miss J. Rhodes.

Bradford. Church Institute (1858). 5000 vols. Issues, 18,510. Income, £800. Staff, 3. Printed dictionary catalogue. MS. catalogue on guard books. Charging, cards. Members, 500. Hours, 10 to 8.

Bradford. Historical and Antiquarian Society (1878).

Bradford. Mechanics' Institute (1832). 20,632 vols. (20,132 lending, 500 reference). Issues, 51,804. Income, £2359. Staff, 6. Printed classified catalogue. Charging, ledger. Members, 1449. Hours, 10 to 8·30.

Bradford. Rawdon College Library (1804). 9000 vols.

Bradford. Yorkshire United Independent College (1756). 10,000.

Braemar, N.B. Public Library.

Braintree and Bocking Literary and Mechanics' Institute (1844). 4219 vols. (4051 lending, 168 reference). Issues, 11,425. Income, £133. Staff, 1. Printed classified catalogue. MS. catalogue on cards. Charging, ledger. Open access allowed. Members, 356. Hours, 11 to 10.

Brampton. Museum and Literary Institute.

Brechin. Diocesan Library of the Episcopal Church of Scotland.

Brickfield, Lancashire. Equitable Friends' Library (1857). Over 1000 vols.

Bridgnorth. Literary Institute.

Brierfield. Co-operative Society Library. 1000 vols.

Brighouse. Mechanics' Institute.

Brighton. Young Men's Christian Association Library.

Brightside, Yorkshire. Co-operative Library (1874). About 1000 vols.

Bristol. Baptist College Library (1683). Over 20,000 vols. Has a good collection of Bibles and early printed books.

Bristol. Cathedral Library. Nearly all of old Library destroyed in 1831 by a mob.

Bristol. Incorporated Law Society (1819; incorporated, 1871), 7000 vols. Has a printed catalogue.

Bristol. Medico-Chirurgical Society.

Bristol. Merchant Venturers' Technical College.

Bristol. Museum and Reference Library (1871; taken over by the Corporation in 1893). 50,000 vols. Issues, 33,158. Income, £2150. Staff, 4. Printed classified catalogue. MS. catalogue on cards. Hours, 9·30 to 9 P.M.; Fridays, 9·30 to 2. Librarian, L. Acland Taylor.

Bristol. Postmen's Library and Reading-room (1894).

Bristol. University College.

Brompton. Reading-room and Library, Yorkshire. Over 500 vols.

Bromsgrove. Literary Institute (1860). 3500 vols. Issues, 10,095. Income, £300. Staff, 1. Printed clasified catalogue. Charging, ledger. Members, 500. Hours, 12·30 to 1·30, and 7·30 to 8·30.

Broughty-Ferry, N.B. Corbet Library (about 1845). Contains over 1500 vols.

Buckie, N.B. Public Library.

Bunbury. Lending Library.

Burnham, Somerset. Free Library. Has a printed catalogue.

Burnley. Co-operative Society Library. 6000 vols.

Burnley. Literary Institute.

Burnley. Mechanics' Institution (1834). 18,500 vols. Issues, 45,444. Staff, 6. Printed subject catalogue. Charging, ledger. Members, 1010. Hours, 10 to 8·30. Librarian, Thomas Hartley.

Burntisland, N.B. Mechanics' Institute.

Burslem. Wedgwood Memorial Institute (1870). About 7500 vols. Has a printed catalogue. See *The Wedgwood Memorial Institute, Burslem*, by Joseph Dawson, 1894.

Burton-on-Trent. Burton Institute.

Bury, Lancashire. Co-operative Library (1860). 15,000 vols.

Bury St. Edmunds. Athenæum. Contains, in addition to its own stock, about 20,000 vols. transferred from the Bury St. Edmunds and West Suffolk Library (1846) in 1896.

Butterstone, N.B. Public Library (1894).
Calne, Wiltshire. Literary Institute.
Calverley. Mechanics' Institute.
Camborne. Mining Association and Institute of Cornwall
    Mining School Library.
Cambridge. Cambridge Union Society (1815). 24,000 vols.
Cambridge. Christ's College (16th century). 13,000 vols. 70
    MSS.
Cambridge. Clare College; originally 1346, present Library
    1550. 7500 vols.
Cambridge. Corpus Christi College (15 c.). 7000 vols.
Cambridge. Downing College (1800). 4000 vols.
Cambridge. Emmanuel College (1584-86). 22,000 vols. Has
    a printed catalogue.
Cambridge. Fitzwilliam Museum (bequeathed by Viscount
    Fitzwilliam in 1816). 10,000 vols. Printed catalogue of
    the music has been published.
Cambridge. Girton College Library.
Cambridge. Gonville and Caius College Library (1348). 15,000
    vols.
Cambridge. Jesus College Library. 10,000 vols.
Cambridge. King's College (1441). 25,000 vols.
Cambridge. Magdalene College (Pepysian Library founded,
    1724; College Library, unknown). Pepysian Library, 3000
    vols.; College Library, 2500 vols.
Cambridge. Newnham College (1882). About 8000 vols.
Cambridge. Pembroke College Library. 15,000 vols.
Cambridge. Peterhouse College. Perne Library founded in
    1597. There was an older Library of an unknown date.
    Contains 8700 vols.
Cambridge. Philosophical Library (1881). 12,000 vols.
Cambridge. Queen's College (1448). Over 30,000 vols. Printed
    catalogue of 1827.
Cambridge. Ridley Hall, Carr Library (1882). 4000 vols. MS.
    catalogue on cards. Charging, cards. Open access allowed.
    Hours, 10 till dusk. Librarian, G. A. Schneider.
Cambridge. St. Catherine's College (1475). 12,800 vols. Printed
    catalogue of 1771.
Cambridge. St. John's College (1511). 50,000 vols., 1000 MSS.,
    23,000 pamphlets. Printed catalogue of MSS. issued in
    1842.
Cambridge. Selwyn College Library.
Cambridge. Sidney Sussex College Library (1598). 5000 vols.
Cambridge. Taylor Library. 2000 vols.
Cambridge. Trinity College (1546). About 90,000 vols., 1918
    MSS. Has printed catalogue of special collections. Has
    the Capell collection of Shaksperiana. Hours, 11 to 3.
    Librarian, Rev. R. Sinker, D.D.
Cambridge. Trinity Hall Library (1350). 7000 vols., a number
    of which are chained to reading-desks.

Cambridge. University Library (1444). Over 500,000 vols. Has a printed catalogue of the MSS., and prints a weekly bulletin of accessions. Librarian, Francis Jenkinson.

Canterbury. Cathedral, Library of the Dean and Chapter. Has over 10,000 vols. and MSS.

Canterbury. St. Augustine's College (1848). 15,000 vols.

Cardiff. Cardiff and County Library (1881). 2000 vols.

Cardiff. Law Library.

Cardiff. South Wales and Monmouthshire College (1883). About 6000 vols.

Carlisle. Chapter Library, the Cathedral (1660). About 4000 vols.

Carlisle. Scotby Library (1884). 1000 vols.

Carmarthen. Literary and Scientific Institution (1840). 5000 vols. Issues, 2400. Income, £200. Staff, 3. Printed classified catalogue. Classification, author alphabetical. Charging, ledger. Members, 200. Hours, 7·30 to 9 P.M. Librarian, P A. Baldwin.

Carsethorn, N.B. Library (1891). About 800 vols. Issues, 1600. Income, £13. Printed classified catalogue. Charging, cards. Members, 98. Open 1 hour once a fortnight.

Cashel. Diocesan Library (founded by Archbishop Theophilus Bolton, 1729-44). 16,000 vols. Has a printed catalogue of 1873.

Castle-Douglas, N.B. Mechanics' Institute. 2300 vols.

Castleford, Yorkshire. Mechanics' Library. 900 vols.

Castlemartyr, Ireland. Lending Library (1895). About 800 vols.

Cathcart, N.B. Couper Institute (1887). 3000 vols. Printed catalogue of 1888.

Catrine, N.B. United Public Library. About 4500 vols. Income, £30. Members, 177.

Chapel-en-le-Frith. Institute.

Chatham. Dockyard Library.

Cheddar. Literary Institution.

Chawleigh, Devon. Library.

Cheltenham. Cheltenham College Library (1866). About 10,000 vols.

Cheltenham. Cheltenham Library (1863). 19,000 vols. Income, £500. Members, 270. Has printed catalogues. Librarian, James T. Presley.

Chester. Cathedral Library (mediæval). 1200 vols.

Chester-le-Street. Co-operative Society Library (1869).

Chichester. Cathedral Library (1660). 4000 vols.

Chichester. Chichester Institute (1829). 7320 vols. (7059 lending; 261 reference). Staff, 4. Printed author catalogue. Charging, ledger. Open access allowed. Hours, 12 to 1; 7·30 to 9.

Chichester. Library Society (1794). 8500 vols. Printed catalogue of 1874.

Chippenham. Jubilee Institute.

Chirnside, N.B.   Library.   Income, £20.   Members, 104.

Christchurch, Hampshire.   Working Men's Institute.

Clayton-le-Moors.   Co-operative Society Library.   About 1000
vols.

Cleckheaton.   Co-operative Industrial Society Library (1879).
4000 vols.

Cleckheaton.   Mechanics' Institute.

Clonakilty, Ireland.   Public Library.

Clonmel.   Literary Institute (formerly Mechanics' Institute,
1842).   3500 vols.   Has a printed catalogue.

Clydebank, N.B.   Public Library.

Coalbrookdale.   Literary Institute.

Coatbridge, N.B.   Literary Association.

Coatbridge.   Technical School and Mining College.

Cockermouth.   Wordsworth Institute.

Coggeshall.   Literary Institute.

Colchester.   Literary Institute.

Coldingham, N.B.   Public Library.

Coldstream.   Mechanics' Institution (1852, previous to which
it was a subscription Library).   4500 vols.   Has a printed
catalogue.

Colmonell, N.B.   Public Library.   1500 vols.   Issues, 2200 vols.

Colne.   Co-operative Society Library.   1700 vols.

Combe, Woodstock.   Library for the village.

Compstall.   Athenæum.

Congleton.   Co-operative Society Library.   900 vols.

Consett.   Industrial Society Library (1868).   About 1000 vols.

Cork.   Diocesan Theological Library, St. Finn Barre's Cathedral
(1629, Lending Library added in 1891).   2030 vols. (530 lending, 1500 reference).   Issues, 179.   Income, £30.   Staff, 1.
Charging, ledger.   Open access allowed.   Members, 40.
Hours, 10 to 6.

Cork.   Library Society (1792).   30,000 vols.   Issues, 72,000 vols.
Income, £520.   Staff, 3.   Printed classified catalogue.
Charging, ledger.   Open access allowed to fiction only.
Members, 420.   Hours, 10 to 6.

Cork.   Queen's College (1849).   31,000 vols.   Income for purchase of books and periodicals, £280.   Staff, 2.   MS. catalogue in guard books.   Classification, subject.   Charging,
cards.   Hours, 9 to 4 in session, 11 to 2 in vacation.

Corstorphine, N.B.   Library, founded in 1856 by Dr. Fowler.
Contains about 4000 vols.

Coventry.   Coventry Institute.

Crail, N.B.   Public Library.

Crayke, Yorkshire.   Parish Library.   700 vols.

Crieff.   Taylor's Trust Free Library (1889).   4460 vols. (4300
lending, 160 reference).   Issues, 21,000.   Income, £300.
Staff, 1.   Printed author and classified catalogue.   Charging, indicator.   Members, 1000.   Hours, 8 to 12, 1 to 3, 6
to 10.

Crompton. Co-operative Library. 3000 vols.

Croydon. County Polytechnic Institute.

Croydon. Literary and Scientific Institute.

Cuddesdon, Oxford. Theological College Library.

Cullen, N.B. Public Library.

Cumnock, N.B. Athenæum (1792).

Cupar, N.B. Duncan Institute.

Cwmaman, Wales. Library (1879). New building opened in 1892. 1400 vols.

Cwmparc, Wales. Library (1880). 1000 vols.

Cwmtillery, Wales. Library (1884). 500 vols.

Cymmer, Wales. Library (1893). Building cost £2400. 500 vols.

Dalbeattie, N.B. Mechanics' Institute. Contains 2336 vols.

Dalry, N.B. Public Library (1863). 2000 vols. Has a printed catalogue.

Dalton-in-Furness. Co-operative Library (1867). 2000 vols.

Dartford. Public Library.

Darvel, N.B. Brown's Institute.

Darwen. Industrial Society Library (1868). 7500 vols.

Dawley. Literary Institute.

Dawlish. Cozen's Institute.

Deal. Deal Institute.

Denholm, N.B. Public Library (1805). The cottage in which John Leyden, the poet, was born has been converted into a home for this Library with the aid of Mr. Andrew Carnegie.

Denny, N.B. Public Library.

Derby. Mechanics' Institution (1825). Has a special building, 1881. 7300 vols. (7000 lending, 300 reference). Issues, 18,000 vols. Income, £250. Staff, 1. Printed classified catalogue. Charging, ledger. Members, 790. Hours: 11 to 2, 6 to 9; Reading-rooms, 8 A.M. to 10 P.M. Librarian, Charles Francis.

Derby. Midland Railway Institute (reorganised 1894). 9250 vols. (9000 lending, 250 reference). Issues, 60,518 vols. Staff, 3. Printed classified catalogue. Classification, numerical in main classes. Charging, indicator. Members, 2100. Hours: Library, 11·30 to 8·30; Reading-rooms, 8 A.M. to 10 P.M. Librarian, Ernest A. Baker, B.A.

Devizes. Literary and Scientific Institution (1833). 1500 vols. Printed catalogue of 1893.

Dewsbury. Co-operative Library (1862). 7653 vols.

Didsbury. Wesleyan College Library.

Dingwall. Public Library, presented in 1895 by Miss Yule.

Diss. Diss Library.

Dodworth. Mechanics Institute.

Dollar, N.B. Dollar Institution (1818). 6000 vols. Issues, 250 vols. Staff, 1. Printed dictionary catalogue. Charging, ledger. Members, 150. Hours, 11 to 12.

Doncaster. Co-operative Society Library. 2250 vols.

Doncaster. Great Northern Railway Free Mechanics' Library (1853). 3000 vols. (lending, 2800; reference, 200). Issues, 4800. Staff, 2. Printed classified catalogue. Charging, ledger. Members, 4000. Hours, 5·30 to 9 P.M.; Saturdays, 4 to 9.

Dorchester. Library, maintained by Col. Williams, M.P.

Dorking. Working Men's Institute (1856).

Doune, N.B. Moray Institute and Library (1894). Includes the old Kilmadock Library of 1865.

Dover. Proprietary Library.

Dover. Working Men's Institute.

Dowlais, Wales. Library (1852). Has a special building.

Downpatrick. Newsroom and Library.

Droylsden. Co-operative Society Library. About 1200 vols.

Dublin. King's Inns Library, of the Hon. Soc. of King's Inns (1788). 60,000 vols. Has printed catalogues.

Dublin. Law Library, Four Courts. New building completed in 1896.

Dublin. Marsh's Library (established in St. Patrick's Cathedral in 1707). Contains 25,000 vols. Has a MS. catalogue drawn up by the Rev. E. Bouhéreau in 1707-14. Librarian, Rev. G. T. Stokes, D.D.

Dublin. Mechanics' Institution (1825). 6000 vols. Income, £600. Hours, 10 to 9.

Dublin. National Library of Ireland (1877, previously it existed as the Library of the Royal Dublin Society). Has a special building of 1890. 130,000 vols. Book purchases, about £1000 per annum. Has a printed dictionary catalogue. Library catalogues for desk use, author. Staff, 11. Classification, Dewey system. Charging, ledger. Modified open access allowed. Hours 10 to 10. Librarian, T. W. Lyster.

Dublin. Royal College of Physicians of Ireland (1711). Has a printed catalogue.

Dublin. Royal College of Surgeons in Ireland (1784). 30,000 vols. Has a printed catalogue, and a MS. catalogue in guard books. Charging, ledger. Hours, 11 to 5.

Dublin. Royal Irish Academy (1786). 72,000 vols., of which 40,000 are books and 1400 MSS. Printed catalogue in preparation.

Dublin. Steeven's Hospital Library.

Dublin. Trinity College (1601). 238,606 vols. and MSS. 4000 vols. in Reading-room for open access. Staff, 12. Printed author catalogue to 1872. MS. catalogue in guard books since 1872. Open access allowed to Fellows and Professors. Has several special collections, i.e., Quin, 1st editions; M'Ghee, Bibles, etc. Hours, 10 to 6, with exceptions.

Dublin. United Service Club Library.

Dublin. Young Men's Christian Association Library.

Dudley. Dudley Institute (1848). 6000 vols. Has a printed catalogue.

Dukinfield. Astley Institute. 5000 vols.

Dumfries. Mechanics' Institute.

Dunbeath, N.B. Public Library (1880).

Dunblane. Bibliotheca Leightoniana, or Leightonian Library (founded by Archbishop Leighton in 1684). About 2000 vols.

Dundee. University College Library (1882). About 2500 vols.

Dungourney, Ireland. Parish Library (1894). About 500 vols.

Duns, N.B. South Church Congregational Library. 2000 vols.

Duns, N.B. Subscription Library (1768). 7000 vols. Has a printed catalogue.

Durham. Bishop Cosins Library (1669). 5964 vols. and MSS. Has a printed catalogue of some of the MSS. Librarian, J. T. Fowler.

Durham. Cathedral Library (mediæval). 15,000 vols.

Durham. Equitable Co-operative Library (1866). 1500 vols.

Durham. Mechanics' Institute (1825). 23,000 vols.

Durham. University Library (1833). 32,000 vols. Printed catalogues of Maltby (1863) and Lightfoot (1891) collections. Librarian, J. T. Fowler.

Dysart, N.B. Public Library.

Ealing. Young Men's Institute.

Earlston, N.B. Reading-room and Library. Income, £33.

East Dereham. Athenæum.

East Grinstead. Literary and Scientific Institute (1888).

East Witton, Yorkshire. Library. 300 vols.

Ebbw Vale. Literary Institute.

Eccles. Provident Industrial Society Library (1867). 9000 vols.

Edale. Reading-room and Library. New building opened in 1894.

Edenbridge. The Institute.

Edinburgh. Advocates' Library (1680). 350,000 vols. Hours, 10 to 4: Saturdays, 10 to 1. Open to any student or reader in quest of information. Librarian, J. T. Clark.

Edinburgh. Edinburgh Subscription Library (1794). Over 40,000 vols. Has printed catalogues of 1846, 1866, 1887, etc. Librarian, George McWhea.

Edinburgh. Faculty of Actuaries' Library (1856). Over 3000 vols. Has a printed catalogue. Librarian, George Lisle, C.A.

Edinburgh. Fettes College (1870). 2500 vols.

Edinburgh. General Register House. Has a Library in addition to the volumes of records.

Edinburgh. Geological Society (1834). 2500 vols. Has a printed catalogue.

Edinburgh. Heriot's Hospital (1762). Over 4000 vols. Has a printed catalogue.

Edinburgh. Heriot-Watt College (formerly Watt Institution, and originally a School of Arts, 1821). 3000 vols. Has a printed catalogue.

Edinburgh. High School Library.

Edinburgh. Juridical Society Library.

Edinburgh. Literary Institute (1872). 10,000.

Edinburgh. Museum of Science and Art (Library opened to the public in 1890). 16,000 vols. Staff, 3. Printed author and class catalogue. Classification, by subjects. Has Patents Specifications, and the Cleghorn Memorial Library of Works on Forestry. Hours, 10 to 4, also 6 to 10 on Fridays and Saturdays. Librarian, C. N. B. Muston.

Edinburgh. New College Library (of the Free Church of Scotland, 1843). 42,000 vols. (40,000 lending; 2000 reference). Issues, 5000. Income, £300. Staff, 2. Printed author and class catalogue. MS. catalogue on slips. Subject classification. Charging, ledger. Members, over 200. Hours, 10 to 2. Librarian, James Kennedy.

Edinburgh. Obstetrical Society Library.

Edinburgh. Pharmaceutical Society of Great Britain. North British branch. 2000 vols. Has a printed catalogue.

Edinburgh. Philosophical Institution (1846). 29,000 vols. Staff, 5. Printed author and dictionary catalogues. Charging, cards. Open access allowed in reference department. Members, 1500. Hours, 9·30 to 8·30. Librarian, H. G. Aldis.

Edinburgh. Royal College of Physicians' Library (1683). 40,000 vols. Has printed catalogues.

Edinburgh. Royal College of Surgeons (1505). About 8000 vols. Has printed catalogues.

Edinburgh. Royal Medical Society (1737). Over 30,000 vols. Has printed and MS. catalogues.

Edinburgh. Royal Physical Society Library.

Edinburgh. Royal Scottish Academy Library.

Edinburgh. Royal Scottish Geographical Society (1884). 5000 vols. Has printed catalogues.

Edinburgh. Royal Scottish Society of Arts Library.

Edinburgh. Royal Society Library (1737). 17,000 vols.

Edinburgh. Signet Library, or Library of the Society of Writers to H.M. Signet (Law Library, 1722; General Library, 1778). About 88,000 vols. Has various printed catalogues. Librarian, Thos. G. Law.

Edinburgh. Society of Antiquaries of Scotland Library (established at end of last century). Over 8000 vols.

Edinburgh. Solicitors' Library, or Library of the Society of Solicitors to the Supreme Courts (1808). 14,000 vols.

Edinburgh. United Presbyterian College (1847). 34,000 vols. Has printed catalogues.

Edinburgh. University Library (1580). Nearly 200,000 vols. and MSS. Contains the Scots Law Library (1815). Has printed and MS. catalogues. Librarian, Hugh A. Webster.

Edinburgh. Working Men's Club Library.
Egham. Literary Institute.
Egham. Royal Holloway College Library.
Egremont. Workmen's Institute.
Elie, Fifeshire. Subscription Library. Contains 4000 vols.
Elland. Mechanics' Institute.
Ely. Cathedral Library (mediæval). 7100 vols. Printed catalogue of 1884.
. Erdington. Oscott College, or St. Mary's College (1838). About 36,000 vols. Has printed catalogue of Incunabula and some MSS.
Eton. College Library (15th century). 23,000 vols.
Eton. School or Boys' Library (1821). 10,000 vols. Has printed catalogue of 1888-89.
Etton, Yorkshire. Parochial Library. 300 vols.
Evesham. Evesham Institute.
Exeter. Cathedral Library (mediæval). 8000 vols.
Exeter. Devon and Exeter Institution (1813). Over 30,000 vols. Has printed catalogues. Librarian, Edward Parfitt.
Exeter. Literary Institute.
Exeter. Technical College.
Eyemouth, N.B. Public Library.
Failsworth. Industrial Society Library (1873). 5056 vols.
Farnham. Farnham Institute.
Farnham. Young Men's Association Library.
Farnworth and Kernsley. Co-operative Society Library. 3750 vols.
Faversham. Faversham Institute.
Ferrybridge, Yorkshire. Library. 300 vols.
Fetterangus, N.B. Chalmers Institute (1895). About 1000 vols.
Fetteresso, N.B. Fetteresso Library.
Finchley. Public Library (1896). 1300 vols.
Findhorn, N.B. Public Library.
Fleetwood. Industrial Co-operative Society Library. 800 vols.
Fochabers, N.B. Fochabers Library.
Fochabers. Milne's Institute.
Forfar. Sheriff Court Library.
Forres. Mechanics' Institute and Library. 4000 vols. Issues, 10,550 vols. Income, £40. Staff, 1. Printed author and class catalogue. Members, 225. Hours, Wednesdays from 9 to 10, 2 to 3 and 8 to 9. Librarian, Wm. Forrest.
Fort Augustus, N.B. St. Benedict's Abbey (1878). About 19,000 vols. Has a MS. catalogue. Librarian, Rev. O. Hunter Blair, M.A.
Fortrose, N.B. Fortrose Library (1854). 2500 vols. Issues, 700. Income, £20. Staff, 1. Printed classified catalogue. Charging, ledger. Members, 50. Hours, 10 to 10.
Fraserburgh, N.B. Mechanics' Institute.
Friockheim, N.B. Reading-room and Library (1875).
Frome. Literary Institute.

Frome. Mechanics' Institute (1858). Over 2000 vols. Has printed catalogue.

Gainsborough. Literary, Scientific and Mechanics' Institution (1849). 3000 vols. Has printed catalogue.

Galston, N.B. Brown's Institute.

Galway. Queen's College Library. 30,000 vols.

Gartmore, N.B. Public Library, 2000 vols.

Gatehouse-of-Fleet, N.B. Public Library (1856). Over 2000 vols. Has a printed catalogue.

Gilling, Yorkshire. Library. 300 vols.

Girvan. McKechnie Library and Reading-room (1888). Over 6000 vols. Has printed catalogues. Librarian, Andrew Robertson.

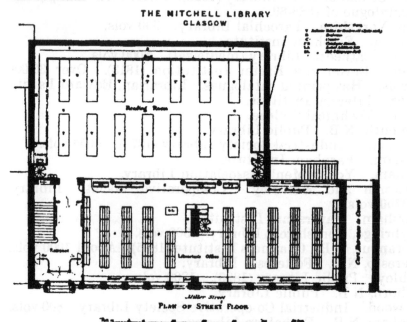

THE MITCHELL LIBRARY
GLASGOW

PLAN OF STREET FLOOR

Glasgow. Accountants' Library.

Glasgow. Anderson's College. Contains the Euing Musical Library, 5500 vols., and a general Library of 10,000 vols. Total, 15,500 vols.

Glasgow. Archæological Society Library.

Glasgow. Athenæum (instituted, 1847; incorporated, 1885). 18,000 vols. Has printed catalogues.

Glasgow. Baillie's Institution (founded, 1863; opened, 1887). 14,065 vols. Issues, 64,886 vols. Income, £1400. Staff, 3. Printed dictionary catalogue. Hours, 10 to 10. Librarian, William Simpson.

Glasgow. Evangelical Union Theological Hall Library.

Glasgow. Faculty of Physicians and Surgeons' Library (1698). 38,000 vols., of which 1000 are for reference. £400 annually spent on books. Staff, 2. Printed author and class catalogue. MS. catalogue on cards. Charging, ledger. Hours, 10 to 6. Librarian, Alexander Duncan.

Glasgow. Faculty of Procurators' Library (1817). 18,000 vols. Has printed catalogues. Librarian, John Muir.

Glasgow. Free Church College (1855). About 25,000 vols., including a valuable collection of Gaelic literature.

Glasgow. Glasgow and West of Scotland Technical College Library (originally the Mechanics' Institute).

Mr. F. T. Barrett, Librarian, Mitchell Library, Glasgow. From a photo by Annan & Sons, Glasgow.

Glasgow. Institution of Engineers and Shipbuilders in Scotland (1857). 2500 vols. Income, £960. Staff, 2. Printed dictionary catalogue. Charging, ledger. Open access allowed. Members, 800. Hours, 9·30 to 8·30. Librarian, Frank Martin.

Glasgow. Mitchell Library (founded, 1874; opened, November 1877). 120,000 vols. Issues, 500,000 vols. Income from various sources, £3300. Staff, 20. Printed dictionary catalogue in guard books, for desk use only. Classification, by subjects. Has special collections of Scottish Poetry and Burnsiana, Glasgow early printing, and Glasgow local literature, etc. Hours, 9·30 A.M. to 10 P.M. Librarian, Francis T. Barrett.

Glasgow. Natural History Society Library.

Glasgow. Philosophical Society Library.

Glasgow. Possilpark Institute.

Glasgow. Queen Margaret College Library. ·

Glasgow. Stirling's and Glasgow Public Library (1791). About 43,000 vols. Income, £800. Staff, 6. Subscribers, 703. Hours, 10 to 10. Librarian, W. J. S. Paterson.

Glasgow. University Library (founded in the middle of the 15th century). Over 200,000 vols. and pamphlets. Has printed catalogues of portions of the Library. Librarian, James Lymburn.

Glasgow. Young Men's Christian Association.

Glossop Dale. Co-operative Society Library. 3045 vols.

Gloucester. Cathedral Library. 1800 vols.

Gloucester. Literary and Scientific Society.

Godalming. Charterhouse School (1803). 10,000 vols. Has printed catalogues.

Godshill, Isle of Wight. Parish Library.

Gomersal. Mechanics' Institute.

Gourock, N.B. Gamble Institute.

Govan, N.B. Thom's Library (1842). 1000 vols.

Granton, N.B. Literary Association.

Grantown, N.B. Library and Reading-room.

Great Bradley, Suffolk. Village Library (1896).

Great Harwood. Co-operative Society Library. 2210 vols.

Greenock. Greenock Library, Watt Monument (1783). About 22,000 vols. Has printed catalogue.

Greenock. Mechanics' Institution (1837). 8000 vols. (7500 lending, 500 reference). Issues, 30,000 vols. Income, £80. Staff, 2. Printed author and class catalogue. MS. catalogue in guard books. Charging, ledger. Open access allowed. Members, 600. Hours, 3 to 9.

Guernsey. Guille-Allès Library and Museum (1856; enlarged 1881-86). 65,000 vols. Printed catalogue of 1891. Librarian, J. Linwood Pitts.

Guildford. Mechanics' Institute.

Guildford. Working Men's Institute.

Guiseley, Yorkshire. Mechanics' Institute. 1500 vols.

Haddington. Free Library (1717). Contains about 4000 vols.

Haddington. Town and County Library.

Hafod, Wales. Library (1884). 1300 vols.

Halesworth. Mechanics' Institute.

Halifax. Dean Clough Institute (1859). 10,000 vols. Has a printed catalogue.

Halifax. Industrial Co-operative Library (1872). 5000 vols.

Halifax. Literary and Philosophical Society.

Halifax. Mechanics' Institution (1825). 15,000 vols. Has printed catalogue of 1883.

Halstead. Mechanics' Institute.

Halton. Chesshyre Library (founded by Sir John Chesshyre in 1733). Contains about 500 vols.

Hamilton, N.B. Mechanics' Institute (1846).

Hanley. Potteries Mechanics' Institution (1826).

Harrow. School. Vaughan Library (1863). 11,000 vols. Income, £150. Staff, 2. Printed author catalogue. MS. catalogue on cards. Charging, ledger. Open access allowed. Scholars of school are members, about 660. Open 4 hours daily.

Haslingden. Industrial Society Library (1874). 1500 vols.

Hastings. Corporation Reference Library in Brassey Institute and Museum (1881). 7000 vols. Issues, 9345 vols. annually. Hours, 10 to 10. Founded by Lord Brassey. Librarian, Edward H. Marshall, M.A.

Hawarden. St. Deniol's Free Library (1894). 30,000 vols. Established by the Right Hon. W. E. Gladstone.

Hawick, N.B. Buccleuch Memorial Institute.

Hayle. Literary Institute.

Hebden Bridge, Yorkshire. Co-operative Library. 2000 vols.

Hebden Bridge. Mechanics' Institute. 2000 vols.

Helensburgh, N.B. Public Library.

Hemel Hempstead. Mechanics' Institute.

Hemsworth, Yorkshire. Parochial Library. 400 vols.

Hereford. Cathedral Library (1380). Has about 2000 vols., most of which were chained. In February, 1896, the foundation stone of a new building was laid.

Hereford. Permanent Library (1815). 8500 vols.

Hertford. Haileybury College (1862). About 7000 vols.

Hertford. Literary Institute.

Heywood. Industrial Co-operative Society Library (1860). 10,550 vols.

Hitchin. Mechanics' Institute.

Holbeck. Mechanics' Institute.

Hollingworth. Co-operative Society Library. 1180 vols.

Holy Island. Reading-room and Library (1870).

Horncastle. Mechanics' Institute (1835). 4500 vols.

Horsforth. Mechanics' Institute.

Horsham Museum. Has a printed catalogue of books lent on a "socialistic" principle.

Horwich. Mechanics' Institute (1888). 7700 vols. (6360 lending, 1340 reference). Issues, 19,000. Staff, 2. Printed dictionary catalogue. Charging, ledger. Members, 1780. Hours, 12·30 to 2·30 and 7 to 9.

Huddersfield. Co-operative Society Library. 3000 vols.

Huddersfield. Mechanics' Institute.

Huddersfield.   Subscription Library.   Over 50,000 vols.

Huddersfield.   Technical College Library.

Huddersfield.   Yorkshire Archæological Association Library.

Hull.   Lyceum Library (1807).   15,000 vols.   Income, £300. Staff, 2.   Printed dictionary catalogue.   Charging, ledger. Open access allowed.   Members, 300.   Hours, 9 to 8.

Hull.   Mechanics' Institute.

Hull.   Royal Institution.

Hull.   Subscription Library (1775).   50,000 vols.   Has printed catalogues.   Income, £890.   Librarian, Alfred Milner.

Huntingdon.   Church of England Young Men's Society. Contains Lady Sparrow's Free Lending Library, gifted about 1864.   There are about 2000 vols.

Huntly, N.B.   Brander Library (founded 1882, opened in 1885). 6200 vols.   Issues, 9000 vols.   Staff, 1.   Printed classified catalogue.   Charging, ledger.   Members, about 200.   Hours vary from 10 to 1, 1 to 4, and 6 to 9 on different days. Librarian, Miss Mary Gray.

Hutton, Somerset.   Parochial Free Library.

Hutton Rudby, Yorkshire.   Mechanics' Institute.   400 vols.

Hyde.   Industrial Co-operative Society Library.   2200 vols.

Hythe.   The Institute.

Ilkley.   Library Company (1872).   4600 vols.   Issues, 15,000. Income, £300.   Staff, 2.   Has printed catalogue.   Members, about 300.   Hours, 10 to 1, 2 to 5·30, 6·30 to 8·30.

Innerpeffrey, N.B.   Library, founded about 1680-91 by David Drummond, 3rd Lord Madderty.   Contains about 3000 vols. An account of this old Library appears in the *Scotsman*, 30th January, 1895.   Issues, 500 vols.

Inverkeithing, N.B.   Subscription Library.

Inverness.   Workmen's Club Library.

Iona, Argyleshire.   Legh Richmond Library, founded about 1820 by the Rev. Legh Richmond.

Ipswich.   Working Men's College.

Irvine, N.B.   Tower Hall Library.

Jarrow-on-Tyne.   Mechanics' Institute (1863).   5000 vols. Issues, 11,500 vols.   Income, £536.   Has a printed catalogue.

Jersey.   Mechanics' Institute.

Johnstone, N.B.   Mechanics' Institute.

Keighley.   Industrial Co-operative Society Library.   2100 vols.

Keighley.   Mechanics' Institute (1825).   12,000 vols.   Has a printed catalogue.   .

Keith.   Public Library (1877).   3433 vols. (3053 lending; 380 reference).   Issues, 9118.   Income, £60.   Staff, 1.   Printed classified catalogue.   Charging, ledger.   Members, 262. Hours, Wednesday 2 till 3; Saturday 1 till 2, 7 till 9.

Kelso.   Kelso Library (1751).   9000 vols.

Kelso.   Mechanics' Institute (1866).

Kendal.   Mechanics' Institute.

Kettering. Church Institute. 1000 vols.

Keswick. Library. Income, £44. Subscribers, 110.

Kew. Royal Botanic Gardens Library (1866). 16,000 vols.

Kilbirnie, N.B. William Knox Institute (1892). 2060 vols. Issues, 3000. Income, £80. Staff, 2. Printed author catalogue. Classification, numerical. Charging, ledger. Members, 250. Hours 3 to 4, and 7·30 to 8·30.

Kilkenny. St. Canice's Library (1692). 2000 vols. A diocesan Library for the use of the clergy.

Kilmarnock. Burns Library in the Burns Monument (1877-82). About 900 vols.

Kingston-on-Thames. Workmen's Club.

Kinross. Tradesmen's Library (1825). Hours, 3 to 9 on Tuesdays.

Kinsale, Ireland. Public Library.

Kirkby Malham, Yorkshire. Library. 1100 vols.

Kirkcudbright. Mechanics' Institute (Library 1777; amalgamated in 1842 and 1854, when Reading-room opened). 5876 vols. Issues, 4655. Income, £66. Staff, 2. Printed classified catalogue. Charging, ledger. Members, 234. Hours, Reading-room, 8 A.M. to 10·30 P.M.; Library, 7 to 9 on Tuesday, 3 to 5 on Friday. Librarian, John Angus.

Kirkcaldy, N.B. Subscription Library.

Knaresborough. Literary Institute. 3000 vols.

Knutsford. Literary Institute and Working Men's Library.

Lamplugh. Parochial Library. Contains about 650 vols. Members, 26.

Lancaster. Co-operative Library (1864). 6400 vols.

Lancaster. Stovey Institute.

Langholm, N.B. Langholm Library (1800). About 8000 vols. Has a printed catalogue. Library endowed by Thomas Telford, the great engineer.

Langley Mill. Working Men's Educational Institute.

Langport. Reading-room and Library.

Largs. Stevenson Institute (1877, reorganised 1894). 3100 vols. Issues, 10,316. Income, £170. Staff, 2. Printed classified catalogue. Charging, ledger. Members, 290. Hours, 10 to 10.

Larne. Newsroom and circulating Library (1873). About 1200 vols. Income, £100. Members, 206.

Laurencekirk. Laurencekirk Library.

Leadhills, N.B. Miners' Library (1741). Contains about 3500 vols. Has a printed catalogue.

Leeds. Industrial Co-operative Society Library (1864). 4000 vols.

Leeds. Law Library.

Leeds. Leeds Library (1768). 80,000 vols. Printed catalogue of 1889.

Leeds. Mechanics' Institution and Literary Society (1824). 20,000 vols. Has a printed catalogue.

Leeds. Philosophical and Literary Society Library.

Leeds.   Thoresby Antiquarian Society Library.
Leeds.   Working Men's Hall (1869).   Contains over 500 vols.
Leeds.   Yorkshire College (1875).   10,000 vols.
Leeds.   Yorkshire Naturalists' Society Library.
Leeds.   Yorkshire Union Village Library (1852).   35,000 vols.
     (32,000 lending, 3000 reference).   Issues, 110,000.   Income,
     £500.   Staff, 6.   Has 205 affiliated village institutes and
     about 100 honorary subscribers.   Hours, 10 till 4.   Supplies
     villages with boxes of 50 books once a quarter.   Librarian,
     Frank Curzon.
Leek.   Literary and Mechanics' Institution.
Leicester.   Law Society Library (1860).   About 2000 vols.   Has
     a printed catalogue of 1890.
Leicester.   Permanent Library (1790).   25,000 vols.   Income,
     £850.   Staff, 4.   Printed classified catalogue.   Charging,
     cards.   Open access allowed.   Subscribers, 600.   Hours,
     10 to 6.   Librarian, Frank S. Herne.
Leigh, Lancaster.   Co-operative Library (1865).   2000 vols.
Leighton Buzzard.   The Institute.
Leith.   Public Institute and Library (1845).   13,000 vols.
     Printed catalogues of 1887 and 1892.
Leslie, N.B.   Young Men's Christian Association Library (1887).
     1300 vols.   Has a printed catalogue.
Letterkenny, Ireland.   Literary Institute.
Leuchars, N.B.   Parish Library (1887).   Building, presented
     by Mrs. Pitcairn of Pitcullo, opened in 1894.   Contains
     about 1500 vols.
Leven, N.B.   Greig Institute (1873).   About 3000 vols.   Has a
     printed catalogue.
Lewes.   Fitzroy Memorial Library.
Lewes.   Mechanics' Institute.
Leyburn, Yorkshire.   Library and newsroom.
Lichfield.   Cathedral Library.   Formed subsequent to the
     siege of Lichfield by the Puritans in 1646.   6000 vols.
     Issues, about 100 annually.   Income, £25.   Printed author
     catalogue of 1888.   Hours, 12 to 2 on two days a week.
Limerick.   Athenæum.
Limerick.   Limerick Institution (1809).   About 2000 vols.   Has
     a printed catalogue.
Lincoln.   Cathedral Library (mediæval).   7000 vols.
Lincoln.   Co-operative Society Library.   5000 vols.
Lincoln.   Mechanics' Institute.   12.000 vols.
Lincoln.   Stock Library.   16,000 vols.
Lindley.   Mechanics' Institute.
Lingdale, Yorkshire.   Miners' Institute.
Linlithgow.   Henry Library.
Linlithgow.   Public Library (1850).   Over 4000 vols.   Issues,
     5000 vols.   Income, £7.   Staff, 2.   Printed numerical cata-
     logue.   Charging, ledger.   Members, 28.   Hours, every
     Tuesday night, 7·30 to 8·30.

Lisburn. Newsroom and Library.

Littleborough, Lancs. Co-operative Library (1864). About 2000 vols.

Littleborough. Technical Institute.

Liverpool. Athenæum (1798). 36,000 vols. Printed catalogues of 1864 and 1892. Librarian, George T. Shaw.

Liverpool. Balfour Institute. About 500 members.

Liverpool. Central Circulating Library Association. Has 2000 vols., which are sent out in boxes of 21 or 90, to village clubs, etc., in the neighbourhood of Liverpool.

Liverpool. Incorporated Law Society (1827). 6541 vols. Printed catalogue of 1892.

Liverpool. Liverpool Library, Lyceum (1758). 98,400 vols. Issues, 92,544 books. Income, £1300. Staff, 5. Printed catalogue of 1889. Charging, cards. Open access allowed. Members, 893. Hours, 9 to 5·30; Saturdays, 9 to 2·30. Librarian, John Forester.

Liverpool. Medical Institution (1779). 16,000 vols. Hours, 10 to 6.

Liverpool. Polytechnic Society Library.

Liverpool. Royal College of Chemistry (1848).

Liverpool. School of Science and Technology.

Liverpool. University College Library (1881). 24,000 vols.

Liverpool. Young Men's Christian Association.

Llanelly. Mechanics' Institute. Has a printed catalogue.

Llandaff. Cathedral Library. About 500 vols.

Llangollen. Newsroom and Public Library.

Llanychan. Church Lending Library. Contains about 600 vols.

Llwynpia, Wales. Workmen's Institute.

Lochgilphead. Library. Contains about 500 vols.

Lockerbie. Public Library (1886). 2000 vols. Income, £20. Staff, 2. Printed classified catalogue. Classification, author alphabetical. Charging, ledger. Members, 100. Hours, Monday, 6 to 8; Thursday, 12 to 1. Librarian, James Morrison.

Loftus, Yorkshire. Mutual Improvement Society. 1000 vols.

London. Admiralty Library (founded before 1700). 40,000 vols. Has printed catalogues.

London. Allan Library. Wesleyan Conference Office.

London. Alpine Club.

London. Anthropological Institution (1844). 4500 vols.

London. Architectural Association (1847). 2000 vols. Has a printed author catalogue. Charging, ledger. Hours, 12 to 7.

London. Ascham Society Library.

London. Athenæum Club Library (1824). About 70,000 vols. Librarian, H. R. Tedder.

London. Bank of England Library and Literary Association (1850). 20,000 vols. Has a printed catalogue.

BISHOPSGATE INSTITUTE, LONDON.

London. Baptist College, Regent's Park (1810). 13,000.

London. Baptist Mission House Library.

London. Battersea Polytechnic Institution.

London. Beaumont Institution, Mile End, E.

London. Bethnal Green Free Library (1876). 34,000 vols. Issues, 40,059. Income, £1081. Staff, 4. Catalogue in MS. Charging, slips. Open access allowed. Hours, 10 to 5, and 6 to 10. A voluntary Library not under the Acts. Librarian, G. F. Hilcken.

London. Bibliographical Society. Has the beginnings of a Library, now amounting to several hundreds of volumes.

London. Bibliothèque de la Providence, in French Hospital, Victoria Park Road (1718). 1500 vols. Printed catalogue of 1890.

London. Birkbeck Literary and Scientific Institution (1823). 12,000 vols. Has a printed catalogue. Librarian, W. H. Congreve.

London. Bishopsgate Institute (1891, opened in 1894-95). 23,535 vols. (18,750 lending, 4785 reference). Issues, 345,000 vols. Income, £2000. Staff, 12. Printed classified catalogue for lending. MS. catalogue in guard books for reference. Classification, by subjects alphabetically in main classes. Open access allowed in every department. Has 15,000 borrowers. Has special collection of London books and prints. Hours, 10 to 9·30, reference; 10 to 8, lending. Director and librarian, Ronald W. Heaton, M.A.

London. Borough Polytechnic Institute (1892). About 5000 vols. Hours, 6·30 to 9·30 P.M.

London. Board of Agriculture Library.

London. Bow and Bromley Institute. 6000 vols.

London. British and Foreign Bible Society (1805). Over 10,000 vols., chiefly Bibles. Librarian, Rev. Wm. Wright, D.D.

London. British Archæological Association Library.

London. British Horological Institute.

London. British Medical Association Library.

London. British Museum Library (1753). Over 1,900,000 vols. Reading-room open, 9 A.M. to 8 P.M. Admission to readers holding tickets only, but these are easily obtained on application. Chief librarian, Sir E. Maunde Thompson, D.C.L., LL.D.

London. British Museum (Natural History) Libraries (1881). Over 70,050 vols. Including a General Library of 24,000 vols., and a Zoological one of 17,000 vols. There are also Botanical, Geological, and Mineralogical Libraries. Catalogue in MS. Contains the Tweeddale collection of ornithological works. Can be used by accredited students, but primarily intended for the use of the museum staff. Hours, 10 to 4.

London. Burlington Fine Arts Club Library.

London.   Carlton Club (1832-36).   22,000 vols.
London.   Central Young Men's Christian Association Library.
      Exeter Hall.
London.   Chartered Accountants' Students' Society Library.
London.   Chelsea Hospital Library.
London.   Chemical Society Library (1851).   13,000 vols.
London.   Christ's Hospital Library.

DR. RICHARD GARNETT, BRITISH MUSEUM.   Messrs. Maull & Fox,
photographers.

London.   Church House Library, Westminster (1888).   15,000
      vols.   Staff, 3.   Has MS. catalogue on cards, author and
      subject.   Open access allowed.   Members, 2500.   Has the
      Julian Hymnological collection.   Hours, 10 to 5; Satur-
      days, 10 to 2.
London.   Church of England Young Men's Society Library.
      About 5000 vols.
London.   City and Guilds of London Institute.
London.   City Liberal Club Library.

London.   City of London College (1848).   About 5000 vols.   Has printed catalogues.
London.   City of London Police Library.
London.   City of London School Library.
London.   Colonial Office Library.   About 13,000 vols.
London.   Compositors' Society Library (1853).   8000 vols.
London.   Congregational Library.   Memorial Hall, Farringdon Street (1875).   About 18,000 vols.   Has a printed catalogue of 1895.   Librarian, Rev. Samuel Newth, M.A., D.D.
London.   Conservative Club Library.
London.   Constitutional Club (1887).   12,000 vols.   Has a MS. catalogue.   Librarian, Horace Horne.
London.   Corporation Library, Guildhall (1425, refounded 1824).   110,000 vols.   Expenditure, £5807.   Staff, 16.   Has a printed author catalogue, and a MS. card catalogue on the Dewey classification with author index.   Attendances, 358,246 to various departments.   Has special collections relating to London, the Clockmakers' Company Library, Library of the Dutch Church, Austin Friars, etc.   Hours, 10 to 9; Saturdays, 9 to 6 in summer months.   Librarian, Charles Welch, F.S.A.
London.   Cripplegate Institute (1896).   25,000 vols. (20,000 lending, 5000 reference).   Open access allowed to Lending and Reference Libraries.   Hours, 10 to 8; Saturdays, 10 to 3.   Librarian, J. Capper.
London.   Cymmrodorion, Honourable Society of.   Library of Welsh books and books relating to Wales.
London.   Democratic Club Library.
London.   Dulwich College, or Alleyn's College of God's Gift (1619).   17,000 vols.   Issues, 1000.   Income, £40.   Staff, 1. Printed author catalogue.   MS. catalogue on cards.   Charging, ledger.   Open access allowed.   Has much theology and MSS. connected with early English stage.   Open to college masters and governors.
London.   English Church Union Library.   4000 vols.
London.   Entomological Society of London (1836).   4500 vols. Has a printed catalogue.
London.   Fabian Society.   Lends boxes of 20 or 30 books to all sorts of working-class organisations throughout the country, at a charge of 2s. 6d. per three months.
London.   Finsbury Park Free Public Library (1894).   2300 vols. (2000 lending, 300 reference).   Issues, 6956.   Income, £150. Staff, 1.   Printed author catalogue.   Classification, Dewey. Charging, cards.   Borrowers, 600.   Hours, 6 to 10 P.M., lending department, 7.30 to 9, on Mondays and Thursdays. Librarian, E. Gunthorpe.
London.   Foreign Office Library.   75,000 vols.   Not open to the public.
London.   Friends' Institute Library.
London.   Garrick Club Library.

London.   Geological Society Library (1807).   19,000 vols.
London.   German Athenæum Club Library.
London.   Goldsmiths' Company's Technical and Recreative
    Institute, New Cross (1891).   6000 vols.   Has printed cata-
    logue.   Librarian, Minnie E. Eastty.
London.   Grand Lodge of Freemasons' Library.   Freemasons'
    Hall.   6500 vols.   Income, £50.   Staff, 1.   Has printed
    dictionary catalogue.   Open to all Freemasons in good
    standing.   Hours, 10 to 5 except Saturdays.
London.   Gray's Inn Library (ante 1555).   14,000 vols.   Has a
    printed catalogue.   Librarian, W. R. Douthwaite.
London.   Gresham College Library.
London.   Guy's Hospital Library (1825).   6000 vols.   Chiefly
    medical works for use of staff and students.
London.   Hackney Theological Seminary Library.
London.   Hampstead Public Library and Literary Institution
    (1833, revived 1882).   10,000 vols.   Has a printed cata-
    logue.
London.   Heralds' College Library.   Chiefly heraldic MSS., etc.
London.   Highgate Hill Free Library and Reading-room (1890).
    About 6000 vols.   Income, £130.
London.   Home Office Library (1800).   About 8000 vols.
London.   House of Commons' Library (1818).   42,000 vols.
    Librarian, R. C. Walpole.
London.   House of Lords' Library.   About 32,000 vols.
London.   Hoxton Library and Institute.
London.   Imperial Institute Library (1893).   10,800 vols.   Staff,
    5.   MS. catalogue in guard books and on slips.   Classifi-
    cation, geographical.   Open access allowed.   Members, 8000.
    Hours, 10 A.M. to 11·30 P.M. ; Sundays, 3 till 10·30.   Librarian,
    H. H. Hebb.
London.   Incorporated Law Society of the United Kingdom
    (1828-31).   35,000 vols.   Staff, 3.   Printed dictionary cata-
    logue.   Subject classification.   Open access allowed.
    Members, 7769.   Hours, 9 to 8; Saturdays, 9 to 4.
    Librarian, Frederic Boase.
London.   India Office Library (established in the India House,
    Leadenhall Street, in 1800).   60,000 vols., including 10,000
    oriental MSS.   Has printed catalogues of books and MSS.
London.   Inner Temple Library (1540).   About 38,000 vols. and
    MSS.   Librarian, J. E. L. Pickering.
London.   Inns of Court Bar Library.   Royal Courts of Justice
    (1883).   15,000 vols.   Staff, 3.   MS. catalogue in guard
    books.   Open access allowed.   Members (of Bar), 8000.
    Hours, 10 to 4·30 during sittings of the court.   Librarian,
    Robert Riches.
London.   Institute of Shorthand Writers' Library (1886-87).
    1800 vols.   Issues, 1400.   Has a printed catalogue.   Charg-
    ing, ledger.   Open access allowed.   Members, 72.   Hours,
    9·30 to 7.

London. Institution of Civil Engineers (1818). About 30,000 vols. Has printed catalogues.

London. Institution of Electrical Engineers, Ronald's Library (1871). 80,000 vols.

London. Iron and Steel Institute (1869). 3500 vols. Printed dictionary catalogue. MS. catalogue on cards. Open access allowed. Members, 1550. Hours, 10 to 5; Saturdays, 10 to 1. Librarian, Bennett H. Brough.

London. Japan Society Library. About 2000 vols.

London. King's College (1829). 30,000 vols. Staff, 2. MS. author catalogue. Open access allowed to some of the shelves. Has special collections (Marsden) of oriental books and (Wheatstone) of works on Physics. Hours, 10 to 8 in term. Librarian, Victor E. Plarr.

London. King's College Medical School Library.

London. Knights of St. John of Jerusalem, St John's Gate, Clerkenwell. About 1000 vols., chiefly on military orders of knighthood and ambulance work.

London. Lambeth Palace Library (founded by Archbishop Barcroft in 1610). 30,000 vols. Has printed catalogue of rare books and MSS. Open free to the public from 10 to 4 on Mondays, Wednesdays, Thursdays and Fridays, Tuesday forenoons, etc. Librarian, S. W. Kershaw, F.S.A.

London. Lambeth Polytechnic Institute.

London. Library Association (1878). Has about 700 vols., chiefly of Library catalogues.

London. Lincoln's Inn Library (1497). 72,000 vols. Has printed catalogues.

London. Linnean Society Library (1788). 50,000 vols. Has printed catalogue.

London. London Institution (1805). 75,000 vols. Librarian, R. W. Frazer, LL.B.

London. London Library (1841). 156,000 vols. Has printed catalogues. Librarian, W. Hagberg Wright.

London. London Working Men's College Library.

London. Marylebone Free Public Libraries (1889). 6000 vols. Issues, 21,582. Income, £324. Staff, 4. Printed dictionary catalogue. Charging, ledger. Borrowers, 530. A voluntary Library not under the acts. Hours, 9·30 to 9·30. Librarian, D. G. Thomson.

London. Medical Society (1773). 13,000 vols. Has a printed catalogue.

London. Merchant Taylors' School Library.

London. Meteorological Office Library (1854). 12,500 vols. Accessions printed in annual reports of the Meteorological Council. Librarian, Robert H. Scott.

London. Middle Temple Library (1641). 40,000 vols. Has printed catalogues of various dates.

London. Morden College for Decayed Merchants, Blackheath, Library.

London.   Morley House Institute Library, Lambeth.   5000 vols.

London.   Museum of Practical Geology (1851).   20,000 vols. Staff, 2.   Printed author catalogue.   Hours, 10 to 4 or 5, according to season.

London.   National Liberal Club, Gladstone Library (1888). Over 15,000 vols.   £300 annually expended on books.   MS. card catalogue.   Open access allowed.   Members, 6000. Hours, 10 A.M. to 11 P.M.   Librarian, Arthur W. Hutton, M.A.

London.   New Church College Library, Islington.   6000 vols.

London.   New College (Congregational) Library, Hampstead (1851).   40,000 vols.

London.   Northampton Institute, Clerkenwell (1896).   About 2000 vols.

London.   Numismatic Society (1836).   2500 vols.

London.   Obstetrical Society (1859).   3000 vols.   Librarian, Miss Agnes Hannam.

London.   Oratory Library, Brompton.   About 20,000 vols.

London.   Oxford and Cambridge Club.   20,000 vols.

London.   Paddington Free Public Library (1888).   3350 vols. (3000 lending, 350 reference).   Issues, 3947.   Income, £143.   Staff, 1.   Printed dictionary catalogue.   Charging, ledger.   Subscribers, 100.   Hours, 11 to 7.

London.   Patent Office Library (1855).   86,000 vols.   Hours, 10 to 10.   Has a fine collection of technical and scientific works to which open access is allowed.   Specifications of Patents of Britain, America and other countries are kept in bound volumes for free reference.

London.   People's Palace Library (1887).   About 12,500 vols. Has printed catalogue.

London.   Pharmaceutical Society of Great Britain (1841). 12,000 vols. (8000 lending, 4000 reference).   Issues, 3000. Staff, 2.   Printed dictionary catalogue.   MS. catalogue on slips.   Classification, Dewey.   Charging, ledger.   Open access allowed.   Members, 6000.   Hours, 9 to 9; Saturdays, 9 to 2, October to July; 9 to 5, August and September. Librarian, John W. Knapman.

London.   Polytechnic Young Men's Christian Institute, Regent Street, Library (1877, removed to Polytechnic in 1881). 7800 vols. (7000 lending, 800 reference).   Issues, 20,970. Staff, 3.   Printed dictionary catalogue.   Charging, indicator.   Members, 1500.   Hours, 7·15 to 10 P.M.   There are also class Libraries in connection with the various subjects taught.

London.   Post Office Library and Literary Association (1859). 5000 vols.   Has a printed catalogue.

London.   Presbyterian Theological College Library.

London.   Public Record Office.   Has a Reference Library for the use of the officers, consisting mainly of works bearing on state papers and public records. Hours, 10 to 4; Saturdays, 10 to 2.

London. Railway Clearing-house Library. About 100,000 vols.

London. Reform Club Library (1841). 45,000 vols. Has a printed catalogue. Librarian, Charles W. Vincent.

London. Religious Tract Society's Library (1799). 12,000 vols. Printed author catalogue. Charging, ledger. Has collection of Puritan Theology, and of editions of Bunyan's *Pilgrim's Progress* in foreign languages. Library accessible only to officers and friends of the society.

London. Royal Academy of Arts Library (1769). About 6000 vols.

London. Royal Academy of Music (1822). 1500 vols.

London. Royal Archæological Institution (1845). 3500 vols.

London. Royal Asiatic Society (1823). 13,000 vols. and 1000 MSS. Has a printed catalogue.

London. Royal Astronomical Society (1820). 10,000 vols. Has a printed catalogue. Librarian, W. H. Wesley.

London. Royal College of Music. Has about 7000 vols. and a museum of musical instruments, etc.

London. Royal College of Physicians (1525). 17,000 vols.

London. Royal College of Surgeons of England (1800). 60,000 vols. Printed dictionary catalogue. MS. catalogue on cards. Open access allowed. Hours, 11 to 7; Saturdays, 11 to 1. During August, open 11 to 6. Shut all September. Librarian, James Blake Bailey.

London. Royal Colonial Institute (1868). 30,000 vols. Staff, 2. Printed catalogue, arranged under colonies chronologically. MS. catalogue in slip books. Charging, ledger. Open access allowed. Members, 4000. Hours, 10 to 5. Librarian, James R. Boosé.

London. Royal Exchange, Lloyd's Library (1844). 1000 vols. Has printed catalogue.

London. Royal Geographical Society's Library (1830). 50,000 vols. Issues, 1500. Staff, 3. Printed author catalogue. MS. catalogue on slips. Classified topographically. Charging, ledger. Open access allowed. Members or fellows, 3753. Hours, 10·30 to 5; Saturdays, 10·30 to 1. Librarian, Hugh Robert Mill.

London. Royal Historical Society (1875). 3000 vols. Housed in St. Martin-in-the-Fields Public Library.

London. Royal Horticultural Society, Lindley Library (1820). 3000 vols. Printed class and author catalogue. Open access allowed to fellows. Members, 3500. Hours, 10 to 5; Saturdays, 10 to 2. Librarian, John Weathers.

London. Royal Institute of British Architects' Library (1834). 10,000 vols. Loan collection (1881), about 600 vols. Has a printed catalogue. Librarian, Alex. Beazeley.

17

London.   Royal Institution of Great Britain (1800).   60,000
    vols.   Printed classified catalogue.   MS. author catalogue
    in guard books.   Classification, subject.   Open access
    allowed.   Members, 1000.   Librarian, Herbert C. Fyfe.
London.   Royal Medical and Chirurgical Society (1805).
    42,000 vols.   Has printed catalogues.   Librarian, J. Y. W.
    MacAlister, F.S.A.
London.   Royal Microscopical Society Library.
London.   Royal Military Academy, Woolwich (1813; burned
    and reorganised, 1873).   14,000 vols.   Has a printed catalogue.
London.   Royal Naval College, Greenwich (1873).   6500 vols.
London.   Royal Observatory Library, Greenwich.
London.   Royal School of Mines Library.
London.   Royal Society (1662).   50,000 vols.   Has printed
    catalogues.
London.   Royal Society of Literature (1820).   8000 vols.
London.   Royal Statistical Society (1834).   30,000 vols.   Printed
    author catalogue.   Classification, author alphabetical.
    Charging, ledger.   Members, 900.   Librarian, John A.
    P. Mackenzie.
London.   Royal United Service Institution (1831).   25,000 vols.
    Has printed catalogues.
London.   Royal Veterinary College Library.
London.   Russell Institution (1808).   18,500 vols.
London.   St. Bartholomew's Hospital, Medical Library (1422).
    13,000 vols.   200 average daily reference issue.   Staff, 2.
    Printed author and class catalogue.   MS. catalogue in
    guard books.   Charging, cards.   Accessible to students of
    the hospital.   Hours, 9 to 5, save during August and a
    week at Christmas.   Librarian, T. F. Madden.
London.   St. Bride Foundation Institute (1895).   Libraries
    consist of a general department, 6500 vols. (a branch of the
    Cripplegate Institute); "Blades" Library, 3400 vols.;
    Passmore Edwards' Library, 4000 vols.   In all over 14,000
    vols.   Issues of general Lending Library, 62,000 vols.
    Income, £500.   Staff, 3.   Printed dictionary catalogue.
    Charging, cards.   Members, 2200.   Hours, 12 to 3 and 5 to
    9; Saturdays, 12 to 5.   Librarian, F. W. T. Lange.   The
    Blades and Edwards' Libraries are for reference only by
    students or members of the Institute.
London.   St. Pancras Public Library (1877).   7000 vols.   Has
    printed catalogue.   A subscription Library.
London.   St. Paul's Cathedral Library (mediæval, but destroyed
    by fire more than once).   10,730 books, 10,446 pamphlets.
    Has a printed catalogue.   Librarian, Rev. Dr. Sparrow
    Simpson.
London.   St. Paul's School Library (ante 1666).   6500 vols.
    Printed author catalogues. MS. author catalogue. Charging,
    ledger.   Open access allowed.   Members of 8th form and
    masters, 200.   Librarian, Rev. J. H. Lupton, D.D.

London.   St. Thomas's Hospital, Medical School Library.
Collection of medical works which can be borrowed by
members of the staff, while students are allowed to use
them for reference.   Librarian, Geo. S. Saunders.

London.   Shorthand Writers' Association Library.

London.   Sion College (1629).   About 60,000.   Classification,
Dewey.   Open to clergymen of the diocese of London.
Librarian, Rev. W. H. Milman.

London.   Sir John Soane's Museum (1837).   8000 vols.
Printed catalogue of 1878.

London.   Society of Antiquaries of London (1555; incorporated
in 1751).   42,000 vols.   Has a printed catalogue of 1887.

London.   Society of Biblical Archæology (1870).   2500 vols.

London.   Society of Telegraph Engineers (1876).   3500 vols.

London.   South Kensington Museum Libraries (1881).   Contains the National Art Library (1852), 60,000 vols.; Dyce
and Foster Library (1869-76), 35,000 vols.; and Science and
Educational Library (1876), 50,000.   Total about 150,000
vols.   Has printed catalogues and MS. desk catalogues.

London.   South London Free Library (1877; suspended in 1891,
reopened in 1893 in a new building).

London.   South-West London Polytechnic Institute, Chelsea.

London.   Sunday School Union Library (1833).   9500 vols.
(8000 lending, 1500 reference).   Issues. 14,000 vols.   Staff,
1.   Printed classified and author catalogue.   Charging,
ledger.   Open access allowed to reference books.   Members, 1450.   Hours, 12 to 9.

London.   Teachers' Guild Library (1885).   8950 vols. (6450
lending, 2500 reference).   Issues, 2624.   Staff, 2.   Printed
• classified catalogue.   Classification by subjects.   Charging,
ledger.   Members, 4300.   Hours, 10 to 6; Saturdays, 10 to 5.

London.   Theological Society of London (1836).   5000 vols.

London.   Toynbee Hall Students' Free Library (1884).   7000
vols. (6300 lending, 700 reference).   Issues, 11,130.   Staff, 1.
Printed classified and author catalogue.   MS. catalogue
in guard books and on cards.   Classification, Dewey.   Open
access allowed to the reference works.   Borrowers and
readers, 500.   Hours, 5 to 10 P.M.; Saturdays, 2 to 10;
Sundays, 11·30 A.M. to 10 P.M.   Librarian, Charles F. New-
combe.

London.   Trinity College (1876).   2000 vols.   Catalogue in MS.
Chiefly works on music.

London.   Tyssen Library, Town Hall, Hackney (1885).   1650
vols.   Printed catalogue of 1888.

London.   University College Library (1826; Library, 1829).
About 105,000 vols.   Has printed catalogues.

London.   Victoria Institute Library (1866).   1500 vols.   Printed
classified catalogue.   MS. catalogue in slip books.   Charging,
ledger.   Hours, 10 to 5.

London.   War Office Library.   26,000 vols.

London. Westminster Abbey. Dean and Chapter Library. About 12,000 vols.

London. Dr. Williams's Library (1716). 40,000 vols. Has printed catalogues.

London. Woolwich Polytechnic Institute.

London. Working Men's Club and Institute Union Library (1862). 4000 vols. (2500 lending, 1500 reference). Issues, 20,000 vols. Staff, 1. MS. catalogue only. Charging, ledger. Members consist of 550 clubs, most of which have Libraries of their own, averaging 500 vols. each. Books distributed among the clubs. No public access.

London. Working Men's College (1854). 4000 vols. Has a printed catalogue.

London. Zoological Society of London (1829). 20,000 vols. Has a printed catalogue.

Londonderry. Foyle College.

Londonderry. Library Association (1809). 20,000 vols. Has a printed catalogue. Librarian, William Tilson.

Longridge. Industrial Co-operative Society Library. 1060 vols.

Longwood. Mechanics' Institute.

Looe, East. Mechanics' Institute.

Loughton, Essex. Lopping Hall Library (1886). Over 2000 vols. Printed catalogue of 1890.

Low Moor, Yorkshire. Harold Club Library. 800 vols.

Lowestoft. Public Library. Income, £221.

Luddenden, Yorkshire. Luddenden Library.

Luddenden. Mechanics' Institute.

Luthermuir, N.B. Village Library. Contains over 500 vols. Members, 140.

Lynn, Norfolk. Stanley Library (1854). 1600 vols. Issues, 21,273. Income, £140. Staff, 2. Printed classified catalogue. Charging, ledger. Open access allowed. Members, 457. Hours, 1 to 7.

Macclesfield. Co-operative Society Library. 1900 vols.

Madeley. Anstice Memorial Institute.

Maerdy. Library (1882). 1700 vols.

Maidstone. St. Paul's Literary Institute.

Manchester. Athenæum Library (1836). 20,182 vols. (19,775 lending, 407 reference). Issues, 70,000. Staff, 4. Printed classified catalogue. Charging, ledger. Members, 3000.

Manchester. Cathedral Library (1869, in place of ancient one). Contains about 1000 vols.

Manchester. Chetham's Library (1653). 52,000 vols. Has a printed catalogue.

Manchester. Conservative Club.

Manchester. Equitable Co-operative Society Library (1865). 3700 vols.

Manchester. Foreign Library (1830). 14,000 vols. Has a printed catalogue. Issues, 4983 vols.

Manchester. Geographical Society (1884). Several thousands of vols. Staff, 2. Open access allowed. Members, 850. Hours, 10 to 4.

Manchester. Geological Society (1838). Has a printed catalogue.

Manchester. Grammar School Library.

Manchester. Incorporated Law Society Library (1820). About 8000 vols. Printed catalogue of 1891.

Manchester. Lancashire Independent College Library (founded at Blackburn, 1816; removed to Manchester in 1842). 13,900 vols. Income, £120. Staff, 1. Printed dictionary catalogue, 1885. Chiefly theological, but has many valuable MSS. and early printed books. Librarian, C. Goodyear.

Manchester. Literary and Philosophical Society (1781). 20,000 vols. Staff, 2. Printed author catalogue. Classification, Dewey. Charging, ledger. Open access allowed. Members, 150. Hours, 9·30 to 5·30.

Manchester. Medical Society (1834). 31,400 vols. Issues, 7210 vols. Staff, 2. Printed author catalogue. MS. catalogue on guard books. Charging, ledger. Open access. Members, 350. Hours, 10 to 6; Saturdays, 10 to 2.

Manchester. Municipal Technical School (1824, formerly Mechanics' Institution). 10,000 vols.

Manchester. Museum (taken over from Manchester Natural History Society and enlarged). 4000 vols. Printed classified catalogue. MS. catalogue on cards. Classification, Dewey.

Manchester. Owens College Library (1851). 63,000 vols. Has a printed catalogue.

Manchester. Portico Library (1806). 42,000 vols. Issues, 16,527. Income, £1071. Has a printed catalogue.

Manchester. Roman Catholic Collegiate Institute.

Manchester. Royal Exchange Library (1792). 32,000 vols. Issues, 19,275. Has a printed catalogue.

Manchester. Ryland's Library. Librarian, Gordon Duff.

Manchester. St. Mary's Hospital, Radford Library (1853). About 5000 vols. Has a printed catalogue of 1877.

Manchester. United Methodist Free Churches' Theological Institute Library.

Manchester. Young Men's Christian Association Library.

Mansfield. Mechanics' Library (1831). 4000 vols.

Mansfield. Subscription Library. 4000 vols.

Marazion. Marazion Institute.

Marlborough. College, Adderley Library (1848). 8400 vols. Printed catalogue of 1889.

Marlborough. Reading Society Library.

Marlow, Great. Marlow Institute.

Maryport. Mechanics' Institute.

Mauchline, N.B. Public Library.

Maybole, N.B. Mechanics' Institute.

Maynooth. St. Patrick's College (1795). 35,000 vols.

Melrose, N.B. Public Library.

Merthyr. Merthyr Public Library (reconstituted 1896).

Merthyr Vale. Library (1880).

Methven, N.B. Subscription Library (1790).

Methven. Trinity College Library, Glenalmond.

Mexborough, Yorkshire. Public Library. 750 vols. Members, 50.

Mickleton, Yorkshire. Subscription Library. 400 vols.

Middlesbrough. Mechanics' Institute.

Middleton, Lancashire. Industrial Society Library (1859). 1500 vols.

Middleton Tyas, Yorkshire. Reading-room. 500 vols.

Middlewick. Library Institute.

Middlewick. Workmen's Institute.

Mildenhall, Suffolk. Literary Institute.

Milngavie, N.B. Mechanics' Institute (1836). About 1500 vols. Has printed catalogue.

Milnrow. Equitable Pioneers' Society Library (1858). 1000 vols.

Millport, N.B. Public Library.

Milnathort, N.B. Milnathort Library (1797).

Moffat. Library Society (1788). 3000 vols. Has a printed catalogue of 1890.

Moffat. Proudfoot Institute (1894).

Montrose. Public Library (1785). 23,000 vols. Issues, 12,012. Income, £211. Has a printed catalogue. Librarian, Wm. Duncan.

Montrose. Trades' Library. Issues, 11,714 vols. Income, £53. Members, 166. Librarian, James F. Balfour.

Morland, Westmoreland. Reading-room and Library. Income, £12 12s. Members, 37.

Morley. Industrial Society Library (1874). 4510 vols.

Mossley. Industrial Co-operative Library (1861). 4444 vols.

Mossley. Mechanics' Institute.

Muirkirk, N.B. Muirkirk Library.

Nairn. Literary Institute (1870). About 1500 vols. Has a printed catalogue.

Neath. Mechanics' Institute.

Nelson. Industrial Co-operative Society Library. 4000 vols.

New Shildon. Mechanics' Institute.

New Tredegar, Wales. Library (1873). Has a special building.

Newbury. Technical Institute.

Newcastle Emlyn, Wales. Emlyn Library.

Newcastle-on-Tyne. Cathedral, Chapter Library.

Newcastle-on-Tyne. Durham College of Science and Art, Library.

Newcastle-on-Tyne. Literary and Philosophical Society (1793). 50,000 vols. (45,000 lending, 5000 reference). Issues, 81,967.

Income, £2000. Staff, 6. MS. catalogue on cards. Classification, Dewey. Charging, cards. Open access allowed. Members, 1800. Hours, 10 to 9·30.

Newcastle-on-Tyne. Royal Infirmary Library. 60,000 vols.

Newcastle-on-Tyne. Rutherford College Library.

Newmains, N.B. Coltness Library.

Newport, Isle of Wight. Young Men's Society Library.

Newton-Stewart, N.B. Mechanics' Institute.

Newtyle, N.B. Public Library. 2000 vols. Members, 80.

Northampton. Polytechnic Institute Library.

Norwich. Cathedral Library (mediæval). 5700 vols.

Norwich. Literary Institute.

Norwich. Norfolk and Norwich Library (1784). 46,000 vols.

Nottingham. Bromley House, Subscription Library (1816). 25,000 vols. Has a printed catalogue. Librarian, Wm. Moore.

Nottingham. Mechanics' Institution (1837). Over 27,000 vols. Has a printed catalogue. Charging, cards. Open access allowed. Librarian, John T. Radford.

Nottingham. Nottinghamshire Provincial Grand Lodge of Freemasons, Library and Museum. Librarian, John Potter Briscoe.

Nottingham. People's Hall (1854). 7000 vols.

Nuneaton. Wood Institute.

Nunnington, Yorkshire. Village Library. 500 vols.

Oakworth, Yorkshire. Mechanics' Institute. 1000 vols.

Oban, N.B. Scientific Association.

Oldham. Equitable Society (1870). 5200 vols.

Oldham. Industrial Society Library (1858). About 12,000 vols.

Oldham. Lyceum Library (1839). 10,000 vols. Issues, 21,466. Income, £1321. Staff, 7. Printed classified catalogue. MS. catalogue on cards. Charging, cards. Open access allowed. Members, 926. Hours open, 8 daily. Librarian, Arthur Tait.

Oldham. Mechanics' Institution (1867). About 2000 vols. Has a printed catalogue.

Ormskirk. Public Library.

Ossett. Mechanics' Institute.

Otley. Mechanics' Institute.

Oulton, Yorkshire. Lending Library. 400 vols.

Ouston. Miners' Institute.

Over, Cheshire. Working Men's Institute.

Oxford. All Souls College. Codrington Library (1710). 71,000 vols. Librarian, C. W. C. Oman.

Oxford. Balliol College Library.

Oxford. Bodleian Library (originally 14th century. Dispersed temp. Ed. VI. Refounded 1598). 570,000 vols. Issues, 121,000 vols. Income, £8500. Staff, 35. Printed author catalogue. MS. catalogue in slip books. Open access

allowed in the older reading-room. Hours vary according
to season; generally 9 to 3, 4 and 5. Librarian, E. W. B.
Nicholson, M.A.

Oxford. Brasenose College (17th century). 12,000 vols.

Oxford. Christ Church Library. 33,000 vols.

Oxford. Corpus Christi College (1516).

Oxford. Exeter College (mediæval). 35,000 vols. and 184 MSS.
Librarian. Charles W. Boase, M.A.

Oxford. Hertford College (c. 1600). 7000 vols. Printed catalogues of 1656 and 1888.

Oxford. Indian Institute (1885). 9000 vols. Has also a
museum of Indian work. Hours, 10 to 1, 5 to 6, and 8 to 9.

Oxford. Jesus College (17th century). 112,000 vols.

Oxford. Keble College (1870). 16,200 vols.

Oxford. Lincoln College (1427). 8000 vols.

Oxford. Magdalen College (1458-80). 24,000 vols. Printed
catalogue of 1860-62.

Oxford. Manchester College (1893). Librarian, L. Toulmin
Smith.

Oxford. Merton College Library (1370). 12,000 vols.

Oxford. New College (mediæval). 17,000 vols.

Oxford. Non-Collegiate Students' Library (1868). 3600 vols.

Oxford. Oriel College (1326).

Oxford. Pembroke College (1625). Contains about 6000 vols.,
of which the Chandler or Fellows' Library has 2500, mostly
Aristotelian literature. Librarian, J. Mowat.

Oxford. Pusey Memorial Library.

Oxford. Queen's College Library (1400). 50,000 vols.

Oxford. Radcliffe Library (1749). 50,000 vols. Has a printed
catalogue.

Oxford. St. Edmund Hall (?).

Oxford. St. John's College (1596). 20,000 vols.

Oxford. Taylorian Institution (1847). 36,000 vols. Has printed
catalogues.

Oxford. Trinity College Library.

Oxford. Union Society (1823). 40,000 vols.

Oxford. Wadham College (1613).

Oxford. Worcester College (1714). 40,000 vols.

Padiham. Industrial Co-operative Society Library. 1530 vols.

Peebles, N.B. Chambers' Institution (1859). 17,000 vols.
Issues, 12,000. Staff, 1. Printed author catalogue. Classification, author alphabetical. Members, 300. Hours, 9·30
to 10, 1 to 2, 7 to 8; Saturdays, 1 to 2·30. Librarian, James
Anderson.

Pembroke Dock. Mechanics' Institute.

Pendlebury. Pendlebury Institute.

Penzance. Penzance Library (1818). 21,576 vols. Issues,
10,650. Income, £142. Has printed catalogue of 1874,
1880, etc. Librarian, George B. Millett.

Perth. Literary and Antiquarian Society.

Perth. Mechanics' Library (1823). About 11,000 vols. Income,
£160. Has printed catalogues.

Perth. Students' Union. Has a printed catalogue, which
contains the books belonging to the late Dr. James Croll,
the geologist.

Peterborough. Cathedral Library. 3000 vols.

Peterborough. Law Society Library.

Peterborough. Medical Society Library.

Pitlochry, N.B. Circulating Library. 1500 vols. Income, £75.
Members, 146.

Plymouth. Incorporated Law Society Library.

Plymouth. Mechanics' Institute (1824).

Plymouth. Plymouth Institution and Natural History Society
(1812). 6000 vols.

Plymouth. Medical Society Library (1794).

Plymouth. Proprietary Library (1812). 40,000 vols. Income,
£600. Staff, 2. Printed classified catalogue. Charging,
ledger. Open access allowed. Members, 280. Hours, 10
to 4·30. Librarian, J. Brooking-Rowe.

Pollokshaws. Campbell Library (1844). 5000 vols. Has a
printed catalogue.

Pontefract. Young Men's Institute. 1000 vols.

Port Glasgow. Moffat Library (1887). About 5000 vols. Has
printed catalogues.

Portadown. Public Library (1872). 3000 vols. Has a printed
catalogue.

Porthleven. Bickford-Smith Institute.

Portsmouth. Dockyard Library.

Preston. Industrial Co-operative Society Library. 9000 members.

Preston. Institution for the Diffusion of Knowledge Library.

Preston. Shepherd Library. Founded as a free Reference
Library in 1759 by Dr. Richard Shepherd. Now forms
part of the Public Library, under a special board of management administering a separate fund. Contains 9000
vols.

Prestwich. Co-operative Library (1865). 3000 vols.

Pudsey. Mechanics' Institute.

Queensferry. Queensferry Library.

Radcliffe, Lancashire. Industrial Society Library (1867).
6241 vols.

Ramsbottom. Industrial Society Library (1866). 4000 vols.

Rawtenstall. Industrial Society Library (1862). 3000 vols.

Reay, N.B. Brubster Library.

Redditch. Literary Institute.

Redruth. Redruth Institution.

Reeth, Yorkshire. Mechanics' Library. 1200 vols.

Reigate. Literary Institute.

Reigate. Mechanics' Institute.

Renton, N.B. Victoria Institute (1887). 5000 vols.

Reston, N.B. Reston Library (1855). About 1000 vols. Founded by Miss Jane Blackwood Mack.

Rhymney. Library (1853). Has a special building.

Richmond, Surrey. Wesleyan Theological Institution (1843). 20,000 vols.

Richmond, Yorkshire. Mechanics' Institute.

Ripon. Cathedral Library (1608). 5000 vols.

Ripon. Mechanics' Institute (1831). 2100 vols. Income, £172. Staff, 2. Printed author catalogue. Charging, ledger. Members, 203. Hours, 7·30 to 8·30 once a week.

Rishton. Mechanics' Institute.

Robin Hood's Bay. Reading-room Library. 300 vols.

Rochdale. Equitable Pioneers' Society Library (1849). 18,000 vols. (15,000 lending, 3000 reference). Has printed catalogues. Librarian, Edwin Barnish.

Rochester. Cathedral Library.

Rossall. School Library.

Rotherham. Literary Institute.

Rothesay. Stewart Institute Library.

Royton. Industrial Co-operative Society Library. About 1000 vols.

Rugby. Co-operative Society Library.

Rugby. Railway Institute.

Rugby. School Library and Temple Reading-room (1878). About 7500 vols. Contains also the Arnold Library of about 2000 vols.

Rutherglen. Public Library (1813). 3000 vols. Issues, 4496 vols. Income, £43. Has a printed classified and author catalogue. Charging, ledger. Members, 76. Hours, 9 to 9.

Ryde, Isle of Wight. Philosophical Society.

Saffron Walden. Literary Institute (1846). 14,000 vols. (13,800 lending, 200 reference). Annual issues, 6456. Income, £175. Staff, 1. Printed catalogue in dictionary form. MS. catalogue in guard books. Classification by subjects. Charging, ledger. Open access allowed. Members, 206. Hours, 11 to 1·30, and 3 to 5; also 7·30 to 10 P.M. on 3 evenings a week.

St. Andrews. University Library (1612). 115,000 vols. Has £630 annually for purchase of books. Staff, 4. Printed author catalogue to 1826, with supplements to 1867. MS. catalogue in guard books. Classification, part Dewey. Charging, ledger. Access to shelves allowed in students' Library. Has about 1500 members. Hours, 10 to 1, 2 to 4. Librarian, J. Maitland Anderson.

St. Asaph. Cathedral Library. 2000 vols.

St. Davids, Wales. Cathedral Library.

St. Leonards. Mechanics' Institute.

St. Neots. Literary Institute.

Salen, Mull, N.B. Library (1884). About 500 vols. Has a printed catalogue.

Salisbury. Cathedral Library (11th century). 5172 vols. Has a printed catalogue, 1880.

Saltburn. Saltburn and Cleveland Institute Library. 350 vols.

Saltney. Literary Institute.

Sanquhar, N.B. Public Library.

Scarborough. Mechanics' Institute (1830). About 5000 vols. Has printed catalogue of 1893.

Settle. Library (1770). 12,000 vols. (11,050 lending, 50 reference). Staff, 1. Printed classified catalogue. Classification, numerical. Charging, ledger. Open access to shelves allowed. Members, 70. Hours, 10 to 1 and 2 to 5. Librarian, M. A. Mason.

Sevenoaks. Library. About 1300 vols. Annual issue, 6300 vols. Income, £80. Staff, 1. Members, 180.

Shaftesbury. Literary Institute (1852). 4000 vols. (3800 lending, 200 reference). Annual issues, 4300. Income, £85. Staff, 1. Printed author catalogue. Charging, ledger. Open access allowed to shelves. Subscribers, 166. Hours, 9 A.M. to 10 P.M.

Shanklin (Isle of Wight). Literary and Scientific Institute.

Shapansey, Orkney. Library (1895). 670 vols. Issues, about 2500 vols. per annum.

Sheerness. Dockyard Library (1851). 4200 vols. Annual issues, 4000. Printed dictionary catalogue. Staff, 1. Charging, ledger. Members, 120. Hours, 1 to 4·30 on Monday, Tuesday, Thursday and Friday.

Sheffield. Athenæum.

Sheffield. Firth College.

Sheffield. Incorporated Law Society Library.

Sheffield. Literary and Philosophical Society (1823). 2600 vols. Printed catalogue of 1887, supp. 1891.

Shepton Mallet. Reading Society.

Shipley. Salt Schools Institute (1870). 9000 vols. (lending, 8080; reference, 920). Annual issues, 25,742. Income, £673. Staff, 3. Printed dictionary catalogue. MS. catalogue on cards and in guard books. Charging, indicator. Members, 500 to 600. Hours, 9 to 8; Saturday, 9 to 5.

Shrewsbury. School Library (1551). 9000 vols.

Sidcup. Parish Library (1881).

Sidmouth. Mechanics' Institute.

Skipton. Mechanics' Institute.

Slaidburn, Lancashire. Reading-room. New building, presented by W. King-Wilkinson, opened in 1895.

Slough. Leopold Institute (1887). 2500 vols. Issues, 5500 vols. Printed author catalogue. Charging, ledger. Hours, 7·30 P.M. to 9 P.M. on Wednesdays; Saturdays, 8 P.M. to 9 P.M.

Slough. Mechanics' Institute.

Smethwick. Literary Institute.

Southampton. Hartley Institution (1862). About 4000 vols.

Southend-on-Sea. Library (1884). 1620 vols. Income, £120. Staff, 1. Printed catalogue. Charging, ledger. Members, 250. Hours, 10 to 9.

Southgate, Middlesex. Reading-room and Library. 4500 vols. Income, £181.

South Molton. Free Library. Has a printed catalogue. Under management of the Town Council.

Southwell. Literary Institute (about 1845). Income, £95. Staff, 1. Members, 90. Hours, 8 to 10 P.M.

Spalding. Mechanics' Institution (1845). 2200 vols. Printed catalogue of 1886.

Stacksteads, Lancashire. Industrial Society Library (1868). 2500 vols.

Stafford. Mechanics' Institute.

Stafford. William Salt Library (1872). Opened in April, 1874. About 15,000 vols. and pamphlets. Has a printed catalogue.

Stalybridge. Mechanics' Institute (1825). 5500 vols. Has a printed catalogue.

Stamford. Stamford Institution.

Stewarton, N.B. Public Library (1810).

Stirling. Macfarlane Free Library (1855). 9000 vols.

Stirling. Smith Institution.

Stockton-on-Tees. Co-operative Library (1873). 1500 vols.

Stockton-on-Tees. Literary Institute.

Stone. Mechanics' Institute.

Stonehaven. Literary Society Library (1828). 3800 vols. Issues, 2000. Income, £40. Staff, 1. Printed author catalogue. Charging, ledger. Open access to shelves allowed. Members, 100. Hours, 6 to 7 P.M. Librarian, Edward Cruse.

Stornoway, N.B. Public Library.

Stourbridge. Stourbridge Institute (1830). 5000 vols. Printed catalogue of 1891. Stourbridge old Library was dispersed in 1894-95, and many of the books containing the bookplate were sold.

Stourport. Stourport Institute.

Stow, N.B. Reading-room and Library. Income about £37.

Stowmarket. Literary Institute.

Stranraer. Athenæum (1866). 3200 vols. Printed catalogue, 1891.

Stratford-upon-Avon. Shakespeare Memorial Library (1877). 10,000 vols. Staff, 7. MS. catalogue in slip books. Annual visitors about 15,000. Has special collections of Shakespeare's works, dramatic literature, etc. Hours, 10 to 6 in summer; 10 till dusk in winter. Librarian, W. Salt Brassington, F.S.A.

Strichen, N.B. Circulating Library (1886). About 1000 vols. Has printed catalogue.

Stromness, Orkney. Public Library. Has a special building and a printed catalogue.

Stroud. Free Library (1887). 4496 vols. Annual issues, 36,524. Income, £128. Staff, 3. Printed classified catalogue. Classification, numerical. Charging, ledger and indicator. Members, 3007. Hours, 9 A.M. till 10 P.M.

Sudbury. Mechanics' Institute.

Sunderland. Co-operative Society Library (1863). 9000 vols.

Sunderland. Subscription Library (1795). Building in Fawcett Street opened in 1878. 20,000 vols. Members, 550. Issues, 26,000 vols.

Swansea. Royal Institution of South Wales (1835). Incorporated 1883. 20,000 vols. Has printed catalogues of 1848 and 1877.

Swansea. South Wales Institution of Engineers' Library.

Swansea. Working Men's Institute (1874). 2005 vols. Has printed catalogue.

Swindon. Great Western Railway Mechanics' Institution (1843). 23,000 vols. (20,000 lending, 3000 reference). Issues, 112,000. Income, £3500. Staff, 6. Charging, ledger. Subscribers, 7229. Hours, 10 to 2, 4 to 6, 7 to 9. Librarian, Alfred J. Birch.

Tain, N.B. Literary and Mechanics' Institute (1851). 1500 vols. Printed catalogue of 1892.

Tarporley. Tarporley Library. Has a printed catalogue.

Tavistock. Public Library (1799). 11,000 vols.

Thornton. Mechanics' Institute.

Tillicoultry, N.B. Tillicoultry Institute.

Todmorden. Industrial Co-operative Society Library (1867). 8250 vols.

Ton, Wales. Workmen's Institute (1895). New building cost £4000.

Tonbridge. Mechanics' Institute.

Torquay. Natural History Museum Library.

Torquay. Vivian Institute.

Tottingham, Lancashire. Industrial Society Library (1869).

Tow Law. Mechanics' Institute.

Trawden Forest. Literary Institute.

Tredegar. Working Men's Institute and Library (1890). 2200 vols. Issues, 5040 vols.

Treharris, Wales. Workmen and Tradesmen's Library (1884). 1460 vols.

Treorky. Pare and Dare Workmen's Institute (1895). New building cost £3500. 700 vols.

Truro. Bishop Philpott's Library. 5000 vols.

Truro. Cathedral Library.

Truro. Church Institute (1884). 1200 vols.

Truro. Cornwall Library.

Truro. Royal Institution of Cornwall (1818). 2000 vols.

Tunbridge Wells. Mechanics' Institute.

Tunbridge Wells. Society of Literature.

Tunstead, Lancashire.   Industrial Society Library (1877).
    1500 vols.
Ulverston.   Ulverston Library (1847).   Income about £20.
Uttoxeter.   Mechanics' Literary Institute.
Ventnor (Isle of Wight).   Literary and Scientific Institute.
Wakefield.   Industrial Co-operative Society Library.
Wakefield.   Mechanics' Institute (1825).   7776 vols. (6922 lend-
    ing, 854 reference).   Issues, 13,731 vols.   Income, £630.
    Staff, 2.   Printed dictionary catalogue.   Charging, indica-
    tor.   Subscribers, 793.   Hours, 12 to 12, and 7 to 9 on
    different week days.
Wallingford.   Free Library and Literary Institute (1844.
    Reorganised, 1871).   4180 vols.   Issues, 5200 vols.   Income,
    £100.   Staff, 1.   Printed classified catalogue.   Charging,
    ledger.   Open access allowed.   Subscribers, 177.   Hours,
    10 to 10.
Walton, Yorkshire.   Walton and Beswick Village Library.
    300 vols.
Wanlockhead, N.B.   Miners' Library (1757).   3000 vols.   Has
    printed catalogue.
Ware.   St. Edmund's College Library (1794).   20,000 vols.
Warminster.   Athenæum.
Waterfoot, Lancashire.   Industrial Society Library (1876).
    1500 vols.
Waterford.   Christian Brothers' College.
Watford.   Literary Institute.
Wath-upon-Dearne, Yorkshire.   Mechanics' Institute.   400
    vols.
Wells.   Cathedral Library (1660).   4000 vols.
West Vale, Yorkshire.   Mechanics' Institute.   2500 vols.
Westbury.   Laverton Institute.
Westerkirk, N.B.   Telford Library (1834).   7200 vols.
Weston Favell, Northamptonshire.   Reading-room and Library.
Wexford.   Public Library.
Whaleybridge.   Mechanics' Institute.
Whitby.   Subscription Library (1775).   30,000 vols.   Income,
    £200.   Printed catalogue.   Open access allowed to books.
    Members, 130.   Hours, 10 to 4 in summer; 11 to 3 in
    winter.
Whitehaven.   Scientific Institute.
Whitehaven.   Subscription Library.   Issues, 7699 vols. annu-
    ally.   Income, £107.
Whitstable.   Whitstable Institute.
Whitworth, Lancashire.   Friendly Co-operative Library (1876).
    2000 vols.
Wigan.   Co-operative Society Library.
Wigtown, N.B.   Mechanics' Institute.
Wilton.   Literary Institute.
Wimborne.   Minster Library of chained books.   Founded in
    1686 by the Rev. William Stone.   Has 240 vols., which

were given for the free use of the Wimborne people, and chained to keep them in the room. One of the few chained Libraries now existing in Britain. Open, 10 to 5, but only visited by tourists.

Winchester. Cathedral Library (1684). 4000 vols.

Winchester. College, Moberly Library (1868). 5500 vols. Has a printed catalogue.

Winchester. Mechanics' Institution (1835). About 8000 vols. Has printed catalogue of 1893.

Windhill, Yorkshire. Industrial Society Library (1875). 1000 vols.

Windsor. Albert Institute Library.

Windsor. Royal Library (founded by William IV.). 75,000 vols.

Winnington. Co-operative Society Library. 700 vols.

Wishaw, N.B. Public Library.

Withernsea, Yorkshire. Institute. 400 vols.

Withington. Public Hall and Library.

Witney. Athenæum Library and Reading-room.

Wolverhampton. Law Society (1847). About 1500 vols. Printed catalogue of 1892.

Wolverton. Science and Art Institute.

Woodbridge. Mechanics' Institute.

Woodbridge. Seckford Schools Library.

Woodside, N.B. Anderson Library (1883). 10,500 vols. Printed catalogue.

Woolfold. Co-operative Society Library. 1300 vols.

Worcester. Cathedral Library (15th century). 3000 vols. Has a printed catalogue.

Worcester. Railway Literary Institute.

Wordsley. The Institute.

Wortley. Working Men's Institute.

Wycombe, High. Free Library (1876). 2300 vols. Income is interest on £3000. Staff, 1. Open access allowed. Hours, 10 to 10.

Wyke Regis. Working Men's Institute.

Yeovil. Everybody's Library. Contains about 1000 vols., and has a printed catalogue.

Yeovil. Mutual Improvement Society of Y.M.C.A. (1840). Nearly 1000 vols. Has a printed catalogue.

York. Archæological Society Library.

York. Cathedral. Minster Library (mediæval). 11,000 vols.

York. Medical Library.

York. Railway Institute.

York. Subscription Library (1794). 32,500 vols. Has a printed catalogue.

York. Yorkshire Law Society Library (1828).

Ystrad Rhondda. Library. New building erected by Mr. Clifford Cory at a cost of £3500. Opened in 1896.

Youghal. Literary Institute.

SOME OF THE PRINCIPAL PUBLIC LIBRARIES OF THE BRITISH COLONIES.

AFRICA.

CAPE COLONY—
 Barkly East, Public Library.
 Beaconsfield, Public Library (1889), 1200 vols.
 Beaufort West, Public Library.
 Bedford, Public Library.
 Calvinia, Public Library.
 Cape Town, House of Assembly Library.
  Incorporated Law Society Library.
  Public Library (1818), 45,000 vols.
  South African Philosophical Society Library.
  South African University Library.
  Y.M.C.A. Library.
 Carnarvon, Public Library.
 Cathcart, Public Library.
 Clanwilliam, Public Library.
 Colesberg, Public Library.
 East London, East, Public Library (1876), 4000 vols.
 East London, West, Public Library.
 Georgetown, Public Library.
 Graham's Town, Public Library (1863), 10,000 vols.
 Kimberley, Public Library (1882), 15,000 vols.
 King William's Town, Public Library (1861), 15,000 vols.
 Lovedale, Lovedale Institution.
  Public Library.
 Malmesbury, Public Library.
 Middleburg, Public Library.
 Montagu, Public Library.
 Mossel Bay, Public Library.
 Port Elizabeth, Public Library (1848), 22,000 vols.
  Y.M.C.A. Library.
 Queenstown, Public Library.
 Richmond, Public Library.
 Riversdale, Public Library.
 Robertson, Public Library.
 Somerset, West, Public Library.
 Sutherland, Public Library.
 Victoria, West, Public Library.
 Willowmore, Public Library.

About sixty Public Libraries in Cape Colony, including some of those above noted, receive annual Government grants varying from £25 to £100.

NATAL—
    Durban, Athenæum Club Library.
        Public Library.
    Estcourt, Public Library, 1000 vols.
    Ladysmith, Public Library.
    Newcastle, Public Library, 3000 vols.
    Pietermaritzburg, Free Public Library, 11,000 vols.
        Maritzburg College (1888).
        Natal Society Library (1851), 10,000 vols.
        Y.M.C.A. Library.
    Pinetown, Public Library.
        Mariannhill Trappist Monastery.
    Richmond, Public Library.
    Stanger, Public Library.
    Verulam, Public Library, 2000 vols.

ST. HELENA—
    Jamestown, Public Library.

AMERICA.

ANTIGUA—
    St. John's, Coke College.
        Public Library (1854), 9000 vols.

BARBADOES—
    Bridgetown, Public Library.

BERMUDAS—
    Hamilton, Public Library.

BRITISH GUIANA—
    Georgetown, Queen's College.
        Royal Agricultural and Commercial Library, 18,000 vols.

CANADA—
    Ailsa Craig, Ontario, Mechanics' Institute, 2000 vols.
    Antigonish, N.S., St. Francis Xavier College (1854), 2500 vols.
    Arthur, Ontario, Mechanics Institute, 2100 vols.
    Aylmer, Ontario, Mechanics' Institute, 2100 vols.
    Ayr, Ontario, Mechanics' Institute, 3200 vols.
    Barrie, Ontario, Mechanics' Institute, 3700 vols.
    Belleville, Ontario, Mechanics' Institute, 3500 vols.
    Berlin, Ontario, Public Library, 3600 vols.
    Bowmanville, Ontario, Mechanics' Institute, 3000 vols.
    Brampton, Ontario, Mechanics' Institute, 2100 vols.
    Brantford, Ontario, Grant Law Library, 2000 vols.
        Public Library, 9000 vols.
    Brockville, Ontario, Mechanics' Institute, 3600 vols.
    Campbellford, Ontario, Mechanics' Institute, 2500 vols.

Charlottetown, Prince Edward Island, Law Library
   (1876), 2300 vols.
   Legislative Library (1848), 3100 vols.
Chatham, Ontario, Public Library, 3800 vols.
Clinton, Ontario, Mechanics' Institute, 2300 vols.
Collingwood, Ontario, Mechanics' Institute, 3900 vols.
Dundas, Ontario, Mechanics' Institute, 5600 vols.
Durham, Ontario, Mechanics' Institute, 2200 vols.
Elora, Ontario, Mechanics' Institute, 7100 vols.
Embro, Ontario, Mechanics' Institute, 2600 vols.
Exeter, Ontario, Mechanics' Institute, 2300 vols.
Fergus, Ontario, Mechanics' Institute, 3100 vols.
Fredericton, N.B., Law Library, 2300 vols.
   Legislative Library, 13,000 vols.
   University of New Brunswick (1800), 4000 vols.
Galt, Ontario, Mechanics' Institute, 4100 vols.
Garden Island, Ontario, Mechanics' Institute, 3800 vols.
Goderich, Ontario, Mechanics' Institute, 2700 vols.
Grimsby, Ontario, Mechanics' Institute, 3600 vols.
Guelph, Ontario, Agricultural College (1876), 5800 vols.
   Public Library, 6600 vols.
   Wellington Law Association (1886), 1200 vols.
Halifax, N.S., Citizens' Free Library (1864), 10,000 vols.
   Dalhousie College (1861), 5000 vols.
   Dalhousie Law School (1883), 6000 vols.
   Garrison Library (1847), 13,000 vols.
   Legislative Library (1859), 22,300 vols.
Hamilton, Ontario, Ladies' College (1860), 1600 vols.
   Law Association Library (1879), 2600 vols.
   . Public Library (1889), 22,000 vols.
Harriston, Ontario, Mechanics' Institute, 2600 vols.
Ingersoll, Ontario, Mechanics' Institute, 2500 vols.
Kincardine, Ontario, Mechanics' Institute, 3200 vols.
Kingston, Ontario, Mechanics' Institute, 5700 vols.
   Queen's College (1842), 21,000 vols.
   Royal Military College, 1500 vols.
L'Assomption, Quebec, College (1833), 12,500 vols.
Lennoxville, Quebec, Bishop's College, 8000 vols.
Lindsay, Ontario, Law Association Library (1885), 1000
   vols.
   Mechanics' Institute, 2100 vols.
London, Ontario, Law Association Library (1879), 2100
   vols.
   Mechanics' Institute, 4000.
   Western University, 4300 vols.
Milton, Ontario, Mechanics' Institute, 3400 vols.
Mitchell, Ontario, Mechanics' Institute, 2200 vols.
Montreal, Advocates' Library (1828), 16,000 vols.
   Congregational College, 5000 vols.
   Diocesan Theological College (1881), 2300 vols.

Fraser Institute (1885), 30,000 vols.
Horticultural Society Library (1876), 1000 vols.
Jacques Cartiér Normal School (1857), 12,500 vols.
McGill College (1855), 48,000 vols.
McGill Medical College, 14,000 vols.
McGill Normal School (1858), 2500 vols.
Mechanics' Institute (1839), 10,000 vols.
Montreal College (1800), 48,000 vols.
Natural History Society (1857), 5800 vols.
Presbyterian College (1869), 13,000 vols.
Wesleyan Theological College (1873), 3500 vols.
Y.M.C.A. (1851), 2700 vols.
Napanee, Ontario, Mechanics' Institute, 2300 vols.
Niagara, Ontario, Mechanics' Institute, 3300 vols.
Niagara Falls, Ontario, Mechanics' Institute, 3300 vols.
Nicolet, Quebec, College (1803), 20,500 vols.
Norwich, Ontario, Mechanics' Institute, 2400 vols.
Orillia, Ontario, Mechanics' Institute, 2400 vols.
Ottawa, Ontario, Archives Library (1872), 7000 vols.
Carlton Law Association (1888), 1200 vols.
Dominion Law Library (1880), 16,000 vols.
Geological Survey (1843), 14,000 vols.
Library of Parliament, 155,000 vols.
Literary and Scientific Society (1853), 2500 vols.
University (1850), 45,000 vols.
Y.M.C.A. (1867), 2000 vols.
Owen Sound, Ontario, Mechanics' Institute, 3000 vols.
Paris, Ontario, Mechanics' Institute, 5400 vols.
Penetanguishene, Ontario, Mechanics' Institute, 2500
vols.
Perth, Ontario, Mechanics' Institute, 2900 vols.
Peterboro', Ontario, Law Association Library (1880), 1200
vols.
Mechanics' Institute, 6000 vols.
Point Edward, Ontario, Mechanics' Institute, 2100 vols.
Port Hope, Ontario, Mechanics' Institute, 2800 vols.
Prescott, Ontario, Mechanics' Institute, 3200 vols.
Preston, Ontario, Mechanics' Institute, 4500 vols.
Quebec, Bar Library (1840), 11,000 vols.
Bibliotheque des Ouvriers (1890), 2000 vols.
College de Sainte Anne de la Pocatiere (1829), 11,000
vols.
College of St. Hyacinthe, 20,000 vols.
Department of Public Instruction (1868), 10,000
vols.
Laval University (1663), 100,000 vols.
Literary and Historical Society (1824), 24,000 vols.
Legislature Library (1867), 50,000 vols.
Regina, Manitoba, North-west Government Library (1888),
3000 vols.

Renfrew, Ontario, Mechanics' Institute, 2200 vols.
Ridgetown, Ontario, Mechanics' Institute, 2600 vols.
Sackville, N.B., Mount Allison College (1850), 5000 vols.
St. Catherine's, Ontario, Public Library, 6500 vols.
St. George, Ontario, Mechanics' Institute, 2600 vols.
St. John, N.B., Free Public Library (1883), 10,000 vols.
    Law Society (1878), 2800 vols.
St. Mary's, Ontario, Mechanics' Institute, 4500 vols.
St. Thomas, Ontario, Elgin Law Library Association.
    Public Library, 6000 vols.
Scarboro', Ontario, Mechanics' Institute, 3000 vols.
Seaforth, Ontario, Mechanics' Institute, 4000 vols.
Sherbrooke, Quebec, Library and Art Union (1882), 3500
    vols.
Simcoe, Ontario, Free Library (1868), 4200 vols.
Smith's Falls, Ontario, Mechanics' Institute, 3500 vols.
Stouffville, Ontario, Mechanics' Institute, 2200 vols.
Stratford, Ontario, Mechanics' Institute, 4800 vols.
Strathroy, Ontario, Mechanics' Institute, 3600 vols.
Streetsville, Ontario, Mechanics' Institute, 2300 vols.
Thorold, Ontario, Mechanics' Institute, 3500 vols.
Three Rivers, Quebec, Seminaire des Trois Rivières (1860),
    6000 vols.
Toronto, Canadian Institute (1849), 8000 vols.
    Education Department (1855), 7000 vols.
    Knox College (1844), 15,000 vols.
    Legislative Library (1867), 70,000 vols.
    McMaster University (1881), 9000 vols.
    Ontario Medical (1887), 3500 vols.
    Public Library (1883), 30,000 vols.
    St. Michael's College (1860), 8000 vols.
    School of Practical Science (1885), 1500 vols.
    Trinity College (1852), 12,200 vols.
    University of Toronto, 45,000 vols.
    Wycliffe College (1879), 8300 vols.
    York Law Association (1885), 2600 vols.
Uxbridge, Ontario, Mechanics' Institute, 4000 vols.
Victoria, B.C., Law Society (1873), 1500 vols.
    Legislative Library (1871), 1500 vols.
    Public Library (1889), 7000 vols.
Waterloo, Ontario, Public Library, 5000 vols.
Welland, Ontario, Mechanics' Institute, 2600 vols.
Westminster, B.C., Public Library (1862), 1500 vols.
Windsor, N.S., King's College (1802), 6000 vols.
Windsor, Ontario, Public Library (1894).
Winnipeg, Isbister Library (1883), 4000 vols.
    Law Society (1877), 4800 vols.
    Manitoba College (1872), 5500 vols.
    Provincial Library (1870), 15,500 vols.
Wolfville, N.S., Acadia College, 4000 vols.

Woodstock, Ontario College (1860), 4000 vols.
    Mechanics' Institute, 4500 vols.
Wroxeter, Ontario, Mechanics' Institute, 2300 vols.

JAMAICA—
Kingston, Institute of Jamaica (1879), 15,000 vols.
    Legislative Council.
    Medical Department.
    Teachers' Association.
    Victoria Institute.

ASIA.

BURMA—
Rangoon, Bernard Free Library, 10,000 vols.
    Literary Society, 10,000 vols.

CEYLON—
Colombo, Ceylon Law Library.
    Ceylon Medical Library.
    Museum (1877), 6000 vols.
    Royal Asiatic Society (Branch) Library (1845).
    Royal College.
    Y.M.C.A. Library.
Galle, Y.M.C.A. Library.
Kandy, Central Town Library.
    Oriental Library.
    Trinity College Literary Association.
Trincomalee, Pettah Library.

CHINA—
Victoria, Hong Kong, Museum.
    Literary Club.
    Royal Asiatic Society, Branch Library.

INDIA—
Agra College.
Allahabad, Anglo-Indian and Eurasian Association.
    Mechanics' Institute.
    Station Public Library.
    University.
Bangalore, Literary Union (1874), 1000 vols.
Benares, College Library, 16,000 vols.
Bhuj, Fergusson Museum.
Bombay, Bhuleshwar Library (1874), 7000 vols.
    Blavatsky Lodge (Theosophical Society) (1879), 1000
        vols.
    Cercle Littèraire Bibliothèque Dinshaw Petit (1886),
        1600 vols.
    Cowasji Dinshaw Library (1875), 3000 vols.
    Dhunjibhoy Framji Library (1860), 4000 vols.
    Dinshaw Petit Kanda Moholla Library (1870), 3000
        vols.
    Jamsetji Nesserwanji Petit Baharkote Improvement
        Library (1869), 1100 vols.

Jamsetji Nesserwanji Petit Colaba Library (1886), 1300 vols.

Jamsetji Nesserwanji Petit Fort Reading-room (1856), 10,000 vols.

Jamsetji Nesserwanji Petit Girgaum Library (1859), 1000 vols.

Moolla Firoz Library (Arabic and Persian) (1842), 2000 vols.

Native General Library (1845), 9000 vols.

People's Free Reading-room (1891), 5000 vols.

Royal Asiatic Society (Branch) (1804), 80,000 vols.

Sassoon Mechanics' Institute (1847), 13,000 vols.

Seamen's Institute.

Victoria and Albert Museum.

Calcutta, Agricultural Society.

Albert Institute.

Dalhousie Institute.

Geological Survey Library, 30,000 vols.

Hindu Literary Society.

Hoogly College.

Indian Museum.

Mechanics' Institute.

Presidency College.

Public Library, 75,000 vols.

Royal Asiatic Society (Branch).

Soldiers' Institute.

University.

Young Men's Association.

Decca, Deccan College.

Lahore, Punjaub Public Library, 80,000 vols.

Lucknow, Railway Mechanics'.

Madras, Agricultural Society.

British Medical Association (Branch).

Free Public Library, 15,000 vols.

Literary Society.

University.

Patna, College.

Poona, College of Science.

Roorkee, Thomason College, 15,000 vols.

MALAY PENINSULA—

Singapore, Mutual Improvement Society.

Raffles Library.

Royal Asiatic Society (Branch).

AUSTRALASIA.

NEW SOUTH WALES—

Bathurst, School of Arts.

Goulburn, Mechanics' Institute.

Grafton, School of Arts.

Kiama, Free Library.

Liverpool, Moore College.
    School of Arts.
Maitland, E., Mechanics' Institute.
Maitland, W., School of Arts.
Milton, Free Public Library.
Newcastle, School of Arts.
Redfern, Free Library.
Shellharbour, Public Library.
Singleton, Mechanics' Institute.
Sydney, Athenæum Club.
    Free Public Library, 85,000 vols.
    Geographical Society.
    Institute of Architects.
    Law Institute of N.S.W.
    Parliamentary Library, 30,000 vols.
    Royal Society of N.S.W.
    School of Arts, 43,000 vols.
    University, 40,000 vols.
    Y.M.C.A.
    Y.W.C.A.
Wagga Wagga, Municipal Free Library.
Windsor, School of Arts.
Yass, Mechanics' Institute.

NEW ZEALAND—

Auckland, Free Public Library (1880), 25,000 vols.
    Institute, Library and Museum.
    Supreme Court Library.
    University.
Balclutha, Athenæum Library.
Bannockburn, Public Library.
Campbelltown, Athenæum Library.
Christchurch, Canterbury College.
    Canterbury Philosophical Society.
    Canterbury Public Library.
Dunedin, Free Public Library, 60,000 vols.
    Otago Supreme Court Library.
    Otago University Library, 10,000 vols.
    School of Arts Library.
    Y.M.C.A. Library.
    Y.W.C.A. Library.
Hamilton, Public Library.
Hyde, Public Library.
Invercargill, Athenæum Library.
Lawrence, Athenæum Library.
Napier, Athenæum Library.
Nelson, Nelson Institute.
Thames, Public Library.
Wellington, Athenæum, 11,000 vols.
    Colonial Museum Library.
    Diocesan Library.

New Zealand Institute.
Parliamentary Library.
Philosophical Society.
Supreme Court Library.

QUEENSLAND—
Brisbane, Mechanics' Institute.
Parliamentary Library, 30,000 vols.
School of Arts Library, 15,000 vols.
Y.M.C.A. Library.
Ipswich, School of Arts Library.
Maryborough, School of Arts Library.
Rockhampton, School of Arts Library.
Toowoomba, School of Arts Library.
Warwick, School of Arts Library.

SOUTH AUSTRALIA—
Adelaide, Library of Parliament (1857), 22,000 vols.
Public Library, 31,000 vols.
University Library.
Y.M.C.A. Library.

TASMANIA—
Hobart, Parliamentary Library.
Mechanics' Institute, 11,000 vols.
Royal Society of Tasmania.
Tasmanian Public Library (1870), 11,000 vols.
Working Men's Club Library.
Y.M.C.A. Library.
Launceston, Congregational Library.
Mechanics' Institute and Public Library (1842), 20,000 vols.
Milton Hall Literary Society.
Y.M.C.A. Library.

VICTORIA—
Ballarat, Free Public Library, 15,000 vols.
Mechanics' Institute, 20,000 vols.
Brunswick, Mechanics' Institute.
Camperdown, Mechanics' Institute.
Castlemaine, Mechanics' Institute.
Diamond Creek, Literary Institute.
Fitzroy, Free Library.
Geelong, Free Library (1876), 6000 vols.
Geelong College Library.
Mechanics' Institute, 23,000 vols.
Kew, Literary and Scientific Institute.
St. Francis Xavier College.
Kyneton, Mechanics' Institute.
Learmouth, Public Library.
Mansfield, Free Public Library.
Melbourne, Athenæum Library.
Australian Club Library.
Congregational College Library.

       Parliamentary Library.
       Pharmaceutical Library.
       Presbyterian Theological College.
       Public Library (1852), 150,000 vols.
       Royal Society of Victoria.
       Trinity College.
       University Library (1855), 22,000 vols.
       Y.M.C.A. Library.
       Y.W.C.A. Library.
   Omeo, Free Public Library.
   Portland, Free Library.
   Sale, Mechanics' Institute.
   Sandhurst, Mechanics' Institute, 16,000 vols.
   Stanley, Athenæum Library.
   Stawell, Mechanics' Institute.
   Tungamah, Public Library.
   Wandiligong, Public Library.
   Winchelsea, Public Library.
   Yandoit, Public Library.
FIJI ISLANDS—
   Levuka, Mechanics' Institute.
   Suva, Literary Association Library.

PRINCIPAL LIBRARIES OF THE UNITED STATES.

(From the Bureau of Education *Statistics of Public Libraries*, 1893, etc.)

ALABAMA—
> Montgomery, State Library (1828), 18,000 vols.
> Spring Hill, College (1829), 18,000 vols.

ARKANSAS—
> Little Rock, State Library (1846), 51,000 vols.

CALIFORNIA—
> Berkeley, University of California (1868), 60,000 vols.
> Los Angeles, Public Library (1872), 42,000 vols.
> Sacramento, State Library (1852), 85,000 vols.
>> Free Public Library (1879), 20,000 vols.
> San Anselmo, Theological Seminary (1871), 19,000 vols.
> San Francisco, Bancroft Library (1858), 60,000 vols.
>> Free Public Library (1879), 79,000 vols.
>> Mechanics' Institute (1855), 71,000 vols.
>> Mercantile Library Association (1853), 70,000 vols.
>> Oddfellows' Library Association (1854), 55,000 vols.
>> St. Ignatius College (1855), 33,000 vols.
>> San Francisco Law Library (1865), 32,000 vols.
>> Sutro Library, 200,000 vols.
>> Theological Seminary (1871), 17,000 vols.
> Santa Clara, College (1851), 22,000 vols.

COLORADO—
> Denver, Mercantile Library (1886), 23,000 vols.
>> Public Library (1889), 31,000 vols.

CONNECTICUT—
> Bridgeport, Public Library (1881), 28,000 vols.
> Hartford, Case Memorial Library, 55,000 vols.
>> Connecticut Historical Society (1825), 22,000 vols.
>> Hartford Library Association (1839), 52,000 vols.
>> Hartford Theological Seminary (1834), 80,000 vols.
>> State Library (1854), 16,000 vols.
>> Trinity College Library (1823), 56,000 vols.
>> Watkinson Library (1858), 45,000 vols.
> Middletown, Berkeley Divinity School (1854), 21,000 vols.
>> Wesleyan University (1833), 40,000 vols.
> New Haven, Yale College (1701), 285,000 vols.
>> Free Public Library (1886), 30,000 vols.
> New London, Public Library (1882), 16,000 vols.

Norwich, Otis Library (1848), 17,000 vols.
Waterbury, Silas Bronson Library (1870), 53,000 vols.

DELAWARE—
Dover, State Library (1830), 21,000 vols.
Wilmington, Wilmington Institute (1788), 26,000 vols.

DISTRICT OF COLUMBIA—
Georgetown, Riggs Memorial Library (1889), 80,000 vols.
Washington, Department of Agriculture (1860), 35,000 vols.
    Department of Justice, 22,000 vols.
    Department of State (1789), 50,000 vols.
    House of Representatives (1789), 125,000 vols.
    Howard University (1870), 20,000 vols.
    Library of Congress (1800), 900,000 vols.
    Navy Department (1878), 25,000 vols.
    Patent Office (1836), 60,000 vols.
    Surgeon-General's Office (1865), 270,000 vols.
    Treasury Department (1875), 21,000 vols.
    U.S. Bureau of Education (1868), 170,000 vols.
    U.S. Coast Survey (1832), 16,000 vols.
    U.S. Geological Survey (1882), 73,000 vols.
    U.S. Naval Observatory (1845), 16,000 vols.
    U.S. Senate Library (1870), 73,000 vols.
    War Department (1800), 13,000 vols.

GEORGIA—
Athens, University of Georgia (1800), 32,000 vols.
Atlanta, State Library (1825), 45,000 vols.
    Young Men's Library Association (1867), 17,000 vols.
Savannah, Georgia Historical Society (1839), 21,000 vols.

ILLINOIS—
Champaign, University of Illinois (1867), 21,000 vols.
Chicago, Chicago Historical Society (1856), 65,000 vols.
    Chicago Law Institute (1857), 26,000 vols.
    Chicago Public School Libraries, 21,000 vols.
    John Crerar Library.
    Newberry Library (1887), 100,000 vols.
    Public Library (1872), 217,000 vols.
    University of Chicago (1890), 380,000 vols.
Evanston, North-western University (1855), 40,000 vols.
Morgan Park, Baptist Union Seminary (1867), 25,000 vols.
Mount Morris, Cassel Library (1881), 16,000 vols.
    Mount Morris College, 25,000 vols.
Peoria, Public Library (1880), 56,000 vols.
Rockford, Public Library (1872), 20,000 vols.
Springfield, Public Library (1836), 28,000 vols.
    State Library (1818), 38,000 vols.

INDIANA—
Bloomington, Indiana University (1820), 20,000 vols.
Crawfordsville, Wabash College (1833), 30,000 vols.
Evansville, Willard Library (1885), 18,000 vols.

Indianapolis, Public Library (1873), 63,000 vols.
State Law Library (1867), 17,000 vols.
State Library (1825), 25,000 vols.
Notre Dame, University, Lemonnier Library (1872), 45,000 vols.
Richmond, Morrison Library (1864), 17,000 vols.
St. Mary's, Academic Institute, 18,000 vols.

IOWA—
Council Bluffs, Free Public Library (1882), 20,000 vols.
Des Moines, State Library (1838), 45,000 vols.
Free Public Library (1883), 20,000 vols.
Grinnell, Iowa College (1848), 19,000 vols.
Iowa City, State University (1860), 33,000 vols.
State Historical Society (1857), 21,000 vols.

KANSAS—
Lawrence, University of Kansas (1866), 21,000 vols.
Manhattan, State Agricultural College (1863), 16,000 vols.
Topeka, Kansas State Historical Library (1875), 64,000 vols.
State Library (1862), 29,000 vols.

KENTUCKY—
Frankfort, State Library (1821), 80,000 vols.
Louisville, Polytechnic Society (1879), 50,000 vols.
Southern Baptist Seminary (1859), 17,000 vols.

LOUISIANA—
Baton Rouge, State University (1861), 20,000 vols.
New Orleans, Public School Library (1844), 17,000 vols.
State Library (1838), 45,000 vols.
Tulane University (1884), 16,000 vols.

MAINE—
Augusta, State Library (1820), 50,000 vols.
Bangor, Theological Seminary (1814), 18,000 vols.
Public Library (1883), 39,000 vols.
Brunswick, Bowdoin College (1794), 58,000 vols.
Portland, Public Library (1867), 60,000 vols.
Waterville, Colby University (1820), 38,000 vols.

MARYLAND—
Annapolis, State Library (1826), 100,000 vols.
U.S. Naval Academy (1845), 32,000 vols.
Baltimore, City Library (1874), 18,000 vols.
Enoch Pratt Free Library (1882), 163,000 vols.
Johns Hopkins University (1876), 85,000 vols.
Loyola College (1852), 30,000 vols.
Maryland Institute (1848), 20,000 vols.
New Mercantile Library (1887), 32,000 vols.
Peabody Institute (1857), 125,000 vols.
St. Mary's Theological Seminary (1791), 26,000 vols.
Mount St. Mary's, College (1808), 16,000 vols.
Woodstock, Woodstock College (1869), 81,000 vols.

MASSACHUSETTS—
    Amherst, College (1821), 76,000 vols.
    Andover, Theological Seminary (1807), 70,000 vols.
        Memorial Hall Library (1871), 19,000 vols.
    Boston, American Academy of Arts (1780), 24,000 vols.
        Boston Athenæum (1807), 245,000 vols.
        Boston College (1863), 24,000 vols.
        Boston Library Society (1792), 30,000 vols.
        Boston Medical Library Association (1876), 43,000 vols.
        Boston Society of Natural History (1830), 31,000 vols.
        Boston University, 33,000 vols.
        Congregational Library (1853), 31,000 vols.
        Massachusetts Historical Society (1791), 130,000 vols.
        Massachusetts Institute of Technology (1870), 33,000 vols.
        New England Historical Society (1845), 75,000 vols.
        New England Methodist Historical Society (1880), 21,000 vols.
        Public Library (1852), 628,000 vols.
        Social Law Library (1804), 25,000 vols.
        State Library (1826), 124,000 vols.
    Brockton, Public Library (1867), 22,000 vols.
    Brookline, Public Library (1857), 40,000 vols.
    Cambridge, Harvard University (1638), 580,000 vols.
        (Has various subsidiary collections.)
        Public Library (1857), 50,000 vols.
    Clinton, Bigelow Free Public Library (1873), 18,000 vols.
    Concord, Free Public Library (1851), 28,000 vols.
    Fall River, Public Library (1861), 40,000 vols.
    Fitchburg, Public Library (1859), 25,000 vols.
    Lancaster, Town Library (1862), 35,000 vols.
    Lawrence, Public Library (1872), 40,000 vols.
    Lowell, City Library (1844), 45,000 vols.
        Middlesex Mechanics' Association (1825), 22,000 vols.
    Lynn, Free Public Library (1862), 52,000 vols.
    Malden, Public Library (1879), 27,000 vols.
    Medford, Public Library (1856), 17,000 vols.
    Natick, Morse Institute (1862), 17,000 vols.
    New Bedford, Free Public Library (1852), 70,000 vols.
    Newburyport, Public Library (1854), 31,000 vols.
    Newton, Free Library (1869), 49,000 vols.
    Newton Center, Theological Institute (1825), 20,000 vols.
    Northampton, Forbes Library (1894), 32,000 vols.
        Public Library (1860), 24,000 vols.
    Peabody, Peabody Institute (1852), 31,000 vols.
    Pittsfield, Berkshire Athenæum (1871), 19,000 vols.
    Quincy, Thomas Crane Library (1871), 18,000 vols.
    Salem, Essex Institute (1848), 210,000 vols.
        Public Library (1889), 31,000 vols.
        Salem Athenæum (1810), 20,000 vols.

Somerville, Public Library (1873), 32,000 vols.
Southbridge, Public Library (1870), 16,000 vols.
Springfield, City Library Association (1857), 94,000 vols.
Taunton, Public Library (1866), 41,000 vols.
Tuft's College, College Library (1854), 38,000 vols.
Waltham, Public Library (1865), 24,000 vols.
Watertown, Free Public Library (1868), 46,000 vols.
Wellesley, Wellesley College (1875), 31,000 vols.
Weymouth, Tuft's Library (1879), 17,000 vols.
Williamstown, Williams' College (1793), 37,000 vols.
Woburn, Public Library (1856), 36,000 vols.
Worcester, American Antiquarian Society (1812), 95,000
    vols.
    College of the Holy Cross (1843), 26,000 vols.
    Free Public Library (1859), 103,000 vols.
    Worcester County Law Library (1842), 22,000 vols.
    Worcester Society of Antiquity (1875), 24,000 vols.
MICHIGAN—
Agricultural College Library (1857), 17,000 vols.
Alma, Alma College, 22,000 vols.
Ann Arbor, University of Michigan (1841), 95,000 vols.
Bay City, Public Library (1870), 16,000 vols.
Detroit, Public Library (1865), 139,000 vols.
Grand Rapids, Public School Library (1861), 27,000 vols.
Kalamazoo, Public Library (1873), 18,000 vols.
Lansing, State Library (1828), 55,000 vols.
Muskegon, Hackley Public Library (1888), 17,000 vols.
Olivet, Olivet College (1846), 40,000 vols.
West Bay City, Sage Public Library (1882), 19,000 vols.
MINNESOTA—
Minneapolis, Public Library (1889), 84,000 vols.
    University of Minnesota (1869) 27,000 vols.
St. Paul, Minnesota Historical Society (1849), 44,000 vols.
    Public Library (1882), 41,000 vols.
    State Law Library (1849), 21,000 vols.
MISSISSIPPI—
Jackson, State Library (1836), 60,000 vols.
MISSOURI—
Columbia, University of Missouri (1840), 38,000 vols.
Glasgow, Lewis Library (1866), 21,000 vols.
Jefferson City, State Library (1833), 20,000 vols.
Kansas City, Public Library (1876) 18,000 vols.
St. Louis, Academy of Science (1856), 16,000 vols.
    Law Library Association (1838), 19,000 vols.
    Mercantile Library Association (1846), 93,000 vols.
    Public Library (1865), 107,000 vols.
    St. Louis University (1828), 35,000 vols.
Springfield, Drury College (1872), 20,000 vols.
MONTANA—
Butte, Free Public Library (1894), 20,000 vols.
Helena, Public Library (1895), 17,000 vols.

NEBRASKA—
    Lincoln, State Library (1867), 24,000 vols.
        University of Nebraska (1870), 22,000 vols.
    Omaha, Public Library (1872), 51,000 vols.

NEVADA—
    Carson City, State Library (1865), 26000 vols.

NEW HAMPSHIRE—
    Concord, Public Library (1855), 16,000 vols.
        State Library (1819), 30,000 vols.
    Dover, Public Library (1883), 21,000 vols.
    Hanover, Dartmouth College Library (1779), 85,000 vols.
    Manchester, City Library (1854), 39,000 vols.
    Portsmouth, Portsmouth Athenæum (1817), 17,000 vols.

NEW JERSEY—
    Hoboken, Free Public Library, 15,000 vols.
    Jersey City, Free Public Library (1889), 49,000 vols.
    Madison, Cornell Hall (1868), 40,000 vols.
    Newark, Free Public Library (1888), 34,000 vols.
        Library Association (1847), 28,000 vols.
        N. J. Historical Society (1845), 30,000 vols.
    New Brunswick, Rutgers College (1766), 33,000 vols.
        Sage Library (1875), 50,000 vols.
    Paterson, Free Public Library (1885), 25,000 vols.
    Princeton, College of New Jersey (1750), 110,000 vols.
        Theological Seminary (1812), 77,000 vols.
    Trenton, State Library (1822), 45,000 vols.

NEW YORK—
    Albany, N. Y. State Library (1818), 225,000 vols.
        Young Men's Association (1833), 22,000 vols.
    Auburn, Theological Seminary (1821), 25,000 vols.
    Binghamton, Central High School, 65,000 vols.
    Brooklyn, Brooklyn Library (1857), 135,000 vols.
        Free Lending Library of the Union for Christian Work (1882), 33,000 vols.
        Long Island Historical Society (1863), 65,000 vols.
        Pratt Institute Library, 40,000 vols.
        Public School Library (1866), 21,000 vols.
    Buffalo, Buffalo Historical Society (1862), 20,000 vols.
        Buffalo Library (1836), 80,000 vols.
        Canisius College (1870), 16,000 vols.
        Grosvenor Public Library (1859), 36,000 vols.
    Clinton, Hamilton College (1812), 40,000 vols.
    Fordham, St. John's College, 36,000 vols.
    Geneva, Hobart College (1822), 28,000 vols.
    Hamilton, Colgate University (1820), 21,000 vols.
    Ithaca, Cornell Library Association (1866), 18,000 vols.
        Cornell University (1868), 140,000 vols.
    Newburg, Free Library (1852), 18,000 vols.

New York, Aguilar Free Library (1886), 29,000 vols.
 American Museum of Natural History (1880), 26,000
   vols.
 Apprentices' Library (1820), 91,000 vols.
 Association of the Bar (1870), 40,000 vols.
 Astor Library (1849), 250,000 vols.
 Astor, Lenox and Tilden Foundations.
 Catholic Club (1871), 20,000 vols.
 College of the City of New York (1852), 27,000 vols.
 College of St. Francis Xavier, 30,000 vols.
 Columbia College (1754), 135,000 vols.
 Cooper Union (1857), 32,000 vols.
 General Theological Seminary (1822), 22,000 vols.
 Harlem Library (1825), 18,000 vols.
 Lenox Library (1870), 65,000 vols.
 Maimonides Library (1851), 45,000 vols.
 Mercantile Library Association (1820), 252,000 vols.
 New York Academy of Medicine (1847), 50,000 vols.
 New York Free Circulating Libraries (1880), 82,000
   vols.
 New York Historical Society (1804), 75,000 vols.
 New York Hospital (1790), 20,000 vols.
 New York Law Institute (1828), 41,000 vols.
 New York Society Library (1754), 90,000 vols.
 Union Theological Seminary (1836), 68,000 vols.
 University of City of New York (1833), 18,000 vols.
 Y.M.C.A. (1852), 45,000 vols.
 Y.W.C.A. (1870), 19,000 vols.
Poughkeepsie, City Library (1843), 20,000 vols.
 Vassar College (1861), 19,000 vols.
Rochester, Central Library (1863), 20,000 vols.
 Reynold's Library (1884), 26,000 vols.
 Theological Seminary (1850), 26,000 vols.
 University of Rochester (1850), 27,000 vols.
Schenectady, Union College (1798), 38,000 vols.
Syracuse, Central Library (1855), 23,000 vols.
 University (1872), 42,000 vols.
Troy, Young Men's Association (1835), 29,000 vols.
Utica, Oneida Historical Society (1876), 25,000 vols.
 Public Library (1893), 23,000 vols.
West Point, U.S. Military Academy (1812), 33,000 vols.
NORTH CAROLINA—
 Chapel Hill, University of North Carolina (1795), 45,000
   vols.
 Raleigh, State Library (1822), 32,000 vols.
OHIO—
 Cincinnati, Hebrew Union College (1875), 65,000 vols.
 Lane Seminary (1833), 17,000 vols.
 Law Library (1847), 16,000 vols.
 Public Library (1867), 211,000 vols.

St. Xavier College (1831), 16,000 vols.
Young Men's Mercantile Library Association (1835), 62,000 vols.
Cleveland, Adelbert College (1826), 40,000 vols.
Case Library (1848), 30,000 vols.
Public Library (1868), 96,000 vols.
Western Reserve Historical Society (1867), 17,000 vols.
Columbus, State Library (1817), 64,000 vols.
Public School Library (1890), 28,000 vols.
Dayton, Public Library (1847), 35,000 vols.
Gambier, Kenyon College (1865), 42,000 vols.
Marietta, Marietta College (1835), 58,000 vols.
Oberlin, Oberlin College (1833), 54,000 vols.
Springfield, Public Library (1872), 17,000 vols.
Toledo, Public Library (1873), 32,000 vols.

OREGON—
Portland, Library Association (1864), 23,000 vols.
Salem, State Library (1850), 18,000 vols.

PENNSYLVANIA—
Alleghany, Carnegie Library (1890), 30,000 vols.
Western Theological Seminary (1872), 25,000 vols.
Altoona, Mechanics' Library (1860), 23,000 vols.
Beatty, St. Vincent Library (1846), 40,000 vols.
Easton, Lafayette College (1832), 23,000 vols.
Germantown, Friends' Free Library (1874), 19,000 vols.
Harrisburg, State Library (1790), 117,000 vols.
Haverford, Haverford College (1833), 28,000 vols.
Meadville, Theological School (1844), 23,000 vols.
Overbrook, Seminary (1832), 23,000 vols.
Philadelphia, Academy of Natural Sciences (1812), 43,000 vols.
American Philosophical Society (1743), 45,000 vols.
Athenæum (1814), 36,000 vols.
College of Physicians (1787), 56,000 vols.
Franklin Institute (1824), 61,000 vols.
German Society (1817), 22,000 vols.
Historical Society of Pennsylvania (1824), 69,000 vols.
Law Association (1802), 25,000 vols.
Library Company (1731), 206,000 vols.
Mercantile Library Company (1821), 177,000 vols.
Mutual Library Company (1879), 44,000 vols.
Presbyterian Historical Society (1852), 20,000 vols.
Spring Garden Institute (1851), 16,000 vols.
Theological Seminary (1864), 21,000 vols.
University of Pennsylvania (1749), 200,000 vols.
Pittsburg, Carnegie Library (1895), 25,000 vols.
Library Association (1849), 22,000 vols.
Scranton, Public Library (1890), 25,000 vols.
South Bethlehem, Lehigh University (1877), 86,000 vols.
Wilkes Barre, Osterhout Library (1889), 23,000 vols.

19

RHODE ISLAND—
    Newport, People's Library (1870), 33,000 vols.
       Redwood Library (1747), 42,000 vols.
    Pawtucket, Public Library (1876), 15,000 vols.
    Providence, Brown University (1767), 92,000 vols.
       Providence Athenæum (1836), 56,000 vols.
       Public Library (1878), 80,000 vols.
       Rhode Island Historical Society (1822), 32,000 vols.
SOUTH CAROLINA—
    Charleston, Library Society (1748), 20,000 vols.
    Columbia, Smyth Library (1831), 32,000 vols.
       State Library, 36,000 vols.
       South Carolina College, 27,000 vols.
TENNESSEE—
    Nashville, State Library (1854), 30,000 vols.
       Vanderbilt University (1875), 21,000 vols.
    Sewanee, University of the South (1869), 38,000 vols.
VERMONT—
    Burlington, Fletcher Free Library (1873), 25,000 vols.
       University of Vermont (1791), 44,000 vols.
    Lunenburg, Cuttings Library (1866), 17,000 vols.
    Middlebury, Middlebury College (1800), 18,000 vols.
    Montpelier, State Library (1825), 27,000 vols.
    Vergennes, Vergennes Library (1876), 23,000 vols.
VIRGINIA—
    Lexington, Washington and Lee University (1796), 30,000
       vols.
    Richmond, State Library (1823), 53,000 vols.
    Salem, Roanoke College (1853), 23,000 vols.
    University Station, University of Virginia (1819), 55,000
       vols.
WASHINGTON—
    Olympia, State Library (1856), 18,000 vols.
WISCONSIN—
    Beloit, Beloit College (1847), 23,000 vols.
    Madison, State Historical Society (1854), 164,000 vols.
       State Library (1836), 25,000 vols.
       University of Wisconsin (1850), 26,000 vols.
    Milwaukee, Public Library (1878), 80,000 vols.
    Ripon, Ripon College (1863), 17,000 vols.
WYOMING—
    Cheyenne, State Law Library (1869), 17,000 vols.

Note.—In a large number of cases the stock of volumes in many of these Libraries consists of a large proportion of "unbound pamphlets". For example, the Essex Institute, Salem, Mass., has 60,000 bound volumes and 150,000 unbound pamphlets. There are numerous other instances of a similar sort.

LIBRARY ASSOCIATIONS AND KINDRED SOCIETIES.

LIBRARY ASSOCIATION.

PRESIDENT, ALDERMAN HARRY RAWSON, OF MANCHESTER.

THE Library Association was founded on 5th October, 1877, at the conclusion of the Library Conference held at the London Institution, under the presidency of the late Mr. J. Winter Jones, then Principal Librarian of the British Museum. It was originally called the Library Association of the United Kingdom.

Its objects are (a) to unite all persons engaged or interested in Library work, for the purpose of securing the best administration of Libraries; (b) to endeavour to obtain better legislation for Public Libraries; (c) to aid and encourage the establishment of new Libraries; and (d) to encourage bibliographical study and research.

The Association has, by the invitation of the local authorities, held its annual meetings in the following cities and towns :—

YEAR.	PLACE.	PRESIDENT.
1878	Oxford	J. Winter Jones (*Principal Librarian of the British Museum*).
1879	Manchester	} Rev. H. O. Coxe (*Bodley's Librarian*).
1880	Edinburgh	
1881	London	His Honour Judge Russell (*Master of Gray's Inn Library*).
1882	Cambridge	Henry Bradshaw (*Librarian of Cambridge University*).
1883	Liverpool	Sir James Picton, J.P. (*Chairman of the Liverpool Public Libraries*).
1884	Dublin	J. K. Ingram, LL.D. (*Librarian of Trinity College Library*).
1885	Plymouth	Edward James (*Mayor of Plymouth*).
1886	London	E. A. Bond, C.B., LL.D. (*Principal Librarian of the British Museum*).

YEAR.	PLACE.	PRESIDENT.
1887	Birmingham	Alderman G. J. Johnson (*Chairman of the Birmingham Free Public Libraries*).
1888	Glasgow	Rev. Prof. W. P. Dickson, LL.D. (*Curator of Glasgow University Library*).
1889	London	Richard Copley Christie (*Chancellor of the Diocese of Manchester*).
1890	Reading	E. Maunde Thompson, C.B., LL.D. (*Principal Librarian of the British Museum*).
1891	Nottingham	Robert Harrison (*Librarian of the London Library*).
1892	Paris	Professor A. Beljame of the Sorbonne *vice* Richard Garnett, LL.D. (*Keeper of the Printed Books, British Museum*).
1893	Aberdeen	Richard Garnett, LL.D. (*Keeper of the Printed Books, British Museum*).
1894	Belfast	Marquis of Dufferin and Ava, K.P., G.C.B., etc.
1895	Cardiff	Lord Windsor.
1896	Buxton	Alderman Harry Rawson, of Manchester.

The 1897 meeting will be held in London, probably in July, and will take the form of an International Conference, at which delegates from the Colonies, various countries in Europe, and the United States are expected to attend. The American Library Association is already co-operating in the work.

The official organ of the Association is the *Library*, which is issued monthly and sent post free to members. In this magazine (edited by Mr. J. Y. W. MacAlister, the Hon. Secretary) appear the papers read at annual and monthly meetings, and a report of the proceedings of the Association, practical papers, reviews, etc.

Monthly meetings are held, usually in London, on the second Monday of each month from November to June, and are reported in the *Library*.

The Association consists of Fellows, Honorary Fellows, Members and Associates. *Fellows*, who are qualified, are elected by the Council, and pay an entrance fee of one guinea, and an annual subscription of one guinea. *Honorary Fellows* pay no subscription. *Members* must be elected at meetings of the Association on the nomination of two fellows or members. The annual subscription is one guinea. Library assistants are eligible for election as *Associates*, but may not vote or hold office. They must be nominated for election by two fellows or members. The annual subscription for associates is half a guinea. All elections are subject to the approval of the Council.

EXAMINATIONS.

The Association has instituted a series of examinations in 1, Bibliography and Literary History; 2, Cataloguing, Classification and Shelf Arrangement; and 3, Library Management. Particulars of these examinations will be found in the *Library Association Year Book*. The honorary secretary of the Examinations Committee is Mr. J. W. Knapman, 17 Bloomsbury Square, London, W.C., to whom all communications should be dd ressed.

Mr. J. Y. W. MacAlister.

SUMMER SCHOOL FOR STUDENTS OF LIBRARIANSHIP.

In June or July of each year is held a summer school, generally in London, when lectures and demonstrations are given in all that relates to literature, bibliography, librarianship and book production. The honorary secretary is Mr. H. D. Roberts, librarian, Public Library, St. Saviour, Southwark, London, S.E., to whom all communications should be addressed. Prizes are given in connection with the meetings of the summer school, which usually last for one week, and it should be the ambition of every Library Committee to send members of its staff to benefit by the valuable training given.

MUSEUM OF LIBRARY APPLIANCES.

A collection of apparatus of all kinds used in Library administration has been made chiefly through the exertions of Mr. J. D. Brown, Clerkenwell Public Library, London, E.C. The specimens were for some years on view at the Clerkenwell Public Library, but were afterwards transferred to 10 Blooms-bury Street, W.C., and are now at 20 Hanover Square, W., awaiting a permanent home.

A large number of interesting and important papers have been published in the *Transactions*, 1877-1884 ; *Monthly Notes*, 1880-1883 ; *Library Chronicle*, 1884-88 ; and in the *Library*, from 1889.

OFFICERS.

Hon. Sec., J. Y. W. MACALISTER,   Hon. Treas., HENRY R. TEDDER,
    20 Hanover Square,   The Athenæum,
        London, W.   Pall Mall,
                                                          London, S.W.

Hon. Solicitor, H. W. FOVARGUE,   Hon. Assistant Sec. :—
        Town Clerk,   Miss AGNES HANNAM,
            Eastbourne.   20 Hanover Square, W.

There is also a Council consisting of president, twelve vice-presidents, three officers, and thirty-two councillors, of whom twelve are resident in London, and twenty in the country.

Rooms and Office:—20 Hanover Square, London, W.

There can be no doubt that the work of the Library Association has done much to improve Library administration and the status of librarians, while its efforts on behalf of improved legislation have also been successful. It was originally founded as the "Library Association of the United Kingdom," but when applying for a royal charter in 1896, the title was altered to "Library Association". It has a membership of about 500, including representatives of all the more important Libraries of the kingdom. A number of Libraries have also joined as members, being, as such, entitled to send delegates to the annual conferences. We think it is the plain duty of every rate-supported Library in the kingdom, with an income of £100 or more, to join this Association for the sake of the publications and the amount of information it gives officially and through its members. A few Libraries pay subscriptions on behalf of themselves and their officers. Whether a Library can afford to pay its librarian's subscription or not, it certainly ought to join the Association on its own behalf. In addition to the publications above noted, the Association issues a *Library Association Year Book* (1s. per annum), and a " Library Association Series," consisting of handbooks on *Library Appliances* (No. 1, 1s.); *Legislation* (No. 2, 2s. 6d.); *Staffs* (No. 3, 6d.); *Music Libraries* (No. 4, 6d.); *Cataloguing Rules* (No. 5, 6d.); *Books for Village Libraries* (No. 6, 1s.); *Adoption of the Public Libraries Acts* (No. 7, 6d.).

Affiliated to the Library Association, though not in any way under its control, are the following local Associations, which have been formed to meet the demand for more frequent meetings and discussions than are afforded by the annual meetings of the parent Association. So far as London and district are concerned, the monthly meetings serve this purpose, hence there is no particular need for a South English section.

LIBRARIANS OF THE MERSEY DISTRICT.

The quarterly meetings of this body were commenced at Warrington in November, 1887. They are held, usually three in each year, upon the invitation of a member, at some place in Lancashire or Cheshire. The proceedings consist of papers and discussions, chiefly on subjects connected with practical librarianship. Meetings were held in 1895-96 at Warrington, Oldham, and Runcorn (also Halton). Membership is open to librarians of the two counties. Subscription, 2s. per annum.

Hon. Secretary—Charles Madeley, The Museum, Warrington.

NORTH MIDLAND LIBRARY ASSOCIATION.

This Association was founded at Nottingham on 26th March, 1890. Its membership is drawn from the counties of Nottingham, Derby, Lincoln and Leicester. Has held meetings, exhibitions, etc., in various towns in the counties mentioned. The membership is about 30. Subscription, 2s. 6d. per annum.

President—W. Crowther, Public Library, Derby. *Hon. Secretary*—J. Potter Briscoe, Public Library, Nottingham.

BIRMINGHAM AND DISTRICT LIBRARY ASSOCIATION.

Established at Aston Manor on 4th October, 1895. Has held meetings at Wolverhampton, West Bromwich, and Stratford-on-Avon, at which papers have been read on various subjects of interest to librarians. The meetings during 1897 will be held at Oldbury, Walsall, Stafford and Worcester. The annual subscription is 2s., but assistants may join on payment of a subscription of 1s.

President—John Elliot, Public Library, Wolverhampton. *Hon. Secretary*—R. K. Dent, Public Library, Aston Manor.

LIBRARY ASSOCIATION : NORTH WESTERN BRANCH.

Formed in July, 1896, by members of the Library Association residing in Lancashire and Cheshire, under Rule 21 of the parent Association. This Association has been formed to discuss questions of legislation, rating, examination of assistants, etc., as they affect municipal Libraries.

Chairman—Alderman Rawson, Manchester Public Libraries Committee. *Hon. Secretary*—Charles Madeley, The Museum, Warrington.

Another society, on somewhat similar lines, was formed in December, 1895, under the designation of :—

SOCIETY OF LIBRARIANS FOR LONDON AND THE HOME COUNTIES.

Several meetings have been held and papers read at different Libraries in the London district.

Chairman—John Frowde, Public Library, Bermondsey, S.E. *Secretary*—Charles W. F. Goss, Public Library, Lewisham, S.E.

In July, 1895, was formed the—

LIBRARY ASSISTANTS' ASSOCIATION,

with headquarters in London and a membership drawn from London and various parts of the provinces. The first chairman was Mr. R. A. Peddie of the Gladstone Library, National Liberal Club. During the session 1895-96, over twenty meetings and concerts were held, at which papers were read by librarians and others. A list of these will be found in the First Annual Report, issued in 1896. There are about sixty members, and the annual subscription is 5s. for senior, and 2s. 6d. for junior assistants. A small Library has been formed in connection with the Association.

Chairman—A. H. Carter, St. Martin-in-the-Fields Public Library London. *Hon. Secretary*—F. Meaden Roberts, St. George, Hanover Square, Public Library, London, S.W.

BIBLIOGRAPHICAL SOCIETY.

Established in London in 1893. Meets for the discussion of papers dealing with bibliography in every department. It also issues monographs on various subjects connected with books, printers, etc., and issues a *News-Sheet* between October and June. Of this, twenty numbers have been published. The objects of the Society are: "The acquisition of information upon subjects connected with bibliography; the promotion and encouragement of bibliographical studies and researches; the printing of works connected with bibliography; the formation of a Bibliographical Library". The membership is limited to 300 from the British Empire and the United States. The actual number of members recorded in the last list is 322.

Annual subscription, one guinea.   Rooms, 20 Hanover Square, London, W.

President—Richard Garnett, C.B., LL.D., British Museum. *Hon. Secretary*—A. W. Pollard, M.A., 13 Cheniston Gardens, London, W. *Hon. Treasurer*—A. H. Huth, Bolney House, Ennismore Gardens, London, S.W.

AMERICAN LIBRARY ASSOCIATION.

Formed in. 1876 at Philadelphia in connection with the Centennial Exhibition.   Previous to this, in 1853, a Convention of Librarians of the United States had met in New York. Annual conferences have been held at the following places :—

1876.	Philadelphia	-	-	-	Justin Winsor, *President.*
1877.	New York	-	-	-	,, ,,
1879.	Boston	-	-	-	,, ,,
1881.	Washington	-	-	-	,, ,,
1882.	Cincinnati	-	-	-	,, ,,
1883.	Buffalo	-	-	-	,, ,,
1885.	Lake George	-	-	-	,, ,,
1886.	Milwaukee	-	-	-	Wm. F. Poole ,,
1887.	Thousand Islands	-	-	-	,, ,,
1889.	St. Louis	-	-	-	Chas. A. Cutter ,,
1890.	White Mountains	-	-	-	F. M. Crunden ,,
1891.	San Francisco	-	-	-	S. S. Green ,,
1892.	Lakewood	-	-	-	W. I. Fletcher ,,
1893.	Chicago	-	-	-	Melvil Dewey ,,
1894.	Lake Placid	-	-	-	J. N. Larned ,,
1895.	Denver	-	-	-	H. M. Utley ,,
1896.	Cleveland	-	-	-	J. C. Dana ,,

The proceedings of these conferences have been published in the *Library Journal*, which was first issued in 1876, and has now reached its twenty-first volume.   The papers, discussions, special articles and general news, which have appeared in the *Library Journal*, constitute it by far the most valuable work on practical librarianship which has ever been published. Where the publications of the Library Association have been devoted more exclusively to bibliography and literary history, the organ of the American Association has been chiefly filled with articles on the practical side of Library work in every one of its aspects, and it must be admitted this has been done thoroughly and with a considerable amount of literary ability.

Besides printing papers and proceedings, the Association has a publishing section through which several important works have been issued ; it was also instrumental in promoting the revised issues of Poole's *Index to Periodical Literature*, the annual literary indexes, etc.   A selection of "best books" has also been made by the Association, which has induced the U.S. government to issue a model catalogue, on three different systems, entitled the *A.L.A. Catalogue.* In every other direction the Association has shown much activity, and in many ways keeps alive the interest and co-operation of its members. Not the least important of these agencies is the State Library Associations or Clubs, which are affiliated to the parent Association. The following is a list of them, as far as it has been possible to ascertain :—

Library Association of Central California : *Secretary*—A. M. Jellison, Mechanics' Library, San Francisco.

Chicago Library Club : *Secretary*—Miss M. L. Bennett, Armour Institute, Chicago.

Colorado Library Association : *Secretary*—John Parsons, Public Library, Denver.

Connecticut Library Association : *Secretary*—Miss Richardson, Public Library, New London.

Illinois Library Association : *Secretary*—Miss Moore, Withers Public Library, Bloomington.

Indiana Library Association : *Secretary*—Miss Ahern, 125 Franklin St., Chicago.

Iowa Library Society : *Secretary*—Miss McLoney, Public Library, Desmoines.

Maine Library Association : *Secretary*—Miss Fernald, State College, Orono.

Massachusetts Library Club : *Secretary*—W. H. Tillinghast, Harvard College Library, Cambridge.

Michigan Library Association : *Secretary*—Mrs. Parsons, Public Library, Bay City.

Minnesota Library Association : *Secretary*—Miss Countryman, Public Library, Minneapolis.

New Hampshire Library Association : *Secretary*—Miss Blanchard, Public Library, Concord.

New Jersey Library Association : *Secretary*—Miss Winser, Public Library, Newark.

New York Library Association : *Secretary*—W. R. Eastman, State Library, Albany.

New York Library Club (established in 1885) : *Secretary*—Miss Rathbone, Pratt Institute, Brooklyn.

Nebraska Library Association : *Secretary*—Miss Jones, State University, Lincoln.

Ohio Library Association : *Secretary*—Miss Doren, Public Library, Dayton.

Pennsylvania Library Club : *Secretary*—C. S. Kates, Free Library, Philadelphia.

Western Pennsylvania Library Club : *Secretary* – W. R. Watson, Carnegie Library, Pittsburg.

Vermont Library Association : *Secretary*—Miss Titcomb, Free Library, Rutland.

Washington City Library Association : *Secretary*—F. H. Parsons, U.S. Naval Observatory.

Wisconsin Library Association : *Secretary*—Miss Stearns, Public Library, Milwaukee.

Milwaukee Library Round Table.

OFFICERS OF THE AMERICAN LIBRARY ASSOCIATION.

President—W. H. Brett, Public Library, Cleveland, Ohio. *Secretary* —R. P. Hayes, Columbus, Ohio. *Treasurer*—G. W. Cole, 473 Jersey Avenue, Jersey City, N.J.

Membership over 500.   Annual subscriptions: Members, $2; Fellows, $5; Libraries, $5.

The rapid development of Library work in the United States has led to the formation of training schools for assistants, and from these many of the recent appointments to Libraries have been made.   The oldest and most important is the

NEW YORK STATE LIBRARY SCHOOL

established at Columbia College, New York, by Mr. Melvil Dewey in 1886, and now forming a section of the University of New York, and carried on at the State Library, Albany, by Mr. Dewey and a staff of librarian-teachers.   On similar lines have been established :—

The Pratt Institute Library School, Brooklyn, N.Y.
Drexel Institute Library Class, Philadelphia.
Armour Institute, Department of Library Science, Chicago.
Amherst College Summer School.   Conducted by Mr. W. I. Fletcher.

Other Institutions and Libraries in America have instituted examinations and classes.

BRAY'S INSTITUTION FOR FOUNDING LIBRARIES,

19 Delahay Street, London, S.W.

Established for the purpose of forming and improving Libraries for the parochial clergy throughout England.   Dr. Thomas Bray (1656-1730), after whom the Institution is named, was active both in England and North America in founding Libraries for the clergy, and he was instrumental in having passed in the Parliament of Anne "An Act for the better preservation of Parochial Libraries in that part of Great Britain called England," 1708.   An account of some of these Libraries, by Mr. T. W. Shore, will be found in the *Transactions of the Library Association* for 1878, pages 51 and 145.

OBITUARY NOTICES.

THE following notices of men distinguished in Library work may be interesting to many who knew them, and they will serve as an introduction to an annual series of biographies of prominent librarians and Library workers. We are indebted to the daily newspapers and to the *Library* for most of the facts given in these notices.

GEORGE BULLEN, C.B., LL.D.,

Keeper of printed books in the British Museum, was born at Clonakilty, Cork, on 17th November, 1816. He was educated at Chigwell Grammar School, and later became a master in St. Olave's School, Southwark, London. In 1838 he entered the service of the British Museum as an assistant, afterwards becoming successively assistant keeper of printed books and superintendent of the reading-room. In 1875 he succeeded Mr. W. Brenchley Rye as keeper of the printed books, and in 1890 he retired. He was made a C.B. in 1891, and in 1890 the University of Glasgow conferred on him the honorary degree of LL.D. He was an active member of the Library Association for many years after its foundation, but is best remembered by his "Catalogue of Books in the Library of the British Museum, printed in England, Scotland and Ireland, and of Books in English printed abroad, to the year 1640," London, 1884—3 vols., and his work in connection with various other catalogues of the British Museum. His death took place on 10th October, 1894.

W. J. HAGGERSTON,

Librarian of Newcastle-upon-Tyne Public Library, was born at Brecon in 1848. He became a junior assistant in the Literary and Philosophical Society's Library, Newcastle-upon-Tyne, in 1867, and in 1872 he was appointed first librarian of the South Shields Public Library. This position he held till 1879, when he became librarian of the Public Library of Newcastle-upon-Tyne. He was a man of immense energy, and on certain easy mechanical lines did a great deal of useful work. His catalogues, however, were of very mediocre merit, and, as is pointed out elsewhere, did real harm to progress in the art of cataloguing by the amount of undeserved notoriety and vogue they received. Newcastle shares with Manchester and Birmingham the credit of having trained more librarians than any other town. Mr. Haggerston died at Newcastle on 6th May, 1894.

THOMAS HURST,

Librarian of the Sheffield Public Libraries, was born at Sheffield on 8th January, 1834. Till 1855 he was a teacher in the Lancasterian Schools at Sheffield, where his mother had been a head mistress. After acting for a short time as a rate collector, he was appointed sub-librarian of the Sheffield Public Libraries in 1856, a position he held till 1873, when he succeeded Mr. Parsonson as chief librarian, an office he occupied till his own death at Sheffield in May, 1894. Mr. Hurst was a man of very retiring disposition, but was greatly respected in Sheffield and among the members of the Library Association. His chief contributions to Library work were a series of catalogues arranged by authors' names, with full subject and title indexes.

T. J. DE MAZZINGHI,

Librarian and curator of the William Salt Library, Stafford, was born in 1809, and was probably the son or other relative of Joseph Mazzinghi (1765-1844), a well-known musician and glee-composer of Italian origin. He was educated at Cambridge, and graduated as M.A. In 1842 he was called to the Bar, and about 1873 became curator of the William Salt Library. He died at Stafford on 18th February, 1893.

JOHN PLANT, F.G.S.,

Librarian and curator of the Salford Free Library and Museum, was born at Leicester in 1819. For some years he acted as curator of a museum at Leicester, and became an active volunteer, in which service he attained the rank of major. In 1849 he was appointed librarian and curator at Salford, a post he held till 1892, when he retired. He died in Anglesey in 1894. His work in connection with Libraries was not distinguished by anything particularly novel, but for many years he was a well-known figure at the annual conferences of the Library Association.

JOHN TAYLOR,

Librarian of the Bristol Public Libraries, was born at Bristol in 1830. For some time he was engaged in business as a retail ironmonger, but in 1862 he was appointed assistant librarian of the Bristol Library Society; succeeding to the post of chief librarian in 1863. When this was amalgamated with the Philosophical Institution in 1871 as the Bristol Museum and

Library, Mr. Taylor continued in office as librarian. He succeeded Mr. J. F. Nicholls as chief librarian of the Bristol Public Libraries in 1883, and held the position till his death at Bristol on 9th April, 1893. Mr. Taylor was as much distinguished for his antiquarian and literary attainments as for his librarianship. He wrote many papers on the local archæology of Bristol and on topics connected with bibliography and literary history, some of which were collected and published as *Antiquarian Essays* by Mr. George of Bristol. This volume contains a short memoir by Mr. George. His principal contribution to practical Library work seems to have been the plan of collecting from different magazines articles on important subjects, and binding them up in volumes according to the subject-matter. This has since been imitated by other Libraries.

ERNEST CHESTER THOMAS,

Secretary of the Library Association of the United Kingdom, was born at Birkenhead on 28th October, 1850. He was educated at Manchester Grammar School and Oxford University. In 1875 he was elected to the Bacon Scholarship of the Hon. Society of Gray's Inn, and in the following year he was studying at Jena and Bonn. He became connected with the Library Association in 1878, when he acted as joint secretary, afterwards assuming the full duties of the office, which he held till 1890. He died at Tunbridge Wells, on 5th February, 1892. A very full and appreciative biography of Mr. Thomas with a list of his various works and translations was written by Mr. H. R. Tedder, and appears in the *Library* for 1892, page 73. It was largely due to the energy, enthusiasm and special knowledge which Mr. Thomas brought to bear on the work that the Library Association lived through the earlier years of its career. He and his friend Mr. Tedder were practically the leading spirits in every new departure tried by the Association, and it was undoubtedly they, and the kindred scholars whom they enlisted in the work, who gave the proceedings of the Association such a high bibliographical character.

APPENDIX.

MR. GLADSTONE ON PUBLIC LIBRARIES.

THE following is the speech delivered by Mr. Gladstone at the opening of the St. Martin-in-the-Fields Public Library in February, 1891:—

I undoubtedly cannot deny that I have a title, though a questionable title, to appear before you in connection with public purposes of great interest to the parish of St. Martin's. Is say questionable title, because I am a little in the condition of a Parliamentary elector who, although properly placed upon the register, has had the misfortune to change his abode. I beg, therefore, you will not look too closely into the nature of my qualification. If I could overlook the comparatively brief term of years since I ceased to have a residential connection with St. Martin's, I might almost aspire to the title of the oldest parishioner, or not be very far from it, for I lived in this parish, with scarcely any intermission, from the year 1837 to the year 1876, inclusively; and I must add that it was not my will, but a prudential regard to circumstances, which caused me to seek a humbler abode elsewhere, but for which I should still be among you, and not one would be able to question my formal right, at any rate, to invite you to recognise me as your coadjutor upon an occasion of very great interest. My first duty is to declare this Library to be open, and I can declare it with the better conscience inasmuch as that office was committed to me in this way—which I think is not always the case with those who declare places open. A key was placed in my hands, and I myself unlocked the door. Under these circumstances, I declare this Library to be open, and I believe it is my duty and privilege, having performed that function, to be the first to profit by the Library. I therefore take the liberty of handing to the librarian a requisition duly drawn and signed, in which I ask, not, indeed, for the Book—that one Book which is to be selected from all others upon its merits, for its dignity and office in a Christian land: there can be no choice as to what that Book should be, but I do not on this occasion ascend to that elevation—and I think I cannot do better than ask for the local tract or treatise on the history of

St. Martin's parish, drawn up by a late respected vicar. Now, sir, having spoken of my own qualification and the defect in it, I must also say that I am very glad to recognise St. Martin's as a parish which I believe to be forward in the promotion of all those undertakings which are likely to give it a distinguished place among the parishes of London. Of the philanthropic improvements which have characterised the last generation, one, and not an insignificant one, perhaps the earliest of them all, was the institution of baths and wash-houses. I think it certainly is forty-five years since I accompanied the then respected vicar of the parish, Sir Henry Dukinfield, to see the baths and wash-houses then in full work in St. Martin's parish, and I am informed, upon what I believe was good authority— well, I was aware they were certainly among the first—I am told they were the very first—institutions of that description founded in this vast metropolis. I hope the honour thus acquired is an honour which will likewise be a stimulus— which has been a stimulus; it has given St. Martin's parish a forward place among the parishes engaged in the foundation of Libraries; it has entitled you to appear in a most useful work by Mr. Thomas Greenwood on the Public Libraries which have now been formed for the use of the population in various parts of the country—here in this work is the front of your Library of St. Martin's figuring and having a distinguished place amongst them. Well, ladies and gentlemen, this is not a very old movement. The Act under which you have been enabled to carry this design into effect dates from the year 1850, when I was myself already beginning to be a somewhat old member of Parliament. The author of that Act is a gentleman of the name of Ewart, a name which I have the honour to bear as a second name, and he is a man whom I very well remember and whom I had the honour and pleasure of knowing. Mr. Ewart, the author of that Act, was a cultivated man, a scholar, highly respected in every relation of life, and his name deserves to be recorded in that he was upon more subjects than one a pioneer, working his way forward, doing the rough, introductory work in his country's interest, in the interest of the nation, upon subjects which at that time very few had begun to appreciate. The appreciation of his work in regard to Libraries which produced the Act of 1850 has been an appreciation gradually progressing. Mr. Greenwood has supplied us with the facts of the case, which are rather simple. The progress for a long time was not very rapid. In the thirty-six years from 1850 onward—that is, down to 1886—133 places had availed themselves of the benefits of the Act. That was not a very large number, not amounting quite, upon the average, to four in each of those thirty-six years. Well, but slow progress in infancy is not always a bad sign. We are not a people whose minds move very rapidly. What we hope is that they move securely, that the progress we do achieve is solid pro-

gress, and that we are not so much given as possibly some
might be to step backwards where we have once found it
our duty to step forward. Now, see the change which has
taken place. We have only four years from 1887 to 1890, and
in those four years no less than seventy-seven places took
advantage of the Act, so that instead of an average of less than
four places in the year we have an average of more than
seventeen places. Now, certainly that is rapid progress, which
I think we ought to regard as satisfactory. No doubt very
many questions arise, which have been ably discussed by Mr.
Greenwood, and upon some of which possibly there may be
differences of opinion. You are aware, for example, that under
the old Acts it was in the power of any qualified person to
demand a poll of the parish upon the acceptance of the Act.
That was not an unreasonable proposition at the time when
it was first embodied in the Act, because this foundation of
Libraries was not like the ordinary recognised functions of
municipalities. It was in the nature of a novelty—of an outside operation; and it was not perhaps unreasonable or
impolitic that the people themselves should be distinctly
consulted upon the question whether they would have a
Library or not. They have availed themselves in various
instances of the privilege of refusing. Mr. Greenwood, I
think, rather complains that in one single year twelve places
declined to have the Act put into operation among them.
Still, until the country has fully recognised that the foundation of these Libraries is an ordinary duty of the local
municipality probably it would not be a bad thing that the
public, the local public, should be consulted upon the question.
There is another great difficulty, undoubtedly, about the
extension of Libraries of this kind from places of comparatively
large population—to which they are now confined—into rural
districts. That is a very serious difficulty, because when you
have a very large population concentrated in a very small
space you can give to the whole of them nearly equal interests
in the Library. It is accessible to all; but where you have in
purely rural districts a much smaller population, distributed
and diffused over a space perhaps twenty or fifty times
larger, there it is very difficult, as persons conversant with
rural districts well know, to put all upon anything like
an equality with regard to their access to the Library; and,
of course, it is to be expected that where people do not recognise either an immediate or prospective benefit to themselves or their families, they should be less inclined to
undertake the burdens which the Act enables them to impose
upon themselves. Well, Mr. Greenwood, who is an advanced
and zealous advocate, has a remedy for all that, and his
remedy is a very simple one. The First Lord of the Treasury
will at once appreciate it. His remedy is a small dose of
public money, a sure and infallible specific, supplying all

20

deficiencies, surmounting all difficulties, and curing all social evils. It may be that in old age one loses one's nimbleness and power to keep up a competition in pace with other men. I am not at all able to follow Mr. Greenwood's zeal in the recommendation that the Consolidated Fund should be the source of supply for institutions of this kind; but I do not wish to give up the case of villages and rural districts. We have in this country a very peculiar distribution of the land. It is held in large quantities. It is held by wealthy men; it is held by men who recognise to a great extent, and who, I hope, from generation to generation will still more largely recognise, the proposition that the possession of landed property entails great social duties; and, instead of the Consolidated Fund, what I hope is that the liberality and the enlightened judgment of these large proprietors who are scattered all over the country will meet the difficulty and enable the villages, either upon their own bases or by affiliating themselves to the town Libraries—which is a plan, I believe, that has been adopted with very great effect in some places—enable them, I say, to meet the case and enjoy the great advantage of institutions of this kind. Well now, I have spoken to you of the progress that has been achieved— of the general progress; but, besides being parishioners of St. Martin's, you are Londoners, and as Londoners it is well, I think, that you should understand how the metropolis stands in this matter. Now, for a long time the metropolis was very stiff, reluctant, and hard-hearted, and a gentleman sent to me only yesterday a letter, written by Mr. Ewart himself, from which I will make a very brief quotation. Mr. Ewart had been cognisant of the fact that in the year 1855 an attempt had been made to induce the City of London, which need not have been apprehensive of an exhaustive burden from the penny in the pound—I believe it was a halfpenny then, but whether a penny or a halfpenny the City of London had declined to accept the Act. Mr. Ewart writes a letter to a friend, in which he says: "I trust that, notwithstanding our recent unsuccessfulness, the Public Library system will flourish even in the City of London". Had Mr. Ewart happily been among us to-day, he would have seen that the faith which he entertained, and which is a very characteristic quality of men who see far into the future and work for the future, has been amply justified. For a long time London was most obdurate; down to the end of 1885—that is, thirty-six years after the Act—London had only two Libraries. But in the month of June, 1890, Mr. Greenwood has shown that instead of two it had twenty-one. That is to say, the rate of increase going on in London was more rapid than in any other part of the country; and what appears likely is that these valuable institutions will in a very short time be strewn so thickly over the whole of this metropolis that there will be no parish without an establishment of the kind. That is a very satisfactory state of things, and if we are content with a moderate but ever-growing success—and that is what a prudent man ought to be content with in this world—I think we may be thankful to see what has been done in this direction, and may look forward to the future with a confident anticipation of still greater achievements. This institution is not an isolated phenomenon. The foundation of Libraries is one among many features of the modern tendency and movement of British society. There is a rough question put by Mr. Carlyle. He says: " How is it there is not a Library in every town ? You will find everywhere the police, a prison, and gallows; why have we not a Library ? " No doubt if we go back a period and look for particular indications of our social system, we find that they are generally of a penal and coercive character. I remember once being in a certain county—I will not name the county—but I was staying in the house of a friend in a certain county, and I said : " You have a great number of gallows in this county ". I forget the exact number, but that was the case in the different rural districts in the old times. They were not merely the ornaments of large towns where there were numbers of prisons and hundreds and thousands of criminals, but they went through the country as a local and parochial institution. I may mention, also, the venerated institution of the stocks which we have almost forgotten. Well, my friend observed to me that I was mistaken. It was not his county, but the neighbouring county. So it was. But on a little further investigation he was obliged to admit that there was in his parish a place called "Gallows-green". That, I am afraid, was only adding conviction to the point in question. But a great change has taken place. We have less to do with the gallows and the prison than we had in former times, and we have more to do with another kind of agency. There is a word which has come into existence since I was young, and which indicates this wide and comprehensive change—the word "sociology"—rather an awkward word, as it is not of pure parentage, but we cannot manage it any better. But it is a very important word which indicates the great system of education which is going over the country. It indicates the foundation of museums, the foundation of art galleries, the foundation of Libraries. It indicates the foundation of institutions having in view the corporeal health and development of the people and the maintenance of their physical properties. Let us not suppose that because we attach importance to the foundation of Libraries, museums, art galleries, and so forth, and because ink and paper are indispensable to human progress, we can separate what God has joined together. You cannot separate the properties of man's body from the properties of his soul. You must develop him as a creature of body, soul, and spirit. And I rejoice to think

that great attention is now given in many cases to these corporeal pursuits also, and that healthful exercise is supplied to
the people.   These gymnasia, or whatever they may be called, I
for my part join and couple with the institutions directed to
manly improvement, and as all being joint ministers in the
great and good work.   I do not venture to say—I do not think
you would approve my thought if I did—that institutions of
this order are institutions which will of themselves enable a
man to attain the highest purposes for which he came into the
world, or will effectually supply all his needs or furnish all that is
required by his infirmities and his sins.   It would be a very great
mistake if we were to place institutions of this kind in competition with the religion which it is our happiness to profess.
They are not designed to compete with that religion, far less are
they to be substitutes for it.   On the contrary, they hold that
religion to be their parent.   It is Christianity which is the
parent of philanthropy—the parent of all the developments
of philanthropy which has taken so many forms in which the
blessed and benevolent principles of the Gospel open and ex-
pand themselves.   We know that not to be an idle boast—not
to be an arbitrary and unsupported opinion, and we do it in
this way.   When we go back to the greatest people of antiquity, when the highest faculties of man were developed, to
an extent probably exceeding any development with which we
are now conversant, these philanthropic developments were
almost unknown.   Never until Christianity came into the
world did they begin, partly by sympathy and attraction, to
make themselves somewhat known.   But the full and large
acceptance of the doctrines of true philanthropy, which the
name "sociology" was intended to embrace and recommend,
was never known to mankind or put in action among mankind.
And it is to the blessed influence of Christianity in my opinion
that we must refer their origin.   But in any case it is in no
spirit of rivalry, much less in a spirit of hostility, that these
institutions found themselves.   We stand here upon ground
which is within 50 or 100 yards of the noble church of St.
Martin.   That is a symptom of the friendly relations which
ought to obtain, and which generally have really obtained,
between the social developments of our time and the still
greater, higher, holier, and more powerful and profound influences which are connected with the Gospel of our Saviour.
But in how many ways are these institutions preparatory to
religion and in how many ways helpful to it?   But these
institutions are enemies of what?   These Libraries, these
gymnasia, these museums, this system of public education,
they are all instruments with which a war is carried on.
War against what?   War against ignorance, war against
brutality.   Brutality and idleness are among the greatest
auxiliaries by which the kingdom of evil and mischief is
sustained and supported in the world.   To put down these

enemies and to restrict their action is a great and enormous good conferred upon mankind. When we speak of brutality persons are apt to think of this now as an idea and a tendency which have become remote. It seems as if it were buried in a long-forgotten past. But it is not a very remote past and not a past very long forgotten. We go back less than 200 years. Pastimes distinctly brutal were the habitual pastimes of the people of this country. Nor do I say that they are to be blamed for it, by members of our present community, when I recollect that cruelty has tended to lodge itself in connection with the thoughtless enjoyments of mankind in all times, and in those times they had little option, they had not employment for the mind. They had severe labour for the body, and when that labour is fixed and presses hard upon the physical powers of man, he must and will find some relief, some alleviation, some refreshment. It is the fault of those who ought to provide him with the refreshment which is better, for the want of which he is driven to the refreshment which is worse. I will not now go into the drink question which is in the minds of everybody. It would be hard to mark a class of persons as the enemies of the public good. But there is no doubt that these institutions are directly in competition with the public-houses of the country. And I will take it for granted that every one of those who hear me wishes them immense success in the prosecution of that competition. It is a very pleasant thing to know that the condition of our labouring population has changed in respect to the means of mental and bodily improvement in two ways. First of all the means—the institutions necessary for the purpose which did not previously exist at all have been largely provided, and are now provided more largely than ever. But there was another difficulty, and that was the hours of labour, such as they were 100 or even 50 years ago, when they were so confined that the hours absolutely necessary for food and the hours absolutely necessary for sleep left no margin in which men of the labouring population could apply themselves to mental improvement. Now, happily, a great change has taken place in that respect, a change which, of course, is associated possibly in some quarters with expectations that are of doubtful prudence and possibility, but these are the mere outlying incidents of every great and beneficial alteration. It can now be said that the hours of labour, for a considerable portion at least of our working population, are fixed within bounds so reasonable, although they still leave the lot of labour sufficiently severe, yet they are fixed within such bounds that when the necessary hours of rest and food are added to them there still remains a margin which is available as real leisure for the working man for the purpose to which he seeks to apply them. Now, there is a competition for the working man who has that margin of time. There is

the competition of evil soliciting him visibly and sensibly in
the streets through which he passes. There may be also a
competition of good in beneficial institutions of every kind
which may afford him the means of employing his leisure,
not only without difficulty or disadvantage, but with the
greatest satisfaction to himself and the greatest advantage to
his family at home, and to the children who may succeed
him. His leisure may be employed in these Libraries, and
how happy it is to see with what zeal and promptitude all
over the country the working population have exhibited their
readiness to take advantage of the opportunities when once
afforded them. There are other uses of Libraries such as these.
I have been promised the power of reference to books here.
A very useful power it is, especially with regard to books
whose series run out into great bulk. To all classes there is
great utility in the power of reference and the uses which this
institution affords, but, of course, it is to the masses of the
community that they are principally valuable, and it is by
those masses that they have been largely, and will be, I believe, still more and more largely, appreciated. There is
one kind of appreciation, ladies and gentlemen, which I
cannot help contemplating with a greater interest than another,
and that is the case of the very young—the case of the intelligent
growing lad, who is just beginning, perhaps only in the humble
capacity of a messenger, perhaps as an apprentice, but in one
or the other beginning to show that he has got in him the
mettle of a man which, if well used, will develop into something valuable and comparatively great for the future. Now,
it is in a Library like this that a youth of that kind may derive
the greatest benefit. His mind is full of material, and it is this
Library and such institutions that may impart the vital spark
to that material, and a visit to which may inspire him with
ideas altogether new, with the idea that his mind is capable of
progress, that his faculties, if applied sedulously and continuously and manfully to a given purpose, will attain a valuable
end. All these things he sometimes learns from the occasions
of life, but there is no place perhaps among all the various
occasions that ordinary life offers—there is hardly any place
where he is more likely to receive that enormous benefit than
he is within the walls of an institution of this kind. I do not
speak of the selection of the books of the institution—a task
very arduous and very difficult, but one which I have not the
least doubt will in the instance before us be admirably well
performed—but on every ground I feel that to take part in
inaugurating, in commending to the public notice and public
interest, this Library, every one of us is discharging a valuable
and important public duty. The very crowd that attended us
on our visit from the vicarage to the doors is a testimony how
the masses of the population of London appreciate an occasion
of this kind. You have got the material—you have got the

human material on which to work—you have got the pecuniary means by which to work; you have put those means into operation—into beneficial operation. I express to you the most earnest desire of my heart to be that prosperity and success in social and moral improvement may attend increasingly from year to year the progress of this Library.

INDEX.

NOTE.—As the various lists of Libraries, municipal and other, are already in alphabetical order (*see* pp. 117-299), it has not been thought necessary to repeat the names in this Index.

326

MUSEUMS

AND

ART GALLERIES,

BY

THOMAS GREENWOOD,

AUTHOR OF "PUBLIC LIBRARIES".

PRICE FIVE SHILLINGS.   450 Pages, Illustrated.

ART JOURNAL.

" A useful and comprehensive account of Museums."

ATHENÆUM.

" A suitable companion to the same author's volume on *Public Libraries.*"

MAGAZINE OF ARTS, 1st January, 1889.

" A volume of great utility and value to all interested in national art education."

ST. JAMES' GAZETTE.

" The contents of this excellent volume tell us all about existing Museums and offer many valuable suggestions for extending their number and improving their character. Such a work was imperatively demanded."

GRAPHIC, 19th October, 1889.

" *Museums and Art Galleries*, by Thomas Greenwood, is so excellent a work that we have little doubt that it will soon pass into a second edition. Mr. Greenwood truly says that the subject is practically without literature, and his own book is a good attempt to fill the gap. There are a few omissions and one or two mistakes; but that is little in such a book covering so large an amount of ground. Museums are becoming of more and more importance, and Mr. Greenwood's book is likely to be the standard work for some time to come."

SPECTATOR, 28th September, 1889.

" Mr. Thomas Greenwood, who some time ago published a book on *Public Libraries*, has followed it up with *Museums and Art Galleries*. Although he is an enthusiastic as regards the educational value of Museums and Art Galleries, and has ideas of his own, which he expresses in special chapters on ' The Relation of the State to Museums ' and ' The Place of Museums in Education,' the value of this book lies essentially in the fact that it tells, in not too guide-book a style, all about the existing Museums and Galleries in the United Kingdom. Mr. Greenwood does not hesitate to tell Municipal Authorities unpleasant truths, as when he warns the Glasgow people that there is a lively prospect of the whole of their collection of pictures being destroyed by fire and that their Museums are situated in an inconvenient and unsuitable position, and neither care nor money has been lavished on the collection. Mr. Greenwood has spared no pains to gather, verify and arrange his facts, and his book is so good that we regret being compelled only to hint at its excellence."

PUBLISHED BY

SIMPKIN, MARSHALL, HAMILTON, KENT & CO., LIMITED.

The **FOURTH** Edition of

PUBLIC LIBRARIES,

A History of the Movement,

And a Manual for the Organisation and Management of Rate-supported Libraries.

BY

THOMAS GREENWOOD,

Author of "Museums and Art Galleries," etc.

OVER 630 PAGES.   *PRICE 2/6.*

LIST OF CHAPTERS.

PUBLISHED BY

CASSELL & COMPANY, LIMITED, La Belle Sauvage, London, E.C.

AND ALL BOOKSELLERS.

The FOURTH Edition of

PUBLIC LIBRARIES,

A History of the Movement, and a Manual for the Organisation and Management of Rate-supported Libraries.

BY THOMAS GREENWOOD,

Author of "Museums and Art Galleries," etc.

OVER 630 PAGES.   PRICE 2/6.

PRESS NOTICES.

DAILY NEWS.—" Mr. Thomas Greenwood has published through Messrs. Cassell's a fourth edition of his volume on *Public Libraries*—a very comprehensive history and survey of the Public Library movement, including descriptions of the management, the organisation, and internal economy of these institutions. Forty-one years have elapsed since the late Mr. Ewart's fruitful measure was passed, and since then no fewer than 238 adoptions of the Act have been recorded. It is still more satisfactory to note that progress is making at an accelerating pace, as shown by the fact that 105 of these adoptions have taken place since the first edition of this work was published five years ago. Mr. Greenwood attributes this gratifying state of things mainly to the clearing of the ground by the Elementary Education Act, which is multiplying readers at a rate hitherto unknown."

SCOTSMAN.—"A new edition of Mr. Thomas Greenwood's book upon *Public Libraries* has been published. The work is re-written in this issue without changing its character. It has become more complete. It was previously the fullest and most trustworthy account before the public of the working and progress of the Public Library movement. The revision has established more firmly than ever its claim to this distinction. The work is not only a history of the movement, but a complete manual of the organisation and management of Public Libraries. The continued improvement of the book cannot but do good service to the cause which it seeks to promote."

DAILY CHRONICLE.—" Mr. Thomas Greenwood's book on *Public Libraries* has been entirely re-written for a new edition. All the facts essential to the chronicle of the movement in each case are recorded. Many of the buildings in which the Libraries are housed have been pictured to illustrate the text. The earlier chapters contain much interesting information regarding the principles and history of the movement. Even the Public Libraries of America and Canada and of Australasia find a place in the book. Mr. Greenwood has laboured indefatigably at his task. He has amassed and digested a portentous quantity of useful information on a subject of deep interest and surpassing importance."

GUARDIAN.—"A material aid in the spread of Public Libraries is Mr. Thomas Greenwood's book on the subject, which contains a history of the movement and supplies an abundance of useful information relating to their organisation and management. In a fourth edition the book has been entirely re-written."

LITERARY WORLD.—" This is a new edition, entirely re-written, of a book by the apostle of the Public Library movement which has already established its reputation. It is a handy manual, explicitly dealing with all branches of its subject, and summarising in historical form all that has already been accomplished. The movement is progressing ' at a splendid rate '. Everywhere the prospect is encouraging, and to Mr. Greenwood thanks are due for gathering results into the convenient form in which we find them."

EDUCATIONAL TIMES.—" In this volume Mr. Greenwood, the veteran advocate of the movement, traces the progress of Public Libraries until last summer, and supplies all the information that is likely to be required by those who are promoting the establishment of such institutions, or are connected with their management. The revised edition, which is entirely re-written, extends to over 630 pages, and is an encyclopædia of condensed information on every phase of the subject ; at the same time the price is so remarkably low that no one interested in the question need suffer from lack of knowledge. We are glad to note the recent activity in London and its suburbs. and the indications that many of the Metropolitan boroughs and parishes are prepared to provide facilities for healthy reading. During the last four years the Act has been adopted in a large number of districts, and this progress has been achieved without any general propaganda."

PUBLISHED BY

CASSELL & COMPANY, LIMITED, La Belle Sauvage, London, E.C.

AND ALL BOOKSELLERS.

Of Special Importance to all interested in Sunday School Work,

AND IN THE

DEVELOPMENT OF VILLAGE LIFE.

SUNDAY SCHOOL

AND

VILLAGE LIBRARIES,

WITH A

List of over 1800 suitable Books, and Hints on Management,

BY

THOMAS GREENWOOD,

Author of "Public Libraries," and "Museums and Art Galleries," etc.

---

96 PAGES, ILLUSTRATED.

Price 1s. 6d. (Cloth). Post Free 1s. 9d.

PRESS NOTICES.

THE LIBRARY.—"The work deserves to be adopted as the text-book for the class of Libraries to which it applies."

GLASGOW HERALD.—"The author gives much valuable information in regard to the organisation and management of these institutions."

SCOTSMAN.—"From Messrs. Clarke and Co., London, comes a small book, in which Mr. Thomas Greenwood treats of 'Sunday School and Village Libraries'. It shows with abundant practical knowledge how such Libraries may best be organised and maintained, and gives lists of suitable books. The work will be found useful to all who are interested in Sunday School work, and in the formation of new Libraries."

CHURCH BELLS.—"Mr. Greenwood is well known as an authority on Libraries, and in this little volume has brought together such a collection of hints and wrinkles as cannot be got elsewhere in a score of volumes. The book should be read by every clergyman who has, or ought to have, a Library in connection with his church. Hints on shelving, cataloguing, choosing and buying books, managing Libraries, etc., will be found adequately and clearly explained."

CARLISLE JOURNAL.—"Mr. Greenwood, who has been a most laborious worker in the cause of Public Libraries, has now turned his attention to the literary wants of villages, and gives many useful practical suggestions for applying them. As a penny rate is no use for villages, he suggests a Government grant in aid, the amount of which could be saved by stopping the waste at South Kensington. His *brochure* contains a carefully selected list of books suitable for village Libraries."

WARRINGTON GUARDIAN.—"This is a useful *brochure*, and one of a somewhat original character. The object is to show how village Sunday School Libraries can be organised and maintained. The rate allowed by the Public Libraries Acts, says the author, is not sufficient for the purpose of establishing and maintaining these Libraries in sparsely populated districts, where the penny has to be calculated on a limited income. The remedy proposed is that of a small Government grant, available through similar channels as the grants to science and arts classes, and for other educational purposes. The whole subject is dealt with in a practical spirit, and those who have the matter at heart will do well to read and ponder Mr. Greenwood's remarks."

Publishers—JAMES CLARKE & Co., 13 and 14 Fleet Street, London, E.C.
And all Booksellers.